CHANGING FACES

A History of *The* **Guardian** 1956–88

CHANGING FACES

A History of *The* **Guardian** 1956–88

Geoffrey Taylor

FOURTH ESTATE · *London*

First published in Great Britain in 1993 by
Fourth Estate Limited
289 Westbourne Grove
London W11 2QA

A catalogue record for this book is available from the British Library.

ISBN 1–85702–100–2

Typeset by York House Typographic Ltd
Printed in Great Britain by Cambridge University Press

CONTENTS

LIST OF PLATES

Preamble

A roll-call of the famous men and women who have written in the Cross Street corridor and reporters' room would be tedious to the reader and too nostalgic an exercise even for us. We shall not attempt it because a newspaper cannot live in the past. It is only as valuable as the words that are printed in it today.

Leading article in the Guardian
on its move to new offices in Manchester,
29 August 1970.

Those sentiments notwithstanding, the *Guardian* has laid the foundations for a heritage industry of its own. Five histories have been published. On the paper's centenary in May 1921, Haslam Mills, chief reporter, wrote a long supplement which was so thorough and lively as to need reprinting in book form. Mills's fluent and unadorned language bridges the years as not all *Guardian* writing of that time has been able to do. Alone among the historians he could, one feels, have made himself at home in Farringdon Road and written for the paper of the 1990s.

Then in 1934 came the standard biography of C.P. Scott by J.L. Hammond. This is instructive, urbane and enjoyable reading for anyone delving into the press of those times. Formally it is about the man rather than the newspaper but since the two were inseparable a great deal of *Guardian* history is included. Third came a compendium of recollections called *C.P. Scott: The Making of the* Manchester Guardian, published in 1946. That marked another centenary (Scott's birth), but since it contained both pre-C.P. and post-C.P. chapters it too could not avoid treating history in the large.

The most important event in the series was the publication of David Ayerst's classic: Guardian: *Biography of a Newspaper*. It was commissioned to mark the paper's 150th anniversary in 1971, when the paper invited six hundred people to dinner at the Dorchester Hotel, an occasion agreeably sumptuous, wholly out of character and costing more than the firm of those straitened years could properly afford.

Ayerst ended on the death of A.P. Wadsworth in 1956 and the accession of Alastair Hetherington to the editorship. He enjoyed a number of advantages, the most important of which was that most of his characters were dead. That meant not only that truth could go untempered by circumspection but that only a pedant would wish to re-examine the material in the hope – a vain one, probably, such was Ayerst's familiarity with historical method – of catching him out. The present writer is by contrast fully aware of the pitfalls on every page.

After Hetherington had given up the chair in 1975 he wrote his memoirs under the title Guardian *Years*. He was characteristically generous about his colleagues, as he was to them personally during his tenure. He was also highly instructive about the way a newspaper's policy takes shape and about the part his *Guardian* played in policy-making in British and wider international affairs. His dictum was that the *Guardian* should be about 'government in the widest sense' and his leaders were a dialogue with the decision-makers. They were placed on Harold Wilson's desk and on J.F. Kennedy's, as Scott's had been on Lloyd George's, and Wadsworth's on Adenauer's, Eisenhower's and Ernest Bevin's (though probably not Attlee's: Attlee was a *Times* man).

An impression may have been given that the *Guardian* is obsessed by anniversaries. That is not entirely true. The present volume was commissioned at an arbitrary moment in the paper's and the company's affairs and was intended to continue the narrative where Ayerst left it. To give a rounded picture of the earlier years it needs to be read alongside Hetherington; certain events as described by him can be amplified, some are seen from a spectator's different angle, some are freshly disinterred and some are omitted altogether. None needs to be basically contradicted.

Fresh difficulties arise where Hetherington leaves off. No one was a more meticulous keeper of records. One has the impression, rifling through, or simply gazing in wonder at, the mountains of his documents boxed and indexed at the Manchester University Library or still in Hetherington's lumber-rooms, that everything ever said to him was jotted down, whether a telephone call from Downing Street, the importunings of a prospective parliamentary candidate or a subtlety in the Common Agricultural Policy raised at the leader-writers' conference. The pencilled notes have remained legible on the backs of press releases from the Liberal party or the Highlands and Islands Development Board.

This wealth of material is not wholly advantageous to a would-be historian because it leaves him no excuse for error. Hetherington's successor Peter Preston, on the other hand, though he wrote copious letters in reply to readers, and took decisions, it seems, every fifteen minutes, transacted almost everything of consequence within the office during casual encounters as he pottered (his term) from one desk to another. When word was not spread by that method he would telephone a foreign correspondent, or circulate a notice by placing it on visual display screens whence it would evaporate when the terminal was switched off.

Even when those excuses have been made, large areas of *Guardian* writing are neglected in this book. They have receded into the limbo-land of events which had neither consequence nor implication; or this writer did not understand them; or at this distance in time it would be a living death to feign an interest. Others agree. John Pringle, formerly of the *Guardian*, whom we shall meet, wrote in *Have Pen, Will Travel*: 'I have not said much about my own work at the *Times* because I was, after all, only a leader-writer and nothing is more boring than the leading articles of twenty years ago.' An anonymous introduction in the Scott centenary volume remarks: 'Almost all his work is buried in newspaper files; and leading articles, like political speeches, rarely survive their hour. The controversies on which Scott wrote, the political situations in which he gave guidance, are already half-forgotten.'

It is the historian's duty, no doubt, to lean over the event horizon and retrieve what has disappeared. But then this narrative does not purport to be a social history of Britain or a political history of the world. It is about how an important newspaper made, and at the time of writing was still making, a large transition in a relatively short time. This was not brought about by the editorial staff alone. It involved everybody: printers, management, tele-ad girls, circulation people . . . The changes have also been in direction as well as scale, towards the journalistic hypermarket in which no consumer's demand is left unmet. In *The Press We Deserve*, edited by Richard Boston (Routledge & Kegan Paul, 1970) Daniel Viklund of the *Dagens Nyheter*, Stockholm, is quoted as saying '"We don't have a popular press. We have everything, serious and popular all together; *Private Eye* and *Country Life* in the same paper."' Other foreign correspondents also lamented the rigid distinction between a popular and a quality press, which they attributed to the tenacity of class in Britain. That is a gulf which Peter Preston appeared, as this narrative ended, to be trying to close. Hence the *Guardian* acted as editorial midwife to the new post-Franco newspaper *El Pais* of Madrid; in turn, when launching into its new design in 1988 it acknowledged a debt to that paper's freshness and style.

The author agrees with the passage quoted at the head of this introduction, and not only because he wrote it at the time. It becomes clear, in writing a book of this kind, that the wind of history bloweth to some extent where it listeth. The result is that some of the best work in the paper is unmentioned and some of its best writers' (and essential desk people's) names do not appear. Their forgiveness is sought. In 1973 Ayerst brought out an anthology of *Guardian* writing throughout its 150 years. One could name several reporters whose work has appeared regularly in recent issues of the Bedside Guardian (published annually since 1952), who will certainly be found in any similar long-term compendium, but whose names are not found here. The author does not reproach himself too heavily for that failure. As the paper pointed out to the Royal Commission on the Press in 1974, one front page contains more words than a half-hour TV news bulletin. Scores running into hundreds of names have appeared in editorial directories since the early 1950s. The features staff alone quadrupled between 1961 and 1988 when it stood (including perhaps a few for whom no other category could be found) at about sixty-four.

SOURCES AND STYLE

Quotations have, where possible, been acknowledged in textual notes. Those used in abbreviated form are:

Ayerst – D.G.O. Ayerst, Guardian: *Biography of a Newspaper* (Collins, 1971)
GY – A. Hetherington, Guardian *Years* (Chatto & Windus, 1981)
Hammond – J.L. Hammond, *C.P. Scott* (biography) (Bell & Sons, 1934)
Mills – W. Haslam *Mills, The* Manchester Guardian: *A Century of History* (Chatto & Windus, 1921)

Unless otherwise stated, written material other than extracts from the paper is normally taken from the company's archives at the John Rylands University Library, Manchester, and its offices at Deansgate, Manchester.

In November 1972 the company changed its name from Manchester Guardian and Evening News Limited (MGEN) to Guardian and Manchester Evening News Limited (GMEN). Both sets of initials are used as appropriate.

The style for names is somewhat arbitrary. In the manner of the time Laurence Scott was usually known as L.P.S., but too many initials on the page would look untidy. He is affectionately remembered as Laurence, and that is how he is normally referred to here. Likewise Alastair Hetherington was referred to as A.H. or sometimes Alastair, but it seems more appropriate to call him Hetherington throughout. Peter Preston and Peter Gibbings are normally given their full names.

A FEW WORDS OF THANKS

The publishers have described this book as an 'authorised' history. That is true to the extent that all the necessary records were made available. At no point, however, has anyone authorised what should be put in or suggested what should be left out. That rare freedom calls for thanks.

The writer has been greatly helped by a lot of friends and colleagues, and by no one more than by librarians. Frank Singleton was the *Guardian*'s man in Manchester for the whole period of this book; his knowledge has been invaluable. In London Helen Martin and Maryvonne Grellier have time and again detached themselves from the present day in order to pursue spent topics. Much of the older and sterner material about the *Guardian* is stored at Manchester University. Dr John Laidlar, Head of Reader Services, and his deputy, Mrs Sen, have guided the writer carefully through that maze. The staff at the London Library, the Skipton public library and newspaper section of the British Library at Colindale have been most helpful. At the office friends have interrupted time-critical work on the urgencies of the hour to recollect thirty-year-old conversations. In the final stages the close eye and exceptional patience of Clive Priddle, managing editor at Fourth Estate, have been invaluable. None of these helpers, as writers always have to say but as this writer says with special emphasis, is responsible for the errors and shortcomings of the book. In personal terms, the author not only appreciates the help of his wife but greatly admires her fortitude at table in the face of boring anecdotes.

GEOFFREY TAYLOR
Litton, North Yorkshire
October 1992

The Guardian *building in Cross Street, Manchester, which was demolished in the early 1970s. The sketch is unsigned but attributed to Ned Owens, then the paper's illustrator.*

CHAPTER 1

Unclouded Face

THE EDITOR of the *Manchester Guardian* died, aged forty-nine, in a boating accident on Windermere in April 1932. He left behind a famous newspaper, a financial threat to its continuance, and a set of riddles about the trade and profession of journalism which were still causing perplexity almost sixty years later.

No one could know what Edward Taylor Scott – Ted Scott – would have made of the paper. It was barely possible to visualise the *Guardian* without the man who had been its editor for fifty-seven years and proprietor for twenty-five. Ted Scott lived in the shadow of his father, Charles Prestwich Scott – C.P. Scott – and although he had nominally been editor since 1929 it was only on his father's death, four months before his own, that the burden of filial obedience could be said to have been lifted. But was it lifted even then? Has not some part of it been passed from editor to editor, and manager to manager, ever since? The questions are not rhetorical only: the nature of the newspaper which C.P. edited and the company over which he presided has determined much that has happened, and not happened, since he and the younger of his surviving sons died within so short a time.

Some warning of the difficulties his successors were to meet can be found in the article C.P. Scott published on the paper's centenary in May 1921, which has become among the most quoted in the history of journalism. They arise not so much from the more celebrated of the lapidary sentiments ('Facts are sacred . . . It is well to be frank; it is even better to be fair . . . nor must the unclouded face of truth suffer wrong . . .')* as from those passages in which Scott discusses the peculiar institution which is a newspaper:

> A newspaper has two sides to it. It is a business, like any other, and has to pay its way in the material sense in order to live. But it is much more than a business; it is an institution . . . Between its two sides there should be a happy marriage, and editor and business manager should march hand in hand, the first, be it well understood, just an inch or two in advance.

* The paragraphs are quoted more fully at the end of this chapter.

C.P.'s biographer records an occasion when, at the age of eighty, he did his evening's work at the office and then took the night train to London. He had breakfast with Lloyd George, spent most of the morning in discussing Balkan questions with the Greek statesman Venizélos, lunched with Lord Cecil, then a minister in Baldwin's government, and returned to Manchester by the afternoon train to write a long leader in the evening.[1] (It was probably this encounter which qualified M. Venizélos for a rare acute accent in the *Manchester Guardian*'s style book; the paper has, until recently, tended to be fairly dismissive of diacritical pretensions in foreigners' names.)

No doubt the day was exceptional rather than routine, and Scott survived to edit the paper at an advanced age partly because the pace was less fevered than it became for his successors. For all his insistence on the sanctity of facts, he paid little attention to mundane considerations like being first with the news. He was content to gather it how he might, provided that he could then give it the interpretation which was what he believed his readers wanted. The regimen of the office could be exacting – certainly the peak of productivity was much later at night than it has been in recent years – but there were long intervals when it was not. During much of the period of eleven years which he spent as an MP he was an absentee editor. He exercised an oversight of policy from a distance but he did not execute it on the spot; the *Manchester Guardian*'s famous stand against the government's policy in the Transvaal and its conduct towards the Boers before and during the war of 1899–1902 was not Scott's only but that of the men who did the writing. Nevertheless the tradition that an editor gives himself to the paper was a Scott tradition which has been consistently maintained. In the case of A.P. Wadsworth, editor from 1944 to 31 October 1956, and a bustling gadfly of a man for many years before, it meant than he burned himself out in the service of the *Manchester Guardian* and died, aged sixty-five, within a few days of his retirement.

The task of fitting the company and the paper for the hard competitive times which were seen to be approaching then rested with two men: the manager, Laurence Prestwich Scott, and the new editor whom he appointed, Alastair Hetherington. The partnership began well and continued well for several years, but within a decade it was placed under such severe strain that it disintegrated.

When the bold principles of May 1921 were asserted their author was both editor and sole proprietor. Two generations later matters had become a good deal more complicated. That Laurence Scott was of the blood royal and Hetherington a relatively recent arrival is not an adequate explanation for the troubles that arose between them. Nor did temperament play a large part, for the two men shared a number of assumptions and neither was given to attitudinising. It would be false to suggest that these differences distorted what the paper was doing, and it would even be permissible to shrug them aside as the inevitable byproducts of any business if they had not figured so large for a couple of years in the 1960s and dealt a serious blow to the staff's morale.* They arose from the peculiar nature of the *Guardian*'s ownership, which was then, and remained, vested in the Scott Trust.

The founder of the *Manchester Guardian* in 1821 was John Edward Taylor. In that age of the proliferating but for the most part short-lived press, a newspaper could be jerked into existence almost in hot pursuit of a single political ideal or to right a few simple but manifest wrongs. It scarcely exaggerates to say that the paper owes its origins to the events which turned St Peter's Field in Manchester into a scene of carnage – the 'Peterloo Massacre' – on Monday afternoon, 16 August 1819. The magistrates had determined to arrest Henry Hunt, the popular orator on the abolition of slavery, the suffrage, total abstention, the high price of food, and other causes of the day, as he addressed a large crowd. They could do this in the presence of the crowd only by sending in a mixed military force of which the first to charge were the locally recruited and ill-trained yeomanry, augmented by the 15th Hussars. In a sword attack, Haslam Mills notes,[2] the wounded are in high proportion to the dead. Within a few minutes 11 people were killed and 560 wounded.

Taylor wrote for a Manchester newspaper, the most influential of the time, the *Gazette*, but it would not appear until the following Saturday. He knew that the magistrates would circulate their own official and, he suspected, inaccurate account. He knew also that the *Times* reporter had been arrested along with Hunt. He therefore sent his own immediate account to a London paper – it is not known for certain which – and his *Gazette* colleague Archibald Prentice sent his account to another. They got in first. The *Times* reporter, Tyas, confirmed their reports when he was released. So did the *Liverpool Mercury* and the *Leeds Mercury*. They were never overtaken by the official version. This adventure helped to crystallise in Taylor's mind the idea of starting a newspaper, which he did in 1821. It was not a newspaper of the extreme radical party, with which Taylor was not in sympathy. 'Some of his backers,' Mills notes, 'expected a weekly tract for the times. They got, instead, a tractarianism much milder than that which continued to issue week by week from the office of the *Gazette*. But with it they got much the best newspaper Manchester had yet known.'

John Edward Taylor's younger son, likewise named, was a minor on his father's death, but after an interregnum during which other members of the family acted as trustees he became sole proprietor in 1858. It was he who appointed his cousin C.P. Scott to the staff in 1871 and to the editorship a year later.

Taylor evidently wished to leave the *Guardian* to Scott in his will, but through a combination of slipshod legal drafting on his part and the acquisitive instincts, natural enough, of others who might have an interest in

---

* Crozier, Wadsworth's predecessor, objected to use of the word on the ground that the final 'e' made 'morale' an unnecessary foreign import. 'Moral' had to be used instead. Crozier kept parts of his diary in Greek.

the property, Scott almost lost control of it on Taylor's death in 1905.[3] In 1914, at the age of sixty-eight, he therefore decided that the only way to safeguard the independence of the paper was to confine its ownership to immediate members of the family and people who worked for it. He transferred the bulk of his shareholding to his two sons, John Russell Scott and Edward Taylor Scott, and his son-in-law C.E. (Charles Edward) Montague, leader-writer and at that time celebrated stylist, though his work is too mannered for today's tastes. A formal agreement was made to ensure that the ordinary shares should not be sold to outsiders and that there should be not fewer than three or more than five shareholders. Montague died in 1928, and the ordinary shares of the Manchester Guardian and Evening News Limited were entirely in the hands of the two brothers.

Ted Scott had become editor, J.R. Scott manager. The two men had agreed, though informally, that on the death of either the survivor should buy the remaining shares from his estate. This arrangement left J.R. Scott as sole proprietor, and he was quick to recognise the crippling extent of the death duties which would be payable if he too died prematurely. Indeed the Inland Revenue were casting predatory eyes on the holding which had been in Ted's name. He therefore sought means of saving his two newspapers, the *Manchester Guardian* and the *Manchester Evening News* (jointly owned until 1905, separated on Taylor's death, and not fully reunited until 1929) in that event. The only satisfactory method that could be devised was to give the two papers away unconditionally. His advisers found such an intention contrary to all their training and experience. Gavin Simmonds, a future Lord Chancellor, said when consulted that 'You are trying to do something which is very repugnant to the law of England. You are trying to divest yourself of a property right.'[4] With Simmonds's help J.R. Scott eventually achieved his aim through the agency of the Scott Trust, which came into being on 10 June 1936. The trustees were Scott himself; Sir Ernest Simon (later Lord Simon of Wythenshawe); W.P. Crozier, who had succeeded Ted Scott as editor of the *Manchester Guardian*; William Haley (later Sir William), editor of the *Manchester Evening News*; Laurence Prestwich Scott, elder son of J.R.; and Evelyn Aubrey Montague, war correspondent, London editor and Olympic long-distance runner.

Revisionism occasionally surfaces about the purpose of the Scott Trust. In a note dated 25 February 1969 Laurence writes:

John Scott had for most of his life been dominated by a father who, latterly at least, was universally acclaimed as a great man. John Scott submitted to this domination, reluctantly but passively. When his father died and he found himself in complete command his only method of judging a course of action in connection with the *Manchester Guardian* was to ask himself: 'What would C.P. have done?' He was utterly convinced of the principle of no interference with the editor, but beyond that his only concern seems to have been with financial viability. Whether he held strong views on proprietorial intervention is not known, but as proprietor he never intervened and as far as I know never contemplated such an idea. Although people talk of the Scott Trust ensuring the principles and independence of the papers, as indeed it does, John Scott in fact created it with little more in mind than escaping death duties and so avoiding any danger of loss of independence through a forced sale.

However J.R. Scott's motives are construed the effect was to secure the two papers against predators. The *Manchester Guardian* was not a money-spinner but the *Manchester Evening News* was, and J.R. Scott could have made himself a rich man by offering the company on the market (to Beaverbrook or Northcliffe, for example). Under the regime introduced by him neither he nor any of the other trustees received payment. It is thus unsurprising that to the Inland Revenue the transaction should appear less as generosity, a concept unfamiliar, perhaps, in that quarter, than as eccentricity. But J.R. succeeded, and he retained the power to appoint and dismiss trustees, who in turn would appoint the management. Thus he remained in every sense the proprietor except that he had forfeited all pecuniary interest in the property beyond the salary he drew for his work in it.

Within twelve years, however, the lawyers were no longer satisfied that every loose end had been as effectively tied as J.R. Scott thought it had, in particular because the 1936 settlement had allowed for the accumulation of income and therefore laid the remaining trustees open to tax liability on his death. Consequently they redrafted the trust deed with at least one important difference. The individual power to appoint trustees would die with J.R. Scott. This change, to which little attention was paid at the time, was of course fundamental to the standing of the 'proprietor'. Indeed the company ceased to have a proprietor. When power to fill vacancies and appoint their successors passed to the trustees collectively the proprietorship had been removed from any one individual's hands. Laurence, as a 'settlor' of the old Trust and a 'beneficiary' of the new, must certainly have appreciated the scale of this change but it was only in later years, when his power was put to the challenge, that its significance had a bearing on the fortunes of the company. At the time it meant nothing to the staff, the newspaper world at large, or the citizens of Manchester. As had always been the case before, Scott was the company and the company was Scott. Laurence was referred to and deferred to as the proprietor of the *Guardian* and, as he would never let people forget, of the *Manchester Evening News*.

One formal instruction, and only one, is given to a new editor of the *Guardian*; it applies equally to the head of the company. It derives from the will of the former proprietor, John Edward Taylor (the second of that name: the first, his father, was the founder of the paper), who died in 1905. The will was a clumsy and ambiguous document, unpardonably so as the testament of a lawyer. It laid down no certain method of perpetuating the firm and drew a distinction between its two newspapers. Referring specifically to the *Guardian*, however, Taylor expressed the 'earnest desire' that the newspaper 'shall be conducted in the future on the same lines and in the same spirit as heretofore'. What did that mean? The paper's circulation was in its sixth successive year of decline. From 48,000 in 1898–9 it had fallen to 35,000, the lowest figure certainly for eighteen years. Profits had also fallen. Within two days in February 1900 Alfred Harmsworth, later Lord Northcliffe, started a northern edition of his *Daily Mail* and Edward Hulton founded his *Daily Dispatch* in Manchester, both selling at ½d, or half the cost of the *Guardian*. The *Manchester Courier*, also a morning paper, had been recast, again by Harmsworth, as a direct competitor.

It seems obvious that Taylor's dictum referred to the editorial content of the paper and specifically to the radical stand it had taken in the Sudan and Boer wars, a policy which had helped to drive away readers. But there is another duty, apart from paying attention to what went on heretofore and potentially contradictory to it, laid upon the editor and manager. Although J.R. Scott's trust deed is for the most part written in the tortuous and punctuation-free language necessary to make it watertight in court, the preamble is in everyday English. It notes that 'It was always the policy [of John Edward Taylor and his family] to devote the whole of the surplus profits of the Company which would otherwise have been available for dividends . . . towards building up the reserves of the Company and increasing the circulation of and expanding and improving the said newspapers . . . ', the other said newspaper being, of course, the *Evening News*. It is not enough, in other words, simply to produce a good and radical *Guardian*. Financial 'reserves', sustained by circulation and diversity, are important too. These were the duties inherited not only by Laurence on the death of his father but also by Hetherington on that of Wadsworth.

Laurence was already thirty-five when his father invited him to join the family firm. The year was 1944. Haley had left the year before for the BBC, of which he soon became Director-General, and J.R. Scott was beginning to feel a shortage of managerial talent. Laurence first had to be extracted from the RAF, which took several weeks of lobbying by W.P. Crozier, the editor who had succeeded Ted Scott, and when he arrived it was to become company secretary. A year later he joined the board of directors, and in 1948, when his father died, the company came under his control. His brother Charles (Prestwich) Scott and his cousin Richard (Farquhar) Scott both held senior posts in the company or its newspapers, the former as personnel director, the latter successively as diplomatic, Washington, and Paris correspondent of the *Guardian* and chairman of the Scott Trust. Theirs was the third generation of the Scott dynasty to hold sway. It was the fifth of the Taylor–Scott family, which continued in unbroken succession from 1821 until – when? It could be 1967, when Laurence was deposed as chief executive; or 1973 when he retired from the company; or 1984 when Richard Scott retired from the chairmanship of the Trust on reaching the age of seventy. The line was broken, and the only link which remained between the family and the newspapers lay in the name of the Trust. There was always a strong presumption that the Trust should contain members of the family, but they came to be a small minority, not immediately concerned with the papers' conduct.

Handsome features and magisterial bearing have been striking characteristics of the last two generations of Scotts which Laurence possessed in full. He was six foot four inches tall, though outreached by his son Martin, who for a short time was employed by the company, at six foot seven. He was a man of courtesy towards all his staff. He did not give the appearance of being a happy or contented man until much later in his life; but then his upbringing had not led him to suppose that happiness or contentment were among life's legitimate expectations. At a personal level the clan has been seriously divided. His childhood and adolescence had been cheerless. He disliked Rugby, his father's and grandfather's school (but not his sons': he saw to that) and after Trinity College, Cambridge, he did not take an allotted place at MGEN, nor did his father offer him one. He joined the railway company, the LNER, as a traffic apprentice. Only later did his thinking turn to newspapers when he became, apparently at his father's behest, a trainee first at the *Financial News*, where he learned sub-editing, and then at the *News Chronicle*, where he was an assistant to the general manager. The traineeship was completed but no offer came to join the family concern.

During part of his time in London Laurence lived at Toynbee Hall and worked at the youth centre there in the evenings. He was nominally a Unitarian, though bearing only lightly the bonds which a previous generation had created between the *Guardian* and the Cross Street Chapel; and although he did not in later life show any evidence of a conventional religious attitude he had been attracted in youth to a German Protestant order known as the Hutterian Society of Brothers. In the mid-1930s, and indeed as late as 1942, he was seriously tempted to join this Bruderhof, as indeed did his sisters May (Davies) and Olive (Rutherford). On 7 July 1935 he wrote to his mother from Toynbee Hall:

> I used to hope that I might one day be a 'great' man in one way or another, by which I mean doing something which leaves a permanent mark on the future, but I have a sinking feeling that it isn't really in me to do that, and I shall spend my life as an ordinary typical middle-class citizen.
>
> It is a pity, if that is so, that I ever came to Toynbee, for living here has given me ideas and knowledge which I should not otherwise have got, and which by drawing me into political and social controversies unfit me for the life of a normal suburban citizen.

His uncertainties surfaced again in a letter to his father only three weeks later asking whether he should not leave Toynbee Hall and study world affairs in preparation for a job with the *Manchester Guardian*. An offer to join the staff at last came in 1937, but Laurence wanted to be sure he would have a specific job to do; when that assurance was not forthcoming he rejected his father's offer and stayed with the *News Chronicle* organisation as circulation manager of its London evening newspaper, the *Star*. When the call at last came, and it was clear that there would be a specific and important job for Laurence, he took it. He became identified with the company and with the civic life of Manchester. Some years later[5] when an importunate reader in Gloucester wrote to Laurence saying he must not allow the *Guardian* to be defeated by the Establishment he replied: 'I am sorry but I am inclined to think of myself as a member of the establishment.'

The Manchester to which Laurence returned had been heavily bombed, but the *Guardian*'s four-square and dignified Cross Street headquarters were unchanged. Double-decker trams (exceptionally noisy trams, for some reason) passed outside, and the ponies and traps continued at a delicate trot from the publishing bay to collect and deliver the *Manchester Evening News*. Not many years were to pass before the heart began to go out of the city, hastened by the post-war decline of the textile trade, but for the time being it was possible to pretend that the former greatness of the city survived. Well-informed daily reports about cotton sentiment on 'Change were written by W.G. Pilkington and (a small anomaly) there appeared on the commercial pages every Monday a notice in keeping with the *Guardian*'s inherited status as the commercial newspaper of record for the region. It bore the ruby heading (the smallest common type: 5½pt.) 'Preston Farm Produce' and said simply: 'Wholesale prices of eggs and poultry were in accordance with Food Control Orders', for which information some enterprising freelance was still earning an honest half-crown more than two years after the end of the war. Some weeks he would add 'There were no eggs on the retail market'; on others 'Retailers sold two eggs per rationed customer at control price'. But if, in the late 1940s, the start of the city's decline had almost imperceptibly begun (a decline, incidentally, which had been reversed by the end of the 1980s) the fortunes of its chief morning newspaper had never been better. The *Manchester Guardian*'s circulation was growing, faster outside its home area than within. It was still required reading in the cotton towns and in north-east Cheshire, as indeed it had long been in Whitehall, but it was becoming increasingly so in Oxford, Cambridge, and those parts of London generically thought of as NW3. The *Guardian* had to satisfy a changing clientele.

Laurence was thus in situ when Wadsworth became terminally ill. It was his duty to appoint a successor. Hector Alastair Hetherington's father was Sir Hector, Vice-Chancellor of Glasgow University, and his own college, after Gresham's School, was Corpus Christi, Oxford. But his first substantial piece of writing was neither an academic thesis nor a newspaper article. It was a work entitled *A Military Geography of Schleswig-Holstein*, of which some one hundred copies are said to be held in the archives of the Ministry of Defence.

This paper, classified as 'restricted', runs to about one hundred pages and describes the soil and other aspects of the terrain important to tanks. It was written immediately after the Second World War when Major Hetherington was an Intelligence officer on transfer to 8 Corps HQ from 11 Armoured Division. He had a close interest in the subject of tank terrain, the tank which he commanded having been destroyed by enemy action north-east of Vire, Normandy, with the loss of one crew member killed and two wounded.

War had begun for Hetherington in the Pay Corps because his eyesight was considered too poor for combat duty when he volunteered. An eventual change of War Council policy allowed him to switch to tanks. He was commissioned in 1942, after two years in the ranks, and took part in both the Normandy landing and the relief of Antwerp, a critical operation in the Allied advance on which he lifted a curtain in the *Guardian* of 1 September 1969, the 25th anniversary. At the end of the war he resumed, though not in the way he had expected, the career in journalism which up to then had begun and ended with three months in the sub-editors' room of the *Glasgow Herald*. He became 'editorial controller' of *Die Welt*.

The military government in the British zone of Germany decided that the country was in dire need of a newspaper. It had put Sefton Delmer of the *Daily Express* in charge, and he had begun assembling an editorial team from his own paper, the *Daily Mail*, and the *Daily Mirror*. Some members of the Control Commission staff then asked whether the new Hamburg-based newspaper should not ideally be a *Times–Manchester Guardian* type of operation rather than an *Express–Mail*. The question was put to members of the Cabinet, which decided in favour of a 'heavy'. Duncan Wilson, an officer in the Control Commission (later to become Ambassador in Moscow), had heard of a young journalist in 8 Corps HQ who might be useful, not realising the depths of his inexperience, and Hetherington was appointed in Sefton Delmer's place. Hetherington had picked up enough German to talk to prisoners of war but scarcely enough to edit a newspaper unaided, so that apart from the locally recruited staff the Foreign Office sent out Werner Burmeister to help him. He was the ideal man, both for *Die Welt* and later, though only for short intervals, for the *Guardian*. At the age of twenty-one or twenty-two he had stood as a Socialist in Berlin in the 1933 election and had had to bolt to Britain soon afterwards, going to the London School of Economics. He was a witty and a learned man, and wrote leaders for the *Guardian* in 1952–3 and again after Hetherington's accession.

After Hamburg, Glasgow again, where he shared tasks with his future economics colleague on the *Guardian*, Harold Griffiths. (Griffiths left journalism in 1967 to join the Treasury. He occasionally boasted that he had known a time when the future editor of the *Guardian* could not spell 'accommodation'.) Anthony Howard alleged of Hetherington[6] that he was 'rather a forbidding figure' on the *Glasgow Herald*. He told a man who had made a trivial error with people's ages in a New Year's honours list: 'You may as well realise, Worsthorne, that you will never get on in journalism if you can't get simple facts right.' Peregrine Worsthorne later became editor of the *Sunday Telegraph*, and it cannot be said in truth that close cordiality was ever maintained between the two newspapers.

In 1950 Hetherington applied to join the *Guardian* and immediately found himself in rapport with Wadsworth. The rapport was strengthened through his having arrived early by train for the interview. With time to spare he went to look round the John Rylands Library in Deansgate; it was one of Wadsworth's joys to be a member of the library's governing council. Wadsworth took him on as a leader-writer and defence correspondent; within three years he had become an assistant editor and foreign editor.

The paper he joined was still the paper moulded by C.P. Scott. It was virtually unchanged in appearance, though still much slimmer because of the long post-war shortage of newsprint, much of which was paid for in scarce dollars. (Newsprint rationing in England did not end until 1956.) It had advertisements on the front page. On the inside pages pride of place went to the several leading articles which, often in quality of writing, when necessary in vehemence of expression, and always in catholicity of subjects, had long marked out the paper from all its regional contemporaries. Its only English competitor in that department was *The Times*, but the *Guardian* still belonged to Manchester. What Scott had said of it twenty-four years earlier[7] was recognisably the spirit of the paper as it gathered itself together after the Second World War. Had anyone recalled it the quotation could have become a slight embarrassment as the years wore on and the ties with Manchester weakened, even severed, but it was not so in the early 1950s. There were papers, Scott said at one of the many bestowals of honour in his later life, which would never be sold and which would rather suffer extinction.

> The public has its rights. The paper which has grown up in a great community, nourished by its resources, reflecting in a thousand ways its spirit and its interests, in a real sense belongs to it. How else except in the permanence of that association can it fulfil its duty or repay the benefits and the confidence it has received?

Thus the *MG* carried not only reports by Alistair Cooke at the United Nations in New York, Terence Prittie on the start of reconstruction in Germany, and Darsie Gillie in Paris on the travails of the Fourth Republic and the Friday transactions of the Académie des Inscriptions et Belles-Lettres, but the sermons of Canon Peter Green in Salford, the proceedings of the Manchester University Senate, and a record of the life and times of the Hulme Hippodrome and the Peak Park Planning Board. The leaders would analyse NATO strategy or African education in Northern Rhodesia, and the correspondence columns would carry regular contributions from the Rev. F.H. Amphlett-Micklewright, Minister of the Cross Street Chapel, or L.F. Behrens, of Barlow Moor Road, Manchester 20, a leading local Liberal and stalwart of the United

Nations Association. There has never been, in England, a newspaper quite like it, though its posture and content would not be unfamiliar to a reader of the *St Louis Post-Dispatch*, the *Milwaukee Journal* or others of the American regional press.

Laurence had already realised, however, as Hetherington soon did also, that a newspaper whose advertising support was drawn almost exclusively from one region of the country could not for ever purport to serve a national readership. Not long after he joined his father in 1944 Laurence took stock of the post-war requirements of the paper so far as they could be seen. He both sensed and showed by market research that the social environment for newspapers was going to change almost as much as it had changed to allow Northcliffe to launch the *Daily Mail* in 1896. Drawing on pre-war experience of the reckless competition in Fleet Street – he almost lived to see the repetition of it when even *The Times* turned to a top people's bingo – and aware that the solid commercial base which the north-west of England had so long provided for the paper could not be relied on much longer, he set himself three targets. One target, rather: to make the *Guardian* a fully national newspaper by printing in London as well as Manchester.

Three things were needed to allow that to happen. News must be put on the front page, the title must be changed by dropping the name Manchester, and some method of duplicating the printing operation, or otherwise getting late papers into London, must be found. The first change he accomplished in 1952 under Wadsworth, though Wadsworth prevaricated to the last (he rebelled against taking decisions on anything except what to put in the paper: those he loved). The second came under Hetherington in 1959. Printing in London did not start until 1961 and in spite of the cheering notices which went up on the board it was an almost total disaster. But that is to anticipate. In 1955 Roy Thomson wanted Hetherington as editor of his then flagship newspaper, *The Scotsman*,[8] which he had acquired in 1953, but Alastair Dunnett was appointed on the advice of James Coltart. In 1956 Wadsworth became terminally ill. Until September he could still organise his staff but his forthcoming retirement was announced on 17 October. Hetherington was appointed to succeed him. He formally took over as editor on 1 November, within forty-eight hours of the invasion of Egypt by Israel with the collusion of Britain and France, and on the day after his thirty-seventh birthday.

Suez became so closely associated with the new editorship in the minds of readers and staff, and has been so constant a theme of Hetherington's own subsequent writings, that there has been some tendency to regard his succession as automatic. Unsurprising, yes; automatic, no. Another strong candidate for the job was P.J. (Paddy) Monkhouse, a second-generation *Guardian* man who had returned from a commission in the Royal Ulster Rifles to be Wadsworth's deputy, and whom many on the staff at the time would have welcomed as their new chief. In addition to bringing his own enthusiasms to the paper (for, among other things, Manchester, for the Pennines and the people who lived there, and for East and West Africa) Monkhouse recruited some exceptional talent which included Brian Redhead, Nesta Roberts, Norman Shrapnel, W.L. Webb and Harry Whewell. Mary Stott, women's page editor, has described her grievous disappointment on learning that he was not to get the job.

> I knew Patrick Monkhouse and admired and respected him more than almost any journalist I had ever met – or indeed have met since. He seemed to me the quintessential *Guardian* man, in his gifts, his attitudes, and above all in his incomparable integrity. I had never accepted the possibility that anyone else might succeed Wadsworth. Because of Hetherington's stand at the time of Suez I was quickly able to tell myself, 'It's going to be all right', for it must in a newly-appointed editor, deprived of the support of his mentor Wadsworth, have taken a degree of courage and integrity one regards as essential in a *Guardian* editor.[9]

Whether or not Monkhouse was more than merely disappointed remained in doubt. To Ayerst he privately confided in later years that he had told Laurence Scott that he was not the right man for the job; to Richard Scott at the time he appeared outraged. Richard, as chairman of the Trust, was asked by Laurence to invite Monkhouse to join that body in what might be thought the somewhat brazen offer of a consolation prize. (This was the earliest of several personally difficult assignments thrust on Richard in his chairman's capacity.) Monkhouse at first declined, then accepted. He continued for several years as a scrupulously loyal deputy editor. Paddy's widow Pamela, whom he had met when she joined the paper as a trainee in 1947, said in retrospect that Paddy might not have resented Hetherington's preferment – but she decidedly had!

Another candidate who had not been forgotten, and had not forgotten the *Guardian*, was J.M.D. Pringle. He had been on the *Guardian* as long ago as 1934, had moved to *The Times*, returned to the *Guardian* as Wadsworth's invaluable assistant editor and leader-writer after the war, and had then gone to Australia for the first of two stints as editor of the *Sydney Morning Herald*. Tiring of that job he was about to leave when he received a cable telling him of Wadsworth's retirement and Hetherington's succession. It is clear from his book that he had secretly hoped that he might return to Manchester as editor but such a course had now come to seem impossible from the Manchester end. In the exchange of letters which followed, Wadsworth wrote: 'I agree that Hetherington will do an excellent job but I should really have preferred that we could have brought you in. Evidently that was not to be reckoned with and there was, of course, the necessity for doing something rather quickly.'[10]

Mary Stott overcame her misgivings. She recounts that she learned to respect Hetherington not only for his qualities as a journalist and his endurance under strain but also (and many others on the staff would echo her sentiments) for his breaking down of the social barriers which for a couple of generations had been a serious disfigurement to the paper's supposed liberalism. The distinction between the Corridor, habitat of the leader-writers, and the rest of the editorial staff had been rigid. Reporters and their wives had, it is true, sometimes been admitted to the newspaper's Didsbury/Withington soirée circuit but sub-editors, rarely if at all. There were officers, NCOs, and other ranks. Wadsworth himself could not be faulted on this score. He had left school at fourteen and come up the hard way, through reporting for the *Rochdale Observer* and improving his history at R.H. Tawney's tutorials at Manchester University; he was merciless in teasing his junior staff for any intellectual shortcomings but he knew no social distinctions as he shuffled about the office in his carpet slippers, sucking his pipe. Unfortunately his wife did not, in her entertaining, follow his egalitarian example and a sharp distinction was drawn between those who were expected at her musical evenings and those who were not.

On giving up the reins Wadsworth wrote to J.E.D. Putz, the chief sub-editor, thanking him for his good wishes: 'I think Alastair will do very well indeed: I expect however that he may be a little more exacting than I have been! Still, we can only trust that wisdom will guide him . . . ' To another friend he confided: 'He is a very serious young man: I hope he will not edit a frivolous newspaper.'[11]

The paragraphs in C.P. Scott's centenary article referred to at the beginning of this chapter read:

In all living things there must be a certain unity, a principle of vitality and growth. It is so with a newspaper, and the more complete and clear this unity the more vigorous and fruitful the growth. I ask myself what the paper stood for when I first knew it, what it has stood for since and stands for now. A newspaper has two sides to it. It is a business, like any other, and has to pay its way in the material sense in order to live. But it is much more than a business; it is an institution; it reflects and it influences the life of a whole community; it may even affect wider destinies. It is in its way, an instrument of government. It plays on the minds and consciences of men. It may educate, stimulate, assist, or it may do the opposite. It has, therefore, a moral as well as a material existence, and its character and influence are in the main determined by the balance of these two forces. It may make profit or power its first object, or it may conceive itself as fulfilling a higher and more exacting function.

I think I may honestly say that, from the day of its foundation, there has not been much doubt as to which way the balance tipped so far as regards the conduct of the paper whose fine traditions I inherited and which I have had the honour to serve through all my working life. Had it not been so, personally, I could not have served it. Character is a subtle affair, and has many shades and sides to it. It is not a thing to be much talked about, but rather to be felt. It is the slow deposit of past actions and ideals. It is for each man his most precious possession, and so it is for that latest growth of time the newspaper. Fundamentally it implies honesty, cleanness, courage, fairness, a sense of duty to the reader and the community. A newspaper is of necessity something of a monopoly, and its first duty is to shun the temptations of monopoly. Its primary office is the gathering of news. At the peril of its soul it must see that the supply is not tainted. Neither in what it gives, nor in what it does not give, nor in the mode of presentation must the unclouded face of truth suffer wrong. Comment is free, but facts are sacred. 'Propaganda', so called, by this means is hateful. The voice of opponents no less than of friends has a right to be heard. Comment also is justly subject to a self-imposed restraint. It is well to be frank; it is even better to be fair. This is an ideal. Achievement in such matters is hardly given to man. Perhaps none of us can attain to it in the desirable measure. We can but try, ask pardon for shortcomings, and there leave the matter.

CHAPTER 2

No Pots in Accrington

STYLES differ. Sir Gordon Newton rarely wrote in the *Financial Times*, but that did not prevent his being a highly esteemed editor. It was reported of Sir William Haley that he had been editor of *The Times* for seven months before he wrote a leader for it.[1] Hetherington enjoyed no such comfortable interval to adjust his weight to the chair. During Wadsworth's illness he had, with his chief's encouragement, fashioned the paper's policies towards the Middle East. Gamal Abdel Nasser had lately been confirmed by plebiscite as President of Egypt. In the growing alarm on the part of the Western powers (including, to begin with, Eisenhower's America) which followed his nationalisation of the Suez Canal, the inflammatory tone of Nasser's rhetoric could not be disregarded, but the *Manchester Guardian* still saw the main question as whether Britain and France could continue in a changed new world with the habits of their imperial lifetimes. The other consideration was that opposition to signs of recklessness on the part of the Prime Minister, Sir Anthony Eden, had to be balanced by a concern for the ultimate safety of the state of Israel.

The paper's relations with Israel have always been uneasy, beset by conflicting scruples. For a man of C.P. Scott's instincts and persuasions (and generation, for the year of the Balfour Declaration was 1917) the powerful advocacy of Zionism in its benign form was an obvious course to take. Persecuted minority? Then protect them!

By 1914 Manchester had become in some respects the capital of Zionism in England.[2] In 1880 the city's Jewish population had been not more than 3,000. By 1900, with the influx of immigrants into the manufacturing towns and mining areas, it was 25,000. The city had a Russian Jews' Benevolent Society, founded in 1904 by immigrants from Berdichev, and the records have lately been found of the Foreign Jews' Protection Society from 1917 to 1919.[3]

With two of his leader-writers, Herbert Sidebotham and Harry Sacher, and two young businessmen, Simon Marks and Israel Sieff (the progenitors of Marks and Spencer), Scott collaborated with Chaim Weizmann in the policy which resulted in the Balfour Declaration designating Palestine as a home for the Jewish people.

Weizmann was a chemist whose talents enabled him to leave his native Russia for several West European universities and finally to take up a teaching and research post in Manchester in the first decade of the century. There he met A.J. Balfour, the future Foreign Secretary, during the general election campaign of 1906 and became friendly with Scott, who introduced him to Lloyd George and others. One reason for the cordial relations he developed with members of the wartime government was that his chemical speciality, which was research into fermentation, enabled him to help in overcoming a serious shortage of acetone, then a vital ingredient in the manufacture of explosives for the Royal Navy. The *MG* leader-writers of the day may not have understood the chemistry but they were riveted by the Zionism. At least, that was the case with Sacher. Sidebotham was also the paper's military analyst, and in those years imperialism was a polity which a radical British newspaper was inclined to modify but not (except in the *Guardian*'s case in Ireland) to repudiate. The military situation, Sidebotham wrote in the paper's leader columns, required a friendly Palestine for the defence of Egypt and the Suez Canal. 'On the realisation of that condition depends the whole future of the British Empire and a Sea Empire.'[4]

Sidebotham did not meet Weizmann until 1916 and his advocacy of a Zionist policy was based 'on grounds of British interest and with the single idea of helping the victory of the Allies in the War'.[5] He was nevertheless an invaluable recruit to the cause and was persuaded by Sacher and other members of the circle to submit a memorandum to the Foreign Office developing his theme. What became of it is not known. The Foreign Office would certainly have found it too extreme; even one of the leading Zionists then living in Britain, Nahum Sokolow, who in Weizmann's absence was charged with promoting the Zionist policy in Whitehall, argued strongly against the maximalist demands being advocated by the *MG* pair. But they continued in their ways. 'Sacher and Sidebotham appear to have been alone in insisting that the formula [to be put before Balfour] should raise the question of a Jewish State, and their drafts never had a chance of being accepted.'[6] Weizmann wrote to Scott on 20 June 1917 to tell him that Balfour had promised to make public the British government's sympathy with the movement but the document was still in the drafting stage and went through at least five versions before it was deemed to have gained the required patina of subtlety.[7] It was issued in the form of a letter to Lord Rothschild on 2 November 1917 and was textually faithful to everything the *Guardian*, if not Sidebotham in his private moments, had been advocating. It is brief enough to quote:

> His Majesty's Government view with favour the establishment in Palestine of a national home for the Jewish people, and will use their best endeavours to

facilitate the achievement of this object, it being clearly understood that nothing shall be done which may prejudice the civil and religious rights of existing non-Jewish communities in Palestine, or the rights and political status enjoyed by Jews in any other country.

But not all Jews living in England were Zionists. Two highly influential members of the community, David Alexander as chairman of the Board of Deputies of British Jews, and Claude Montefiore, president of the Anglo-Jewish Association, strongly opposed 'the claim that the Jewish settlements in Palestine shall be recognised as possessing a national character in a political sense'. This implied, they said, that the Jewish communities of the world were incapable of complete social and political identification with the nations among whom they dwelt.

> Emancipated Jews in this country . . . have no separate aspirations in a political sense. They hold Judaism to be a religious system, with which their political status has no concern, and they maintain that, as citizens of the countries in which they live, they are fully and sincerely identified with the national spirit and interests of those countries. It follows that the establishment of a Jewish nationality in Palestine, founded on this theory of Jewish homelessness, must have the effect throughout the world of stamping the Jews as strangers in their native lands, and of undermining their hard-won position as citizens and nationals of those lands.[8]

This letter was repudiated by Chief Rabbi Hertz, and the provincial Jewish communities, of which Manchester was the biggest, played a large part in deposing Alexander.

Scott's response in the *Guardian*'s leader columns was one of joy at 'the fulfilment of an aspiration, the signpost of a destiny'. Without a national home the Jews would never have security. 'The example of Armenia and the wiping out of a population fifty-fold that of the Jewish colonies in Palestine was a terrible warning of what might at any time be in store for these.' But nothing better illustrates how even the wisest and best-intentioned can be deceived about the working out of their schemes. The only reference to the Arabs is a glancing one: 'Other conditions are involved, and are stated or implied in the present declaration. The existing Arab population of Palestine is small and at a low stage of civilisation. It contains within itself none of the elements of progress, but it has its rights, and these must be carefully respected.'

Under Crozier's editorship, from May 1932 to June 1944, support for Zionism became the inevitable response to Nazi persecution, yet in the view of some of Crozier's contemporaries it was also in danger of becoming his King Charles's Head. Wadsworth did not change the paper's line on Israel but he pursued it with less vigour. John Pringle, his assistant editor immediately after the war, says of Wadsworth that

> He saved the *Guardian* by making it more lively, more entertaining, more realistic, and a far better *news* paper. He quickly dumped those causes, like pacifism, Zionism, internationalism and the official Liberal Party, which however noble and idealistic they had once been, had become so many albatrosses slung round the *Guardian*'s neck. He was splendidly impatient with bores.[9]

Ernest Bevin, Labour's post-war Foreign Secretary, and a man already imbued when he took office with the orthodox Foreign Office irritation about Zionism, was one of the people Wadsworth most admired. And it was Bevin who encapsulated the post-war British dilemma in a speech in the Commons on 26 January 1949:

> I do not want to arouse controversy, but ever since I have had anything to do with it [the Palestine problem] I have been conscious of one fundamental fact, that the Balfour Declaration promised the same thing to two peoples. If partition is difficult now it is because the statesmen in those days did not face the problem fearlessly, resolutely and finally. If they desired a National State for the Jews and not, as they said, a National Home, I cannot understand why they did not carve out a piece of territory and then say, 'This is Jewish and that is Arab' . . . It was no service to posterity to take refuge in contradictory statements to Arabs and Jews, leaving this problem to go on for thirty-two years under successive governments and never bringing it to a final issue.

Wadsworth wrote only occasionally on Palestine; his preoccupation abroad was with the beginning of the Cold War, and at home with the industrial and economic fortunes of the Labour government. He encouraged others to take an interest in the Middle East. Chief among the others became Hetherington, who as defence correspondent and foreign editor found himself increasingly engrossed in Middle Eastern affairs to which he brought no intimate prior knowledge but to which he gave, now and for his entire period with the paper, a great deal of his attention.

The divisions of the Middle East were rapidly reflected in the British political leadership and newspaper-reading public. Party political persuasion at home had no relevance to the fortunes of the Levant (nor did it thirty years later when, in the *Guardian* office, a senior member of the staff who voted the straight Left ticket on virtually every issue was also a committed Zionist). In 1956 Hugh Gaitskell, leader of the Labour party, had to be cajoled, not least by Hetherington and the *MG*, into the position of stern critic of the Eden government, though he held fast to that position having reached it.

Not all Gaitskell's colleagues were equally convinced. Among them was the Labour MP for Manchester, Cheetham, who spoke at length in the Commons debate of 31 October 1956. Towards the end he said:

> If certain Arab aggressive intentions are not going to be moderated, then I am certainly not among those who would invite the Israelis to sit back quietly and be hacked to pieces, as their enemies mobilise on all sides ready to slay, bomb and ruin them, their consolation being to bathe their mortal wounds in the crocodile tears of the leader writers and cartoonists of the *Manchester Guardian*.
>
> I, for one, could say many things in criticism of the sanctimonious humbug of those on the sidelines, who are rather like Othello . . . who said of Desdemona that he would kill her first and love her after. I think the *Manchester Guardian* would sometimes like to do that with the Israeli people and the Israeli Government; it is willing to admire and love them after they have lain down peacefully, qualifying under all the rules of the best north-western Liberal school for a good conduct medal, but having sold the pass of their kingdom and sold the right of their people to live in peace, freedom and progress. Nobody on this side of the House need be ashamed of defending the rights of the Israeli people to exist.

Next day the *MG* dutifully reported the words, and Alastair Hetherington, who must be cast as the Moor in the metaphor of Harold Lever MP, though that is marginally better than being Iago, formally became editor.

During the summer of 1956, and specifically from 26 July, when Nasser nationalised the Canal, Hetherington had become increasingly alarmed by what he saw as Eden's dangerous irrationality. His fears were amplified by messages from the US State Department via the *Guardian*'s Washington correspondent, Max Freedman. The reporting from the Middle East was in the hands of Michael Adams, based in Egypt, who had not at that time formed the vigorous attachment to Arab interests for which he later became well known but who wrote consistently and knowledgeably about the strength of nationalism under Nasser and who helped to shape the paper's unhesitating and outspoken opposition to the use of force by Britain and France.

President Eisenhower's special envoy on Middle East matters, Robert Murphy, had been in London and had reported to Secretary of State Dulles that the British government was preparing to seize the Suez Canal by force and without delay. That was not common knowledge. It must be assumed that Freedman had been told in confidence because he did not put it in his dispatch for the paper but sent it as a private message to Hetherington and Richard Scott, the diplomatic correspondent. The effect was not as strong as it would have been had the story, sourced from Washington, appeared on the front page, but Scott made the best use he could of it by suggesting that Mr Dulles's purpose in paying an unexpected visit to London was to 'counsel more moderate action' than that which Britain and France had favoured.

Hetherington, however, used the information as the basis of a long leader on the possibility of military action which appeared on 2 August, almost three months before hostilities in fact began. He said:

> The Government is right to be prepared for military action at Suez. If Colonel Nasser were to close the canal – but only in that event – British troops should move in. At present there is no possible warrant for using force . . . What Colonel Nasser has done may be awkward, commercially damaging to the West, and perhaps even part of a plan for creating a new Arab Empire based on the Nile. But it is not ground for armed action – unless he closes the canal, or seizes the British maintenance bases there [left over from the British evacuation of Egypt under a treaty of 1954] or turns against his neighbours. We must be ready for action, but we must not launch it without cause . . .

Hetherington's argument against the use of force in collusion with Israel (as he suspected, and as was later shown) was of a piece with the paper's pragmatic assessment of where 'British interests' lay. Like Wadsworth, who at this period was still intellectually engaged with the paper, though he could no longer be physically in control, he had a feel for what was right for it. Wadsworth had supported Bevin in steering the Labour party away from the sentimental attachment to the Soviet Union and hostility to the United States to which it was naturally inclined. 'Atlanticism', as it came briefly and unhappily to be called, was a position to which Hetherington also was naturally sympathetic, and it was the easy confidence and understanding between the two men which, among other things, qualified Hetherington in Wadsworth's eyes to succeed him as editor.

More than pragmatism, though, was involved. When faced with what he took to be an issue of political morality Hetherington had little hesitation. In the early days Michael Kennedy, for a long time Northern editor of the *Daily Telegraph* and (should one say but?) a firm friend of the *Guardian*, playfully asked him while they were sharing a railway journey why the *Guardian* always took the other side in colonial disputes. (The spur to this question was almost certainly the Nyasaland (Malawi) emergency of 1959.) Hetherington coloured sharply, as he frequently did when discomposed, and replied that he too came from a country which had been looked down upon as second rate and known domination from outside.*

Asked in later years what, apart from Suez, had been his most difficult editorial decisions he replied that Suez had not been difficult at all. He had

---

* Hetherington did not dispute the recollection but qualified it by saying that the Scots had suffered as much from Scottish landowners and their own internal feuds as they did from the English. [Private sources.]

had good information and no doubts. Hindsight confirms that response. The policy with which he launched his editorship could not have taken any other form without contradicting all that had gone before. From the time the Suez crisis began, with the withdrawal of American and British help to Egypt for the building of the Aswan High Dam and the subsequent nationalisation of the Canal, the *Guardian* had argued against the standard imperial reaction of putting Nasser in his place by force. A generation or more later such an argument may not appear especially novel, but in 1956 Britain was still an imperial power, governing large swathes of Africa and Asia, operating a network of alliances in the Middle East itself, and in general expecting to have its wishes heeded. It was not therefore to every reader's taste when, on 31 October, the day after Britain and France had issued their threat to intervene militarily 'in whatever strength may be necessary', the *MG* wrote:

> The Anglo-French ultimatum to Egypt is an act of folly, without justification in any terms but brief expediency. It pours petrol on a growing fire. There is no knowing what kind of explosion will follow . . .
>
> The Prime Minister sought to justify the ultimatum by saying that we must protect our shipping, our citizens, and 'vital international rights'. But what possible right have we to attack another country? The British and French military action threatened in the ultimatum, if carried out, will be flagrant aggression . . .

On the next day the leader was headed 'A Disaster'.

> The world must be told clearly that millions of British people are deeply shocked by the aggressive policy of the Government. Its action in attacking Egypt is a disaster of the first magnitude. It is wrong on every count – moral, military, and political. It is a severe blow to Britain's reputation, to the Atlantic alliance, to the United Nations, and, not least, to Britain's prospect of material prosperity. To recover from the disaster will take years – if, indeed, it is ever possible . . .

Eden became a very sick man and in his suspicion of the BBC went so far as to order an instrument to be drawn up for taking it over. His concern was to stop repetition in the World Service of British press criticism of his government's actions.[10] The endeavour inevitably failed; the press summary, which went out three times in the early part of the day, British time, had for so long been part of the daily broadcasting format that to have dropped it would have aroused world-wide suspicions. However, the BBC had actively to resist pressure for Richard Scott to be excluded from among the regular World Service commentators.

It would have been even more difficult to stop the reporting of Parliament, where Hugh Gaitskell, leader of the Labour Opposition, had lately come to speak in much the same terms as the *Guardian* (at least partly, it would seem, at the instigation of Mark Arnold-Forster, in his capacity as political reporter,

COMRADESHIP IN HUNGARY

Khrushchev sent Soviet tanks into Hungary while the world's attention was diverted by the invasion of Suez. The Hungarians, led by Imre Nagy, had been turning against Soviet Russia and moving towards a position of neutralism. The Russian response, depicted in this Low cartoon of 12 December 1956, was uncompromising and brutal.

who had been sent on a mission to Gaitskell by Wadsworth).[11] That had not always been the case. He had made himself a hostage to accusations of inconsistency by his speech in the Commons debate of 2 August when he had said: 'It is all very familiar. It is exactly the same as that we encountered from Mussolini and Hitler in those years before the war.' (The *Guardian*, while recognising that Nasser was intemperate, unpredictable and a threat to Israel, had argued against the comparison with Hitler and his occupation of the Rhineland.)

The *Guardian* was not without allies in the press; it would be wrong to present its crusade as single-handed. The *Observer* under David Astor had long been highly critical of what it saw as the government's failure to understand the strength of Arab nationalism and hostility to imperialist activity in the rest of the Third World (though that term had not yet been invented). Among the national dailies the *Daily Mirror* and *News Chronicle* opposed the operation, though they were one day less quick off the mark. Freedman's early warning to Manchester in August about the possibility of armed force served the *Guardian* well in making the office think the then unthinkable. When the invasion finally came the *Observer* had bitterly to confess that it had not believed 'our Government [would] make a military attack in defiance of its solemn international obligation . . . We had not realised that our Government was capable of such folly and such crookedness.'

The extent of collusion between France and Israel and between Britain and France is now a matter of record, and the clandestine meeting at Sèvres between politicians and officials of the three countries is now known to have been the occasion when it was put in place. Credit for the first hard evidence goes to James Morris in the *MG* of 20 November 1956. Israeli censorship had prevented his filing from Tel Aviv, so he went to Cyprus to do so. What he reported was that French Mystère aircraft flown by French pilots in French uniform had played an important and possibly decisive part in the Israeli offensive across the Sinai desert, destroying Egyptian trucks and armour with napalm. Darsie Gillie, Paris correspondent, was able to piece together some of the political evidence of collusion although the full import of Sèvres was not then known.

Michael Adams, along with other British correspondents in Cairo, was put under house arrest, or as he more accurately put it (27 November) was luxuriously interned in the Semiramis Hotel. When he was expelled 'the security officer was goggle-eyed and a shade impatient . . . "You have so many friends here – and you must leave the country?"' Adams grieved for all the other British and French passport-holders and the Jews, even Egyptian ones, expelled. Many, Levantines and Maltese for example, had acquired their nationality by accident and now left their homes with twenty Egyptian pounds to represent a life's work. Morris, who had been in Tel Aviv, was lamenting the dismal prospect faced by Israel. Shipping to Eilat was still vulnerable to Egyptian interference:

> But the Israelis are perhaps optimistic if they suppose they can squeeze any concessions out of Egypt at all. Many of them think that by giving the Egyptian Army a bloody nose they have strengthened their national position in the Middle East; they do not yet realise that in the eyes of most of the world it is they, not the Egyptians, who deserve to suffer sanctions. Indeed, though they complain of United Nations incompetence, their manner towards the representatives of that organisation is often insufferably arrogant.
>
> There can be little doubt that the Powers now in the ascendant in the Arab world intend one day to obliterate Israel and are already doing their best

towards that end. But the Israelis do not seem to know how to convince the world of that fact, or retain the international sympathies so easily commanded by the hideous agonies of recent Jewish history.

Morris encapsulated there a great deal of *Guardian* sentiment about Israel at the time and since.

Like the speech at Agincourt the opening leaders of Hetherington's reign – the 'act of folly' and the 'wrong on every count' – were designed to stiffen sinews, though in an opposite cause. Among most, not all, in the office they had that effect, and those who read them eagerly at their desks and in corridors when the first editions came up felt towards their less inspirited colleagues, on that and other papers, as did Henry towards the gentlemen in England now a-bed. But if it was St Crispian's day at the *Guardian*, for many of its traditional readers it was a day of shame.

In times of crisis a circulation manager will normally know how to distinguish between the genuine loss of readers and a momentary loss of nerve on the part of newsagents and reps. Reports of cancellations feed on one another and have a cumulative effect. Tales of woe are magnified out of proportion. In this case many of the reports of disaffection were genuine enough, at least in the *MG*'s traditional heartland, and were reflected in some of the letters to the editor which the paper printed.

The paper's two main circulation reps on its home ground were Norman Shaw and Syd Markey. Shaw, who looked after North Manchester and the cotton belt beyond, was a former compositor who, like others of his kind, not only worked for the paper but loved it. He must have sold a thousand copies on the strength of his personality alone. (At a party conference at Blackpool he had a stand next to one of his competitors. He said of their different approaches, 'It's my job to sell the *Guardian*. It's his job to stop *The Times* falling into the wrong hands.')

Norman Shaw was greatly proud of the *Guardian* during Suez, but the people he was dealing with were not. That was the case not only with customers but with neighbours where he lived in Grasscroft, a superior part of Saddleworth. South-east Lancashire was already at the start of the huge social and economic changes which have since transformed it, but in 1956 it was still the practice for every household of substance to take the *MG*, whether it was read or not. Houses were bought and sold through it. Births, marriages and deaths were incomplete without a notice in it. It had to be on the hall table. At Suez the fashion abruptly changed. 'It became a dirty word,' Shaw recalled. 'It became the fashion to stop the thing. People used to say "I'm never going to have it in the house." It hit me in the pit of the stomach.'

This was also the experience at the time of the circulation manager, W.J. Lascelles, who at day-to-day encounters in Manchester would be hearing much the same thing. He in turn reported to Laurence Scott. But the figures themselves, when they were counted at the end of the month, tell a different story. The *Guardian*'s alleged heavy loss of readers during Suez is a myth. That is not to say it is untrue but that the truth it tells is not as it seems. Nationally the paper showed a substantial increase in sales as a direct result of Suez, and although sales in the North-west did not follow exactly the national trend they did not show the dramatic fall of popular legend but rather a small increase. Some people stopped the paper but rather more started it. It took time for the North–South discrepancy to open up, but it did so; between the beginning of 1956 and the end of 1959 the circulation in London and the Home Counties grew by more than one-third and the North-west remained much as they had been. (Detailed figures for the Suez months and for the years 1956–9 are given at the end of this chapter.)

Other things were contributing to the switch of readership. Norman Shaw used to have four or five quires of *Guardians* delivered in Oldham to mill offices alone, a quire at that time and place (it varied, like the gill) being twenty-six copies. In the 1940s it was said of Oldham that it had as many mills as days of the year, and by the end of the 1980s it barely had half a dozen; 1956 saw it at a half-way stage. The readership, not only in the mill offices, was largely lower-case conservative and on the whole did not wish to be disturbed. On a later occasion, of which the details are unimportant and forgotten, the editorial department had launched what it considered a significant and challenging series and the circulation department had ordered a 'box-out' – the trade term for the extra and unordered supply of papers to newsagents, on a sale-or-return basis, in the expectation of increased demand. Shaw wrote in his weekly report to the circulation manager that the series was no doubt important but 'it cracked no pots in Accrington', and that would have to be the verdict on the paper's performance during Suez too.

Laurence Scott told Hetherington of the bad news he was receiving from Lascelles. He also told him not to let the figures influence his editorial judgment, thereby endorsing at the very start the rule of managerial non-intervention. Hetherington always spoke and wrote gratefully of Laurence's support in what was thought at the time to be a dangerous policy, yet was this not the very kind of break with the past for which Laurence had been looking? If the *Guardian* was to cast its Mancunian skin, what better occasion to choose than a question of principle like Suez?

Another man with anxieties of his own was the No. 3 in the composing room, Mr Bigglestone, whose first name not many people would have presumed to use. He was in charge of the floor and the 'stone', the long metal table where type was made up into pages. He would not, if he could help it, allow a page to go to press which did not meet his stringent standards or which derogated seriously from the way things had been done before.

For C.P. Scott, and to some extent his successors, the paper's leading articles had been the prime purpose of its existence. They were the place where readers could expect to find every topical subject, and some fairly arcane ones, fairly analysed and an opinion, forthright or tentative according to its importance and the evidence available, put forward. Scott established the format in which they were written, and which survived well into Hetherington's era. The first leader was normally of three paragraphs (thesis, antithesis, synthesis; or prosecution, defence, verdict) and of about 900 words in all. The other leaders, of which there might be three, four, or even five, would be either in two-par form or 'shorts' of one par. One of Lawrence Bigglestone's jobs was to attend to the production and physical appearance of the paper, and especially of its leader page. Indeed the *Guardian* had been highly fortunate in its composing room overseers: H.O. Rouse, a disciplinarian who inspired terror in every compositor and most of the junior sub-editors, and a much milder professional, Arthur Wailes, who did more of the actual work. They produced a paper which for the most part was typographically faultless. Bigglestone, the third of the group, had the painful duty on Sunday night, 4 November, of setting out the main leader across two columns instead of one, which resulted in an awkward and messy page. He complained that Hetherington had made more changes in four days than previous editors had made since he joined in 1919. A slight exaggeration, but given that front-page news had had to be thrust on a procrastinating Wadsworth by Laurence Scott over a period of months if not years, the charge had some substance.

There would be times in the future when some of his senior staff thought Hetherington leaned too heavily towards the Israeli side of the Middle East conflict, but that was not the view in 1956 of the large Jewish community in north Manchester who made up part of Harold Lever's constituency. The Israeli Embassy, glad to find at least one loyal and outspoken ally in the city which had nurtured Zionism, invited Lever to visit the country. He did not wish to go empty-handed and called on his friend, the sculptor Jacob Epstein. In 1926 Epstein had been commissioned by a group of subscribers to make a bronze bust of C.P. Scott for presentation to the City of Manchester. Lever asked him whether the mould was still in being. Epstein agreed that it was, though the commission had specified that only two castings should be made, the other going to the *Guardian* offices. He promised, however, to see what he could do. The result was that in the summer of 1958 another cast was made and shipped to Israel in honour of Chaim Weizmann, the first President of Israel. At the last report it was standing in the entrance hall of the Weizmann Archive at Rehovot near Tel Aviv. In due course Mr (then Lord) Lever decided to forgive the paper its sanctimonious humbug and put his financial advice at its service by joining the board of the Guardian and Manchester Evening News Ltd in 1979.

GUARDIAN CIRCULATION

Omitting August as unrepresentative the total 1956 figures (line 1), those for the North-west (Manchester, Lancashire, Cheshire and North Derbyshire) (2), and those for London and the Home Counties (3) during the months of Suez were:

	JAN.–JUNE	JULY	SEPT.	OCT.	NOV.	DEC.
(1)	163,585	160,989	164,473	171,751	182,720	177,671
(2)	79,262	75,039	76,102	79,008	80,568	77,971
(3)	30,003	30,445	31,460	34,010	39,284	38,411

The pattern in succeeding years was:

	1957		1958		1959	
	JAN.–JUNE	JULY–DEC.	JAN.–JUNE	JULY–DEC.	JAN.–JUNE	JULY–DEC.
(1)	176,924	172,518	178,393	176,928	182,233	190,134
(2)	77,214	75,067	77,315	75,851	78,098	78,634
(3)	37,298	36,025	37,230	37,348	38,181	41,301

CHAPTER 3

Innocents at Home

PRINTING in London, an ambition seventy-five years old, began on Sunday night, 10 September 1961. Preparations for the event were wholly inadequate and the strain it imposed on the staff, especially the handful of editorial people brought down from Manchester, was immense. Within three years Laurence was beginning to lose his faith in the paper's ability to survive, and by 1965 he had lost it. In both that year and in 1966 he tried to bring about a merger with *The Times*. The defeat of that effort, in which the intervention of his cousin Richard Scott, chairman of the Trust, was decisive, led to a complete reorganisation of the paper's management. That in turn produced, by the end of the decade, a new and successful design and an expansion of the paper's coverage – though even as late as 1970 Laurence was still hankering after a merger. Resemblances to the *Manchester Guardian* diminished only piecemeal, but diminish they did.

Distribution from London as well as Manchester had been one of three essentials which Laurence had set out for his father, John Russell Scott, soon after joining the company in 1944. The first had been to put news on the front page. That had been accomplished in the autumn of 1952, in conditions of such editorial secrecy that immediately before edition time on the first Sunday night the sub-editor charged with handling the front-page lead, Graham Deakin, had to ask the chief sub whether any decision had yet been taken about what typeface should be used for the headline. The second move had been to drop the name of Manchester from the title, a decision which virtually everyone on the paper in September 1959 knew to be essential but which many lamented. (It was clearly not the name of the city they pined for because most of them came from outside: it must have been the remembrance of their youth, and that rare combination of modesty, earnestness and fun which constituted the *Manchester Guardian* they had longed to work for.)

The first attempt to print in London was aborted in the 1950s, though it was not the first time the idea had crossed anyone's mind. C.P. Scott had promoted it in 1884, before he became proprietor, and in 1914 he went into the proposal seriously enough to discuss it with Lloyd George and to entertain prospects of raising £250,000 to finance it.[1] The aim then was the same as in the 1950s and 1960s – to make the *Guardian* a fully national paper and increase the circulation. Laurence revived the idea, and starting in the late 1940s Charles Markwick, the company's chief engineer, worked with Muirhead and Co., Ltd. to devise a photocopier capable of transmitting whole pages from one printing centre to another: the early prototype of the fax now in everyday use. The *Guardian* would be set into type in Manchester, transmitted to London by telephone line, and printed at a plant in Pocock Street, near Waterloo Station, which the company bought for the purpose in December 1952. When the project was costed in 1950 the extra for London printing by facsimile (£113,000) was just over half what it would cost to employ full teams of editorial and production workers at the London end.

Laurence talked informally to trade union secretaries and reported that the meetings had been 'without exception reasonable and helpful'. He had, however, neglected to talk to the most important union of all, the London Society of Compositors, forerunner of the National Graphical Association. More than a decade later, on the BBC *Panorama* programme (2 January 1967), he rejected a suggestion from James Mossman that the unions had been obstructive. The *Guardian*, he said, had funked it.

> Mossman: I was told the unions turned you down flat on modern devices?
> Scott: No, this is not true at all. A lot of people say this but it's untrue. The true fact is that we funked it.
> Q: On the grounds of what – union objections?
> A: We were afraid of what the unions would say, but to be fair to them we never asked them and they're entitled to say, as they do, that we were never asked, we might have agreed. I thought they wouldn't agree.

Mossman asked whether the method had not been tested and adopted elsewhere, as indeed it had. It had been successfully tried between the Manchester office and the *Berlingske Tidende* in Copenhagen and then bought to produce the Japanese newspaper *Asahi Shimbun* simultaneously in Tokyo and Sapporo.

> Mossman: Shouldn't one have fought that issue then?
> Scott: I think if we had been a lot bigger and wealthier organisation we might have fought it but we thought we were too small.

At the time of this interview Laurence was deep in negotiations about a retrenchment programme arising from the paper's crisis in 1966, and it is likely that if he erred in talking to Mossman he did so on the side of tenderness towards the unions. In a much earlier retrospect on the facsimile project, written for the guidance of the board in January 1957 when yet another scheme for London printing was being advanced, Laurence wrote:

> The project was repeatedly discussed during 1953 and 1954, but the directors could never bring themselves to take the plunge. They were deterred by three

fears, the fear (then widespread) that Beaverbrook was about to start a third evening paper in Manchester, the fear that the Trade Unions were currently very belligerent and would make a lot of trouble, and the fear that it was generally unwise to take such a large financial risk on borrowed money. The decision was postponed, but it was always expected that [London printing] would be revived before long.

He therefore produced a proposal for flying the flongs (the papier-mâché impressions, also called matrices or mats, of a page from which the metal cylinder is cast for loading on to the press) from Manchester to London and printing there under contract with the Argus Press. In a long memorandum the cost of the different options was estimated thus:

	1957 £000	(=1990 £m.*
Telephoto (i.e. fax)	247	(2.230
Argus scheme	144	(1.300
Traditional		
with Union good will	380	(3.431
with Union ill will	435	(3.928

* approx. The paper cost 2d and postage for letters 3d.

By 'traditional' is meant the duplicated process of sub-editing and setting in each city. The document foresaw a number of trade union snags, of which it believed the most serious to be demands for compensation by men not employed in London.

> If we succeed in printing in a second centre without the aid of compositors or readers, then the same system might be adopted by the London papers and their staffs dismissed . . . Also, the London daily papers, who remunerate their compositors by piece work, have agreed to pay for everything in the paper whether set by compositors or not, so it would not be a new thing to demand that we pay for the setting of the paper in London even though none is done or even nobody employed to do it . . . I take the view that a claim of this sort is more likely to be made than not.

Laurence was quite looking forward to a scrap with the unions. He proposed going straight away to see the London Typographical Society (secretary Robert Willis), which had a strict 'No setting no printing' policy and inviting his response. He hoped the battle would be won or lost before the project was started and without a stoppage. But he also thought that 'it would do us no harm and might do the industry a lot of good if we make it a public quarrel, provided we conduct it fairly. I should like in that case to explain in the columns of the paper exactly why we are not able to print in London.'

He did not, however, want the scrap to be with the other newspaper houses.

Singly I do not think that they can harm us, but jointly as the NPA [Newspaper Proprietors' (later Newspaper Publishers') Association] they can be very awkward . . . The NPA has some degree of control over certain 'newspaper trains' and full control over many road services shared by their members. If they feel malevolent they could prohibit our use possibly of the trains and certainly of the road services . . .

As a provincial paper the *Guardian* was not a member of the NPA. Nor did Laurence want to join, partly because he did not believe in paying unnecessary subscriptions or spending the company's money on lavish entertainment, and partly because 'they long ago sold the pass' to the London compositors' trade union. (The *Guardian* did eventually join in the person of Laurence, whose colleagues thought he began to enjoy the appurtenances.)

When to the noise of grinding between the LTS and NPA millstones was added the not uncommon sight of fog at Ringway or Croydon, which was the airport Laurence originally referred to, the aeronautical scheme began to look less attractive. In 1958 it was abandoned, in spite of Laurence's initial enthusiasm, but the need to go to London remained. The minimum profitable circulation for a daily paper was constantly rising. Either the paper had to be popularised or it had to reorganise itself to be delivered everywhere early in the day.

Laurence therefore remained on the lookout for a deal with another company and in April 1960 he reported that he and Lord Thomson were playing a poker game – a dangerous metaphor in the context because the 'rough-neck Canadian' as he liked to call himself[2] probably came from the superior school. Thomson, already a big-time newspaper proprietor though he had not yet acquired either his peerage or his *Times*, was losing £100,000 a year on his *Evening Chronicle* in Manchester, which he had acquired as part of his deal with Kemsley, but 'Every time we meet,' Laurence wrote, 'he mentions his wonderful profits, implying that he doesn't need the £100,000. Every time he raises London printing for the *Guardian* I say we are in absolutely no hurry. We are both bluffing.'

Not only was the *Evening Chronicle* losing money but confident rumours were being heard of a so-called Operation K in which Lord Beaverbrook would launch a third Manchester evening paper from his printing works, modelled on his Fleet Street Lubianka, half a mile from Thomson's building in Withy Grove. Moreover the *Manchester Evening News* needed a new building in which to put new plant. Its maximum print was 32 pages and it needed the occasional 48 to accommodate the classified ads. Thomson wanted Laurence to buy or lease Withy Grove from him but it was a dreadful building and,

Laurence wrote, 'if we take over Withy Grove we should own the biggest newspaper plant in England, we should be the largest printing employer in Manchester, and . . . we should have to enter the NPA and conduct our trade union affairs through them . . . I do instinctively dislike the idea.' The London-based employers were grouped, then as later, in the NPA; the provincial employers, of which MGEN was still one, were members of the Newspaper Society.

The upshot was that MGEN effectively bought the *Evening Chronicle* from Thomson, though the formal arrangement was that the two papers kept their identities and were published by a jointly owned company, North News Ltd. Laurence seems genuinely to have hoped to keep the *Chronicle* going. ('In the background must remain the knowledge that the Scott Trust is a non-profit-making body and that the trustees would prefer not to see the *Chronicle* closed if it can reasonably be continued.')[3]

The hopes may have been more pious than practical, to judge by the depletion of choice in other provincial cities. With the two Manchester evening papers no longer in competition large savings in overheads, especially distribution, were immediately possible. Anxieties about Beaverbrook began to recede. Nevertheless, within three years the *Evening Chronicle* was closed. The last edition was the late night final of Friday 26 July 1963, which led on the destructive earthquake at Skopje, Yugoslavia. The paper contained no reference to its own death, but in a stroke of genius the sub wrote the last banner headline: Wiped Out!

In the early years after Sir Edward Hulton, of the second generation of the publishing family, had launched it in 1897, the *Chronicle* had been profitable, but it had steadily lost ground to the *Manchester Evening News*. Even after it came under North News ownership the *Chronicle* had to contend with the higher production costs of Withy Grove which turned out four daily and three Sunday titles and experienced the trade union clout expected in such a house. Thomson's poker players had looked at their hands and extracted from MGEN (or North News) a contract to print the *Chronicle* for twelve years. The terms of its closure were that Thomson should be paid £1,720,000 in compensation, which in the early 1960s would have been recognised everywhere as a respectable sum. (The *Guardian*'s cover price was 4d; postage 3d.) Laurence was apologetic:

> The payments to be made to Thomson . . . appear very large. Some justifica-
> tion of them may seem desirable . . . First, it is fair comment that, as things
> have turned out, the original North News agreement was unfortunate. It
> should have contained provision for terminating the *Chronicle* printing contract
> in less than twelve years should that paper go out of existence. We mistakenly
> overlooked this risk, assuming that the *Chronicle* had a life of at least ten years.[4]

Other circumstances of the closure were equally unhappy. The Typographical Association's journal, under the heading 'The Cannibals of Fleet Street', lamented that 'Not since the death of the *News Chronicle* has the basic weakness of newspaper economics – over-reliance on advertising revenue – been emphasised so starkly.' The association recommended an all-round increase in cover price. The commentator Francis Williams (Attlee's public relations adviser, former editor of the *Daily Herald*, future life peer) was no happier:

> The *Manchester Evening Chronicle* was compelled to close, although it had a circulation of over 250,000, which was two-and-a-half times that of the average circulation of provincial evening newspapers in Britain. This large sale and the paper's manifest popularity with a great number of readers proved useless in attracting advertising because it consistently ran second in circulation to the *Manchester Evening News*. As a result its advertising revenue fell to a level where it was operating at a loss of over £300,000 a year. Similar circumstances brought evening paper closures in Birmingham and Nottingham in the same year. If you can only run second you might as well not run at all.[5]

But there was more than one deal to do with Thomson. The other was that the *Guardian* should print on his *Sunday Times* presses in Gray's Inn Road, which would otherwise be idle for six days of the week, and should rent office space in the same building. This contract was to run for fifteen years from 1961 and the rent, fixed before inflation had made the indexing of such an item almost automatic, meant that at the end of that time, in the mid-1970s, the *Guardian* was still paying a mere £18,000 a year for 14,000 square feet of office space. (Was not Laurence aces high after all?) But if the 1961 agreement was financially one of the most attractive the company had made, in every other respect it was fairly disastrous, and those who were charged with carrying it out, which meant principally the editorial staff, were soon to find themselves reeling from the culture shock.

It was not only that the physical conditions caused not entirely facetious mutterings in the NUJ chapel about the Factories acts, though they contributed to the drain on self-confidence which many of the staff, especially the sub-editors, soon underwent. The existing Londoners among the staff had nearly all been specialists, critics, or a higher echelon of reporters – working in possibly cramped but well-established and familiar offices in the traditional newspaper setting of Temple Bar. They now left for the graceless surroundings of the old Kemsley House, renamed Thomson House, a workplace only, devoid of civility and almost of identity. Brian Jones was one of only six sub-editors who made the leap from Manchester. Later in a vigorous and successful but restless career, he became for a few years a deputy editor of the paper. Recalling the move from Manchester to London he wrote: ' "Office" was hardly the word to describe the public lavatory architecture favoured by Kemsley, a style adopted presumably on the principle that the place would never need re-decorating: the walls just needed hosing down from time to time.'[6] The NUJ chapel was more patient than the management had any right to expect. The move was made in September 1961; only at the end of January 1963 did the Father, Victor Anant, courteously remind Laurence of the sufferings undergone. 'That this chapel,' the resolution said, 'whose members have been prepared to put up with unsatisfactory working conditions during the transitional period of London printing, is now of the opinion that these difficulties should have been resolved after eighteen months.'

Only one other Manchester journalist travelled south to join the new venture, and that was Nesta Roberts to be news editor. London had never had a news editor because it did not set out to report news. It wrote articles about developments. The coordination of this activity was within the remit of the London editor, Gerard Fay, the last of several distinguished bearers of that title, a graceful writer himself and, in the Irish sense of his forebears, a lovely man. Nesta was both a reporter and a sketch-writer. Later on she did some vivid work for the paper as Paris correspondent at the height of the student 'événements' of 1968. But she was not an administrator and there is no doubt that she was miscast. When she joined the paper in May 1947, from a weekly in South Wales, the reporters did not have individual telephones, nor was there one in their room (or Room: it was given a capital R, that it might enjoy parity of esteem with the leader-writers' Corridor). The telephones were in cubicles outside. Like most of the others, Nesta found this a satisfactory arrangement because no extraneous assault on the senses interrupted the work in hand, but it gave her less than ample preparation for the competitive world awaiting her.

Nesta had been highly valued by Wadsworth, Monkhouse, Pringle and others on the paper since she started writing 'back-pagers' for it at the age of nineteen. The back-pager, now a long vanished art-form, was an essay of about a thousand words which even through the privations of a six-page paper during and after the war had been kept to give relief from the compulsions of the news columns. After a short time in Manchester Nesta began to specialise in social services reporting. She became deputy news editor there less because her inclination lay that way than through seniority. When she went to London she had, apart from a few free-standing specialists as lobby, diplomatic, parliamentary and labour correspondents, a reporting staff of six. Most of the talent in all departments in Manchester (John Anderson, Geoffrey Moor-house, Mary Stott, David Marquand, Anthony Tucker, Harry Whewell as news editor, David Frost for rugby and Denys Rowbotham for cricket) stayed in what was still the head office. Nesta Roberts served in her unwonted capacity for two and a half years before returning to her speciality in the social services, this time with the title to go with the job. 'I simply wanted to stop being news editor,' she said afterwards.[7] She could not think, after she had been at it a short time, why she had been appointed. She concluded that the appointment was diplomatic, to prevent people from jumping off Waterloo Bridge. No one did so in her time, 'though I several times felt like it myself'.

Hetherington remained in Manchester and indeed was insistent that the

editorship would stay where it was. The thinking behind London printing
had not changed much since the early days of Markwick's fax machine or
Laurence's aerial flongs. The paper would be Manchester-based and Manches-
ter-edited. It would print in London in order to get later news and arts notices
into the paper. It would benefit from a rail and road service starting in the
South as well as the North. Otherwise the changes would be as few as possible.
Putz, the night editor, would transfer to London and would there recruit a
new subbing team. Horace Milner, the production director, would recruit the
printers. They, like their counterparts in Manchester, would breathe in the
indefinable atmosphere of the *Guardian* and take pride in doing so. Additional
costs would be taken care of by increased circulation.

These were, of course, flimsy assumptions on which to launch a national
paper, as Hetherington knew. In July 1960, while spending a few days at
Borwick Fold, his retreat in Westmorland, he received a letter from James
Callaghan, then known as the MP for Cardiff South and a friend of the trade
unions, which took up an earlier conversation:

> There is a tide in the affairs of men –
>   Are you following the difficulties of Odhams and the TUC?
>   This is your moment.
>   If you are prepared to become a paper of the Left (no need to be bound to the
> Party) you can rapidly increase your influence and circulation.
>   The 50's belonged to the Tories.
>   I believe the 60's will belong to us.
>   If you are serious about printing in London and willing generally to be
> friendly I believe you would have a sympathetic reception from the TUC. I have
> already taken soundings and can initiate discussions as soon as I get the
> Memorandum you promised to send me.

Hetherington replied the next day, 7 July, with a four-page summary of the
paper's three options for London printing and some idea of the costings. The
Markwick–Muirhead facsimile method could be made to pay with a sale of
300,000 to 350,000 (the current sale being 200,000). Teletypesetting (see
below) would need 500,000 circulation, and a full conventional printing
house, with its panoply of sub-editors and compositors, 750,000 or more. He
recounted the tentative talks with the trade unions and the uncertainty they
created but pointed out that even if the unions were cooperative, as Callaghan
was suggesting, other Japanese newspapers had followed the *Asahi Shimbun*
into facsimile, so that Muirheads were now so busy with other orders that they
could not deliver to the *Guardian* in much under two to three years. Finally he
went into detail about the paper's present distribution arrangements, involving a special train to Crewe. He acknowledged Callaghan's soundings and
agreed that 'with the troubles at the *Herald* [which then owed nominal
allegiance to the TUC but was run commercially by the Odhams publishing

group: it was later transmuted into the *Sun*} this might be an opportune moment'. He went on:

> But of course the *Guardian* could never have any sort of formal or informal commitment to the TUC or the Labour party. I should greatly like to see a strengthened radical opposition, with hope of forming a government in the not too distant future, and others in the *Guardian* feel the same way. As before, we'll do all that we can to help in that direction. More than that, however, I couldn't say.

A copy of this correspondence was clearly sent to Laurence because on 8 July a rocket was dispatched from Manchester to Westmorland:

> I am very perturbed about your discussion with Callaghan. I don't believe that he or anyone else can do anything to help us over London printing, and if they could I should be strongly opposed to accepting their help.
>
> Odhams Press have at no time, so far as I am aware, had the slightest help from the Trade Union movement in the form of easing their printing or production problems.
>
> The terms and conditions under which we shall print in London will be settled by negotiation between management and trade union and it would damage the negotiating power of management to have well-meaning but ineffectual intervention on its behalf by third parties.
>
> The way in which the TUC has been of help to the *Daily Herald* has been by persuading loyal trade unionists that they have a duty to read their paper. If such persuasion were used on behalf of the *Guardian* the knowledge that it was being done would seriously undermine our status as an advertising medium with those advertisers to whom we are now trying to appeal.
>
> There is also the political angle, that if we accept any kind of favour from the Labour Party or the TUC it puts us under some kind of moral obligation to them, and the serious thing is not that we incur it (since we may make our own stipulations) but that the facts and circumstance may become generally known.
>
> I am even frightened by the fact that you should be discussing the subject in this kind of way. Your letter to Callaghan is I believe substantially correct but I cannot see why he should be in possession of all these facts and figures, particularly as you do not make it clear that some of the facts you give relate to 1952 and are by no means true today.

In the event circulation, which was projected to be 300,000 within a year or two, did not reach that figure until 1970, though there were a few buoyant years from late 1962 to the end of 1966 when it pulled ahead of *The Times*. Production costs for the first six months were £81,000 (17 per cent) above Laurence's estimate and advertising revenue was £43,000 (5.5 per cent) down. A projected gross profit of £25,000 became a loss of £175,000.

The difficulties were not diminished by the chosen production method involving the technical innovation mentioned to Callaghan and known as duplicated teletypesetting, or TTS for short. In the right conditions this can be a useful method of exchanging small quantities of type between offices. *The Times* had used it, in one direction only, for setting copy from the House of Commons. In the *Guardian*'s case the system was used for the nightly production of almost the entire newspaper, half from London and half from Manchester. (The pages not set on the night were prepared in advance, almost always in Manchester, and sent to London in mat form by train.) TTS was movingly, and fairly, described by Putz as the most God-awful printing system ever invented.

In theory TTS was judged admirably suited to the *Guardian*'s requirements. It depended on a linotype or monotype operator in either London or Manchester using a keyboard which, instead of causing metal type to issue direct from the machine, produced a punched tape. This was fed into a black box which transmitted the contents of the tape to a typesetting machine in the office of origin specially adapted to receive it, and also over a telephone link to another black box at the other printing centre, which produced an identical tape. The distant tape was then fed into a distant type-caster. Identical slabs of type were thus produced at both ends from one keyboard operation. A row of linotypes operating on a TTS system was a ghostly sight, like a speeding car without a driver. In front of each linotype was an empty chair, and as the machine received the tape all the moving parts of the machine – the keys similar to those on a typewriter keyboard, the arms which lifted the cast line of metal, the rotating axle which restored the metal templates to their housing at the back of the machine – went up and down or from side to side as usual except that no one was controlling them.

At that time the paper's foreign department was housed in Manchester so that nearly all foreign and much feature material was set in Manchester to balance the preponderance of home political and City news set in London. The cardinal weakness of the method was that it magnified electronically the errors which normally arise in keyboard operation, and since the proofreaders' corrections took half an hour to reach one end from the other the paper was full of misprints, or literals as newspaper people like to call them. Thus was the long-standing title of *Grauniad* born in the pages of *Private Eye*. Moreover since compositors were paid for making corrections to other compositors' work the inducement towards accuracy in the original setting was less emphatic than it might have been. The *Guardian* stuck with this system for fifteen years.

Within a day or two of the start of production the inevitable notice went up on the board: A Good Start. It was nothing of the kind. A large part of the composing room staff had been brought in from the highways and byways, if for no other reason than that the end of the summer is the most difficult time for recruitment. The sub-editing staff, too, apart from those who had volunteered or been pressed to leave Manchester, were if not entirely raw then unaccustomed to the paper and uncertain whether its bold venture would succeed. An old-established chief messenger, Harry Nelson, had crossed from Fleet Street but the newcomers included men who would have been better cast as footpads from an *Oliver Twist* pea-souper. (One, coming upon the deputy editor eating supper from a tray at his desk, said: "Ere! Every time I come in 'ere yer feedin' yer f– face!') The head messenger in Manchester, Steve Daly, slight of build but strong in authority, had eventually to be briefly seconded to help to bring order, and since he had been Army lightweight boxing champion of Northern Command his advice to the other messengers was influential.[8] Gerard Fay brought his reluctant band of specialists, arts critics and assorted wordsmiths from Fleet Street. Ken Murphy, cricketer and philosopher, brought his barrowloads of cuttings and began to re-establish his library. It was magnificent but it was not what Fleet Street meant by a circulation war.

That is not to say that the other papers were initially unfriendly. Indeed they expressed some interest in the arrival of this extraterrestrial. It was not until a year or two later, especially when the *Guardian* had had hard things to say about the behaviour of the press in the Vassall scandal, and had itself fallen down badly in the ensuing Profumo case, that the others began to turn nasty. The *Observer* ran a profile on 10 September 1961, the day before London printing began, which showed some prescience about the struggles to come:

> Though the large commercial risk involved has been endlessly calculated and weighed (largely by the chairman himself, who will have done it as expertly as anyone in the newspaper business could), it will hang over each issue for some time to come. Nearly 500 extra staff taken on, a substantial account to pay Roy Thomson for the printing contract and office space, a big jump in overheads generally: this is the size of the adventure.
>
> Coming at a time when Fleet Street echoes with woe about the outrageousness of newspaper economics, there is a touch of daring about the move that doesn't quite square with the vague public image of a staid and circumspect Scott tradition.

Laurence had been in hereditary office for thirteen years, the appointed Hetherington for five. There was therefore an inescapable truth at the end of the *Observer*'s profile:

> The difficult area in the relationship, of course, is where business demands and editorial planning inevitably merge. No newspaper has found a way of leaving its editor entirely free from considerations of profitability . . . C.P. Scott laid it down in a famous dictum that 'an editor and business manager should march hand in hand, the first, be it well understood, just an inch or two in advance'. Laurence Scott has reversed the marching order, but preserved *The Guardian*'s reputation.

That judgment was accurate in September 1961; six years later it would have had to be drastically revised.

CHAPTER 4

'Our Special Correspondent'

WHEN the paper was missing editions or relying too heavily on news agency copy, as it often was in the penury of the early 1960s, it depended heavily on the quality of the sub-editing. The subbing can often make or ruin a story. Everyone knows if the sub gets it wrong; no one knows when he has saved the paper from a blunder. Arguably it was the subbing which did much to rescue the *Guardian* from itself on its London adventure, and it was especially galling for Putz in London that his opposite number in Manchester, the night editor there, W.R. Taylor, was able to change pages and update the news as the paper always had done, whereas the people whom the paper was trying to convert into regular readers in London and the Home Counties had to make do with a second-best product. Readers had been prepared to excuse the omission of late news, sports reports and art notices when they knew the paper was printed 180 miles away, but not when it had boasted of being able to compete with the other nationals.

This did little for the morale of the London subbing team, and turnover was high. With loss of morale went a lack of that self-confidence which the subs had always enjoyed in Manchester. When the other papers' early editions came into Gray's Inn Road the *Guardian* would start making unnecessary changes because it assumed the others must be right and itself wrong. There were even occasions when *The Times*, doubtless for different reasons, changed as well, so that the two papers in effect swapped lead stories. Yet in spite of all their frustrations the senior subs — Putz and Michael Hides, later Philip Osborne, Colin Henderson and Peter Large — gritted their teeth, worked a bit harder and a bit longer, and performed the nightly miracle. They helped in keeping up a dialogue with readers which, production faults notwithstanding, was probably more intimate than that achieved by any other national newspaper, except perhaps its closest rival in that respect, the *Daily Mirror*.[1] The success of this collective effort depended much on the arts and women's pages but also on the paper's specialists and reporters at home and abroad.

Chief of these, on a paper like the *Guardian*, is the political correspondent, who later, under the heavy inflationary pressure on titles during the 1970s and

80s, became known as the political editor. Francis Boyd, tall, solidly built, volatile in temper, filled that office when he resumed his work for the paper at the end of the war in 1945. Newly arrived sub-editors would be advised by the chief sub-editor, N.J.N. Dixon, that 'All our correspondents are treated with respect, but the political and parliamentary correspondents are treated with the greatest respect.' In other words: Don't alter their copy. (The parliamentary man at the time was Harry Boardman, succeeded by Norman Shrapnel.) His other injunction was: 'Always leave a spare adjective in case something even more extraordinary occurs.'

Harold Wilson, in his capacity as student of the press, was sometimes very complimentary to *Guardian* staff. On 28 February 1966 he told Hetherington that he had thought of calling in Francis Boyd because Boyd would try to understand his position, and when Boyd had a scoop it was usually a very good one. This was presumably soft soap, which Wilson frequently applied unashamedly in his meetings with Hetherington, and which Hetherington came to recognise and withstand. Wilson could equally well be scathing about Boyd, as indeed about other Lobby correspondents and newspapers. On 18 April he asked Hetherington what was going to happen to *The Times*. It was a terrible paper, he said, and would have to improve its quality a great deal.

Wilson would have been on firmer ground in confining himself to Boyd's scoops. He had beaten the field on an important development in 1960, when on 20 July the *Guardian* had carried his exclusive and at the time astonishing forecast that Lord Home would be appointed Foreign Secretary by Macmillan in succession to Selwyn Lloyd:

> It would be a bold stroke if Mr Macmillan were to follow Neville Chamberlain's example [in appointing a peer, Halifax, in 1938] . . . but Mr Macmillan likes a large flourish . . . The more one considers this possible solution of Mr Macmillan's problems of finding a successor to Mr Selwyn Lloyd the more probable it seems.

Macmillan duly announced the reshuffle on 27 July, with Edward Heath as Foreign Office spokesman in the Commons. Boyd, like his successors Ian Aitken, Julia Langdon and Michael White, kept to a strict rule of confidentiality which in his case lasted longer than the Cabinet's thirty years. He never did disclose his source for that useful exclusive. 'Oh, Home, yes. I remember. A man told me in the back of a taxi.'

Boyd's work provided the bedrock of the paper's influential political reporting for a good twenty-five years, and especially in the period Wilson was talking about. He also had a direct influence on the paper's fortunes in general as a member of the Scott Trust from 1961 to 1975. He had joined as long ago as 1934, from the *Leeds Mercury*, and the fact that he had not been to university (though nor had Wadsworth) seemed to rankle with him for much of his career. It was as well that Leeds University gave him an honorary degree shortly before his retirement. He was knighted in 1976. Nobody could ever persuade him how valuable a man he was. Hetherington describes him,[2] not with the greatest felicity, as a 'reliable carthorse beside Ian Aitken's racehorse qualities', Aitken for some years being his younger rival in the paper's political team. Another metaphor might have been that Boyd was a stock bowler who never deviated from a good line and length, whereas Aitken could and did use spin – possibly even the 'finely flighted, richly wristed spin' in a phrase of Denys Rowbotham's, cricket correspondent until his death in 1968 at the age of fifty-two, which has gone down in *Guardian* lore. Aitken became a power in politics, looked to for reassurance by the Left, trusted for his scruple by the Right.

Boyd's political colleagues at the time, notably Edward Greenfield, stuck to the animal metaphor and thought of Boyd as Eeyore, always putting the gloomiest construction on anything that was said or not said to or of him. He would frequently write four or five stories a night from the House of Commons – a white paper, Prime Minister's questions, written answers, Lobby talk, government prospects, possible opposition reshuffles – but if, solely to distribute the load, the news desk assigned some other member of the political staff to a job he would moan that that proved he wasn't wanted. He cannot, one assumes, have been serious but he kept up a remarkable pretence.

Boyd's reintroduction to Westminster after the Second World War could well have constituted an episode of *Dad's Army*. He had joined the Royal Artillery and been posted to an anti-aircraft battery for the defence of Bristol. The quartermaster officer for this battery was a certain Captain Ernest Marples, who entered Parliament in the 1945 election and eventually became Minister of Transport from 1959 to 1964. For many years thereafter an aerosol slogan on a bridge over the northbound M1 proclaimed 'Marples must go'. Why he should go was never clear to motorists observing the notice – possibly it was his acceptance of the Beeching report slashing the railways – but it long survived his departure from office after the 1964 election.

Towards the end of the war, Bristol having been defended by the battery, two incidents involved Marples and Boyd. One of Boyd's thermometers was broken, and as lance-bombardier in charge of an A-A gun he needed to know the temperature of a shell before it could safely be fired. He therefore asked the quartermaster-sergeant for a new thermometer. The sergeant refused this request on the ground that the thermometer might be needed by somebody. Marples, the officer, had a desk at the other side of the hut, and Boyd remonstrated with him against this illogicality, saying that he was in fact the somebody by whom the thermometer was needed. 'Certainly, Boyd, certainly,' Marples replied, and the thermometer was duly provided.

The second incident came when the battery had to move from one site to another. Marples told Boyd he had an important job for him. A series of three-ton lorries was coming into camp that morning to transport the equipment, and he wanted Boyd to mount the running board of a cab which would accompany them and direct the driver to each shed in turn – shed one, shed two – so that the incoming lorries could be told where the sheds were. 'I'll try to do that, Sir,' Boyd replied, and duly pointed out the sheds. The operation was evidently carried out without hitch. When Marples, a fellow-Yorkshire-man, entered Parliament and found Boyd was in the House as Lobby correspondent for the *Manchester Guardian* he recalled these occasions and would introduce him to Tory colleagues with the words: 'I want you to meet Boyd here. He's an extraordinarily good administrator.'

Interesting things were happening overseas in the early 1960s, even more so than at home. The *Guardian*'s first staff appointment in Africa was Clyde Sanger, who came from *Drum* magazine in Lagos and the *Central African Examiner* in Salisbury, which he had edited for a time. While in Salisbury he had worked in opposition to the federal regime of Sir Roy Welensky and the Southern Rhodesian regime of Sir Edgar Whitehead, and in close tandem with Terence Ranger, then a young lecturer at the University College of Rhodesia and Nyasaland who published a radical periodical called *Dissent* and later became Rhodes Professor of Race Relations at Oxford.

Sanger left no doubt of his commitment to African rule in the countries he covered, or to his attachment to particular African parties therein. Kenya had two parties, the KANU (Kenya African National Union) of Jomo Kenyatta and the Kikuyu (but also of Tom Mboya, a Luo), and the Kenya African Democratic Union (KADU) which was more representative of the smaller tribes. (The present writer, who as foreign editor at the time was Sanger's 'control', also wrote about Africa, mainly in the leader columns. He had grounded himself in African affairs by working in Lagos for a few years on the Mirror Group's newspaper there. Sanger supported KANU. His control, in a romantic sort of way, had more time for the little people in KADU. Sanger, of course, won; rightly so.)

One of Sanger's most far-sighted deeds was to arrange for a complimentary copy of the *Manchester Guardian Weekly* to be sent to Kenyatta during the later stages of his imprisonment and subsequent administrative detention on charges of managing the Mau Mau rebellion in the 1950s. On release Kenyatta expressed his thanks for the gift, though whether such improving reading influenced his presidency when independence came is another matter. From being 'the leader to darkness and death' in the words of the Governor, Sir Patrick Renison, he became, in the eyes of the Europeans, the embodiment of moderation and propriety. It is just possible that the *Guardian*'s friendly gestures helped: they had begun a good deal earlier when the paper had taken an interest in Kenyatta and Joe Appiah of the then Gold Coast (Ghana) at the pan-African conference in Manchester in 1945. It was a year later that P.J. Monkhouse, later deputy editor, rejoined the paper after war service and set about making Africa one of the paper's specialities.

The few years of intense nationalist activity in East Africa, Northern Rhodesia (Zambia) and Nyasaland (Malawi) in the early 1960s coincided with the start of the much more protracted emergency in Southern Rhodesia. Sanger covered both regions. On occasion he would file a story about Kenya or Uganda from Nairobi early in the morning and then take a flight to Salisbury and file another about Rhodesia from there, sometimes charming his way, which he was very good at, on to an Alitalia or other foreign airliner in defiance of the strict cabotage rules.* His house was in the bush outside Nairobi, and like Eric Silver's in Jerusalem in a later era, was among the first places where visiting firemen (from other papers as well as the *Guardian*) would call to be brought up to date with events.

It was Sanger's excellent idea to appoint a black African as the paper's stringer – the first for any British national paper – in Salisbury. He was Nathan Shamuyarira, then editor of the *African Daily News*, a paper banned by the Winston Field government of 1962–4. (We shall meet Shamuyarira briefly later in a less happy context.) His coverage was authoritative but also brave. He had to contend not only with the hostility of the government but with the terrible faction fighting and house-burning which broke out between the Shona and Ndebele[3] in the African townships of Harare and Highfields. What he did not write for use as 'From our Correspondent' (bylines for stringers had not yet come into use) he sent privately to the paper for use in another form. Thus the leader column could take a much less heavy line against the Salisbury government's emergency legislation to control the violence than it might have done had it not had Nathan's inside knowledge of what it was like on the ground. He would drive white journalists through the townships during times of trouble at undoubted personal risk to himself, for if he had had even a minor brush with a pedestrian in those crowded streets the car and its occupants would have been set upon. One of the ironies of the paper's connection with Shamuyarira was that when a visitor from head-quarters wanted to visit a die-hard settler family who had written an impassioned letter to the paper saying that Africans would never be fit for self-rule, it was Nathan who gladly lent his car for the long journey south to Fort Victoria.

It would be incorrect to suggest that the *Guardian*'s African coverage was solely or even mainly in the hands of those mentioned. Scarcely an African conference took place in the heady independence days of the 1960s without the attendance of Hella Pick, Patrick Keatley, or both. Hella gradually became responsible for almost the entire gamut of interests of the Foreign Office outside the Far East and Latin America as diplomatic editor. Patrick Keatley, though he too eventually bore the title of diplomatic correspondent, was Commonwealth correspondent for the main part of his career. He was Canadian but his deepest interest was Africa, and it is fair to say that scarcely

* The rule, largely abandoned, prohibited carriers from flying passengers between two places both under another jurisdiction.

an African politician of consequence came to London without calling to see
Pat and Eve Keatley.[4] Patrick was able to knock out as much copy as required
on any African subject, however obscure, at a moment's notice. He was an
ebullient member of the staff, with a huge laugh, and was never known to
bear a grudge or say a harsh word (except about white Rhodesians).

Only two omissions from a totality of the virtues prevented Keatley from
being a paragon among newspapermen. The first was that nobody could stop
him from telling lengthy anecdotes however late the hour or urgently needed
the copy. Ask him how much he was writing and he would tell you about
taking afternoon tea with the Pakistan High Commissioner. The other
difficulty was that he was rarely to be found. In addition to his full-time, or
supposedly full-time, job at the *Guardian* he took advantage of the paper's
benign attitude to moonlighting except that he did it by daylight. John Cole,
as news editor, would extract a promise from him that he would finish his
piece before leaving the office. 'Sure thing, J.C.,' Keatley would reply. But
ten minutes later, when the copy was needed, Macavity's not there. He would
be tracked down either at Bush House, broadcasting for the BBC World
Service material the *Guardian* was anxious to put in its columns, or doing a
think-piece for Canadian television. At the end of one particularly contentious
Commonwealth conference, when Simon Kapwepwe of Zambia flew home in
dudgeon after calling Harold Wilson a racist, that fact had to be tacked on to
Keatley's report because he was busy on the box.

Clare Hollingworth, war correspondent, lived when in Paris in a commo-
dious flat converted from a warehouse in the Rue 4 Septembre. She and her
journalist husband, Geoffrey Hoare, had bought it, she said, with a bonus
paid to him by the *News Chronicle* for his work on the escape of Burgess and
Maclean. Journalists often take pride in believing their homes to be bugged,
but hers was literally so. It was full of insects and their larvae (collected mainly
in the Bois de Boulogne by Geoffrey) which were being reared in tanks and
jars, and the walls were lined with pictures of them taken by Clare. To
complete the household they had living with them a young Frenchwoman,
Janine Poirier, who worked at the British Embassy to improve her English and
made probably the best cassoulet north of Castelnaudary. Staff were glad of an
excuse to visit Paris.

Clare Hollingworth's work in Algeria during the civil war, and especially
in the closing stages in 1962, was highly valuable in two ways. She had good
contacts in the Government, among 'the Muslims' (as the nationalist insur-
gents were quaintly described at the time), and in the deadly underground
(and often more overt) operation of the OAS.* These enabled her to get
political as well as eye-witness exclusives – including the terms of the

---

* Organisation de l'Armée Secrète, set up in 1961 by General Salan and three other officers
after a frustrated coup against President de Gaulle.

constitution for Algeria proposed by the French. She also managed to capture the full deadliness of the war by going to the heart of it, by literally marching towards the sound of the gunfire and regularly walking alone through the casbah. She may have been right to conclude that a European woman was safer doing that than a European man would have been. She was more likely to have slops poured over her head (as she did) than to be killed. All the same, some of her male colleagues thought she ran needless risks. By the standards of the time the atrocities were horrific, as when she reported the scene when the OAS launched five three-inch mortar shells into an Arab crowd,[5] though they became almost commonplace in the Beirut of the 1980s.

She perplexed the editor in the early months of 1963 by airmailing a story from Beirut about the disappearance of Kim Philby. Not surprisingly he was hesitant to use it because the Prime Minister had officially denied that Philby was the 'third man' who had tipped off the spies Burgess and Maclean. Philby's innocent return from nomadic wanderings with a desert tribe would have cost the paper a fortune in libel damages. According to Hetherington's account she filed the story on 15 February; according to Hollingworth she filed it 'immediately' she had carried out her checks in Beirut after Philby failed to turn up for a dinner party on 23 January.[6] It had still not surfaced, in the *Guardian* or elsewhere, by the time Hollingworth returned to London in April. It was now three months since the disappearance, the highly suggestive circumstances of which she had investigated at the time, and the paper therefore took the risk with a carefully constructed story, appearing on an inside page on a Saturday, 27 April. Between the lines Hollingworth made it clear that Philby had fled to the Soviet Union, while ostensibly saying how strange it would be if he had done such a thing. The *Guardian* had never been at home in the looking-glass world of spooks but this little scoop, followed up dutifully by the other papers, was eventually confirmed by Edward Heath as Foreign Office man in the Commons on 1 July.

One of the main Hannen Swaffer press awards for 1962, that for Woman Journalist of the Year, went to Clare Hollingworth for her work in Algiers, and the qualification 'woman' in the title was one to which she did not take exception but which struck others as slightly offensive. She received also the Granada *What the Papers Say* award for the best news reporting of the year, which was a less invidious distinction. Brian Inglis, chairman of the judges, said of her: 'For more than two months [she] stuck it out in nerve-wracking conditions, and all the time she kept sending back reports which were models of judgment and accuracy.' In fact she was in and out of Algeria many times over many years. No bias ever showed because she did not possess any. Nor did she seem drawn to Algeria, as Sanger and Keatley were to Africa, by the impact of a great historical process in the making. She was excited by it as a war. The downside to that strict detachment was that she almost came to love war for war's sake. Writing later[7] about her coverage of a Kashmiri war for the *Guardian* in 1965 she said:

The town and the bridge were being shelled and big V-shaped clouds of smoke and dust rose from craters into the hot air creating a haze over the ruined streets. Our driver put his foot down and we bumped and rocked through the town amid the crash of high explosives. I remember that as we emerged from the target zone into the scrubland beyond I turned to my companions, exclaiming 'Now *this* is what makes life worth living!'

Early in 1963 she had become defence correspondent rather than a free-ranging war correspondent, but she was always less happy at a strategic studies seminar or a NATO briefing than pounding along with the artillery. Her future career lay in helicopter journeys (sitting on bullet-proof vests, she would always insist) for the *Daily Telegraph* rather than the *Guardian*.

James, later Jan, Morris sandwiched a longish spell on the *Guardian* between the first part of his career as a *Times* correspondent and the later, mainly as a writer of books. He joined in mid-1956, when he was based in Cairo, saying he had decided to switch from *The Times* because it would not let him write the books he wanted to write.[8] He was in the right place to do some conspicuous work, as has been seen, during Suez, and he went on from there to travel the world. He had a fine talent for choosing the words best calculated to annoy the conventional stereotype of a Left-leaning *Guardian* reader. Among the places he visited was Oman in the days of the former Sultan, Said bin Taimur. Sultan Said was eventually deposed by his son, Sultan Qaboos, in July 1970 in a coup confidently alleged[9] to have been organised by MI6 in the days when Britain still held sway at that end of the Gulf. Oman in the 1950s was at its most feudal and Said bin Taimur has since been regarded by all progressive Arabists as a grotesque and insufferable tyrant, but Morris wrote of his downfall:[10]

I was one of those who, being only intermittently distressed by the political conditions of Oman, rather liked him. I liked his wary doe eyes and his gentle voice . . . His face was a stylised face, with its fringed beard and its calculating mouth, and his supple but portly figure spoke of oiled baths, frankincense, and the more decorous pleasures of an abstemious harem.

Among others Fred Halliday, Professor of International Relations at the London School of Economics, took strong (perhaps over-austere?) exception to this kind of writing in his essay on news management by the Foreign Office, security services and counter-insurgency.[11]

Widening his horizons beyond the Middle East Morris went to Australia and wrote a series of thirteen LPAs (leader page articles) during the summer of 1962. The fifth, on Sydney, appeared on 7 August.

. . . For most Sydney citizens the purpose of life may be summarised in the parade of the life-savers on Manly Beach, all bronzed open-air fun on Saturday afternoons, and perhaps it is this paucity of intent, this lack of lofty memories or aspirations, that makes this metropolis feel so pallid or frigid at the soul.

This and what seems to be a shortage of kindness. The people of Sydney will usually greet you warmly enough, even heartily, but compared with the great immigrant cities of the New World – Montreal, New York, or São Paulo – this place feels cruelly aloof. Perhaps it is the origins of Sydney that invoke this sensation – for, in spite of the sophistries of her society ladies, she was founded by the scum of England only six generations ago. Perhaps it is the expressions on the faces of those ladies themselves, so steely, scornful, accusatory, and plebeian, as though they are expecting you (which Heaven forbid) to pinch their tight-corseted behinds. Perhaps it is the intolerance of one citizen to another, sour bus conductor to irritable passenger, cross-patch waitress to indifferent customer. Sydney does not reach out, as New York once did, to receive 'your tired, your poor, your hungry masses yearning to breathe free'. No great ideals of politics or humanity animate her, no visions of nobility, but only starker impulses of self-advancement or survival.

Nor does she even feel content. She seems full of reproach, sneer, and grumble. The immigrant from Europe or England all too often feels resented. The dinkum Aussie all too often seems to cherish racial prejudices of the nastiest kind. The sleazy bars of the place, looking like public lavatories and smelling of slopped beer, exude no genial good cheer, but only a mindless and sometimes rather frightening sense of male collusion. A proud new bridge collapsed in Melbourne the other day but the *Sydney Daily Telegraph*, in its editorial on the matter, offered not a breath of sympathy, nor even a kindly joke, but only a column of crude and spiteful mockery. The people of Sydney like to think of themselves as 'a weird mob', but they strike me as weird not in any free-and-easy, gallivanting way, but only in a sort of twisted uncertainty and isolation.

He went on to list some exceptions to the general stricture, but they hardly counted in Sydney at the time. Half a page of letters appeared on 16 August, most of them verging on apoplexy. Two were from Sydney; one, from Mr Eric Lambert of Halstead, Essex, asked: 'What sun-singed, singletted, beer-swilling wag from Woolloomooloo has once again gone and rubbed a Pom up the wrong way?' Even so, the Australian papers lost no time in asking for reprint rights.

On Monday 22 October 1962 began the most anxious week in world affairs since nuclear weapons had come into being. That at least became the received view in the years immediately afterwards. The Cuban missile crisis itself is scarcely remembered nowadays, except as an historical reference point. Even at the time it probably alarmed the news professionals in press and broadcasting, in constant touch with their sources in Washington, more than the consumers of news behind their papers or in front of their sets. (There were more journalists and fewer broadcasters then: the *World at One*, for example, had not come into existence.)

The crisis occupied the entire attention of Hetherington in Manchester and Max Freedman in Washington, with Leonard Beaton as defence correspondent, Victor Zorza as kremlinologist, and assorted specialists, foreign editors, news editors, telephonists and messengers in attendance. Freedman was a Canadian, reared on the *Edmonton Bulletin* and the *Winnipeg Free Press*, who had been taken on in Wadsworth's time, partly as a counterpoise to Alistair Cooke in New York. He declined the chance of the editorship in Winnipeg, preferring the *Guardian* job in Washington. In the White House press corps it was said of him, not in the least unjustly, that his recreation was to read the Congressional Record and that for debauchery he turned to the judgments of the Supreme Court, and especially of his friend Chief Justice Frankfurter.

T.S. Matthews, observing the paper of the early 1950s, wrote that if it were possible to name its most generally popular feature, a likely choice would be Alistair Cooke's dispatches. 'And yet this laughing cavalier (would C.P. Scott altogether have approved of him?) does not quite seem to fit the generally Roundhead tradition of the *Guardian*.'[12] Freedman, Matthews wrote, gave the impression of origins even more distant than Canada – 'say, the late eighteenth or early nineteenth century. Though he is capable of Johnsonian irony and Landorian eloquence, he is never light, either of mind or heart . . . C.P. Scott would certainly have approved of him.' This placement of Freedman's epoch was accurate, for he let it be known that his most admired guide to the language was Edmund Burke; Cooke's was H.L. Mencken, whose judgment he quoted that there are no boring subjects, only boring writers.

It may thus have been unavoidable that, after an early period of collaboration, silence should descend between Freedman and Cooke, and it originated at Freedman's end. In the early 1960s there was no communication between the *Guardian*'s two US correspondents. Any organisation that had to be done – and there was plenty, if only to ensure they did not cover the same story, which often happened nonetheless – was done through the Manchester office. Hetherington was probably less at ease with Cooke, partly one supposes because of the cavalier qualities noted by Matthews, and encouraged Freedman. The encouragement was not wasted. Freedman was certainly one of the best-informed people on the White House run, a personal friend of Kennedy and Lyndon Johnson, and gave the paper a relentlessly, remorselessly good news service.

That is to say, he did so most of the time. He had a habit of disappearing without warning. On 7 November 1960 Hetherington wrote to him:

> I was delighted to see the cable from you last night after the long silence. I've been much bothered about your position. I know you hate writing letters, but I wonder if you could tell me how things stand.
>
> I hope I'm not being unreasonable when I say that a silence of three weeks by one of our two staff correspondents in the United States at the height of a presidential election – and without any explanation – is a bit troubling. I know

that the arrangements between you and Alistair Cooke are difficult. We have tried hard here to abide by the agreement on division of labour. I'm not aware that it has been breached. If it has, I wish you'd tell me. I did ask you that in my last letter, but I've had no reply.

The division of labour came about after Freedman, without consulting anyone, had engaged D.W. Brogan* to cover the Democratic nominating convention in Los Angeles. Party conventions had traditionally been Cooke's occasions; Hetherington agreed that they should remain so and that Cooke should cover the United States at large, but that as a quid pro quo Freedman should have the capital to himself. Cooke (with the title of Chief US Correspondent) was effectively prevented from writing from there. He bridled against this restriction, suggesting that he must be the only foreign correspondent in the world who was not allowed to write from his capital city.

Freedman sent a pained response to Hetherington, on 9 November, written in a childish hand on wide-ruled paper as from an exercise book:

. . . You are never unreasonable . . . but I find your statement both unexpected and perplexing . . .

Unless I am morbidly sensitive or strangely stupid, it remains my clear and painful memory that I was placed under special instructions to regard everything related to the primaries, the nominating conventions, and the Presidential campaign as forming no interest of mine . . . It is true that sometimes I broke through this prohibition (otherwise I would have burst) but I always felt that my copy was regarded as an intrusive and unwelcome burden.

These matters have not been easy for me. I asked my bookman to tell me how much I had spent since January in his shop on books dealing with American history, literature, economics and politics. The figure comes to just over $2,335. Yet all this knowledge, for the *Guardian*, remained completely unused . . .

I have borne with tight-lipped silence and humiliation the repeated rebukes of my American friends who wonder why my writing for the *Guardian* is limited to routine, unlettered, and marginal themes, and almost never to the subjects which are known to engage my mind and interests. Yet there was a time, in the remembered past, when my copy, I trust, was not wholly without value.

I have been eager to write on the new Administration with authority and in detail; and have for many weeks been preparing myself for this task. For me this task began the day after the election – when my quarantine came to an end.

After the 'quarantine' was over and Freedman returned to Washington from a retreat in New England he made up for lost time. On 12 January 1961 he filed

---

* Sir Denis Brogan, Professor of Political Science at Cambridge, was a long-standing contributor on American politics.

1,000 words on the State of the Union speech, which was reasonable, but without warning telephoned another piece 3,800 words long, intended for the same night's paper, about Secretary of State Dean Rusk. The foreign desk cabled him appealing to him not to do it again, and followed the cable with a letter pointing out that the two pieces would have occupied five-sixths of the entire foreign space allocation for the night, and that at £1 a minute the fifty-six minute telephone call had cost about two weeks' pay for the sub who was handling the story. It should be said that Cooke had once spent nearly a sub's week's pay in dictating his recipe for a hamburger which someone in the office had requested at a time when that delicacy was a less familiar part of the British cuisine.

The Cuban crisis came about because US reconnaissance showed that nuclear-capable Soviet missiles were being installed there, directed against the US. The Soviets denied this, but the photographic evidence was unmistakable. Kennedy 'quarantined' the island (i.e. blockaded it, though the term was not used because a blockade would have been illegal under international law) and at the end of a frantic week his implied threat to use 'any' force necessary led Khrushchev to agree to dismantle them. America's critics, including the *Guardian* as the week wore on, maintained that Khrushchev was demonstrating the similarity between 'defensive' Polaris bases at Holy Loch on the Clyde and 'defensive' Soviet installations in Cuba. On the Saturday before the crisis ended the *Guardian* said military action against Cuba 'would seem to most of the world to be as much a piece of aggression as the British and French attack at Suez'.

Freedman was able to keep in close touch with Lyndon B. Johnson throughout the week – theirs was an odd relationship, the bookish and the beery – and since LBJ was on the National Security Council the *Guardian* had material, some of it alarming, about the missiles being readied in their silos, as well sourced as anything in Fleet Street. This included a leader-page article nearly three columns long 'based on the papers and thoughts of the President's executive committee'. It appears that Kennedy, throughout his preoccupation of that week, was closely briefed on the foreign reaction to what he was doing. Hetherington visited Washington not long afterwards and went through the crisis with the State Department, with LBJ, and finally with Kennedy himself. LBJ made the point strongly that nobody had known what would happen, and that even those most knowledgeable about the Russians had not been able to tell how they would react to the blockade. When Hetherington said to Kennedy that perhaps he had been too critical in the later stage the President said that perhaps the *Guardian* had not been too far wrong, but that its greatest flaw had been its failure to realise that the Russians were still expansionist, and were looking for any weakness in the West that they could exploit.

Freedman ceased to be Washington correspondent the next year, 1963. He first became a weekly columnist but gradually faded from the *Guardian*'s scene. During his time in Washington he remained a man of towering grievances. When told during the afternoon's planning call from Manchester to his office in the *Washington Post* building about a good story in that morning's *Times* from Louis Heren, he replied: 'I will do a trade with the *Guardian*. I will go on writing for it and the *Guardian* will not mention Mr Heren's name.' Freedman died, a greatly talented but evidently not very happy man, in 1980 at the age of sixty-three.

Cooke covered the founding of the United Nations for the *Guardian* as locum tenens for Bruce Bliven, editor of the *New Republic*, who at the end of the war was the paper's only regular American correspondent. It was not day-to-day news he covered; more week-to-week or month-to-month; Wadsworth paid him £500 a year and asked him not to cable if a letter would serve.[13] On a visit to Manchester Cooke was invited by Wadsworth to join the staff, on which he served from 1946 to 1972, providing the most versatile service about everything American. In 1950 readers of the *Guardian* (and of the syndicated service it supplied to the *Glasgow Herald*) were alone in Britain in following, through Cooke's daily reports, what proved to be a crucial episode in American political – and psychological? – history: the trial of Alger Hiss. Wadsworth used columns of rationed newsprint to unfold this bizarre story of the betrayal – the alleged betrayal – of American secrets by a senior government officer. It was probably those reports which established Cooke as required reading at the British universities, but he went on to write about anything American he could lay hands on: jazz, the Metropolitan Opera, a big fight, a presidential nominating convention (his favourite subject of all, he later told Hetherington), golf, baseball, the state of the dollar – but the list is almost inexhaustible and familiar to anyone who has ever listened to the radio or watched his TV series.

Relations between Cooke and Hetherington had ups and downs, mainly ups, but Hetherington repeatedly asked, probably rightly, whether Cooke was giving enough attention to the evolving South. He took up the theme when they met in England (at Chester, for some reason) in October 1962. Hetherington's file note records:

> I said . . . we weren't getting enough first-hand reporting. This used to be the great strength of what Alistair himself did. He used to travel the country and tell us what was really going on in the minds of people in different parts of the United States. The failure, however, to have anyone at Oxford, Mississippi, at the critical moment* was an outstanding example of what was going wrong

---

* In one of the early civil rights struggles James Meredith, a black, made three unsuccessful attempts to enlist at the state university and was finally escorted in by 300 US marshals. Violence spread all over the town and reporters were attacked by the mob.

now. Either Cooke or Weatherby [*Guardian* features man in New York who specialised in race relations stories] ought to have been down there . . . As it was we were getting the *New York Times* beautifully rewritten by Alistair Cooke, but that wasn't enough . . . Secondly we couldn't rely on what was promised . . . If we sent Weatherby somewhere we knew we'd get something, but at present we never knew what to expect.

In a sense it is very unfair to select this passage from what was in general one of the most productive partnerships in British journalism. It is quoted to show when an editor has to edit, and how it is done. He can let 'the man on the spot' decide for nine-tenths of the time, but when the tenth tenth arrives he has to assert what he believes are the paper's interests.

Hetherington wrote to thank Cooke profusely for his handling of Kennedy's assassination and the subsequent events. Cooke wrote a long reply[14] about his own reaction to the event:

I don't recall ever being so depressed by the reading of English and European papers: the foul deed released something very ugly among even very intelligent people in Europe, and the implicit but raging anti-Americanism of so much of the high-fallutin stuff (the desperate need to see a sinister plot, to see this country as a jungle, to lump all Americans with the inhabitants of Dallas, and all the people of Dallas with that idiot of a police chief) is disturbing indeed. I just saw a piece by James Cameron about the coming Civil War, America rent by 'vicious hate', the population rushing about scrawling swastikas on Jewish shop windows . . . this is the very essence of the thing he affects to despise . . . so violently against violence, so hateful against 'hate'. [The ellipses are Cooke's.] I meant to say on my own account that I thought [the *Guardian*'s] editorial side stayed wonderfully sane and balanced through all the worst days.

Cooke's letter also said, though, that 'the truly frightening thing' was the immediacy and fullness with which the TV networks could move into an event of that kind. Yet he had in fact been able to cover the story better from the box than if he had been there.

General Clifton [of the White House staff] had coaxed me through the previous weekend to go along to Texas, and my name was down. But I had done 82 flights in just over two months, and I thought it more important to say what the trip was about (the Texas political troubles) than to hop four places in two days. It was a stroke of luck that I wasn't along, except – and this is always the snag – for the dateline. The White House press corps was thirteen cars behind the President, and by the time they swung round the bend and through the tunnel, the main cars were on their way to the hospital. Not one member of the press bus guessed the truth, though they were puzzled by people lying on the ground. They turned off the freeway and went to the Trade Mart, where he was to make the speech. They got a little restless and the Hearst [*Chicago Tribune* etc.] girl, having to file for evening papers, went into a telephone booth, called

her office in New York and said the first take on the speech would be a little
late. Her dumbfounded news editor was incredulous, told her the truth, and
she rushed out of the booth and told the corps. They were then a couple of miles
from the hospital and as stranded as the men in the trenches in the First World
War. Some took off for the hospital, and most retreated to bars (they had no
hotel reservations in Dallas since they were winding up that night in Austin)
and made fast notes from the TV.

The networks had had cameras overlooking Kennedy's route. From his
apartment in New York Cooke, with his family's help, monitored three
networks and filed faster and more fully than he could have done from the
spot. The letter ends by bidding a warm welcome to Hella Pick and Richard
Scott, both of whom had forthcoming New York and Washington assignments after Freedman's departure. How different from Max.

After Cooke had left the staff in 1972 Hetherington proposed 'a little
dinner' for him next time he was in London. He replied gratefully accepting
but said, 'I feel embarrassed and uneasy at the prospect of breaking bread with
people I do not know, especially [he mentions two illustrious *Guardian*
names] whose *Guardian* is demonstrably not my *Guardian*.' His other request
was that 'a private room at a gemütlich restaurant would be fun, don't you
think?' He would like if possible to avoid Hetherington's club, the Athenaeum, where the food 'still immortalises English club food between the
wars'.

CHAPTER 5

The Trig Point

NO doubt the word 'fuck' had previously been slipped into type by a mischievous printer, and the copies of the paper which got out before the presses were stopped would, in the standard phrase, have 'changed hands on the Stock Exchange at five shillings a time'. But when 'fuck' made its first appearance by editorial design the reaction was much as if it had been used in the Speech from the Throne. As well as surprise there was some outrage at this breach of the ancient taboo; a Tory MP, Dudley Smith of Brentford and Chiswick, unsuccessfully applied to the Attorney-General for the *Guardian* to be prosecuted for obscene libel.

Wayland Young (Lord Kennet) was able to use the word in his column of 4 November 1960 by courtesy of the jury at the Old Bailey, which had just acquitted Penguin Books of a charge under the Obscene Publications Act, and of the succession of expert witnesses who had defended Lawrence's language in *Lady Chatterley's Lover*. Since the trial has been repeatedly documented on radio and television its novelty can scarcely be recaptured, but what Wayland Young wrote was:

> I for one was brought . . . to realise that those tremendous pages of level and open eloquence had for years been living unremembered in my head as surely as the Authorised Version or Shakespeare themselves . . . The hero among the witnesses was Richard Hoggart. I think he made history. In his own evidence, using the word in its correct and proper sense, he said the point Lawrence made was 'Simply this is what one does – one fucks'. If ever the English language comes to be at peace with itself again, thereby giving people freedom to be at peace with themselves, the credit will be Lawrence's first but Hoggart's soon after.

The column appeared on a Friday. Kenneth Tynan in the *Observer* had to wait until Sunday, but Bernard Levin in the *Spectator*, who was also able to get into print on Friday, showed an engaging bashfulness, eschewing the f-word and merely opening his long column with the lesser profanities 'Shit and arse', and even then in quotation from prosecuting counsel.[1]

Hetherington was editing the paper from the Manchester office and Young had, as usual, delivered his copy to London. The lawyers were sent for because although the jury had acquitted Penguin it was not certain where a newspaper would stand in using similar language. John Notcutt of Lovell, White & King put to Gerard Fay, the London editor, a technical rather than substantive legal case against publication of the word; but he and Fay himself, like others in the office, bridled on grounds of taste. The decision rested with Hetherington, who had to use the column as it stood, negotiate a change with the writer, or remove it altogether: that was the understanding on which the regular columnists worked. Hetherington had himself been recruited, along with the Bishop of Woolwich and many more, as an expert witness for the defence. Though he might have liked longer to ruminate he had little doubt and indeed not much choice. It would have been too late, even if he had been so inclined, to renegotiate the column. To drop it would have exposed the paper to ridicule. He therefore left it alone, and it came to stand as a trig point from which the landscape of the coming decade could be surveyed. Hetherington and his successor, Peter Preston, issued numerous reminders to the staff that this and the other newly enfranchised four-letter words should be avoided unless the need for exact quotation was persuasive, but the canon came to be observed with diminishing respect. In a general coarsening of language, 'balls' came to be an acceptable headline word in the late 1980s.

Whether Wayland Young and Richard Hoggart reflected widespread popular usage at the time was a matter of controversy in the correspondence columns and among some of the staff. Mary Stott, the women's page editor and formerly a sub on the *Manchester Evening News*, who was then in her fifties, wrote that she did not know what the word meant,[2] and that no man of her acquaintance, certainly not her husband (Ken Stott, Northern editor of the *News Chronicle*), would have dreamed of using it in her presence.

The episode led to one of the *Guardian*'s most acrimonious encounters with the Press Council, and to one of the earliest documented disagreements between Hetherington and Laurence Scott. The Press Council had been set up in July 1953 on the recommendation, four years earlier, of the first Royal Commission on the Press. It was not at that time, or for many years to come, an especially awe-inspiring body, and although its behaviour in the *Lady Chatterley* case was certainly discourteous and probably improper, the paper made heavy weather of it.

The row began when, some weeks after the trial, the Council decided off its own bat to consider the action of three papers. Late on Wednesday afternoon, 15 February 1961, the *Guardian* learned from the Press Association tapes that, along with the *Observer* and the *Spectator*, it had been censured at a meeting the day before. The use of certain four-letter words, the Council said, was both objectionable and unnecessary. 'The Press, in general, demonstrated how a court case of this kind can be adequately and broadmindedly covered without debasing standards of decency.' This verdict, however, had been

HORNER   The Puckerbrow Dig

The Guardian *carried its first strip cartoon in 1964, one of a long series by Arthur Horner, who had previously created the character Colonel Pewter for the* News Chronicle. *His genre is reflected in this strip from 13 October 1965. Copyright © Arthur Horner, 1965.*

reached not only without any invitation to the papers to submit comments but without their being told that the case was being heard.

Hetherington ran a fairly mild leader, saying he heeded the rebuke while disagreeing with it, and defending the Young column. There the matter might have rested had not Frank Singleton, editor of the *Bolton Evening News* and a staunch friend of the *Guardian*, first announced[3] that he had 'passionately dissented' from the Press Council's decision, and then resigned from the Council after receiving a letter from the chairman, George Murray, accusing him of a breach of confidence.

It was common in Hetherington's reign for the leader column to have the last word in a controversy or for admonitory letters to the editor to carry a footnote in rebuttal. (The practice was not, of course, Hetherington's innovation. Previous editors had used editorial footnotes, and Wadsworth's too were sometimes argumentative, above the space-saving formula, in caps and small caps, ED. GUARD.; people were sad at Ed Guard's ultimate retirement.) On this occasion the leader column took two somewhat heavier swipes at the Press Council and its procedure in response to letters from Mr Murray[4] and this time antagonised not only Murray but Laurence. The leader of 25 February said: 'So far as we know the *Guardian* has never been asked to take part in the council's work. It will not do so while the council's procedure and constitution are unchanged.'

Laurence's note to Hetherington[5] shows an irritation which was to grow into antagonism. Laurence wrote:

> I did raise an eyebrow when I read from my sick bed that you had committed me not to join the Press Council.
>
> As a matter of fact I have been against joining the Press Council, but for

totally different reasons. My feeling is that if the Press Council is to have any
influence on the popular press then that influence will be reduced if the Council
includes more than a tiny fraction of the quality newspapers among its
members.

Not having the benefit of your inside information when I read my *Guardian* I
am afraid that I got a rather unhappy impression from the whole affair and I
wonder whether some of our readers may not have done the same.

Whereas public figures have to put up with misrepresentation and mis-
reporting in the press, and if they complain in a letter are always corrected by a
subsequent last word from the editor, we seem to give the impression that we
are not mature enough to accept the position. I felt that our original statement
of attitude was excellent, but somehow to go back to it and start picking holes
in Murray's letter appeared very petty minded.

This departure from the rule of managerial non-intervention was possible
because the leader had committed the company as well as the editor.
Hetherington records himself as being 'jolted' by the rebuke.[6] Peter Preston,
when editor, virtually abolished footnotes on the ground that the paper had
plenty of chances to make its views known. An angry reader would usually
have the last word, even if what he said was factually incorrect.

The *Guardian* of that time is often reckoned to epitomise the 1960s as a
turning point in British social history in the same way that Dawson's *Times*
embodied the appeasement of Hitler in the 1930s, and usually the parallel is
intended to be equally disparaging. There is something wrong with this over-
simplification, even though it has some truth. The 1960s were not, of course,
a self-contained decade. The mood they have come to represent started a good
five years earlier, if not before, and the 1960s continued to reverberate
throughout the 1970s. Osborne's *Look Back in Anger*, which could be taken as
the starting pistol for the 1960s, appeared in 1956, and Philip Hope-
Wallace, the *Guardian*'s drama and opera critic, didn't like it either at the
time or in retrospect. He was quick to detect a trend and hold it up to the
light. In 1966 he wrote of

> the younger generation who imagine that apart from Shakes and Shaw, the
> drama in this country sprang like Minerva, but rather less well armed or wise,
> from the brain of Osborne in 1956 . . . I seriously think there are plays by
> Granville-Barker and Galsworthy which are now likely to seem actually *less*
> dated than Osborne's earlier invective and belly-aching or Pinter's teasing
> doodles. We seem to be approaching the condition of the musicless musical. I
> do not believe if you laid all the current musical notions in all the current
> musicals in London, as Miss Parker might have said, end to end, you would
> finish up with enough material for a Chopin nocturne.[7]

To have Eric Newton as art critic, Hope-Wallace on theatre and opera and

Neville Cardus on music was the *Guardian*'s three-card trick. Certainly the paper was always at the sharp end of arts criticism. It had been there since the days of Samuel Langford and the Hallé and C.E. Montague at Miss Horney-man's theatre in Manchester and indeed it continued there in years to come. Cardus continued to contribute until not long before his death in 1975. In his prime, which was spent watching Lancashire or listening to Stravinsky in the 1930s, he was one of the most important reasons for reading the *Manchester Guardian*. His fame was made in Manchester, but after his return from Australia in 1947, where he spent the war years since January 1940, he covered very little there. His later notices in London were drafted at rehearsal, completed, sometimes to the annoyance of people in adjoining seats, at performance, and sent to the office in a Harrods hired car. In the end he became an embarrassment to the features department which by then was in full stride and it was not too soon when he settled for the occasional ceremonial piece and let the work proper fall to a new generation, mainly Colin Mason and then Gerald Larner in Manchester and Edward Greenfield in London.

Hope-Wallace is described by Veronica Wedgwood, who edited an antho-logy of his work, as the best conversationalist of his generation. He must have spoken, then, as he wrote – and his notices were for the most part delivered into a telephone immediately after the curtain. He was of that happy band of homosexuals whose renown came from their urbanity, wit and high talent; he would have been thoroughly put off by the demonstrative 'gayness' which later came to fashion. A friend and colleague wrote of him:

> He worshipped words but drew no hard distinction between their written and spoken form. Indeed his real genius lay in conversation. For many years some of the best talk in London could be heard at his favourite table at El Vino's in Fleet Street. His noble head, his mellifluous voice, his thesaurus of anecdotes and the shafts of wit, sharp but never cruel, which he played on the personalities of the day, attracted a gifted circle of writers, editors, lawyers, and public men, over which he presided with grace, generosity, and a quiet but unmistakable moral authority.[8]

So Cardus and Hope-Wallace were unlikely torchbearers to the permissive revolution. Who else was around to influence the paper in that direction? Hetherington's interests, in spite of his evidence in the *Chatterley* case, were predominantly political and military; he was a physically vigorous man who took his relaxation seriously (and his staff were well advised to do the same) on the Lake District fells rather than in the library, the concert hall or the West End theatre.

The first two features editors, the men with whom any initiatives for a change in social mores would have had to lie, Brian Redhead (1959–62) and John Rosselli (1962–4), were men of different talents but neither held any brief for what he might consider flip or meretricious. Redhead had a flair for experiment, change and challenge which he channelled into typographical innovation and design. At a time of relatively small papers he devoted large areas to blank space. This did not endear him to the news subs, scrabbling to find room for an extra item, but the device was attractive to readers and to critics in the trade. (Arthur Christiansen, the master artificer who edited the *Daily Express*, wrote enthusiastically about it in the *World's Press News*.) Redhead was the upstart Geordie who proclaimed his intention of becoming editor within weeks of his arrival. He was undoubtedly the *Guardian*'s cheeky chappie, but he was a keen admirer of that newspaper (perhaps slightly more in retrospect than at the time) with *Manchester* in its title, which was still in being when he joined.

Rosselli not only admired the *Manchester Guardian*; he personified it. He took over the features department, but by this time in London, when Redhead left for an early short stint with the BBC. He was the son of an Italian Social Democratic leader murdered under Mussolini, educated in the US and Cambridge, sometime leader-writer and literary editor of the paper. He was a man of courage, diligence and terrifying intellectual mien.

After not much more than two years in the job Rosselli had exhausted himself. He had in fact set himself standards more exacting than the paper was beginning to need, and he worked with a small staff, several of whom were still in Manchester. One characteristic incident rankled with him. In 1955, before the features department had been properly gazetted and he was in charge of the then Miscellany page, he used as the page lead an article by Denis Saurat, former Professor of French at University College London, on a movement for the revival of the *langue d'oc* in south-west France, then chiefly led by poets but with nationalist aims. This is what he thought the paper was about. But the London papers were strikebound at the time and the *Guardian* was exploiting that fact. Hetherington, in charge that evening as assistant editor, evidently objected to a page lead on so esoteric a subject at such a time and, according to Rosselli, repeatedly reverted to the topic.[9]

In 1964 Rosselli left for the academic world. Half of his reason for going was the physical exhaustion. As to 20 per cent it was his interest in the new horizons of higher education (specifically at Sussex, where he went to lecture in politics), but there remained, as to 30 per cent, a strong feeling that the *Guardian* had committed itself inexorably to a type of development which he did not want to see or belong to. He reasoned that by the costly decision to print in two centres the *Guardian* had bound itself not only to the target circulation figure of 300,000 (the sale was 245,000 in 1961 and 277,000 in 1964) but probably to half a million. This could be achieved only by 'broadening its appeal'. He did not want that to happen, as he feared it would, by the paper's pandering to a marketing department. He wanted the *Guardian* to be in effect *Le Monde* in an English setting: essential reading for members of what he was not afraid to call the intelligentsia, whether they liked its politics or not. It would be radical, vigorous, philosophical, inquiring.

Others in the office took much the Rosselli line, including John Maddox, the science correspondent, and David Marquand, leader-writer, both of whom left about the same time as Rosselli, though not as part of any concerted defection. Victor Zorza, the kremlinologist, was of a Mondiste persuasion (though he wanted as many readers for his column as possible and eventually got them by syndicating it). So were Harold Jackson and several other influential reporters. Those in rather more doubt did not necessarily want to popularise the paper but were suspicious of comparisons with *Le Monde*. It was true that that newspaper had never spent a penny on advertising or carried a single photograph, that it relegated hard news to a special and fairly lowly section, and that it was to a very high degree readable; but it was catering not so much for a different clientele as for a similar clientele but with different expectations, in a country where national newspapers did not have the foothold they had here.

Although he left comparatively early in the *Guardian*'s transition Rosselli remained a strong influence on individual members of staff, partly through personal friendships and partly because he would write the occasional theatre notice. In the 1980s he rejoined the paper briefly in summer as a relief leader-writer. And that was odd because one of his long-standing arguments was that the serious papers no longer needed their multiple leading articles, or needed them only on the rare occasions when there was something to say. 'The Rosselli solution', as it became known, was dusted down a few years later when the *Guardian* ran into crisis, but the immovable obstacle remained: that the British press is different from the French.

On the news desk in the first half of the 1960s were, in London, Nesta Roberts, assisted by Harold Jackson and succeeded by John Cole, and in Manchester Harry Whewell. Each of them would follow a story wherever it led, but none of them would follow a trend. The main feature writers were Geoffrey Moorhouse and Terry Coleman, the first renowned for the strength of his descriptive writing and what seemed an instinctive rapport with the wide interests of readers, from Anglican hymnody to the Test match film library at Lord's or the workings of a nuclear submarine; the second, as time went on, for his interviews, which drew criticism from his more modish colleagues because they said he was too Right-wing. Michael Frayn's funny pieces in the transformed Miscellany column were against the grain of the 1960s rather than with it: he held a whole new profession up to mock in his public relations character Rollo Swavely. ('Have you ordered, by the way? They do an awfully good tournedos here, you know.')

We may find later that if the *Guardian* did not start the permissive revolution, it cheered it on its way. In the meantime a couple of sexual episodes arose of the kind deplored and enjoyed by the newspaper-reading public, from one of which the paper emerged handsomely, from the other in distinct disarray.

They are reported here because the result of them was that the paper's editorial headquarters were transferred to London.

In October 1962 an Admiralty clerk, William Vassall, was sent to prison for eighteen years for spying for the Russians. He had been trapped in homosexual activity in Moscow and blackmailed. The Prime Minister, Harold Macmillan, announced a Civil Service inquiry into the matter and George Brown, Deputy Leader of the Labour party under Gaitskell, giving vent to the solemnity which at that time invariably accompanied an event of the kind, said such an inquiry was inadequate 'in the light of what one understands to be involved here'. The *Guardian*, though worried that Vassall had gone undiscovered for so long, did not understand anything to be 'involved here' beyond the evidence which led to the conviction. Specifically it saw no need for a grander inquiry. What George Brown was getting at was an exchange of letters between Vassall and Thomas Galbraith, a junior minister in the Scottish Office who had previously been a civil lord of the Admiralty. The innuendo was that Vassall's relations with Galbraith also needed examination. The *Sunday Express* led the field and a week later the *Sunday Pictorial* 'flaunted', in the *Guardian*'s word, its possession of the letters. On 7 November the committee set up by Macmillan published all the letters and the *Guardian* commented next day:

> Mr George Brown and the *Daily Express* look a little foolish this morning. The terrible letters from an unidentified minister and a civil servant to William Vassall, which were going to make the Vassall case 'blow up' in the Government's face, turn out to be trivial and unimportant . . . The idea that these were a cause for censuring Ministers is absurd . . . An ugly smear has been wiped out.

Galbraith resigned nevertheless. The *Guardian* found this an unnecessary response to a 'scurrilous' campaign. It returned to the attack on 10 November, observing that it alone among newspapers had been troubled by the part played by the press in hounding Galbraith and accusing the *Express* of vicious conduct and the *Sunday Pictorial* of muck-raking. This was tough and honest journalism in which Hetherington was seen at his best, defending ministers with whom he was politically out of sympathy.

The *Mirror*, no slouch itself in the powerful use of English, replied with an attack on Hetherington personally of the kind with which he was later to become familiar: the hoary comparison of past greatness with sad present decline. Under the title 'The Guardian – of what?' the *Mirror* wrote:

> *The Guardian* was a magnificent newspaper, vibrant in ideas and originality, swift and sure-footed in leadership; it has swapped its majestic virtues for vacillation and timidity. Even fussiness. Worse, a smugness has settled around it thicker than a London (or Manchester) fog.
>
> The decline of a newspaper's influence is sad at the best of times. When that

newspaper is *The Guardian* we are on the verge of a major tragedy; a revival is surely overdue. Where is that voice that breathed o'er Eden during the Suez fiasco? It is curiously stilled.

The *Mirror* twisted the knife by rehearsing an episode which had caused some dissent among *Guardian* staff: its recent doubts about entry into Europe on the terms which might then be obtainable. Hetherington himself had worried about this change of policy and the *Mirror* took clear aim: 'The *Guardian*'s Common Market shuffle is depressing enough: it accused Mr Gaitskell of "a sad retreat" – and then retreated so rapidly itself in the same direction that it was waiting there when Labour stumbled round the corner. It sounded The Last Post, but not Reveille.'

This attack was less easy to shrug off when Francis Williams, whose normal sympathies would be with the *Guardian*, supported the *Mirror* in his *New Statesman* column:

> The *Guardian* is of course perfectly entitled to its opinion that the Galbraith letters are unimportant. What seems to me more difficult to understand is the unbridled nature of its attack, not only on the *Express* and the *Pictorial*, but on practically the whole of the rest of the press as well, for disclosing all the information on this matter that came into its possession and persisting in the demand for a much fuller inquiry and more substantial publication of the facts than Mr Macmillan was originally anxious to have . . .
>
> Sympathy for a no doubt personally pleasant, if rather absurd junior minister is all very well. But issues of much greater importance are involved. It seems to me that in this matter, as in the Burgess–Maclean case, the newspapers have done what it is their business to do.

In response to the clamour Macmillan had, in spite of his earlier reluctance, set up a judicial inquiry under Lord Radcliffe, which reported on 25 April 1963. It found unequivocally for the ministers under attack. There had been no improper relations between Vassall and Galbraith; Lord Carrington, First Lord of the Admiralty, was acquitted of the negligence alleged by newspapers against him. The conduct of the press as a whole had not been among the tribunal's terms of reference but the papers which had been in the forefront of the campaign emerged badly from individual findings, where specific allegations were shown to be groundless.

Macmillan restored Galbraith to the government and in May proposed a permanent Security Commission to look into spy cases. But Labour was not interested in Macmillan's commission. What Harold Wilson and his security adviser George Wigg knew by then, but Macmillan did not, was that another scandal, involving the Secretary for War, John Profumo, was ripening. The *Guardian* did not know either, and when told refused to believe. The decency of one year was the naïvety of the next.

The *Guardian* accepted Profumo's personal statement to the Commons on

HORNER The Puckerbrow Dig

22 March in which he denied having an affair with Christine Keeler, who was similarly involved with the Soviet military attaché, Ivanov. Every other newspaper in Fleet Street either knew or suspected that the denial was untrue. Hetherington too might have known had he been closer to the Fleet Street and Westminster gossip. But he was not much given to gossip anyway, and he still lived in Manchester. His visits to London, though frequent, were for sterner purposes. He records[10] that Wilson tried to alert him to the rumours but it seems that no one in the London office did so. The paper was compartmentalised. The political staff, reading their order papers at Westminster, were not on the same circuit as the El Vino bon viveurs. An inbuilt suspicion of scandalmongering had justified itself in the Vassall case. Everyone knew that Hetherington had his own sources in the Commons and it was assumed that he knew about the rumours and had decided to discount them. When Profumo's letter to Macmillan, acknowledging the lie to the House, was published on 5 June Hetherington was attending a conference in Stockholm and therefore did not write that night's comment, which said the Profumo disaster should be allowed to sink as quickly as possible into oblivion. No doubt the country would have been spared a lot of humbug if that advice had been taken, but the *Guardian* was not in a strong position to give it. Hetherington found the leader 'too emollient', as well he might at the time.

The episode added to the conviction that he could not stay in Manchester. Early in 1964 he moved house, contrary to all protestations when London printing had begun. The move would have had to happen, but the privilege of turning the *Guardian* into a fully national newspaper belongs to Christine.

CHAPTER 6

Towards a Merger . . .

PLENTY was happening. Readers would not have suspected anything was wrong. But the years leading up to the paper's crisis in 1966–7 were years of strain for the editor (an editor has few people outside his family to talk to) and the manager. The strain transmitted itself to the editorial staff by a sort of osmosis. Printing in two places was costing £500,000 a year more than Laurence had estimated.* He wanted changes in the paper – to popularise it, but he was not yet ready to use the term – but was constrained by the inherited convention. Hetherington was under no such inhibition in criticising management. He was the only director who did not owe his continuance in office to Laurence. Once an editor has been appointed he cannot be dismissed except by the Scott Trust, and then it would need a scandal to remove him. There was much for Hetherington to criticise, especially in the marketing and advertising departments. It seems odd even at a distance that on the day the *Chatterley* trial opened the *Guardian* should carry an almost half-page ad for the *Daily Telegraph* – 'The Paper you can Trust', which 'provides all you can wish in a newspaper' – selling at 2½d. The *Guardian* was 3d.

Historically 'marketing' had been a concept somewhat foreign to the *Guardian*; even in January 1954 Richard Scott, as trustee, had written to Laurence about a plan to put £50,000 into 'developing' the paper, and urged that more of 'so large a sum' should be spent on editorial improvements and recruitment of additional staff rather than on promotion. As for the promotion itself,

> I wonder whether a close enough personal eye is being maintained on the manner in which this development money is being spent. Are all the advertisements put out on our behalf by [the agency, later dropped] scrutinised by a responsible member of the staff? Is it really felt that advertising of the M.G. on the backs of London bus tickets justifies the expense or is the proper medium for

---

* Postage was then 4d, or 1.6p. The *Guardian* went up to 5d (about 2p) in November 1964 and stayed there until 1968.

trying to sell a commodity like the *Guardian*? I of course am ignorant about such matters . . .

Similarly in advertising, for three or four years after London printing started the classified ads at the top left of page 2 were still dominated by old Manchester stand-bys – Gibb's Bookshop, Sam's Chop House and Gaskell's Baths. The pages of property advertising at weekends, though they were lucrative enough, were devoted almost entirely to the south Manchester commuter belt. Printing quality was poor.

The paper had not been installed in London for more than four months before the inevitable frugality campaign began. The first of the decade's frequent downturns in the economy at large had coincided with the period when the *Guardian* should have been expanding. When Hetherington came to draw up notes for a meeting with the Scott Trust (which he had conspicuously not been invited to join) in April 1962 he put a bold face on the paper's modest successes but said the specialists were showing frustration that the new regime had not given them greater scope. He looked like losing a quarter of them in the autumn. Zorza had resigned three times in nine months and might finally be leaving, Frayn was going to the *Observer*, Maddox to the Rockefeller Institution, Morris to his books, and possibly Beaton to the *New Scientist* (though Beaton didn't go: he went to Brussels instead to cover the Common Market negotiations). Teletypesetting was not working properly. The *Guardian* was consistently six pages smaller than *The Times* and *Telegraph*, the advertising reps were not selling space, and staff salaries needed to be 30 per cent higher to keep important specialists, subs and reporters.

For the similar gathering of 1963, held in January, he noted that sales were down by 2,000 in the North, though up 6,000 in the South. The paper was stale. The sport was pedestrian, the financial news unreliable, the features unreadable. Then he put in parentheses: 'But these are exaggerations; and remember the paper's successes', including 'Shrapnel almost every week'. (Norman Shrapnel, the parliamentary sketch-writer, was and remained one of the paper's most valuable assets.) But a hate-the-*Guardian* campaign had been running, W.J. Lascelles, the circulation manager, was getting dismal reports from his reps, and the ads were not arriving.

His diagnosis was that the paper, then costing 1d a day more than the *Telegraph*, was not giving value for money. There had been two years of excessive pressure on himself as editor, in spite of the 'enormous help' of his assistant and later deputy, Harford Thomas, and there wasn't money to employ enough reporters and subs. The solutions he toyed with were to replace Gerard Fay as London editor because, though Hetherington spoke of his talents, he wasn't in the right job; to appoint a Manchester editor, possibly the 'willing and loyal' Paddy Monkhouse, specifically to improve the last two Northern editions; and to take on some new advertising display reps. Astonishingly there was still no suggestion that either he or Harford Thomas should move to London. A mixture of these solutions was eventually applied. Monkhouse was asked to supervise expanded coverage of the Manchester area, but Mancunians were no longer interested. They didn't regard the *Guardian* as 'their' paper any more.

There are, of course, fashions in the public perception of newspapers. No praise had been too high for the *Guardian* in 1956 and in 1961 but the change of mood continued throughout 1963 in such arbiters of fashion as *Private Eye*, the TV satire show TW3 (*That Was The Week That Was*) and *The Spectator*. The bitterest attack of them all was made in *The Spectator* of 20 September 1963 by Clive Irving. The piece gathered into one long and rich philippic the long-standing jibes to which the staff were accustomed: ' . . . the tweedy, materially self-denying philosophy, political ambiguity and decision-funk-ing, unctuous moral postures, woolly leaders, front-page pictures of sunsets on Windermere, the refusal to acknowledge the existence of horse-racing and the news sense so selective that it amounts to perversity'. When Peregrine Worsthorne wrote carping words about the *Guardian* of the 1980s the staff were in good enough fettle to shrug them off, even to enjoy them. They would not have bothered too much in their old Manchester fastness. But in 1963 pieces like Irving's sapped the self-confidence the paper needed to do the things it was good at: domestic politics, Europe, America and Africa, the arts, the unexpected features. And the hurt was the greater because the thrust of his argument was against the paper's non-fulfilment of its new national ambitions.

In fact, the 'front-page pictures of sunsets on Windermere' were already almost a memory – to many readers a sad and precious one, because they typified a paper which had refused to be stampeded into conformity – though with the deteriorating presses both in Gray's Inn Road and Cross Street, decent picture reproduction was becoming impossible. But Irving made the valid point that in the days when readers took the paper because of its very detachment – its 'refreshing northern attitudes' as he succinctly put it – the fact that it was never really a *news*paper was not important. Now things had changed. Two years in London had been long enough to cover teething problems, and 'its virtues seem now to be so few that they no longer compensate for the eccentricities of character'.

Irving's gibes were palpable even on the 'woolly leader' front. On Gaits-kell's death in January 1963 the *Guardian* had taken what he called the 'unrealistic course' of backing James Callaghan for the leadership against Harold Wilson and George Brown. Brown was deemed too erratic and too offensive in manner; Wilson had been a party intriguer. On the first ballot Wilson got 155 votes and Brown 88. Callaghan, with 41, dropped out. Hetherington then switched to Wilson, but with a gift to his detractors in the words: 'Much can be said in favour of either candidate; something can be said against both.' Hetherington's leaders were normally bold, vigorous and well informed. How could a man of good judgment write such a parody? But it was of a piece with the almost youth-club jollying in staff circulars – 24 April 1970, for example, headed 'Full steam ahead, but one hand near the brake'. (And plenty of sugar in the cocoa? That would be frank without being fair.)

Laurence wanted a lighter paper, one which would appeal to business and draw in the ads. There is not much documentary evidence for disagreements between him and Hetherington because this was not the sort of thing to put in writing. But what little evidence there is – in a retrospect he wrote in December 1966, for example, on the abortive negotiations to merge with *The Times* – leaves no doubt that he felt frustrated in his position of responsibility without power – responsibility for the company without the power to do anything about the *Guardian*. Two or three years previously, not long after the closure of the *News Chronicle*, a Mr Binyon had written to Laurence to say he would like to take the *Guardian* instead but found it hard work. Laurence replied: 'I agree with you and should very much like there to be a popular quickly read version of the *Guardian* – the paper is getting far too large and its articles are too long for a great many.'[1] (At that time the paper averaged 16 or 18 pages, with 12 pages on Saturdays.)

After further argument with Laurence, Hetherington offered to resign in January 1964 but Laurence replied 'No – emphatically'. But something was going to break. His assumptions had been wrong. In May 1961 he had set out the minimum circulation figures which would allow the *Guardian* to increase advertisement rates (at that time £5 a column-inch compared with £10 on *The Times*) and thus make the London operation viable. The figures are.

	FORECAST	ACTUAL
October 1961	260,000	264,695
March 1962	280,000	266,595
October 1962	290,000	269,925
March 1963	300,000	268,429
October 1963	310,000	267,648

In other words two years in London had increased the circulation by less than 3,000. Ad rates could not reach profitable levels. Hetherington was needling him, while refusing to be needled back.

By 1964 Laurence was looking for some new way out of his predicament and suggested bringing in editorial people to take over functions of management. The three he suggested were W.R. Taylor, the night editor in Manchester who had been both sports and news editor; Mark Arnold-Forster in London, another man who had shown his ability to work across departments; and John Cole, the news editor. He also suggested that Hetherington should take more holiday – eight or twelve weeks a year, for battery-charging.

For reasons unexplained Laurence dropped the idea of appointing editorial people to the management. That is strange because the same year, 1964, he called in Management Selection Limited (MSL) to advise him what to do and they came up with the same suggestion. He had been worried for years about the quality of management. As long ago as 1956, in a short memo to fellow directors headed 'Brains', he said: 'It has occurred to me that today not one of the half-dozen senior executives of the company has got serving under him a man whom we would regard as capable of doing the executive job even as well as the present incumbent.' ('Even as well!') The consultants quickly realised that they were dealing with management in a most unfamiliar sense of the term. Managers had all the usual duties, but the design of the product was a matter for the editor alone, 'and is aimed at an object beyond straightforward profit, and not necessarily to be pursued by normal commercial means'. The writer of the report went on:

> . . . The *Guardian* Editor's appreciation of the importance of commercial considerations to his platform is striking . . . but the effect of editorial policy cannot but be disappointing on occasion to advertising, promotion and circulation managers . . .
>
> [London] has proved not just a geographically convenient contract giving bearably-priced printing and distribution for the South . . . but an insistent force sucking *Guardian* staff, company top management, and common funds to Gray's Inn Road as it were through an internally abrasive tube, removing during the passage that sturdy Manchester coating which gave the *Guardian* its precious advantage of manifest disassociation from the London press . . .

MSL also quickly learned a lot about the still surviving Scott family influence and wished to see it extended by bringing members of the fourth generation of Scotts, which effectively meant Laurence's sons Martin and Jonathan, into the business, at least experimentally. The consultants also gave warning that Laurence should share responsibility – specifically with his deputy managing director, Kenneth Searle. But probably the least expected conclusion (and for journalists, had they known about it, the most gratifying) was the one Laurence had reached and discarded some months earlier: bring in the editorial.

> If an editorially acceptable journalist could be persuaded – even pressed or, to start the ball rolling, plainly enticed – to manage the *Guardian* circulation for a term, and if further management roles could be similarly carried for periods – as of secondment – by editorial staff (by reason, ultimately of some devotion to the paper) much advantage could be gained . . . The editorial staff are the *only* staff who exercise a skill unique to the business: they should be the steel framework of the undertaking.

Laurence duly appointed Searle, whom he had recruited through a firm of talent scouts in 1958 and with whose management qualities MSL were much impressed, to be his joint managing director, himself remaining chairman. He was leonine in feature and of Laurence's stature both physically and metaphorically, with the professional manager's inbuilt advantage of height. The rough division was that Laurence would take care of the *Guardian* and labour problems and Searle would look after the *MEN* and the new building in Manchester. But he rejected outright MSL's idea of bringing in editorial people. He may have been wiser than he knew. Journalists as a rule prefer journalism. To get people of quality the enticements would have had to be large and the secondments short. Laurence accepted most of MSL's suggestions but not the most important. That was that outside directors should be brought in to allow an impartial view of the company's performance. They wanted 'two or three valuable contributors from outside – at least two from London – say a merchant banker on finance, a distinguished (and recently retired) trade union general secretary, and a contemporary company organisation expert'. As things stood, they rightly said, the board was there 'mainly to meet statutory requirements and to provide a dignified honorific for executives who are felt by the Chairman to merit it . . . In truth the board is a rubber stamp' – wielded, it was made clear, by the chairman. Laurence accepted the criticism but said some other means must be found of meeting it. In any case, he wrote, 'while I would welcome any good outside director, the qualities I should ask in him would be so high that I should not expect it to be easy to find even one such man'.

Laurence's merchant bankers were Lazard Brothers; his adviser there was Mark Norman. During 1964 and 1965 Norman considered that the *Guardian*'s losses were unrealistic and pressed him 'to consider what the ultimate outcome might be and . . . expedite whatever seemed to me the best solution'.[2] Laurence conceded that in logic there was not room for both *The Times* and the *Guardian* and that the two should merge, 'with us on top'. He reflected that since *The Times* would crack financially before the *Guardian*, such a merger did not seem impossible.

On 23 June 1965, therefore, Laurence wrote to Gavin Astor, chairman of The Times Publishing Company, what he said would, but for 'recent rumours', have seemed an impertinent letter:

> In my opinion in today's context any question of rivalry or competition between *The Times* and the *Guardian* is unimportant. The country needs both of us. What is important is the struggle between *The Times* and the *Guardian* on the one hand and the *Telegraph* on the other. We produce better newspapers, but they produce a better advertising medium.
>
> If in this struggle there is any way in which we can usefully cooperate I shall be very ready to do so. I have no positive suggestion except that if you feel the same and if we both transmit this feeling to our senior executives something useful might emerge.

Astor replied that he much appreciated that 'such an interesting subject' had been raised. He had shown the letter to the *Times* editor, Haley ('who knows your situation as well as he knows ours'), and both agreed that the struggle was with the *Daily Telegraph*. It would be useful to see whether there were 'ways in which we might cooperate and help each other without losing our independence of character or of ownership'. A meeting was accordingly held at Astor's house (chosen 'for security reasons') on 21 July of which Laurence's handwritten note records:

> They suggested looking one day at the possibility of printing the *Guardian* in London at Printing House Square and *The Times* in Manchester in our new building. I suggested putting our sales together to see what a promotion campaign for both papers jointly would offer to advertisers. This idea was taken up gently, but nobody in fact ever pursued it.

August was blank, but on 8 September Laurence met Haley and told him that his private answer to questions he had been asked in the City was that if in ten years' time the *Guardian* could approach 500,000 and *The Times* 400,000, they would still be in existence. But if not it was very possible that there was not room for them both. In that case the right course was a merger.

By October Laurence, having refined his ideas further, discussed them with his legal adviser, Ben Hutchings of Lovell, White & King. Sooner or later either *The Times* or the *Guardian* was going to get into financial difficulty. *The Times* was probably weaker than the *Guardian*, which had the profits of the *MEN* behind it, but if it were taken over by Roy Thomson or some other organisation with large sums of money, it could become much stronger, 'in which case we should be the ones who got into serious difficulty first'.

The merger might never come off. That would depend on what concessions the Scott Trust was willing to make, though here Laurence thought the *Guardian* had a slight advantage in that 'neither the Scott Trust nor I personally am in the least concerned in saving face'. (The Trust deed does not forbid the sale or closure of the *Guardian*. It is a policy which is protected, not a paper: 'The Settlor is desirous of securing . . . the continuation of the said policy . . . whether the Company shall continue to own the said papers or may have disposed of the same and acquired other papers . . . ' The formula appeared in the 1936 deed and was repeated verbatim in the 1948.)

The idea of a merger, sooner rather than later, had obviously begun to excite Laurence. He said that he, who had always been a full-time working newspaperman, would like to have the dominant position in practice, whereas Astor would 'take the main position in the public eye': i.e. Astor would be 'president' and Laurence chairman. Haley, who was then sixty-four but very fit, would be editor, to be succeeded on his retirement, in perhaps five years' time, by Hetherington.

Richard Scott, Washington correspondent and chairman of the Trust, knew roughly what was going on. He was probably the only man on the paper who did. He and Laurence had discussed a merger in an abstract way earlier in the year when Richard was home from Washington, but Richard took fright at what was being contemplated and wrote to Laurence from Washington on 22 October:

I am surprised that things appear to be developing as rapidly as they seem. I certainly agree that if we really have to face up to a situation which we contemplated in our talk at your house this would pose the biggest issue we have yet had to face. It would certainly be one for the Trust to consider and I agree that it is not a strong body as at present constituted . . . I would assume that you would feel it desirable to inform AH at a reasonably early stage so that, whether invited to join the Trust or not, he would be able to give us the benefit of his views. I think his view would be important to the Trust in discharging its duties of preserving the essential character of the paper.

These events took place in 1965. Hetherington had been editor since 1956 but was not a member of the Trust, for even though Richard was chairman, and had been since 1956, Laurence was the dominant member and did not want him on the Trust as well as the board. Hetherington resented this pointed exclusion and made no secret of his feelings. It was not until 1970, when the balance of power at the top of the company had shifted, that he was appointed a trustee, although both his immediate predecessors, Crozier and Wadsworth, had been members throughout their editorships, the latter chairman after the death of J.R. Scott in 1948.

It was 3 November of 1965 before Laurence 'dropped a small bomb on my head', in Hetherington's words, and told him of his feelers towards *The Times*. He said he feared that if the *Guardian* did not talk to *The Times* then the *Financial Times* or *Telegraph* would. The two men met again two days later at Laurence's house at Alderley Edge, and Hetherington made it clear he did not want Haley as editor. Laurence suggested, for the first but not the last time, a divided editorship in which Hetherington would look after the leader page and the specialists and Haley the rest of the paper (a familiar formula on American newspapers). Hetherington was not enthusiastic and put forward a counter-notion: they should appoint Jo Grimond as editor. Grimond, Hetherington notes, 'was thinking of relinquishing the Liberal leadership and wanted some kind of executive role'.[3] Laurence did not regard such a wish on Grimond's part as adequate qualification to edit the *Guardian*. Most people on the paper would have thoroughly agreed with him. A note of the meeting[4] has him saying that if he was going to appoint another editor of the *Guardian* it would be John Cole.

Hetherington and Haley met several times to work out how the hybrid newspaper would work and although both agreed that it *could* be done neither was in the least enthusiastic. At the same time managers from the two sides, Searle for the *Guardian* and George Pope for *The Times*, met to draw up a financial prospectus. Within a short time Laurence accepted that the project was too vapid to pursue. He would have a struggle with the Trust, pliant though it was at the time, and he no doubt sensed that Hetherington, if his talks with Haley were not satisfactory, could rely on the support of the editorial staff in opposing it. Laurence and Astor then went off to the Caribbean for a Commonwealth Press Union beanfeast, but when Laurence returned on 15 December it emerged that neither had thought it worthwhile to raise the question of a merger.

Laurence was right to suppose that Astor had larger ideas, though *Times* biographers do not disguise that the profits of the *MEN* were looked upon with interest. James Bishop, in his unofficial history (Chapters 25 and 26 of *The Story of* The Times), says it became evident that the *Guardian* was the least logical partner; a merger, however presented, would lead to the demise of one paper or the other. More serious talks between *The Times* and the *FT* were abandoned in September 1966. Iverach McDonald, in the official *Times* history (1984) (pp. 412–13), says that 'When it came to the point no one could precisely envisage a paper that combined the formality of *The Times* and the informality of the *Guardian* . . . '

The two companies let the talks lapse. Laurence conceded[5] that the Scott Trust would have difficulty in swallowing Haley as editor. He decided, though, that it would be tactful to attribute the failure to fear of what the Monopolies Commission might say rather than to editorial difficulties, and Haley, replying to him in Astor's absence,[6] fell in with that stratagem.

Laurence began the next year, 1966, in a gloomy frame of mind by selling half the company's investments in anticipation of a Labour victory in the impending general election. A note to directors in February said he expected a heavy assault on prices and incomes, and that any company dealing in products of national importance would find its profit margins pared. On 11 March he wrote to Hetherington: 'I like very much your present series of leaders in which you debunk the pompous and the extravagant claims of all the political leaders . . . ' Labour did win on 31 March, with a much increased majority (96 against 4 in October 1964) and within a few days Laurence again wrote to Hetherington to say that, talking to people at large, he had the impression that the public was now a little tired of politics. He went on:

> You asked me a little while ago whether I could tell you what I enjoyed in the *Daily Telegraph* which was not in the *Guardian*, and so far as this morning's issue is concerned, Monday 4 April, the answer is six columns of non-political news and pictures on the front page compared with four-and-a-half columns in the *Guardian*. Incidentally I could also add five individual stories in the *Telegraph* which were interesting but either missed or crowded out of the *Guardian*. These were (1) Moonship plays the Russian Anthem; (2) Girl Drowns in Remand Home Escape; (3) Dog breeds being made unrecognisable;

(4) £550 flat in Mayfair; (5) The Longleat Lions – and particularly the picture of them.

He neglected to add that the *Telegraph* had thirty pages that day, the *Guardian* sixteen.

Before long Laurence returned to the subject of a merger, this time in a six-page memo setting out the pros and cons and leaning towards the pro. He had clearly given up hope that the *Guardian*'s losses (£500,000 a year; cover price was 5d (2p); postage 4d) could be substantially reduced. Thus the *Guardian* continued its dependence on the *MEN*. This, of course, was legitimate company policy which Laurence himself had been happy to defend. Back in Wadsworth's time he had talked frankly about it.

> The editor and I have a fundamental cleavage . . . He wants the *Guardian* to pay its way and hates living on the profits of the *Evening News*. I believe that we have no option . . . I also believe that a proper purpose of the Scott Trust is, by making large profits on the *News*, to produce a better *Guardian* than would be possible if it were a purely commercial product.[7]

But the scale of the dependence showed no lessening. Money needed to be spent on the *MEN* if it was to go on being profitable. Laurence now wrote:

> The *News* needs a new building, and finance for this must be given priority and must rank before the needs of the *Guardian*. This finance, which will have to be borrowed within two years, will put the *Guardian* into the danger area, the area in which a bad downward lurch of trading conditions could jeopardise the existence of the paper.

Laurence was once again beginning to see the choice as between the *Guardian*'s total disappearance and some attenuated survival in a joint quality newspaper.

Everything that happened in the economy in 1966 added to his worries – and to everybody else's, of course, but MGEN did not appear well placed to stand the strain. The balance of payments began the year in deficit; on 1 February bank loans were frozen; on 7 February the Board of Trade imposed stiffer hire-purchase controls; the Budget in May brought in a Selective Employment Tax; the seamen went on strike; a run on the pound was checked in June only by a massive effort involving eleven central banks; Frank Cousins (brought into the government by Wilson as a trade union heavyweight) resigned in protest against incomes policy; Bank Rate (minimum lending rate) went to a then unprecedented 7 per cent on 14 July; and a week later Wilson announced a wage freeze and a stiff dose of deflation.

After this battering Laurence sent up another of the many flares launched from his office around that time with a similar aim – to illumine the papers' landscape – and with similar headings: The Scott Trust, The Future of the Trust, The Purpose of the Scott Trust, The Purpose and Principles of the Scott Trust, The *Guardian* Today and Tomorrow, The Future of the *Guardian*, The

Position of the *Guardian*. This one, however, in August 1966 was entitled simply Report by LPS. It brought to light a couple of very serious weaknesses in the company's position which most people did not know about and then did a demolition job on the editorial content of the paper.

The first commercial weakness was in property. 'Finding ourselves closely associated with some very successful and very reputable people' in the property development field, Laurence had 'taken it upon myself to go in fairly deeply'. This was a reference to a company called Milbury Estates, into which the *Guardian* had walked by mishap, along a road paved with the best intentions.

In 1931 John Scott, Laurence's father, as billiards player and philanthropist, bought an interest in a Manchester company, Temperance Billiard Halls Limited, on both his own behalf and the company's. He became chairman of the billiard halls for a while. This benign little concern, designed to keep the men off the streets, remained in obscurity until 1958 when it became part of a takeover by a company called Jasper. By that time Temperance Billiard Halls had itself widened its field and was joint owner, with the London company Newcombe, of the property company Milbury Estates, In the resulting reshuffle of shares MGEN acquired a stake in Milbury Estates, of which Laurence, in his private capacity, became chairman. He made no money out of it, but the company's shareholding and cash advances grew to such a point that when Milbury fell on evil days during the stop-go economic cycles of those years it became clear that, for the *Guardian*, returning were as tedious as go o'er. Good money followed bad.

Laurence did not give details in his August memorandum but from July 1960 onwards MGEN provided increasing sums in loan capital. By December 1965 it held a bundle of stock and unsecured promissory notes for accumulated loans of £200,000. Laurence had also sunk company money (£10,000 in shares and £150,000 in an unsecured loan) in another firm, Salvesen Properties, but eventually a rescuer hove in sight and took both shareholding and loans off the *Guardian*'s hands. The rescuer's name – the South Georgia Whaling Company – did not mean much at the time but it came to fame later when the dismantling of its miserable hutments in the South Atlantic precipitated the Falklands War.

Another anomaly in the company's position disclosed by Laurence was its venture into local weekly papers and contract printing by way of Comet Newspapers (Manchester) Ltd which had been set up in business at Lowton St Mary, near Leigh in Lancashire. Here again Laurence did not go into fine detail but Comet Newspapers was owned not by MGEN as a company but by the Scott Trust through the company's London solicitors acting in the name of Serjeants' Inn Nominees. It had been set up in secrecy in order that the print unions should not realise its parenthood, for if they had done it would not have stood a chance. (It didn't stand a chance in any case, but that is another matter.)

Comet Newspapers first came to light in February 1965 when Laurence informed the Scott trustees of a project evolved in consultation with a Mr Ronald Richards to publish a group of weekly newspapers. He proposed that the share capital should be kept low, say £10,000, and the remaining finance should be supplied by MGEN through trading agreements. The Trust, of course, agreed. In March he elaborated for the trustees and directors the means by which the operation was to be kept secret. A separate bank account for the new company would be set up and Stanley Porter, a relatively new appointment to the staff, ultimately finance director of the group but then a financial assistant to Laurence, would be the sole signatory for cheques. He was not responsible for the company's operation. The cheques 'will carry no identification other than his name which would enable the recipients to identify them either with the *Guardian* or with Comet'.[8] Further clandestine measures were set out in the document. In September Laurence informed the Trust that the issued share capital was two ordinary shares of £1 each, one held by Mr Richards and the other by Serjeants' Inn Nominees. He now proposed that the remaining 9,998 unissued shares should be subscribed on behalf of the Trust and held by Serjeants' Inn Nominees. And the Trust, of course, agreed.

The operation was run almost literally in hole-in-corner fashion from a small office at the junction of Deansgate and Blackfriars Street in Manchester, which no one from the *Guardian* must be seen entering. (Stanley Porter was seen, because the *Guardian* and *MEN* lift-man worked there part time.) Porter was the only go-between for Laurence and Comet. When money had to be transferred from the MGEN's ancestral account with Williams Deacon's Bank in St Ann Street to start the Comet account at National Westminster it was done by a bank draft payable to bearer and handed to Porter. This was illegal and was immediately recognised to be so by the receiving bank. Such a document had the status of a banknote, and in England only the Bank of England could issue such a thing.

Innocent fun. But by 1966 Mr Richards had resigned and Laurence decided to tell the Trust[9] that it was time for the hole-in-corner operation to cease and for the *Guardian* to come out openly as the parent company. Comet failed badly in the end, and its failure contributed to the downfall of the MGEN's two most senior executives — Laurence and Searle. It had a rogue press. Successive managers could not turn the project round. It was intended to produce colour inserts for the *Guardian*, the *Daily Mail*, and anybody else who could be persuaded to buy, but the colour was not good enough. It did successfully print the *Guardian Weekly* for a while, but that was insufficient reason to hang on to it. Laurence's gloomy report of August 1966 said:

We have made a loss on this of around £100,000 . . . Whereas we originally hoped to complete an investment by now of £400,000 and to see a profit by early 1967, today it looks like an investment of £450,000 ready by next December, and the prospect of a loss in 1967 and a break even on running costs with no return on our investment in 1968. The trouble with this is the timing . . .

It was indeed.

Laurence was undecided whether to treat the obvious financial emergency of the coming autumn and spring as temporary or as the occasion for 'long-term and irreversible changes'. The temporary measures would mean not replacing staff, cutting promotion budgets and reducing the proportion of editorial content. The long-term would include getting rid of Comet 'even at a large loss', scrapping the *Guardian Weekly*, printing in London only, running fewer editions of both the morning and evening papers, and 'any of the policy changes', he added delphically, 'that could arise from re-thinking the *Guardian*'s basic position'.

In one respect at least Laurence had had his way with the editorial content of the paper. The previous year, 1965, had seen the retirement of Richard Fry,[10] one of the outstanding City editors, not of the *Guardian* only but of the press in general. Under him the City office had been virtually freestanding and its columns within the paper self-contained. (Hetherington delegated readily, especially in subjects like the City, sport and the arts, in which he was not very interested.) Laurence had been keen to get William Davis, who had built up a large personal following as City editor of the London *Evening Standard*. The formal meeting took place at the Athenaeum, Hetherington's club, but Laurence's was the spirit behind the acquisition. Davis shocked them both, according to his own account,[11] by asking for a Jaguar, but he took a lower salary than he was receiving from the Express group. He could afford to. He was a man of formidable energy who combined the job of financial editor (he changed the title) of the *Guardian* with much radio and TV activity, including that of presenting *The World at One*. He rapidly changed the City pages, and his picture every day marked another break with the reserve of former years. He replaced the commentaries on economic affairs, domestic and foreign, in which Fry had excelled, by a simple emphasis on what he took to be the thing people were most interested in, namely money. He wanted to call it The Money Page, like *The Money Programme* which he launched on TV. The editorial establishment jibbed at that, but he did launch the first family finance page in a national newspaper, which went on to grow in importance long after his time. His whirlwind impact on the *Guardian* ended as abruptly as it had begun and he left in 1968 to be editor of *Punch*.

In his August 1966 manifesto Laurence said the choice was between struggling on and losing very large sums of money or accepting that 'there is not room in the country for two high quality papers, in which case one of them must become more popular, or else one of them must go out of existence, or else they must merge'.

The 'more alert and intelligent members of the population', to whom the *Guardian* had to sell, could be divided into those mainly concerned with commerce and industry and those concerned with politics, education and social and cultural life.

> Editorially the *Guardian* has always been more concerned with the second group . . . This is in the very bones of its tradition, but it does not help to create a newspaper that appeals to the first group – and our survival might depend on creating a newspaper that does so appeal . . . Nearly all our editorial staff belong by inclination and experience to the second group, and can only write in the idiom and with the general outlook of that group. Some of them tend to belittle the ethics and outlook of the first group . . .

As an example of this, Laurence went on, Richard Fry had written for the few City men who were also intellectuals. William Davis wrote for the first group as a whole, 'and there is no doubt that some of our present increase in circulation is due to the writing of William Davis'. He then came to the point, expressing his views in the familiar euphemism of what 'some people feel':

> that our politics do obtrude and that this is why we make so little progress in circulation. They say that our reporting is not always politically impartial, but even more they say that in our leading articles we have lost our independence and have become committed supporters of the Labour Party whom we only criticise reluctantly and tenderly. I have no doubt that this impression, true or not, has been one of the basic reasons for our declining sale in Manchester.
>
> The same criticism put in a different way lies in the view that we have fallen into the trap which we always feared when we started London printing, and which was one of the great arguments against it. Too many of our editorial staff have got too close to the top politicians and civil servants, can see too clearly the problems and difficulties with which these people are faced, and consequently have lost the clarity of view which is more easily maintained at a distance.

Hetherington had rehearsed these arguments with Laurence before. His response now[12] was to say that they possibly represented not points to stimulate discussion but real feelings on which Laurence wanted action to be taken.

> If that were to be so, the action must be as obvious to you as it is to me. You must replace the editor. John Cole would be no good as a substitute in these circumstances. Bill Davis or Brian Redhead would be possibilities; both are able and energetic men, and neither has strong political beliefs. There may be other candidates too.

But if, he went on, the new editor's brief were to be based on the criticisms as set out

> then you would destroy the *Guardian* as it has existed for the past seventy years. Again, I tried to make that point [in conversation] in May; and if you want to

advocate that course then I am bound to oppose it. Commercially it may be sound. In terms of the *Guardian*'s character and significance in British life, it is wrong.

He received a kind and sympathetic reply. Part of Laurence's problem as a Fleet Street chairman was that he was a kind and sympathetic man.

> I am finding it hard to make up my mind and to close it to uncertainty and doubt, and the memorandum was partly an effort to help me to do so and to invite other people to help . . . I do appreciate that all this puts you into an unhappy position, that nagging from your chairman can only be irritating and that what you really want is to be left in peace and to get on with the job. Perhaps even I might be giving the paper the best chance of success if I simply back you through thick and thin and cease to worry. But if this appears to mean a 10 to 1 chance of merging with *The Times* on their terms, then I think, I do have a duty at least to ask myself whether there is any alternative.
>   You ask whether I really believe in the points of view which imply editorial criticism. The answer I suppose is that I do not wish to change the essential character of the *Guardian* any more than I wish to change the editor, but that in my opinion these points do each have a marginal validity and some recognition of this need not change the character of the paper . . . I might never have written my memorandum if the *Guardian*'s profits for May and June had not been so depressing.

Circulation for May was 285,519, down 1,000 on April, and the *Guardian*'s trading loss was £24,109; for June the circulation was 281,438 and the loss £52,114. In spite of what was to come Laurence would surely have been remiss if he had failed to sound warnings about the downhill slide of circulation and the uphill struggle against costs.

Because of the way the company was built he had few to confide in. The directors were his nominees and with one exception were not of his stature. Relations with his brother, Charles Prestwich Scott, the personnel director, and his cousin Richard, chairman of the Trust, were correct rather than warm. His wife Constance was gravely, and as it proved terminally, ill. The exception on the board was Kenneth Searle, but even here a close rapport was lacking; now that Searle was responsible for the *MEN* and Laurence for the *Guardian* the sort of advice Searle would give was of the kind reflected in the manifesto. What was happening in management in 1966 was a reprise of what had happened editorially in 1961. The gentle reticences of Manchester days were not the culture of Fleet Street.

Was there substance to Laurence's criticisms? Some in the office at the time remarked on the frequency of Hetherington's meetings with Harold Wilson and the length of time taken to dictate the subsequent notes. (Between the October 1964 general election and August 1966, when Laurence wrote his memo, they had thirty-two recorded meetings. They had 106 meetings

Power cut

'The worst blow the Guardian *had struck against the Labour party,' according to Marcia Williams. The cartoon appeared on 24 March 1964 during the power workers' strike. Copyright © Papas, 1964.*

altogether – not all at Downing Street or the Commons, though most were – yielding notes of about 250,000 words.) Hetherington was also strongly influenced by R.H.S. Crossman, the Labour luminary and *Guardian* columnist from whom he rented digs in Vincent Square before his move to London. He was usually on his guard in Wilson's company and noted when Wilson used the somewhat transparent flattery of a cutting from that day's leader column on his desk.

He took a round rebuke from Marcia Williams (Wilson's political secretary, later Lady Falkender) for a cartoon by Papas. There was a power strike; on 24 March 1964 Papas depicted Wilson as three light bulbs, the first smiling, the second frowning, and the third blacked out. Marcia Williams said it was the worst blow the *Guardian* had struck against the Labour party and the effect would be seen in the next Gallup poll. Hetherington no doubt resisted Wilson's blandishments, but no one was to know how effectively. (He discussed with Wilson how the paper would cover a general election.) Although he got on well with certain people in the Tory party he consulted them much more rarely – Maudling, for example, whom he liked and respected, he saw only a handful of times and Heath thirteen times between November 1963 and October 1974.

He was also harnessed to a staff which, given the nature of the paper, had attracted some highly articulate Left-wing people, though Hetherington's own undoubted radicalism was more in the old Scott mould. He confessed himself daunted[13] by the appearance before him every afternoon of 'this solid phalanx of Left-wing leader-writers' who included over a period of a few years Richard Gott, Jonathan Steele, Walter Schwarz and John Palmer. Of all these people of high and long standing on the paper Palmer was perhaps the most complicated. He was for a time the editor's administrative assistant and later became best known for his work as European editor in Brussels. Roy Jenkins, when chairman of the EEC, didn't care for him personally (he called his more critical pieces the produce of Château Palmer) but he comments[14] on an evening meeting in 1978:

> We got on in a reasonably friendly way, which is not least an improvement on a year ago. I had in fact been extremely nice about him (although I have no idea whether he knew that) to Peter Preston ten days before, saying, which is indeed the truth, that he was much the best informed of the British correspondents in Brussels.

Palmer also did important stints as number two in the City office and would almost certainly have become City editor had his politics not been outré, even by the tolerant standards applicable to *Guardian* leader-writers. He was a leading member of one of the ultra-Left groupuscules and could not escape the factional in-fighting familiar there. This was not reflected in his highly regarded copy. He was the model of the soberly dressed and highly articulate professional. But colleagues were puzzled, almost as though F.R. Leavis or A.J. Ayer should have spent their leisure hours composing horoscopes. One incident, certainly, substantiates Hetherington's complaint about the phalanx. On a spring Sunday afternoon Palmer, Steele and Gott all turned up in the office fresh from an anti-American Vietnam demo in Trafalgar Square at which they had all officiated and Palmer had been a speaker.

CHAPTER 7

. . . and Back Again

LORD Thomson announced his takeover of *The Times* on the last day of September 1966. He threw the *Guardian* camp, which was still debating with itself the niceties of a merger in which it would come out on top, into the utmost confusion. The *Mirror* summed up the attitude of the other Fleet Street spectators: 'There is no reason at all why *The Times* should not become a professional newspaper. The *Guardian* will certainly be obliged to adjust its corsets.' When Laurence went to see Thomson a few days later he found him looking extremely pleased with himself. 'You could have had it if you had wanted,' Thomson told Laurence, and that did not raise his spirits.

They discussed what should happen next. Thomson wanted to move *The Times* to Gray's Inn Road from its old home at Printing House Square, Blackfriars, which would mean that the *Guardian* was printed by its main competitor. Would Laurence have any objection to that? He said he would not, but wrote to Thomson two days later, on 6 October, reversing that answer after talking to Hetherington. But Laurence went off on another tack and told Thomson that the *Guardian* could not afford to go on printing in two centres. Thomson took this to mean a return to Manchester, but Laurence said no: it would have to be London. The reluctant option, though, of reverting to the *Manchester Guardian* was in his mind and was hinted at in another of his gloomy *aides-mémoire* (The *Guardian* Today and Tomorrow) put out as soon as Thomson's deal had been announced.

Denis Hamilton, then editor of the *Sunday Times*, was quoted in the *World's Press News* as saying that negotiations between the Astors and Thomson had begun two years earlier and been revived in the middle of August after a lapse. Had the *Times* people been stringing Laurence along the previous year; or were they seriously looking for an alternative to Thomson? The *FT* negotiations were clearly more serious. James Bishop seems right to observe that of all the suitors for *The Times*, the *Guardian* was the least 'logical' and that the talks with it were no more than exploratory.

Thomson's *démarche* of Friday night opened another period of managerial and editorial exertion, ferment even, at the *Guardian* which lasted for the rest of the year and well into next. On Sunday afternoon Hetherington posted an order of the day on the boards, 'Points for action', which, while affirming that nothing about the paper's news values and balance of interests had changed, conceded some ground to Laurence. He pencilled a few notes on the file copy he retained. Of his long-standing definition of the paper's interests ('Government in the widest sense'), he noted: 'But don't overdo it.' Page one, the public version said, needed variety – at least one short 'top' and one or two lighter (though not, he insisted, trivial) items lower down. To news editors and their deputies he wrote: 'Are we using our reporters properly? Why do good men write sometimes only two stories in a week? Are we wasting too much time on remote social-conscience items (e.g. rent rebates)?' And lower down:

> We lose readers needlessly by casual blasphemy, snide comment about company directors and business men, and at times an apparent obsession with the perverted or sordid. When a writer has something valid to say, let him say it. But let us avoid heedless and gratuitous offence. Remember there's nothing immoral about making profits, so long as adequate goods and services are provided.

Hetherington was evidently rattled.

Laurence, meanwhile, was concerned with drafting an appeal to the Monopolies Commission. Thomson was aggrieved that the government should refer the deal to the commission at all. The merger of his *Sunday Times* with the Astors' *Times* was to be hedged around with safeguards which looked impressive and which certainly precluded Thomson's treating it as another licence to print money. 'I was being put on trial,' he wrote, 'by the decision of the English Establishment to see whether I and my money were worthy of their trust to the extent of being allowed to take care of their leading Establishment paper, the paper that the "top people" read.'[1]

Thomson was therefore not especially pleased when Laurence sent him an advance copy of the *Guardian*'s submission and the two of them, with Hetherington, had a stormy meeting. The submission was drawn up by Laurence and the lawyers, but some of the phrasing seems to derive from Hetherington. It said that although the *Guardian* had no objection in principle to the takeover it was worried about the effects. Hitherto the Thomson organisation, as contract printers of the *Guardian*, had had every incentive to help it and to wish for its success,

> but from now onwards this will not be so and indeed the Thomson Organisation would stand to gain considerably by putting us out of business . . . [Thomson's] have the power not only to give us a visible push, but equally to inflict death by a thousand pinpricks, and to do this to some extent at lower executive levels without the knowledge or consent of Lord Thomson or the *Times/Sunday Times* directors. The *Guardian* is fully prepared to meet the competition of *The Times* as a newspaper, but unfair increases in our costs and

The Guardian Office
Manchester
October 17, 1956

Dear Putz,

Thank you very much indeed for
your most kind letter. We have had
a good time together and many things
to look back on.   I think Alastair
will do very well indeed: I expect
however that he may be a little more
exacting than I have been!   Still,
we can only trust that wisdom will
guide him.   I am not, however, feeling
particularly religious at the moment.
I am more concerned to get a bit better.
Still, I think by dropping the humbug
of trying to edit the paper from one's
bed things may become a little brighter.
I can only thank you and everybody
for their kindness.   It has softened
the blow a great deal.

                    Yous ever,

One of the last letters of
A. P. Wadsworth, editor from 1944
to 1956, dictated from his sick-bed.
In it he commends his successor,
Alastair Hetherington, to J. E. D. Putz,
Chief sub-editor. Wadsworth's retire-
ment was announced on 17 October 1956.
He died two weeks later.

ABOVE: As time went on the paper's
letterhead became more assertive.

LEFT: Putz (right) with Patrick
Monkhouse, Wadsworth's deputy.

TOP: Alastair Hetherington at his desk in Gray's Inn Road after he had moved his headquarters there in 1964.
BOTTOM: Peter Preston, who succeeded him in 1975.

ABOVE: The London office in the Fleet Street of the 1950s.

BELOW: The printing centre on the Isle of Dogs, built in the 1980s.

Mary Stott, editor of the women's page 1957–72, and (right) her columnist
Gillian Tindall, whose picture Hetherington considered austere and Victorian.

FROM LEFT TO RIGHT: Simon Winchester, Harold Jackson and Simon Hoggart,
the nucleus of the *Guardian*'s early reporting team from Northern Ireland. They
were in London for the annual Granada press awards in 1972, in which their work
was particularly commended.

Tom Stuttard's picture of the radio telescope at Jodrell Bank tracking the Soviet *Luna II* satellite in 1966. For this picture he used a Practisix Reflex with an 8 cm lens, balanced on top of his car, with a thirty second exposure at F4. No flash. Stuttard was photographer for the paper from 1925 to 1971.

Ceremonial occasions. Willy Brandt, Federal German Chancellor, and Edward Heath, Prime Minister, were guests of honour at the *Guardian*'s 150th anniversary dinner. Behind them are Laurence Scott (left) and Alastair Hetherington.

BELOW: Patrick Monkhouse (left) explains composing room technicalities to Leonard Behrens, an eminent Mancunian liberal, and his wife, accompanied by Jo Grimond (second from right) leader of the Liberal party. On his right is Harford Thomas, who succeeded Monkhouse as deputy editor. Grimond became both a director of the company and a member of the Scott Trust.

Guardians of Manchester. Harry Whewell (TOP), northern news editor, and John Course (MIDDLE), head of the northern features department where large amounts of material for both London and Manchester printing were prepared each night. Whewell became northern editor and Course succeeded him in that post in 1987.

BELOW: Brian Redhead leaves the *Guardian* in 1968 to become editor of the *Manchester Evening News*. Listening to the cheeky chappie are (clockwise from left), Whewell, John Rowe Townsend, Joe Minogue, Hetherington, W. R. Taylor, Tom Bartholomew (father of the NUJ chapel) and Margaret Smith.

The last generation of Scotts to control the *Guardian* and its associated papers: Richard Farquhar Scott, chairman of the Scott Trust and Laurence Prestwich Scott, chairman of the company.

unreasonable difficulties or delays in our production could well result from the
new situation.

The *Guardian* therefore asked the commission to stipulate measures to protect
the paper from the rapacity of Thomson executives. These included an
undertaking by Thomson to let the paper transfer to Printing House Square
and receive there all the space and facilities it had at Thomson House on the
same terms and conditions; an option for the *Guardian* to renew its printing
and housing contract with Thomson's (due to expire in 1976) for another
twenty years, with the *Guardian*, but not Thomson, free to break it at five-
year intervals; and an option for the *Guardian* to buy Printing House Square at
an arbitrated price. Taken together the terms of the *Guardian* approach
managed to combine an impression of nervous insecurity on its own part with
gratuitous insults to Thomson.

Several schemes were floated for the future of the *Guardian* at that time,
including the quaint one that it should take over the *Sun* – not the Murdoch
Sun of later years and fame but a worthy publication put out by the *Mirror*
group as successor to the *Daily Herald* and intended as improving reading for
blue-collar workers. Laurence rejected this, explaining that the *Guardian*
could not afford to damage its ABC1 profile. Nothing came of the schemes,
but the process of arguing them through added to the tensions between editor
and chairman.

One of the more plausible, which emerged from a meeting of *Guardian* and
Observer people on 24 October, was that the two papers should form a joint
company to buy Printing House Square from the *Times* Astor family and that
both should print there, thus poking an enjoyable stick in Thomson's eye
because he would lose the *Guardian* printing contract at Gray's Inn Road
without gaining the *Observer*'s at PHS. This was not fully explored because
there was not time: like other suggestions current it was made informally and
although the *Observer*'s trustees toyed with the idea it was not subjected to
management scrutiny.[2]

Another plan, advocated by David Astor, the *Observer*'s editor and proprietor, was that Laurence should put to the Monopolies Commission the
misgivings about the *Guardian* which he had been venting privately to his
friends in the City and say that the arrival of the dreaded Roy confirmed his
fears. Even though *The Times* might prefer to be taken over by Thomson it
could weigh strongly with the Monopolies Commission that approval of the
Thomson deal would be fatal to the *Guardian*. The result would be a merger of
the two papers under the *Guardian*'s proprietorship, but keeping the title of
The Times, upon which the present owners would insist. The editor would
have to be someone other than Haley or Hetherington. Sir Gordon Newton,
editor of the *FT*, and Lawrence Gandar, former editor of the *Rand Daily Mail*,
were both suggested – the first as probably preferable to *The Times*, the second
to the *Guardian*. The *Observer*, it was implied, would join the merger.

This proposal did not reach its final form until it was too late to be considered[3] – the *Guardian* was on the point of settling the crisis in its own way – but an element of it which never found its way into the record was that upon Hetherington's leaving the editorial chair when the two papers were merged under Haley, Newton, Gandar, or even Pringle from Sydney, David Astor would make way for him to become editor of the *Observer*. This was a part of the plan, Astor said, which he never managed to communicate to Hetherington because he was too choleric to listen. 'He saw the whole thing as a wicked plot to use the *Guardian* to save *The Times*,' Astor said. 'I thought the opposite: I thought I was using the Monopolies Commission to save the *Guardian* and perhaps the *Observer*, and *The Times* would vanish, so that their name would be there but their policy wouldn't.' The proposition entered *Guardian* folklore as an attempt by the *Observer* to make itself secure with the profits of the *MEN*. And indeed, however altruistic the *Observer*'s stated intentions, that would have been the effect.

At an early stage of this tumultuous activity Hetherington wrote to Richard Scott in Washington warning him that Laurence might suddenly act on his own. Richard came to London to be on hand. Innumerable consultations ensued inside and outside the paper's offices, between editor and management and among editor, management and interested parties at the *Observer*. But the staff were not told. On their way back from a meeting with the *Observer* on 19 October Hetherington told Laurence that Stanley Porter had asked for his agreement to talk to members of the editorial staff about the financial implications of printing in one centre and he had refused, saying that he and Laurence should first tell the staff what was happening. But Laurence said it was too soon for 'the John Coles of this world' to know. But there weren't so many John Coles apart from John Cole, the news editor, and it seems certain that he was the one person on the staff in whom Hetherington felt able to confide.

Fairly late in these acrimonious proceedings another contender entered the lists. In early November Laurence received an approach from Claud Morris, an engaging journalist and business entrepreneur who had rescued, or at least prolonged the life of, a moribund local newspaper at Ystalifera, Glamorgan, and gone on with the help of Lord Thomson to build a publishing group in that part of the world. At one stage he and Thomson were associated in an unsuccessful attempt to secure a commercial TV contract in Wales, but he had had a row with Thomson and had come to the conclusion that Thomson would be a thoroughly bad thing for *The Times* and the country. Morris was now proposing that a consortium should be formed to make a rival bid for *The Times*. He wrote to Laurence on 8 November enlisting his help and said he had talked in the last few days to Gavin Astor, David Astor, and Deloitte Plender Griffiths & Co., his own accountants. He had £250,000 of his own money to put in the pool and was confident of raising another £3,000,000.

Laurence had Morris up to his house at Alderley Edge the following weekend and not only joined the consortium but took charge of it. Hetherington offered to be there but was told that was not necessary, and indeed Laurence handed over a letter to Morris which stipulated what Hetherington had asked him to stipulate.

'If you want to go in with us,' Laurence said, 'you must accept our terms. If we come in I want to put my full weight behind the project and I want it to have every chance of success.' First there must be solid and influential City backing. Without this he was not prepared to go ahead and there would be no hope of support from the Monopolies Commission. He went on:

> I can offer experience and know-how, but only the City can offer respectability. (Gavin is also most respectable, but David like myself is not.)
>
> The City must have an appreciable share in the investment and it must be the right people in the City. We need at least five first class names, each representing an important group. So far you have only one in this category . . . I can and will help, but you must do the leg work.
>
> To be absolutely honest I am less than enthusiastic about the *Observer*. The idea that they should be included is good; there is a simple logic in grouping a daily and a Sunday paper together, and their inclusion will I think improve our chances of success. But they bring no financial strength. On the contrary the *Observer* is in a difficult financial position, likely to be much worse when Thomson really sets about them as he will, and they want to come in primarily because they want the prop of our financial resources and the economy of being printed as a partner instead of as a customer.

He was not prepared to work in double harness with another management and wondered whether the *Observer* were aware of this. There was no justification for offering the *Observer* more than 10 per cent of a consortium. The *Guardian* should have 40 per cent, Gavin Astor 15, and Morris 10. The City should have at least 25 per cent. He urged Morris to satisfy himself whether the *Observer* management was reconciled to losing the power to appoint and dismiss its editor. Then he turned to the editorship of the merged newspaper:

> This is one of the most important questions in the whole exercise. The first editor of a *Times/Guardian* will set its tone and its traditions, and being nearly irremoveable he will wield tremendous power. The Commission is an exceptionally able and astute body,[4] and they will see this and they will not rest content with a vague statement. They will press hard to know who it is likely to be and they will find out. This being so we do ourselves damage and not good by trying to evade the issue. Moreover if it is an issue on which the consortium could disagree then we had better know this before we get together and not find out painfully under cross-examination in front of the Commission. As for me I am convinced there is only one candidate. Alastair Hetherington is far abler than any other man in sight (except conceivably and unfortunately Denis Hamilton). Moreover I know that I can work with him and he with me.

Lest there should be fears that '*The Times* and all it stands for will be submerged' Laurence gave Morris a copy of a prospectus for the merged paper which Hetherington had drawn up, incorporating points from John Cole and the deputy editor, Harford Thomas, and which contained sentiments every bit as noble as the Astors or C.P. Scott could have desired.

The day after Claud Morris had written to Laurence he appeared before the Monopolies Commission and told them all about the consortium, though if Laurence was going to be involved he would clearly have preferred to brief the commission himself. Morris did not receive an altogether sympathetic hearing (a) because he had not at that stage had any discussions with the *Guardian*, (b) because he could not name the people in the City who would be putting up the money, and (c) because he invoked a number of names without apparently securing the sanction of those concerned.

> Chairman: You mentioned [the name of a supporter], who unfortunately died. Had you anybody else in mind?
> Mr Morris: Among the newspapers we have had in mind the *Liverpool Daily Post*, the *Birmingham Mail*, and Westminster Press provincial newspapers, as a subsidiary, of course, of the Cowdray interest, and we had in mind specifically an investment in this by a special consortium of the Federation of British Industry, also a special consortium of the TUC.
> Chairman: . . . You have no means of knowing whether or not any, or all, of the bodies or people that you have in mind would be willing to come into this or not?
> Mr Morris: There is a strong interest on the part of the *Observer*.

Where, the chairman asked again, would the money come from?

> Mr Morris: Either from Lord Cowdray or from the City.
> Chairman: What does the 'City' mean?
> Mr Jones: Were you thinking in terms of about 60 per cent equity capital and 40 per cent loan capital? Was that how you were proceeding?
> Mr Morris: I feel that the actual details would have to be worked out. We had in mind a share capital of three millions and loan capital around two millions, roughly.
> Lord Francis-Williams: When you say from the 'City', do you mean that you would approach merchant bankers and see if you could get an investment?
> Mr Morris: We have approached and confirmed this matter.
> The Chairman: Confirmed by whom? This is confidential. We must try to see the basis of this.
> Mr Berry: We saw Mr David Montagu of Samuel Montagu. This money could be found, but they said as far as newspapers were concerned Lord Cowdray was the one man who has got the money available.
> The Chairman: Cowdray has not been approached?
> Mr Berry: No.

The Mr Berry who accompanied Morris and was considered a member of the consortium was Anthony Berry, the youngest son of Lord Kemsley and a director of Kemsley Newspapers when Thomson secured control of that group in 1959. The deal included *The Sunday Times* of which Berry was assistant editor from 1952 to 1954. He was assumed to be acting with the consortium on behalf of the merchant bankers Leopold Joseph, but according to the *Daily Telegraph* of 19 November 1966 he said he was acting in a personal capacity and that Leopold Joseph were not involved. Donald Tyerman, lately retired as editor of *The Economist* and a co-opted member of the commission, told Hetherington privately that the consortium was 'a very hypothetical exercise' and that Morris's idea of an independent newspaper would prove to be different from the *Guardian*'s.

Laurence kept in touch with Gavin Astor – they were friends – and told him[5] he had never known a time when rumour was so wild or so incorrect. But he now believed the Monopolies Commission was not happy with the extent of the Thomson takeover and he was considering approaching the commission specifically for a merger of the two papers. Gavin Astor replied that surely it was in the public interest that no title should be abolished.

The day after Laurence's meeting with Morris, Monday 14 November, Hetherington flew to Israel by long prearrangement to interview Abba Eban, the foreign minister. It was the worst time to go and he thought he had secured an undertaking from Laurence that nothing would be decided while he was away. However, by the time he had hurried back to London early on Wednesday afternoon Laurence was in process of staging a coup. The Trust was already in session at his flat at Cadogan Place, Richard Scott having once more flown the Atlantic, at Laurence's urgent request, to preside. Laurence presented a gloomy report about finances, in the recession which was still biting, and said that if the October trend continued the year's loss on the *Guardian* would be £900,000 (cover price 5d, postage 4d) which the company could not afford. He secured a free hand from the Trust to do as he wished.

Laurence was by now committed to the consortium and the merger. He told Hetherington that the consortium had decided that he was unacceptable as editor and that at lunch that day he, Morris and Richard had toyed with the idea of inviting a senior but inactive person like Geoffrey Crowther, former editor of *The Economist*, to take charge, with a managing editor and a leader-page or policy editor under him to do the work. In fact this was little more than idle chatter since there was not at any stage a serious possibility that the Monopolies Commission would turn away the solid Thomson offer in favour of anything so hastily conceived, and ill conceived, as the ideas Morris and Laurence were dangling before them.

But Laurence had a fallback position if the consortium failed. He had four courses to suggest: to popularise the *Guardian* and give it a sale of 450,000; to pull out of London and revert to being the *Manchester Guardian*; to struggle on a bit longer, though in the knowledge that *The Times* was bound to win; and to close the *Guardian* and develop the *Guardian Weekly* as an independent political organ in its place.

This meeting produced the breakdown between the two men. Hetherington accused Laurence of breaking his word and insisted that Richard should reconvene the Trust, which Richard undertook to do, though for practical reasons not before the following Monday. Hetherington then wrote a memo of some 3,000 words denouncing Laurence's activities, which he posted on 17 November to every member of the Trust. He often wrote at great length: in this the wordage may have been even more than usually justified. The trustees had information and ideas put before them which they had not heard from Laurence. Monkhouse telephoned Hetherington to say that the document altered the whole complexion of what was being proposed.

The manifesto questioned whether Laurence was capable of standing up to Claud Morris. Two of the three conditions he and Laurence had agreed, Hetherington said, had been abandoned, in that the five merchant banks had shrunk to one, the least distinguished, and 'our editor' had been dropped. The third condition had been modified in that the *Observer* was to have 15 per cent of the shareholding instead of 10 per cent.

> My objection is not because I personally have been set aside. During the talks with *The Times* a year ago, as Laurence will confirm, it was I who suggested the 'third party solution' [i.e. appointing Jo Grimond] . . . If, then, our editor and editorial point of view are unacceptable so most probably is any attempt to perpetuate, even with restraint and reasoned expression, our ideas on social welfare and reform . . . And, presumably, this point of view must take care not to offend Claud Morris or other important partners. Are we really ready to accept that the new paper should soft-pedal subjects that the *Guardian*, uniquely, has cared about – what can be done for the forgotten people in this country, about their poverty, housing conditions, the sheer filth of their surroundings and the drabness of their lives? . . . My view is that discussion with Claud Morris ought to have been abandoned when he refused Laurence's three conditions. I still believe that the *Guardian* ought to withdraw.

In any case, Hetherington argued, were the finances as bad as they were portrayed? The *Guardian*'s past two months had been appalling; companies looking for quick cash savings during the credit squeeze had cut their advertising. It did not follow that advertising would remain at this level next year. The company had made a profit of £200,000 in the six months to September and could not do worse than lose £200,000 in the six months to March. It had investments, not counting trade investments such as its holding in Anglia TV, of £1,250,000. Reserves were substantial, even allowing that money would be needed for the new building in Manchester. He was not, he said, asking for a long period of subsidy but only that a premature decision should not be taken on the basis of two bad months.

Remember that if the *Guardian* is killed, say, in June or July, 1967, the *Manchester Evening News* will be well able to finance its new building out of its own profits in a fairly short time. Remember also that if the *Guardian* is killed now, or in the next two or three months, those who have done it may by next summer wonder why they were so hasty.

By cutting costs, shedding staff, perhaps finding cheaper printing arrangements, limiting all salaries (including those of directors, except *MEN* directors) to £3,500[6] or even by returning to Manchester and ploughing on with a lower circulation 'I believe that we can keep going – making the *Guardian*'s voice heard and providing employment for many of our current staff. Let us try this rather than capitulate.'

It is astonishing that nothing of all this leaked to the rest of Fleet Street; it was Saturday 19 November, when the crisis was almost over, before even the *Daily Telegraph*, usually first on the scene when an ambulance arrived at Another Newspaper, disclosed 'a possible bid for *The Times* newspaper in competition with that from Lord Thomson'. But then not many people in the office knew; one who did, John Cole, had to tell the editor privately that even if he were acceptable to the consortium the proposition for a merger would not be acceptable to the editorial staff.

Laurence's reply may have been unconvincing but it was a document as straightforward as the man. Claud Morris, he said, was a man of driving energy and strong convictions.

> He is convinced that given some chance to control it he could make a success of a *Times/Guardian*, and he has to a large extent sold himself to me. In accepting this idea of the consortium I am accepting that Claud Morris would have a large say in what happens thereafter. And I know that what would happen would be strongly opposed by Alastair.

The ultimate choice was between a *Times/Guardian* dominated by Thomson, with 'us' publishing the *MEN* and perhaps a political weekly, and a *Times/Guardian* dominated by Claud Morris and associated with the *MEN* and perhaps the *Observer*. 'Both in our interests and in the national interest I prefer the latter.'

Laurence frequently acted on the principle that a soft answer turneth away wrath. Instead of allowing himself to be goaded by another of Hetherington's onslaughts against managerial inefficiency Laurence said he accepted some of the comments, although others he regarded as only the age-old discontent of the editorial side of any newspaper. 'But the core of his complaint is valid; it is that we would do much better if we had a driving, forceful man full-time at the top of the business side of the *Guardian*, that my traditional approach of giving independence to departmental heads is too gentlemanly for this ruthless world.' There were inefficient old servants in the advertisement and circulation departments, on the production side and 'even' on the editorial side. If the company purged by seniority these would be among the last to go. A new and forceful manager would be needed to deal with them, but 'few good men would willingly join our staff today'.

At rock bottom, though, Laurence said, there was a clash between himself and Alastair:

> He believes that the *Guardian* today is a very good paper (some say never better) and that given better management we should have a fair chance of pulling through. I fear that the *Guardian* (excellent as it certainly is) is excellent only in the eyes of 300,000 people and that the last five years have demonstrated the inability or unwillingness of the present editor to produce a paper that would be excellent in the eyes of 500,000 people. I regard managerial weakness as unimportant beside that fact.

Matters now came quickly to a climax. Laurence wrote to Hetherington to maintain the civilities but to insist that the *Guardian* as a London paper had failed. Claud Morris scurried round the City looking for backers. Hetherington had further talks with David Astor about what would happen if the Monopolies Commission turned down the consortium and the *Guardian* went out of business. He also talked to Richard Scott and Richard reconvened the Scott Trust. Everything now depended on it. It was called upon to do something it had never done before: to make a choice.

In the years before the crisis the Trust had been treated and had therefore acted more like the nominated Legco of a nineteenth-century dependency than a newspaper proprietor. In February 1965 it had been 'informed', according to the minutes, about the management's Comet project but it had not been consulted and had simply agreed to do what Laurence asked. Before that, its exertions had been even more limited. It is true that in October 1962 it had heard a report from the editor, at his suggestion, on the paper's policy towards the Common Market but the report had been heard in silence, no reference was made to it, and slightly to the editor's embarrassment, no questions were asked.

Otherwise the matters recorded in the Scott Trust minutes, though doubtless of substance at the time, were not of a kind to impinge heavily on the fortunes of the Trust's newspapers in the long run. In October 1962 it was agreed to give 100 guineas towards a memorial to the late Canon Peter Green. In April 1963 a covenant of £40 a year to the John Rylands Library was authorised, and a gift of £15 for the provision of lunch at a match to be played between the English Schools Cricket Association and a Public Schools XI at Aigburth. From October 1961 to September 1964 the only matter of moment appears to have been whether or not to endow a bookshelf and other furnishings in the common room of a new youth hostel in Longdendale to which £300 would be devoted. Even then, unfortunately, it was reported in 1964 that 'difficulties had arisen'.

Some years later, when things were calmer, Laurence wrote to Richard that 'The ideal trustee is one who is best pleased when the Trust is not called on to do anything', and indeed in the relatively uneventful and newsprint-rationed post-war years, when the main thing the *Manchester Guardian* had to do was to go on being itself, the trustees could and did let Laurence run the business on traditional family lines. Even in the early 1960s Monkhouse, who led a very busy and productive editorial life in the office, found in the Trust another outlet for his many charitable and especially outdoor activities. But when the crisis came it was Monkhouse and Richard Scott who bestowed a new role on the Trust and transformed it within a few weeks into an effective watchdog over the interests of the *Guardian* and the *MEN*.

The crucial meeting at which this transformation took place was held at 45 Cadogan Place on Monday 21 November. It was the first of three within thirty-six hours. Before either Hetherington or Laurence spoke Richard Scott himself made a powerful opening statement which left no doubt where he believed the Trust and the Scott interest to lie. Mr Morris, Mr Berry, Mr Astor of *The Times*, Mr Astor of the *Observer*, and the consortium's potential partners in the City regarded it as essential, he said, that the *Times/Guardian* should be tailored to the tastes of *Times* readers. The new edifice which the consortium was planning was 'assuming more and more the character of a mausoleum in which the relics of the *Guardian* might be preserved with decorum and without loss of face to nourish and sustain a more thriving *Times*'. He concluded:

The maintenance of the *Guardian* is virtually the sole function of the Trust. We are not required to express our views on the economic fight to be, or the day-to-day arrangements for publishing our papers. These are questions for the Board. But ours is the chief responsibility for ensuring that actions are not taken which might jeopardise the essential character of the *Guardian*. If we fail in this, we are out of business. And we are not back in business again, however successful the consortium with which we are associated, if it fails to speak with the voice of the *Guardian* and to preserve its essential character.

The trustees then heard an oral version from Hetherington, who was there by invitation, of the manifesto he had circulated during the weekend, and a clearly inadequate riposte from Laurence, who had to confess that the company's cash reserves were much more slender than Hetherington had assumed and the balance sheet of the previous March had suggested. On top of a loss of £100,000 on the Comet weekly newspaper, now abandoned, £500,000 had been put into the printing plant at Lowton which, 'whether this was a wise investment or not', had already swallowed some £500,000. He did not specifically mention the company's investments in and loans to Milbury Holdings and Salvesen Properties but said the MGEN's property holdings could not be realised before 1969 – or rather that, although in theory they could be realised, the money was not there. That amounted to about another half million.

The effect of Richard's opening remarks was decisive, not only for the strength of his argument but because any waverers among the trustees no longer felt themselves required invidiously to choose between a Scott and an outsider. They thereupon reversed the decision of a few days earlier and agreed that the consortium should be dropped unless large City support was forthcoming, the *Observer* took only a small share, and Hetherington was editor of the new paper. Richard recognised the anger welling up inside Laurence from the way the tip of his nose went white (a phenomenon similar to that sometimes seen in Hetherington, whose face would become puce). But Laurence conceded defeat.

It was all over. The board met that afternoon. In the laconic language of board minutes 'It was agreed that the proposed merger was not a practical proposition. A statement for publication was agreed.' In the evening the Trust met again and endorsed the statement. The editor read it to his staff. The *Guardian* would carry on alone. Cheering broke out.

It was all over, that is to say, bar the nastiness to come. A board meeting that afternoon heard Hetherington say that 'Laurence is the kindest, most honourable, and in many ways the most enlightened of newspaper proprietors . . . But the events of the past year, and above all the events of the past three weeks, have undermined my confidence in Laurence as chairman and managing director of our company.' Whereas on paper they had a cash reserve of more than £1,350,000, some £700,000 was locked up in property companies and half a million was earmarked that winter for the Comet plant at Leigh.

> Thus the survival of the *Guardian*, a great and historic enterprise, may be jeopardised next spring for the sake of a futile and useless venture – one that we ought never to have started, and one that, when we saw the way it was going, we ought to have killed stone dead many months ago. We are all to blame: directors and trustees. Laurence consulted us. We were weak, and we let him go on. But we must ask ourselves what sort of leadership, what quality of judgment, and what quality of management we have been given.

Hetherington's no-confidence motion started the process which eventually brought Laurence down.

The cost of the 'belt-tightening' (a phrase not unfamiliar already to *Guardian* staff) was high and its impact felt immediately. Laurence convened the general secretaries of the unions in the Printing and Kindred Trades Federation, put to them the losses the paper had suffered and expected to go on suffering, and made it plain that the paper's survival depended on a 25 per cent cut in labour costs before the end of January, to be achieved largely by redundancies. Evidently the unions had good reason to believe Laurence was not bluffing, and by and large the cuts were achieved. The editorial

department suffered more severely than any, losing 18 per cent of its staff –
thirty-five people – including some who could not really be spared as well as
some whose departure was not a great loss.

The last important union to settle, as anyone familiar with the practices of
the time could have guessed, was SOGAT, the Society of Graphical and Allied
Trades, which had introduced an extra refinement into its machinery for
dealing with newspaper managements by having joint general secretaries,
R.W. Briginshaw and T.J. Smith. Laurence had originally asked on 6 December 1966 whether he might have the union's decision by 1 January. In
illustration of the causes of heart disease and early retirement among Fleet
Street executives at that time it is worth quoting from a letter from
Briginshaw to Laurence dated 23 January 1967:

> Further to the telephone conversations that Mr Smith and myself have had with
> you and also in reply to your communication of January the 20th, we have to
> convey to you that the decision of the SOGAT Executive Council following
> lengthy discussion when they were in receipt of reports from the various
> Branches concerned with matters that had been raised by you affecting the
> *Guardian* is that they will seek guidance and early decision if it is obtainable
> from the Joint Board for the Newspaper Industry concerning matters that are
> arising in the industry piece-meal. The idea of the Joint Board was that an
> obligation had been placed on both sides of the industry to give attention to
> problems that had emerged since the Board authorised the investigation that
> was carried through by the Economist Intelligence Unit who have now just
> reported, as you know. Certain problems facing some newspapers have been
> accentuated by a number of factors.
>
> So far as the *Guardian* is concerned, you have emphasised that the problems
> of this newspaper are in your view extremely urgent, but this union is also the
> recipient with others, we believe, of a number of urgent pressures from other
> newspapers. The situation is confused and it is understandable that the SOGAT
> Executive should want the position cleared up as to how the Board are going to
> deal with matters for the industry and how soon, and as to how far it is the
> collective wish of the Board that they should abdicate major responsibilities
> that they appeared to have desired to take on in the beginning to direct and
> unilateral negotiations between newspapers and unions . . .
>
> In your communication of January the 20th, you emphasise your view that a
> meeting ought to take place between yourself and representatives of this
> Society. We have agreed administratively that arrangements should be made to
> accede to your request in this regard and Mr Smith and myself will seek as best
> we can to respond to our mutual conveniences in this regard.

Laurence's nose-tip may well have gone white again. He replied next day that
he could not understand what the letter meant, but that in all his experience
he had met nothing like it. Harold Wilson told Hetherington he thought a
suitable job for Briginshaw would have been Governor of the Seychelles, but

that kindly thought was never brought to fruition. Wilson also said he had told Lord Goodman (chairman of the *Observer* trustees and of the Arts Council, at whose offices some of the negotiations with the *Observer* were held) to 'stay with' the consortium but in the end to see that it died. There would be a *Times/Guardian*, Wilson said, only over his dead body. Laurence and SOGAT, however, made up their differences. Laurence wrote an emollient letter when a manning agreement had been reached and T.J. Smith, now sole general secretary, wrote on 22 March 1967: 'Our Executive . . . were glad that our Chapels in Division A were able to help the paper out of its difficulties not only because of the employment which the paper provides, but also because it is indispensable to the British way of life.'

The crisis had several immediate results in the way the company was run. Kenneth Searle, as joint managing director with Laurence, took over control of the *Guardian*. The chairman of the Trust would in future be entitled to attend board meetings, though without a vote. Outside directors were appointed for the first time – Jo Grimond, who had recently ceased to be leader of the Liberal party, and J.M. Clay, a director of Hambros Bank. MGEN became a parent company with operating companies for the *Guardian*, the *Manchester Evening News*, and eventually a proliferation of smaller concerns.

Was Searle, then, the 'driving, forceful man full-time at the top of the *Guardian*' for whom Laurence had wished? He certainly brought an approach unfamiliar to Cross Street when in October of 1967 he decided to strike, using as his instrument a detailed account for the board of Laurence's handling of the property investments. After listing the numerous stages in the Milbury and Salvesen saga he wrote: 'The official MGEN record of these events is surprisingly inadequate and at this distance in time only fading memory can tell us whether many of the points were undiscussed or merely unrecorded. There is no minute to support any of the following decisions . . . ' and he went on to list nine occasions on which loans were granted, interest rates reduced or repayment dates extended. Some of his longer-service colleagues, Searle wrote, would recall, 'perhaps with a belated twinge of conscience', the cursory way in which Laurence's investment summaries had been accepted until the auditors 'suggested [in 1965] that a slightly more formal approach to these important financial matters would be appreciated'. With almost Mark Antonine suavity Searle wrote of the directors' willingness to stand aside. 'We left Laurence to shoulder the whole weight of these responsibilities almost on his own and, typically, he willingly undertook this task single-handed . . .' Then there was the 'abysmal series of failures and inadequacies' of the Comet venture and – a dig at Hetherington instead of Laurence here – 'the sanctity of the editorial prerogative and the consequent reluctance of our corporate predecessors to discuss any matter which could conceivably be tucked in under that very wide umbrella'. In not very coded language Searle concluded that editorial matters should not be barred from discussion by the board, that the company needed a full-time finance director, and that Laurence should cease to be both chairman and chief executive.

Searle was not alone in these sentiments. Those concerning Milbury and Comet were shared, of course, by Hetherington, and also, to the others' surprise, since he was thought to be a Laurence man, by the editor of the *MEN*, Tom Henry. A cabal of these directors, with Richard Scott from the Trust in the chair, met at Gray's Inn Road on 27 October to decide how best to ease Laurence out of the company. With them was Peter Gibbings, who had recently joined the *Guardian* from the *Observer* as part of the management reconstruction; he confined himself, as would befit a newcomer, to the effect that any new hierarchical system would have on the *Guardian*. Hetherington and Henry were in favour of dismissing Laurence altogether, in Henry's case unceremoniously on the ground that as long as he had a desk in the building he would interfere. Searle thought he could handle the matter more gently. He said Laurence was suffering from strain and that the company would be severely damaged in public esteem if it were seen to be dismissing 'Scott of the *Guardian*'. He was in favour of keeping him as non-executive chairman.

Richard came to the rescue. He said he had already forewarned his cousin of the disquiet of the directors. To dismiss him now, when he had had all the anxiety of Milbury and his wife was gravely ill, could destroy him. It would be inhuman. Once again at a crucial time in the *Guardian*'s affairs Richard took the lead and found a way through the crisis. Laurence would remain as chairman, but in a strictly non-executive capacity. It would be made clear to him that his power of yea and nay was at an end.

Next day, a Saturday, the cabal concluded its discussion on the terrace of the National Liberal Club. It decided on the Richard–Searle formula and Richard, upon whom the painful duties of the *Guardian* seemed regularly to fall, took an afternoon train to Alderley Edge to inform Laurence of his colleagues' decision. Laurence met Richard at the station and they talked in the car. Richard told him that the next board meeting would accept, in view of the burden of his other commitments, his decision to retire from executive office. It would place on record its deep appreciation of his unsparing work on the company's behalf and would warmly look forward to his return in six months' time as non-executive chairman. Laurence was not angry. He was relieved. He had surmised what the choice before the cabal had been and had feared a different outcome. Scott remained at the *Guardian*. The Monopolies Commission said Thomson could take *The Times*.

CHAPTER 8

Sea Interludes

He made a personal discovery in the art of dead-reckoning which should find its place with the flight of birds, the appearance of seaweed, and all the trivia by which the primitive navigator made a guess at his position. He shaved in sea water; and when the soap lathered more easily he knew the water was fresher and that the boat was in the vicinity of melting ice. – William Golding reviewing *Vinland Voyage*, by J.R.L. Anderson (Eyre & Spottiswoode), *Guardian*, 6 June 1967

Complexity is in the nature of anything that he is involved in. – Laurence Scott on J.R.L. Anderson

Surely only Anderson, set to teach Indian gunners the simple trigonometry of height-finding, would have written for them, having learned the language in three months, an Urdu text-book in which the sides of right-angled triangles became cousins of varying degrees, maintaining a constant family relationship. – *Guardian* obituary after Anderson's death at the age of sixty-nine on 21 August 1981

John Anderson was successively a reporter, correspondent in Germany, Labour correspondent, leader-writer, and assistant editor. He created the industrial reporting department in Manchester. He commissioned and wrote dozens of industrial features, some in the form of supplements, which brought in lucrative advertising. But the job he liked most, and to which he probably appointed himself, was that of yachting editor. He doubled the post with that of motoring editor, in which capacity he wrote on Mondays a succession of 100-word tips to drivers about the need to carry multiple bits of makeshift equipment for use against every possible hazard of the road or weather. People passed his room with care, for he could stop them in the manner of the Ancient Mariner and ask their views on some project he had been thinking up for the paper. During these conversations he would either be practising golf shots with imaginary clubs or leaning head in hand on his lectern saying 'Oh my God, it's all too, too much'.

Anderson had a genius for two-way contact with the readers. Most summers during the 1960s he would organise a competition for schools to take part in, and if it could involve some element of seamanship so much the better. In 1960 Francis Chichester had won the *Observer*'s single-handed trans-Atlantic yacht race, and a couple of years later Chichester, who had admired Anderson's yachting pieces in the *Guardian*, offered to sell the paper a daily story by radio about his next solo crossing in which he was planning to better his 1960 time.[1] Anderson and the Marconi company between them developed a ship-to-shore radio system powered by battery which was capable of transmitting over trans-Atlantic distances and in June 1962 *Guardian* readers were treated to a daily account of this famous voyage.

Chichester had not only to navigate his yacht, *Gipsy Moth III*, but learn the arts of radio telephony, transmitting to a receiver at Goonhilly Down in Cornwall when conditions were right, or direct to the GPO radio terminal at Brent, North London, when they were difficult. Anderson kept up a daily commentary for readers on the niceties of the voyage. Nothing was left to chance nor the readers left uninformed on the smallest detail. A few days out of Plymouth Chichester found himself host to a wounded pigeon which had taken refuge on *Gipsy Moth*. Solemnly the *Guardian* reported that it had put the problem of the pigeon to the Curator of Birds at the London Zoo, the RSPCA, and the Severn Wildfowl Trust. The voyage was a huge success for the paper and for Chichester, who did set a new record. His wife Sheila flew to New York to welcome *Gipsy Moth* as she passed the Ambrose Light vessel in the harbour on US Independence Day, 1962. With her was Rex Hearn, manager of the New York office, and Alistair Cooke in jaunty straw hat and striped blazer.

This radio-telephone technique was used again in 1963 when the *Guardian*–Post Office team, recruiting additional specialists from the Muirhead company, transmitted the first small-boat ship-to-shore pictures. They were taken by a medical doctor, David Lewis, who was testing his catamaran between England and Iceland for an eventual voyage from South America to Easter Island, much in the manner of Thor Heyerdahl's journey on the raft *Kon-Tiki*. This too provided the *Guardian* with a schools competition. The technique was never to be put to the test, however, in the adventure intended by the author William Golding. He had contracted to send the paper an account of his voyage in July 1967 from England to Le Havre, by canal to Marseilles, and thence to Greece. However, his yacht *Tenace* sank in the Channel on the second day out from Shoreham after being in collision with a 7,000-ton Japanese cargo ship, the *Heian Maru*. Mr Golding was not available for comment that night. Mrs Golding was quoted in the paper as saying 'My husband is still very upset at the moment.'

The next important stimulus to Anderson's antennae was the publication by Yale University in October 1965 of what was said to be a medieval map showing that Norse settlements on the American eastern seaboard were visited by a papal legate, Bishop Erik Gnupsson, as early as 1117, or nearly four centuries before Columbus sailed in 1492. The location of the settlement shown on the map was Vinland, and accordingly Anderson mounted a nautical expedition which would retrace the route supposedly taken from Greenland to America by Bjarni Herjolfsson and Leif Eiriksson, for which he insisted that the oral evidence had 'lived on' in the great Icelandic sagas[2] at the close of the tenth century.

For the purposes of this voyage the *Guardian* chartered, and eventually bought, the 45-foot Bermuda-rigged cutter *Griffin*, which Anderson described as 'a fine example of East Coast wooden shipbuilding, tough, and well-maintained throughout her life'.[3] She had been the club yacht of the Royal Ocean Racing Club; Anderson now fitted her out with a Marconi Kestrel radio-telephone powered by Exide batteries, so that he, like Chichester, should send daily reports to the *Guardian*. Anderson was leader of the expedition and he secured the services of Peter Haward as skipper and sailing master, with four other members of the crew. Haward, as Anderson reported in the paper, was not only an accomplished seaman but the son of a former editor of *The Pioneer*, Allahabad. After a number of further explanatory articles *Griffin* set sail from Scarborough on Monday 2 May 1966 and, to foreshorten many a saga on the way, made her landfall at Martha's Vineyard in Massachusetts on Monday 27 June.

Suspicions were naturally voiced about the authenticity of the map, beginning in the *Sunday Times* of 6 March 1966. Yale had paid the equivalent of £100,000 for it, but far from being 'the greatest treasure in the Yale map collection', as it was originally described by that university's curator of maps, it was feared by cartographers to be a forgery. These doubts were eventually amplified in 1974 when analysis of ink samples suggested that the map was 'a 20th-century fake rather than the work of a 15th-century Swiss monk'.[4] Whether the map is genuine or not must be left to specialist opinion. There is other evidence (for example from coins[5]) of early Norse penetration of North America. In any case Anderson was not to be deterred, nor the *Guardian*. The map had provoked a famous jaunt and a jolly schools competition. The coincidence of Vinland and Martha's Vineyard was perhaps a little unsubtle, but never mind. Anderson's voyage proved, in a negative sort of way, that the legends were not necessarily false. *Griffin* was laid up in Massachusetts, and harbour-masters from Fairhaven and New Bedford continued to send in regular bills for wharfage dues to a harassed company secretary in Manchester. Nearly two years after the voyage, in the spring of 1968, *Griffin* passes out of the *Guardian*'s log, it having been agreed in December that she should be sold, though not, Anderson was assured by the editor, in any offhand or callous manner[6] and only when a suitable owner could be found.

After Vinland, back to Chichester. This time the *Guardian* came unstuck. It signed a contract, jointly with the *Sunday Times*, to take Chichester's copy by radio-telephone on a single-handed round-the-world voyage. Anderson launched the project and the paper carried long reports. Then after he had reached Sydney, silence. It was all explained by Anderson.[7] The initial contract covered only the outward journey. When Chichester had reached Australia new arrangements were needed and the *Guardian*, which had undergone its financial crisis, could not afford them. Accordingly *The Times* signed up Chichester and had by far the best of the bargain. The outward journey had been tedious; the return, battling round Cape Horn, was exciting in the extreme. A disaster which he narrowly avoided made *The Times* lead story. On his return Chichester was knighted in the Great Square of Greenwich Naval College, when the Queen used Sir Francis Drake's sword.

This was hard for John Anderson but it never showed through his stoicism. Instead he launched himself into another and cheaper project in collaboration with Japan Air Lines. He gave *Guardian* readers their first insight into the haiku: the verse of thirteen syllables spread over three lines which, he assured the editor, was 'one of the purest and simplest, yet most effective forms of cultural expression and communication ever devised'.[8] So for several weeks in 1967 energies were put into this metrical form which has enjoyed sporadic popularity ever since.

Randolph Churchill, in the *Spectator* of 2 June 1967, was scathing, not about Anderson, whose pioneering of the radio link he warmly praised, but about the *Guardian* for not seeing Chichester home.

> It is comical for them to say that at that time they were 'in the throes of an economic crisis' . . . Chichester's contract for the return voyage called for two articles a week: one for the Sunday paper and one for the daily. Thus *The Times* were able to print eighteen pieces on Chichester. This works out at £83 an article . . . All this talk of bigger cheque books is farcical. Any half-prosperous newspaper could have found £1,500 out of the petty cash.

Hetherington took a different view. In a note to Peter Preston, features editor, on 3 June 1970, he said, of a suggestion for printing a nautical extract from one of John Anderson's subsequent books,[9] 'Perhaps unfairly I should say that I'm a bit allergic to Chichester.'

After a stalwart career with the paper Anderson faded out rather than left and went to run a marina and a restaurant near Abingdon. He had been born in what was then British Guiana, where his father was a colonial civil servant, but the family retained its English roots. Hence his move from The Old Hall, Marple, near Manchester, via London, back to Berkshire. 'When you've owned land in the Thames Valley for eight hundred years,' he told a colleague, wiping a hand across his forehead, 'it imposes certain obligations.'

CHAPTER 9

In Strife: Vietnam

ALMOST simultaneously with the management upheavals of 1966–7 the editorial staff were engaged in a more familiar type of argument, usually agreeable but this time painful, about what to say in the paper. The story did not unfold tidily and it would do violence to try to impose tidiness in retrospect. The disputed subjects were Vietnam and Palestine.

Before the start of the Six-Day War in June 1967 Frank Edmead, leader-writer, had established an editorial line on Palestine against which all future comment would have to be measured. Most people on the paper would have said he had done the same for Vietnam. The editor altered course on both these subjects. The shift on Vietnam was more conspicuous, and noises of dissent reverberated for a long time. But it was the shift on Palestine which led Edmead to resign. On Vietnam Hetherington may since, whether necessarily or not, have given some ground,* but in 1967 the two men, having examined the situation, came up with different responses.

Vietnam was not, of course, a British 'sphere of influence' (the term was still in use) in the way that the Middle East was. The *Guardian* did not have staff correspondents permanently stationed there during the first years of the mass American intervention under Kennedy and Johnson, with Robert McNamara as Secretary of Defense. Any direct influence on American public opinion by its visiting reporters could scarcely be compared with that wielded by the American networks in 'the first television war'; but it was far from negligible. Then, as later, the *Guardian Weekly* (or *Manchester Guardian Weekly* as the American edition for long continued to be called) circulated in American universities. Secondly all British press reporting, in this case the *Guardian*'s, influenced British public attitudes. And thirdly the paper's reporting shaped its editorial stance, and was thus one of the influences on the way the British government, which during the crucial years was Harold Wilson's, addressed its American ally.

---

* '. . . my misjudgment (if it was a misjudgment) over Vietnam . . .' (Guardian *Years*, pp. 294–5).

The tone of the *Guardian*'s reporting is expressed in a piece from Saigon by Clare Hollingworth, defence correspondent:

Today, in spite of American bombing of targets in North Vietnam and the danger of the local struggle becoming a major war, there is a military stalemate: the Vietcong are in complete control of the major part of the country but unable to dislodge the Americans and the Vietnam Government from the principal towns. This stalemate could continue indefinitely. By maintaining a formidable range of sophisticated and powerful weapons and nearly forty thousand men, the Americans have dug themselves in – often literally – in an effort to secure their firm hold on Saigon and the six main air bases.

It is evident that the Americans had made little preparation for (and had little understanding of) the kind of limited war now in progress in South Vietnam. Senior American officers in Saigon complain that the Pentagon have been so preoccupied with nuclear strategy since the end of the Korean war that they have given but scant attention and thought to guerrilla or subversive war of the kind, for example, the British fought in Malaya. They certainly had evolved no tactics to compete with the latest refinements of Mao Tse-tung techniques which the Vietcong had developed and adapted during the long years of fighting since the end of the Second World War.

The Vietcong can easily deploy considerable effort at little cost to themselves while the Americans are forced to expend resources on a vast scale. The rebels have the sympathy of a large majority of the Vietnamese or local tribesmen in the areas where they operate. They have a superb intelligence network and it is quite impossible for a foreigner to distinguish between a Vietcong rebel and Vietnamese soldier because they are the same people, and they dress, talk and generally behave in an identical manner. The terrorist can and frequently does walk safely in the streets of Saigon . . . [1]

Hollingworth's assessment of the military situation in this and subsequent reports reinforced the a priori judgments about the war in the paper's Corridor in Manchester, where several leader-writers, and in this case especially Edmead, were still based. He was a Quaker who had done his service during the Second World War first on a farm and then driving for the Friends' Ambulance Unit in Europe. (His section leader in the war zones was Gerald Gardiner, later the QC who defended *Lady Chatterley's Lover* and became Lord Chancellor.) He joined the *Guardian* in 1950 along an uncommon route through the *Eastern Daily Press*, Norwich. Hetherington, on taking over from Wadsworth, transferred Edmead from the reporters to the leader-writing staff, where he kept watch over large swathes of territory in the Middle East and non-Soviet Asia. He compiled, from a copious reading of the British and continental press and from the BBC monitoring service, detailed records of what was going on within his jurisdiction, and entered these in small green pocket-books, one for each country. It was an era when the serious dailies and weeklies were expected in their leader columns to keep readers abreast of events far removed from the centre of British concerns. Edmead and his leader-writing colleagues worked at one remove from academe on one side and from Whitehall on the other. He would write on several days a week, and if nothing spectacular was happening in the more glorious provinces of his empire he would press the claims of its frontiers in Burma or Kuwait. He could be heard intoning Chinese syllables behind his closed door, the better to understand his sources. At the end of the 1950s he was a conservationist before the term had become fashionable, refusing to use the car which had been left to him. Years later, teaching English at the University of Xi'an, he found himself dreading the 'horrible Utopia' in which every Chinese, like every Westerner, had a car.[2] That would scarcely be relevant except to demonstrate an unswerving, sometimes unnerving, fixity of principle which Edmead now applied to the American intervention in Vietnam.

Another member of staff whose involvement with Vietnam took an exceptional course was Richard Gott, who was to become a mainstay of the paper for at least another two decades. At a time when, apart from rare and unexpected Etonians, most of the editorial staff were grammar school products, Gott brought to his Wykehamism a rare combination of total severity in politics and immense jollity in conversation. He said that if the term had not been misappropriated in Germany he would call himself a National Socialist. He was strongly opposed politically to the American involvement in Vietnam and temperamentally to the Wilson government's support for it (less than wholehearted though that was). It was a natural course, therefore, that when a by-election came about in Hull North in January 1966 Gott should formally resign from the leader-writing staff of the *Guardian* and stand as candidate for an ad hoc grouping called the Radical Alliance, hoping to shake the Labour party's grip on the seat.

This 'talented young man', in the words of the *Annual Register*, 'fought a vigorous campaign and some feared he might win enough Labour and Liberal support to command a substantial vote and, perhaps, give the Conservatives victory'. Labour, taking fright, sent in its dreadnoughts in the couple of weeks before polling, and the fright had at least one long-term result. Barbara Castle, the Minister of Transport, put out in London on Tuesday 18 January a list of important road works her department planned to undertake. That same evening in Hull she announced in addition that the city was to have a road bridge across the Humber as soon as development plans had been agreed. Should he wish to (and he might, because he personified another unusual combination: Left-wing politics and a fondness for fast cars) Gott* could thus

---

* In his entry for Monday 21 April 1969 Richard Crossman (*Diaries of a Cabinet Minister*, Vol. 3, Hamilton and Cape, p. 449) says the bridge had been decided on ten years before the traffic justified it. 'This was something Barbara and I have promised in order to win the Hull by-election in March [sic] 1966 and, ironically, the money was found by deducting it from the Development Areas, to the fury of Willie Ross [Scottish Secretary].'

fairly claim to be if not the only, at least the proximate begetter of the Humber Bridge and hence of the supposed County of Humberside.

Reporters at the campaign, though not especially from the *Guardian*, thought Gott was going to pile up a substantial vote on 27 January. On the Monday before polling a youngish reporter called Peter Preston wrote an LPA applying a cold douche to the Radical Alliance's electoral euphoria, but welcoming the relief from the 'utter greyness' of recent by-elections:

> But the greyness permeates deeper – to the type of candidate. Mr Richard Gott is not blighting Mr [Kevin] McNamara's life because of Vietnam. He will be very lucky to poll his thousand votes. Mr Gott's real importance in Hull North is more damaging and more subtle, because everything that he does well, Mr McNamara does not. Mr Gott is completely at ease with the press. He is extremely lucid and firmly committed. He is matey on the doorsteps and impressive on the platforms. He has made a tangible impact. Quite a few Labour supporters are looking on and thinking wishfully that he ought to be their official candidate. For where are the Government's tame Gotts?

In 1978 Preston appointed Gott to be features editor. Further to illustrate a continuity in the *Guardian*'s affairs, Gott's election agent in 1966 was John Gittings, who had been his fellow research assistant at the Royal Institute of International Affairs when Gott served there from 1962 to 1964. Gittings later became the paper's China-watcher, flirted with Maoism, and was present in Beijing for the full shock of the Tiananmen Square massacre. He held, among other posts, those of foreign news editor and chief foreign leader-writer.

A leader on the same day as Preston's LPA was cautionary but sympathetic:

> Mr Richard Gott . . . is over-optimistic in the peace plan he puts before the voters of Hull North in his election address. 'There could be real negotiations tomorrow,' he says, if, first, the Americans stopped bombing North Vietnam for good; second, they stopped sending massive reinforcements of men and materials; and, third, they accepted the Geneva Agreements without quibble. The third proposition may be true, but it is unlikely to be fulfilled 'tomorrow', because it would imply American withdrawal. The first two would not satisfy the Vietcong; they want nothing less than the expulsion of the foreigner from Vietnamese soil.
>
> These two propositions are nevertheless strongly to be urged . . . The alternative is a resumption of the ruinous course which the United States has been pursuing up to now – in which, whenever its latest expedient fails (through misunderstanding of the issues) it can see no remedy other than to expand the war still further and thus make the next failure all the more damaging. If the wheel continues to roll on in this way it will crush all Southeast Asia, and perhaps more.

Friday morning brought the result as the lead story: the Radical Alliance candidate polled 253 votes. Labour, in the person of Kevin McNamara, polled

24,479, increasing its majority from 1,181 to 5,351. Gott rejoined the *Guardian* staff, which no one seriously thought he had left.

The by-election had coincided with an order by President Johnson for a bombing pause in North Vietnam, after a Christmas truce, and with a 'peace offensive' in which American envoys visited the major capitals to secure support for his negotiating formula. In an LPA written immediately after the election Gott had predicted that the bombing would resume, which it did next day. The Foreign Office (incumbent Michael Stewart, who then and later was held by the *Guardian* in thorough and reciprocal disesteem) announced that 'HM Government understand and support the decision of the US Government to resume the bombing . . . ' The *Guardian* asked:

> At what point will the bombing, if it continues to grow in scale, become intolerable to the British Government as Vietcong methods rightly seem to be already? . . . One can understand why the Foreign Office should 'understand' the resumption of bombing; and that ought to have been enough. The additional phrase 'and support', with the rest of the statement, may be read to mean that by its suspension of the bombing for 37 days, and by its 'peace offensive', the United States Administration is, in the view of the British Government, absolved from further responsibility for the war. Perhaps Mr Stewart does believe that. But it is not only the more left wing of his party colleagues who disagree. Nor (though he may be tempted to think so) is it only 253 voters of Hull North . . .

During the three-day truce for Tet (the lunar new year) which fell in January, Defense Secretary McNamara announced that if the Vietcong expanded operations the US would send more troops. Michael Wall, reporting for the paper from Saigon, had reached that conclusion from observations on the ground. He wrote:

> The scale of the American involvement and the pattern of its development are clear evidence that once the decision had been taken that a stand had to be made in Vietnam it was accepted that the war might be long, costly, and a far wider and more serious conflict than a guerrilla war in South Vietnam . . .
>
> There is not and never will be such a thing as a battle front. The only hope of victory is to physically weaken and tire and reduce the Vietcong forces, to seek out, destroy, and replace with something better . . . their infrastructure in the villages. It is a more complex and difficult task than faced the British in Malaya. It will take many years to complete unless there is a politically negotiated settlement. The Americans are preparing for a long struggle and none of the military minds here are hopeful that peace will come to Vietnam the easy way.[3]

Hetherington tackled Wilson on Vietnam at their frequent meetings, though it was not by any means the only subject recorded. On 28 February 1966, for example, when they were discussing the *Guardian*'s election coverage ('I said that Peter Jenkins would be assigned to him, as last time. We thought that Peter had done a very good job, and I hoped that he would give Peter all possible help') Hetherington proposed an interview for publication on Wilson's fiftieth birthday in March. 'I thought it important,' he notes, 'that we should try to say something about Wilson's underlying beliefs in order to answer the criticism that he had no real principles and no deep objectives. It was a criticism that came, among others, from Jo Grimond, who had reiterated his complaint that Wilson did everything "off the cuff".' On 8 June 1966 Hetherington notes:

> I said that his greatest difficulty was Johnson. It seemed to me that the President simply didn't understand what was happening in Vietnam. He was out of his depth and lacked elementary information. Wilson said that wasn't so. Johnson understood very well what was happening in Vietnam. He 'tortured' himself about it every day, but he simply couldn't see his way ahead. He hadn't any real policy there.
>
> I said I understood his (Wilson's) difficulties and could see that the British Government had to treat the issue of Vietnam as secondary. We couldn't afford to quarrel with the Americans too much about it. Nevertheless, didn't he think that the time had come to speak out openly? . . . He said that at the time the bombing of the north started he'd made the strongest representations to Johnson. They'd had some very tough conversations on the telephone and he had been pretty brutally rebuffed.

On 27 June Wilson discussed with him whether it might not be better to break with Johnson and look for peace in Vietnam through the Soviet Union.

The rest of 1966 confirmed the fears of those expecting the conflict to be amplified. The *Guardian* maintained its consistent attack on the handling of Vietnam, with only an occasional obeisance to the acuteness of the American dilemma. The Soviet Prime Minister, Alexei Kosygin, visited Wilson in London early in 1967 and the two men tried to exert separate leverage on Hanoi and Washington. It failed, giving substance to the *Guardian*'s thesis that a settlement must come from inside Vietnam. The paper argued also[4] that Wilson would be better employed trying to persuade the Americans to get the National Liberation Front (the Vietcong) to the conference table than in seeking Soviet mediation.

At the same time Johnson tried to bring about a ceasefire and was rebuffed by the North Vietnamese. Like everybody else the *Guardian* was disappointed but was less than even-handed in dividing the blame; Ho Chi Minh, it said,[5] would have had some reason to regard agreement to American 'demands' (the ending of infiltration of troops and supplies across from the North) as 'surrender'.

Not long afterwards Hetherington took the opportunity to distance the paper from Wilson, in circumstances which Wilson might not have expected and which may even have helped to fuel the paranoia for which his administrations became renowned. Back in October 1966, when Hetherington had gone to see him on the 28th, Wilson had said he would like to give dinner to various newspapers at Chequers. His reason, according to Hetherington's notes at the time, was that he wanted to establish a new link direct with some of the senior newspaper people. He was 'fed up with the Lobby' because there had been so many leaks, because the quality of some of the correspondents was very low, and because he 'knew for certain that anything he said to the Lobby was now getting back to Heath within a matter of minutes'.

Hetherington told him that he still had great reservations about the Lobby system, though not for the same reasons.

> I didn't like stories with no directly attributable source. Where a source could be given, it was far better to have something on the record or with the source stated. It was more honest towards readers. I also thought there was a great danger of phoney 'thinkpieces' which weren't really based on any information from Ministers, but were written off the top of a man's head.

There was some argument about who should be at the dinner, Wilson having taken a dislike to Francis Boyd, the political correspondent, but a *Guardian* team went to Chequers for the night on Sunday 19 February 1967. It consisted, along with the editor, of John Cole, Francis Boyd, Ian Aitken, Mark Arnold-Forster and Peter Jenkins. Gerald Kaufman was there to support the PM. They talked about Vietnam for three and a half pages of close-typed Hetheringtonian notes before going on to the Common Market, sterling, Rhodesia, incomes policy, defence and 'miscellaneous points'. The talk threw some light, incidentally, on the hazards of global statesmanship by telephone. During Kosygin's visit he and Wilson were tired out 'because the world was not on Greenwich time. Kosygin was getting messages from places eight hours ahead of us where [Wilson] was having to talk to Washington, which was five hours behind us.'

As though to show that he was not susceptible to blandishments Hetherington dropped one of his blockbusters, two weeks later on Monday 6 March. (A leader of 1,500 words or more would often appear on a Monday because the editor, who was normally in the office on Sunday, had fewer claims on his time.) It was headed 'Where is the Government going?' and asked:

> What is wrong with the Labour Party – both the Government and its backbenchers? . . . Pragmatism is all very well. The Prime Minister is a master pragmatist. For a Conservative Government pragmatism alone may be enough. For a Labour Government – as for most Liberals – it is not . . .
>
> On Vietnam the Government has spent too long making excuses for inexcusable American action. Mr Wilson, it is true, has repeatedly tried to mediate – helped latterly by Mr George Brown. Their latest effort, during Mr Kosygin's visit, was genuine and valid. Momentarily, it seemed to have a chance of succeeding. If President Johnson is now rudely unappreciative, as

reports from Washington suggest, then that ought finally to convince Mr
Wilson and Mr Brown that it is time publicly to tell the whole truth about
Vietnam. Why they refrained from doing this months ago baffles and angers
many of their supporters . . .

This kind of thing was much approved of in the office, or most of the office.
The leader was the editor's own but this part of its argument was Edmead's
who, as the exponent of Vietnam policy from day to day, was carrying people
with him much as Hetherington had done at Suez. Then the change came
about.

Hetherington was invited by the newspaper *Asahi Shimbun* to take part in a
symposium of editors at Kyoto in May 1967. It was not to be devoted entirely
to Vietnam or even Asian politics in general, though in the event they
dominated the sessions. He took the chance to visit Vietnam first, and
naturally enough both the Americans and the South Vietnamese set their stall
out. There was nowhere he could not go and no one he could not see, up to and
including General Westmoreland, the US military commander. To bring the
editor of the *Guardian* on side would rank as one of the propaganda coups of
the war. That, at any rate, was the reading given to Hetherington's trip by the
more cynical of his critics, and it became something of a tragedy that they
appeared superficially right whereas fundamentally they were wrong.

Hetherington *was* impressed by what he saw of the American effort in
Vietnam, but through his intellectual analysis of it, not because of the way it
was presented. He was an unlikely candidate for conversion either by specious
argument or, with the background of a tank commander and defence
correspondent, by military flummery. After an active week of travel and talk
with Americans and Vietnamese he attended the conference in Kyoto at which
the other papers represented were *The Times*, the *New York Times*, the *Christian
Science Monitor, Asahi Shimbun* itself, the *Times of India* and *Le Monde*.

The Times, characteristically, had a reporter at the conference and the
Guardian, characteristically, did not. Among the more suspicious members of
the staff there was a degree of impatience to learn whether their editor had
been got at by the Americans. The first of his LPAs did not appear until 10
May, but the day before that *The Times* carried a conference report which said:

> Mr Hetherington was all for a longer pause [in the American bombing of North
> Vietnam] . . . but after a recent visit to South Vietnam he understood far better
> the American reluctance for another pause so long as Vietnam gave no sign of
> willingness to stop supply and infiltration of the South . . .
>
> Mr Hetherington admitted that his South Vietnam visit had left him no
> longer quite sure that the Americans ought to leave Asia to the Asians, and
> cease propping up helpless regimes. He had been impressed by the civil efforts,
> and the extension of the areas of security. He reckoned that for more than half of
> the South Vietnamese people the likeliest way to a peaceful life lay in 'the
> Americans completing their military preparations'.

He saw new distinctions in escalation. He was against the bombing of the
North, but he felt it would be justifiable for the Americans to bring in 200,000
or 300,000 more troops to extend and prevent Vietcong hit and run raids.

The idea of bringing in yet more troops, and on such a scale, was contrary to
everything the paper had previously argued, and especially to the received
view that however repugnant the hostilities, they were still a Vietnamese
affair which would not be remedied by outside intervention. The staff in
London and especially in this case Manchester, where the foreign department
was still based, had no report of their own to go on; all they had was a much
crisper version put out by Reuters which quoted Hetherington as saying that
certain changes would be needed in the paper's policy. Details of what those
changes might be had to wait until the next day.

In the first two of the four LPAs which followed, Hetherington described as
minutely as space allowed the impact of the war on two small towns in the
Mekong Delta, one of which had suffered under heavy mortar fire and was now
in a supposedly 'secure' area, and the general election held in these difficult
conditions. His second article concluded:

> What I do not doubt, after meeting some of them, is the devotion and
> determination of a number of Arvin [South Vietnamese Army] officers and their
> American counterparts. The Vietnamese want to establish a stable, non-
> Communist system and in trying to achieve it they are taking great personal
> risks to themselves and their families. The Americans are risking their lives too;
> they also are as concerned with civil operations as with military . . .
>
> Vietnam is a beautiful, cruel, and puzzling place. Its people have lived with
> civil war for 20 years. Would they be better off if left to Vietcong rule? I do not
> know, but I greatly doubt it. Anyone who advocates it must reckon what it
> would cost in the killing and uprooting of many thousands of men and women
> who have worked with the Americans. It would be worse than all the misery
> and bloodshed that have come already.

The next two articles, appearing a week later, asked such pertinent questions
as 'Can the US win?' and recounted discussion on escalation with American
generals and on civil reconstruction with Vietnamese 'Revolutionary Development' teams. But Hetherington had to reckon not only with a growing
scepticism, as Britain itself withdrew from foreign commitments, about the
efficacy and ethics of such an enterprise but with the prevailing anti-
Americanism of the British intellectual Left and even Centre at that time,
amplified by attacks on the war in the US itself. In conversation he perhaps
did not help his case by using American military jargon, including the
pronunciation 'zee' for the 'z' in DMZ (the demilitarised zone between North
and South).

After this series Hetherington wrote another LPA on 29 June which was
clearly prompted by the drubbing he had received. He started with a series of

the typical quotes he had heard on social occasions: 'Been in Vietnam, have you? Must be a gruesome place. Frightful what the Americans are doing, isn't it? Burning all those villages, and bombing all the time, and killing all those children . . . ' and 'Not sure? What do you mean, you're not sure? Everybody knows about it. You published Martha Gelhorn, didn't you? And you've read Mary McCarthy?[6] It's frightful, I tell you . . . ' He goes on: 'Friends are incredulous when I start to say that the American record is not entirely black. And when I begin to qualify my own statements – Vietnam being an extremely complex place – people at times look at me as if I had taken leave of my senses.'

Noting the Gelhorn series (six pieces which the *Guardian* had published in September 1966 and later reprinted as a pamphlet) he wrote:

> Martha Gelhorn's articles have described – with strict accuracy, so far as I know, for nobody has challenged her reporting – the horror of crowded provincial hospitals, understaffed orphanages, and refugee camps. It is evident also that articles such as Martha Gelhorn's have been a powerful influence in keeping Americans conscious of the need both to avoid civilian casualties and to improve their civil aid programme.*
>
> But it ought to be acknowledged that – again, so far as I can tell – the number of civil casualties from napalm, phosphorus, and high explosive is now much reduced. Among the generals (I talked to four separately) and among fighting units the need for restraint and the importance of civil reconstruction were constantly mentioned. This is true even though restraint means that more Americans are killed and wounded.

He concluded, in words which needed at least as much courage as those he wrote at Suez:

> No doubt it would have been better if the Americans had never committed themselves militarily in Vietnam. That is not the point today. They have committed themselves and they have gone too far to turn back . . .
>
> A peaceful and settled life is what people in Vietnam probably want most. It is what we, too, ought to want for them. Given the situation as it is today, will they attain peace more quickly if the Americans abandon Vietnam, leaving it to further chaos and continued civil war, or if they stay until their task is done? Answers will differ. Mine is that the Americans ought to stay. It in no way excuses the bombing of the North or the failure to let President Johnson's own

---

* Martha Gelhorn had reported war in Spain, China, Finland, Germany and elsewhere. She went to Vietnam as a freelance. 'No newspaper in the US would publish the series of articles for American readers, "Everywhere I was told they were too tough for American readers." Eventually the *St Louis Post-Dispatch* took the two mildest ones. Miss Gelhorn had to turn to Britain to get the others published. They appeared in the *Guardian* [Sept. 1966] and ended Miss Gelhorn's career as a war correspondent. When she applied for a visa to return there, her request was refused.' – Phillip Knightley, *The First Casualty*, Deutsch, 1975.

peace initiative in February mature, but unqualified condemnation of what the Americans are doing in Vietnam is unjust.

The *Guardian*'s change of tack was still a talking point in Saigon when Ian Wright was posted there as resident correspondent in the autumn of the following year, 1968. Wright already had overseas experience. After working as an agricultural officer in Kenya he began on the *Guardian* as a news sub and was posted to the features department. He went to Uganda to write a piece for the travel pages, and while there discovered that a bloodbath was taking place in the neighbouring southern Sudan. He went to the area and wrote about the upsurge of Muslim–Christian conflict centred on Juba. It was on the strength of this first-hand material that he was posted twice to cover the nationalist upsurge against the British in Aden. During spells in London he acted as film critic. Wright returned from Vietnam in August 1970 to become foreign editor, greatly expanding the paper's coverage, in part by syndication arrangements with overseas newspapers. Later, as managing editor and a director of the *Guardian* operating company, he presided over the paper's transition to the new technology.

Before Wright's posting, and between other foreign forays, Harold Jackson had a spell in Vietnam. He soon found that although the editor had reached his own conclusions about the value of the American presence and the conduct of the war he never interfered with or questioned Jackson's own dispatches, based as they were – for he too was a pacifist – on a quite different assessment of events.

CHAPTER 10

In Strife: Middle East

THE Middle East divided people once again, though on less predictable lines. Hetherington's notes have Wilson grumbling on 12 June 1967 'that the Labour people who were doves over Vietnam were mainly hawks over the Middle East on the Israeli side. They did not seem to see any contradiction.'

Terence Prittie, who led for Israel in this controversy, joined the *Guardian* early in 1946. He was engaged by Wadsworth to write about cricket in succession to Neville Cardus, who had not yet returned from Australia. Before the year was out Prittie was sent to Germany and was the paper's chronicler of the recovery under Adenauer until he returned to London in 1963 as diplomatic correspondent. He was an enjoyable writer on cricket again (especially Middlesex) and on German wine.

The Hon. T.C.F. Prittie MBE (Military), to use the full honorifics of correspondence at the time, was a scion of the ascendancy, the younger son of the barony of Dunalley in Co. Tipperary, who lent his sympathies to Irish nationalism and wrote an appreciative letter to the *Irish Times* on the death of Eamon de Valera. He was a convert to Zionism and one of its important exponents in England from the end of the Second World War until his death in 1985. He had known Germany as a student in the 1930s, and during the war escaped six times from its prisoner of war camps. He not uncommonly affected the manner of a Bertie Wooster, yet was a confidant of Wadsworth; a natural conservative who would occasionally wonder at the meaning of the strange signs of liberalism all around. Perhaps there is a limit to the number of nationalisms to which a person can easily adapt: at all events he took, in private, a distinctly and indeed one-sidedly Israeli view of the Middle East conflict and referred to Arabs in uncomplimentary terms. After he left the *Guardian* in 1970 he devoted himself almost entirely to fostering relations through the pressure group Britain and Israel, entertaining at the Travellers' Club. He wrote a biography of the Israeli Prime Minister, Levi Eshkol.

At the other extremity, ideologically speaking, of the fertile crescent was Michael Adams, sometime (from 1956) staff correspondent in the Middle East and then for a short period in Italy, who left the staff in 1964 but continued to write regularly on Arab, especially Palestinian, affairs. In some ways his career matched Prittie's. He was born in 1920, Prittie in 1919. He too was a German prisoner of war. Prittie went to Stowe school, Adams to Sedbergh.

To hold the ring in the news columns was the foreign editor (Taylor, this writer) and in the leader columns, once again, Edmead. It is doubtful whether there has ever been full agreement for long between editor and leader-writer on the Middle East, whether under Wadsworth, Hetherington or Preston. To reduce the 1967 controversy to somewhat simplistic terms, Edmead believed that Nasser had fallen into an Israeli trap; Hetherington believed he had dug the trap himself, hoping to catch the Israelis in it and heap revenge on them. It is probably true also that Hetherington tended to see local conflicts in geopolitical terms as ultimately part of the East–West confrontation, whereas others treated them as expressions of regional rivalry.

On Monday 29 May 1967, a few days before the start of the Six-Day War, Edmead devoted the first of a series of signed columns on the foreign page to the increasing tension. The column gave him added freedom to that he already enjoyed in the leader columns. He probably sensed that Hetherington was impressed, as in future years was Preston, by the democratic appurtenances of Israel faced with enemies among whom, as a later *Guardian* leader observed, Machiavelli would have gone unemployed on account of his gullibility. Both editors gave more weight than their specialist writers to Israel's internal democracy. The column in question addressed the conflicting rights of Jews and Arabs and the historic justification for the Zionist claims. Then came the dialectical half-nelson from which no subsequent *Guardian* leader-writer was able to escape:

> Non-Zionists may surely ask why, if Jews claim the right to return after two thousand years, the Palestinian refugees have no such right after only 20 years. To them the phrase 'If I forget thee . . .' has a literal and personal, not just a figurative, meaning.
>
> But that leaves out practical arguments overwhelmingly convincing to many non-Jews. Zionists maintained in 1917 that without a homeland of their own Jews could never feel secure, and 19 centuries of their history as a minority in a Christian world bore them out. But even they could not realise how appallingly their argument would be proved right 20 years later. The millions of Jews killed by Hitler seemed to make the case for a Jewish national home unanswerable.
>
> Yes, answer the Arabs, but why on Arab soil? Why should our compatriots be punished for the wickedness of Christians? And this argument too looks legitimate. Moslems have not generally persecuted Jews. At the receiving end Zionism looked like yet another European colonial movement: settlers flowed in, to acquire eventually much of the land and all the political power. Throughout most of the colonised world, including Algeria and other Arab

lands, the indigenous peoples have either checked or reversed that process. In South Africa, Rhodesia, Palestine, and a few other places they have not: that does not mean that they will not keep trying . . . They fear expansionism; in any case, acquiescence in what they take to be the injustice of a permanently Zionist Palestine seems as much out of the question to many Arabs as acquiescence in Mr Ian Smith's Rhodesia to many Africans.

It was not the done thing in those days, when British opinion was much less critical of Israel than it later became, to draw so direct an analogy between Israel and Rhodesia. It was all the more adventurous to do so in a newspaper which had been highly critical of successive white regimes in Rhodesia but had also done much, if in an earlier generation, to make straight a highway for the Zionists. Edmead, having made the comparison, did not press it. There were fundamental points of difference between the Zionist and Rhodesian declarations of independence and, as he wrote, 'even those who most uncritically accept the justice of Arab claims must realise that their fulfilment would generate infinitely more misery than it would remedy – among Arabs as well as Israelis'.

The immediate cause of the crisis (one may be excused from embarking on the ultimate cause) was a series of belligerent speeches by President Nasser; the acceptance by the UN Secretary-General, U Thant, of his demand for withdrawal of the UN peacekeeping force of 3,400 men which had patrolled the Gaza Strip and the Israeli–Egyptian border since 1956; and the threat by Egypt to close the Gulf of Aqaba to shipping bound for the Israeli port of Eilat. In the leaders before fighting began the emphasis differed from Edmead's in his signed column. On 2 June, for example, a distinction was being drawn between 1967 and 1956, and the blame was being firmly attached to Egypt.

> There is no point in being over-optimistic. Egypt may be intent on goading Israel into a desperate act. We have *Al Ahram*'s [the Cairo newspaper's] word for it – a reliable word in this context – that Egypt is now confident of victory in a direct confrontation. That confidence must, of course, be due partly to the belief that the Soviet Union will neutralise any American or other attempts to intervene. If this is a correct reading, and if the Russians continue to support the Arab states, diplomacy stands very little chance of success. But it must be tried. Only when it has visibly failed can other methods be justified.

This time the *Guardian* had made slightly more adequate provision for covering the crisis on the spot. It had Michael Wall in Cairo, though like Adams in a previous war he was prevented from filing while the fighting went on; Harold Jackson in Israel doing the work of three or four men;[1] David Hirst in Beirut (in future to become the *Guardian*'s anchor-man in the Middle East, and probably the most experienced of all foreign correspondents there); and the highly versatile Richard Scott in Washington, tying up the diplomatic loose ends of the Middle East and of Vietnam at the same time. Prittie, though partisan in person, was objective enough in print. He had good Israeli sources and was able after three days of war to report how Israel would handle a victory. Adams weighed in with an equally well-founded leader-page article[2] on the Arab position.

> For the Arabs, defeat will impose strains even more intolerable than those which have tormented them ever since the violent imposition in their midst of a Jewish State . . . The resentments, the bitterness, the all-pervading sense of frustration and humiliation which they knew then will be redoubled now. The first victim will be the short-lived mood of solidarity in which they faced Israel for the third time in 20 years. In the ensuing search for scapegoats, no Arab leaders will be secure.

Adams correctly deduced, however, that Nasser would not quit of his own accord, and pointed out that his revolution had been based on Egyptian, not Arab, patriotism. It had been designed to transfer power from the class which had misused it to representatives of 'the people'. (Nasser did in fact offer to resign, but was immediately swept back into office by popular enthusiasm. He died in 1970.)

Because of the *Guardian*'s recent financial crisis, and also because at that time it was contrary to the paper's inborn frugality, its staff overseas did not compare in size with that fielded by *The Times* and the *Daily Telegraph*. In the Middle East *The Times* had three staff men, the *Daily Telegraph* five, including two in Beirut, plus stringers. But the *Guardian* could shine on big occasions by its use of comprehensive 'intros' rounding up the day's and night's events, updated edition by edition until, if need be, 2.30 a.m. Sometimes they were written by a senior sub – John Perkin was head of the foreign subs' desk – and often, especially on a foreign subject and even more especially on a military one, by the editor. The paper could thus present every day a crisp and cohesive front page and plenty of informed comment inside.

The Times and *Daily Telegraph* both had staff men in Moscow, but that advantage was largely neutralised by Victor Zorza, dissecting in his room in Gray's Inn Road or his home in Putney (he later moved nearer Heathrow, where he insisted he could have quicker access to the air-freighted Moscow papers) wherein lay the meaning and wherein the dross of Soviet pronouncements. In a long analysis on the front page of Thursday 1 June, the day before war began, Zorza examined Soviet naval movements:

> Russia's imminent dispatch of her warships to the Mediterranean, which made the main headlines in so many of the world's newspapers yesterday, has not even been mentioned in the Soviet Press. So far as their public statements go, the Russians are certainly approaching the Middle Eastern crisis with great caution.
>
> The question is whether this public caution reflects also the private view of

the Soviet Government, or whether it is merely a cover under which the Kremlin is privately egging on the Arabs and is proceeding with its own preparations to confront the US in the Mediterranean . . .

If they want their revenge for Cuba and Vietnam, a compromise solution which gives each side in the Middle Eastern quarrel a little of what it wants would be no good. The Russians would have to insist on a clear and decisive victory for the Arabs. Any such victory would mean that Israel's chances of survival have been greatly jeopardised.

This the Western Powers are unlikely to concede, and the Russians are not likely to fight for it. The reason why they did not make a more determined stand over Cuba and Vietnam is that they did not want to risk war. There is no reason to assume that they are prepared to risk it now . . .

The most that the Kremlin is likely to do is to encourage the Arabs to engage the Western Powers militarily, while it cheers them on from the sidelines.

Part of Zorza's technique as a kremlinologist was to compare what the words actually said with what they might have said but didn't, or sometimes with what people, by wishful thinking, took them to have said. Certainly a background in Soviet politics was an advantage, but the method lends itself to any textual criticism. Nasser had not said, as first reported in the West, that the Soviet Union 'will stand by the side of Egypt in battle'. 'According to Cairo Radio, he quoted Mr Kosygin as saying that "the Soviet Union stands with us in this battle". This is, therefore, not a promise to give direct assistance to Egypt in the event of future hostilities but a vague and generalised statement of support for Egypt's present stand.' And so it proved.

Not all pro-Zionist readers thought so, but the leader line in Hetherington's hands shifted slightly in the immediate aftermath* of the Israeli victory. On Monday 12 June a long leader weighed up the not very bright chances of a settlement and included the words:

[Israelis] will not give up the Sinai peninsula, the west bank of the Jordan, or the heights overlooking the upper Jordan valley until they know what the Arabs will accept. If there is no peace settlement, will they ever give them up? Their minimum demands must be free passage through the Tiran Strait and the Suez Canal, a more logical frontier east of Tel Aviv, ready access to the Old City of Jerusalem, dissolution of the Palestine Liberation Army, and agreement on the future of refugees. These were the kind of terms that the Israeli Government appeared to have in mind a few days ago. The champagne of victory, however, has gone to some heads. Voices have been raised in Israel to insist that the Old City must be held, that most of Jordan's west bank must become Israeli territory, and that an Israeli garrison must be stationed at the Tiran Strait. It

---

* A word formerly forbidden in the style book 'except in the sense of a second mowing'.

will be neither surprising nor wholly wrong if these demands become Government policy. But the chances of successful negotiation have to be weighed.

Edmead in his column the same day did not argue this point, except to say that one condition of Israel's acceptance by the Arabs was that it should be believed when it denied being expansionist. 'Earlier in this crisis Mr Eshkol's Government showed that it realised this, and disavowed territorial aims. But victory brings powerful temptations.' Privately at the time, however, Edmead was very depressed by his own assessment of the prospects. The Israeli occupation of the West Bank, he told incredulous colleagues, would still remain after another ten years! That was impossible, they thought. 'International opinion', in which they had encouraged themselves to put their trust, would never allow it.

Edmead became progressively more unhappy with the editor's line. The editor offered him a break from leader-writing in the reporters' Room but he had decided to leave. The break was amicable, at least in retrospect, in that the two men respected each other; Edmead felt able to say many years later that in his memoirs Hetherington had treated their differences very fairly, 'indeed admirably and astonishingly so'.[3] At the time Christopher Driver, then features editor, voiced the opinion of others in the office that 'you can't hire people like that; you have to grow them'. The ostensible reason for Driver's letter was to reject a pay increase on the grounds that the paper was hard up and he did not wish to be singled out. But he was drawn into direct criticism of Hetherington's methods:

> Since I've started speaking out of turn, can I also suggest that your own interests and sympathies are now too narrowly focussed for the paper's good (mine, perhaps, too widely). We are shaking off irreplaceable individualists at an alarming rate* and the latest and most lamentable, Frank's, looks to the rest of us directly attributable to the fact that generals and politicians have your ear more than historians or students of Asian behaviour. (I doubt whether your arguments on Vietnam will outlast a year, let alone a decade) . . .

(On the question of pay Driver noted that John Course, his counterpart in Manchester, 'had been overworking grossly'. Driver himself, when overworked, would take his paperwork on the train to Manchester but by a protracted route, no longer practicable, from St Pancras instead of Euston.)

Controversy carried over in 1968. Walter Schwarz, one of the *Guardian*'s polymaths, as became evident in later years, had taken over the main Middle East leader-writing burden, with contributions from the editor and Mark Arnold-Forster. Hetherington was henceforward heavily engaged in Middle Eastern matters, with occasional visits to the region for interviews on both

---

* Probably a reference to Rosselli, Maddox and Marquand and further signs of unrest from Zorza.

sides. Mark, though less heavily involved, made a point of seeing statesmen who came to London, in particular that frequent visitor the Crown Prince Hassan of Jordan, younger brother of King Hussein. On the ground, while Israel settled down to the long process of consolidating its occupation of East Jerusalem, the West Bank and Gaza, Michael Adams made increasing use of his contacts in those territories for pieces in the *Guardian*. (Successive Israeli administrations allowed highly critical *Guardian* writers a free hand.) It was not long, however, before hostilities broke out between Adams and the paper.

The opening shot was a long dispatch from Jerusalem dated 25 January 1968 in which Adams wrote:

> In the measures it is now taking against the civilian Arab population in the Gaza Strip, the Israeli army of occupation is disregarding the provisions of the 1949 Geneva Convention for the protection of civilians in time of war.
>
> In response to a series of minor incidents in the last three weeks the Israeli Army has imposed collective punishments on the population (mainly refugees from Palestine) regardless of age or sex. They include curfews lasting several days during which no proper provision is made for the distribution of food and water, arbitrary arrests, and the random demolition of houses and property belonging to civilians in no way connected with incidents.
>
> When I left Gaza this morning three refugee camps housing 100,000 Palestine refugees were under day and night curfew, and there was sporadic shooting in the streets of Gaza city which served no apparent purpose beyond the intimidation of the civilian population. UNRWA [the United Nations Relief and Works Agency], which is responsible for the welfare of refugees in the Gaza Strip, is not told in advance of the curfews which have been succeeding each other for the last two or three weeks . . .
>
> I had my ups and downs during four years as a prisoner of war in Germany, but the Germans never treated me as harshly as the Israelis are treating the Arabs of Gaza Strip, the majority of whom are women and children.

A few weeks later[4] Adams reported that pressure was being put on Arabs to leave the West Bank for Jordan, so that Israel should have 'the dowry without the bride'. He recounted the case of a woman who was turned into the street with her five children while her husband was arrested and her house blown up, all of which she was told later was caused by mistaken identity:

> The result — and it is difficult to believe that it is not the result intended — is to terrorise the local population, especially those who have small children or elderly dependants, and to encourage them to leave the area and make the sad pilgrimage to safety beyond the Jordan . . .
>
> It is certainly true that intermittently over the past eight months serious attempts have been made (and they are still being made) to terrorise sections of the Arab population in different parts of the West Bank — and the result has been and still is the continuing flow of refugees across the Jordan River.

The Israelis vehemently deny this interpretation of events. In two weeks of careful investigation in Jerusalem and the West Bank I found no impartial observer who did not support it.

Another such piece, stripped across seven columns on the foreign page, appeared on 4 March under the headline 'Bulldozers the symbols of Israel's mastery' and described among other things the building of new Israeli housing on Arab land on Mount Scopus, overlooking the old city of Jerusalem. The two pieces were preceded by a personal letter to the foreign editor. 'I cannot over-emphasise,' Adams wrote, 'the seriousness of the position of the Arab inhabitants under Israeli occupation.' He then listed the names of a number of distinguished neutral witnesses to Israeli mistreatment of Arabs and said: 'I suggest that if some private approach could be made to the following people you could get verification of a state of affairs which I only came to accept as the reality after much scepticism.'

There matters rested until 1 May when, partly because Taylor was absent in Eastern Europe, Adams dealt directly with the editor and had a row with him on the telephone. The next day Hetherington wrote to Adams accusing him of lack of objectivity and complaining in particular about the closing passage of a piece Adams had sent in on the mood of the Arab world. A piece nevertheless appeared next day, implicitly accusing Britain of not having honoured the promise in the Balfour Declaration to protect 'the civil and religious rights' of the Arab population of Palestine. The original may have been more robustly phrased, though in general Adams scored his tempestuous points in the gentlest of language.

The Martha Gelhorn whose pieces were graven into the Vietnam controversy went to Israel and the occupied territories for the *Guardian* in July 1967. In a three-part series she was unimpressed with Arab complaints. She sat in the circle and drank coffee with some of them:

'Bethlehem was bombed all day!' one cries. But there is Bethlehem, intact and rosy in the afternoon light. 'The Jews came to every house in Nablus, shooting. Our youths defended their homes. Two hundred were killed, women, children, boys, at least 200.' And there are the houses, solid, unmarked, of cut stone, and on a later visit calmer counsel reduced the number of civilian deaths to 19; still incredible. Where? How? We agree that there was no fighting here . . . that the town is untouched except for a few buildings at the southern entrance . . . No records; no circumstantial evidence. It is comforting to feel certain that people are alive and well whom propaganda has killed . . .

The Six Day War scarcely touched the Arab civilian population. I am not talking about emotions. I am talking about real war: death and destruction. The difference is self-evident, like the difference between civilian life in London and New York during the Second World War . . .

I submit that a total of *two hundred civilians*, Arab and Israeli, everywhere, throughout the war, is the highest conceivable number of noncombatants killed. All the dead are to be pitied and mourned; none should be exploited for propaganda.

The pieces appeared on 24, 25 and 26 July. On 27 July the lead letter to the editor was from Michael Adams, and the rest of the Palestine lobby was equally outraged. Martha Gelhorn, however, did not have the last word.

The break with Adams, when it came, was about the biblical village of Emmaus, where in St Luke (ch. 24) two of the disciples were joined by Jesus after his Resurrection. The village was known to its twentieth-century Arab inhabitants as Imwas. Adams submitted a piece which Hetherington refused to print, and according to Adams's account, not disputed by Hetherington, there took place on Friday 24 May a 'conversation . . . in which you told me that you would not publish any more of my reporting from the Middle East because, you said, "I no longer feel able completely to trust what you write". To be told, after an association that has lasted for twelve years, that I am no longer thought trustworthy on my own subject is painful.'[5]

Adams had discovered that the Israelis had destroyed Imwas at the end of the 1967 war. Hetherington did not dispute that, but complained[6] that Adams had said nothing in his piece 'about the raids on Israeli territory launched from villages close to the border between 1949 and 1967, nor about the intermittent shooting and mining that took place after the June war (and indeed is still taking place in some districts)'. Had these facts, Hetherington asked, 'no part in drawing a complete picture'?

Hetherington justifiably referred to all the highly critical pieces which had appeared and regretted that the reference on 25 January to German prison camps had not been cut out. Adams's specific answer about Imwas was that there had been no trouble from the village because it was surrounded by Israeli territory and was far too vulnerable to engage in such activities. The parting was civilised, with an invitation to Adams to lunch. After an interval Adams again wrote for the paper, and continued to do so for many years, but it was always made clear that his pieces were regarded as philippics and not simple reportage.

In the fullness of time Adams was to be borne out in many of his fears about the direction taken by the state of Israel. In the view of many colleagues, however, he allowed his concern for the Palestinians, though it was magnificent, to become an obsession. But he genuinely felt that the outside world did not understand what was happening on the West Bank and Gaza, and even when relations were at their worst and his judgments were disputed, there were very few on the paper who did not admire him.

Later in 1968 Hetherington, as courteously as ever but by now probably wearily, exchanged notes with Taylor about a highly charged though no doubt substantiated piece by David Hirst in Beirut. This, appearing on the centre spread, described the 'powerful impetus to scholarly and dispassionate research into the Palestine problem', of which 'impressive evidence of the new

Middle East wars. Arab armies attacked Israel on the Jewish Day of Atonement (Yom Kippur), 6 October 1973. As before, the superpowers continued to pour arms and aid into the Middle East. This cartoon, which appeared on 17 October 1973, shows Nixon, left and Brezhnev, right. Copyright © Les Gibbard, 1973.

sophisticated approach' had been given at an Arab conference on human rights in Beirut. Of the research bodies represented one was the Institute for Palestine Studies, not affiliated to any government or group, and another a research group formed by the PLO.

The theme of the piece was a report drawn up by Sabri Jiryis, a Christian Palestinian lawyer, about the Kafr Kassim massacre of 1956 in which 'Israeli soldiers systematically killed 49 Arab villagers as they returned home in ignorance of a curfew which had been imposed at short notice'. The perpetrators were tried, sent to gaol, and quickly let out. The brigadier who gave the orders was found guilty of 'a merely technical error' and a Lieutenant Joubrael Dahan, convicted of murdering forty-three Arabs in one hour, was no sooner released from prison than he was appointed 'officer responsible for Arab affairs' in the city of Ramleh. Other sections of the report deal with torture, looting, etc., and the whole is described as 'dispassionate, scientific, well documented, and clearly presented'.

An Alderman Russell of Newcastle wrote in to complain and Hetherington noted, in his covering memo:

It is intemperate, of course, and in line with the persistent Jewish criticism of anything mildly reasonable about the Arabs. I did, however, have some misgivings about David Hirst's piece of December 12 just because he seemed to be accepting almost uncritically the truth of allegations made at the Arab regional conference on human rights. Do you think a mild and gentle word of warning would be wise or not?[7]

The Adams episode has two unhappy sequels – or three. The *Sunday Times* published, in a slightly different version, Adams's account[8] of the destruction of Emmaus/Imwas. The *Guardian* still got in first because Harold Jackson, looking at Israel and the West Bank a year after the war, discovered the story independently, and the paper published it a few days before[9] the *Sunday Times*. According to Adams the *Guardian* editor's office telephoned an apology and an offer (wounding unless very tactfully put) to pay for the original unused piece. Finally the village of Imwas, or Emmaus, having been first bulldozed and then landscaped by subscriptions from Zionists in Canada, was renamed Canada Park. It became a picnic site for Israelis and a haunted place for Arab Palestinians.

CHAPTER 11

'The Clerking Side'

S EVERAL months were spent in reorganising the company after the misadventures of 1965–6. The two papers were given separate managements. Masses of documentation passed between Cross Street, Gray's Inn Road, and Serjeant's Inn off Fleet Street, where the law firm of Lovell, White & King had its not totally impecunious being.

The first effect, however, was seen at the *Guardian* fairly early. During the abortive talks with the *Observer*, the *Guardian*'s team, Hetherington in particular, had been impressed by the contributions of Peter Gibbings, then an *Observer* director. He was invited to join the *Guardian* in order to be managing director as soon as the subordinate company was formed. The company had long ceased to pay much attention to the scholastic origins of recruits but it happens that Gibbings had been to Rugby, where a number of journalists and managers had been nurtured since C.P. Scott's time.* After Wadham College, Oxford, and service with the 9th Queen's Royal Lancers, Gibbings was called to the Bar at the Middle Temple, and worked in the circulation department at Associated Newspapers. It took very little time for Gibbings to make his mark. He wrote to Hetherington giving his first and fairly detailed prescription for turning the paper round before he had formally joined the staff. Eventually it was not only the paper but the company which he transformed. The small and, in the context of the 1970s and 1980s, anomalous little publishing house became a big and profitable one.

Gibbings was a keen professional. It cannot seriously be supposed that he shared the *Guardian*'s politics, but he saw in them the means of exploiting a niche in the market. His vigour and diplomacy were admired by his fellow chief executives (proprietors, some of them) in Fleet Street. He was also good-natured. He was exacting, though probably no more so than a manager needs to be. Was he ruthless? He may have been over-sensitive to a position in which he was senior to Laurence Scott's elder son, Martin, who had begun to equip

---

* W.T. Arnold, Arthur Ransome, P.J. Monkhouse, Evelyn Montague, E.D. Simon, Darsie Gillie, Christopher Driver, as well as three later Scotts – John Russell, Ted and Laurence.

himself for an important role in the family concern. At all events as Peter Gibbings rose through the echelons Martin left to begin a successful new career as tutor in management, enjoying in spacious rural Hertfordshire a working environment unlike the composing rooms and metal foundries where he had first learned his managerial skills. Many years later he became a member of the Scott Trust.

Gibbings in turn made his first critical appointment when he persuaded G.P. (Gerry) Taylor to make the unusual transition from one side of the trade, where he was media director of the advertising agency Ogilvy and Mather, to the other as advertisement director of the *Guardian*. Taylor and his predecessor could scarcely have been more unlike. William McMillan had been advertisement director of the sole company since 1948, having previously been in Germany promoting the *Manchester Guardian Weekly* and in the New York office. Mac was unruffled by the world, dignified, relaxed, patrician; he maintained in John Street, near and parallel to Gray's Inn Road, as imposing an office, partly because his wife was an interior designer, as any in the *Guardian*'s possession. Advertising at the Manchester end was left to his deputy there, Arthur George. Gerry Taylor, by contrast, had what came to be called street cred. He knew his marketing and promotion. He knew how to bring in the ads. In defence of the paper's interests he stalked, as it were, stealthily and sideways through the agencies like the man in the computer game, back to the wall and shooting both ways at every corner. He was one of the few people appointed to management in those years who had taken the *Guardian* as his own paper.

Another of the new operating company directors was Michael Jack (M.G.A. Jack), who had been circulation manager under W.J. Lascelles and now became circulation director, with Brian Connor in Manchester to persuade northern readers not to desert. Michael Jack did not join as an established *Guardian* reader. He made it clear, without entering into the merits of the *Guardian*'s stand at Suez, that he disliked Hetherington's repeated invocation of that triumph in later years. Michael Jack did not disguise his politics, sometimes to Hetherington's annoyance, but Laurence insisted that he was appointing a salesman, not a politician. Jack's view was that although he was a Tory, and would never vote any other way, the *Guardian* provided a splendid opportunity to sell newspapers. He was constantly encouraged by Laurence. Jack was bemused when, in the early days of Thomson, *The Times* had stormed ahead of the *Guardian* and by June 1969 had a half-yearly sale of 437,000 against the *Guardian*'s 292,000. Laurence told him not to worry. *The Times*, he said, was expanding the quality market, and in the long run the *Guardian* would be the beneficiary. So it proved, and Michael Jack went on to see the paper reach more than half a million.

Not everyone on the editorial side followed these proceedings with enthusiasm. A few who had known and admired the modesty of the *Manchester Guardian*'s managerial arrangements would have preferred them to remain unchanged. Staff based in London and Manchester were told at meetings what was happening, but the foreign correspondents had to have things explained by telephone. Nesta Roberts, then in Paris, absorbed the news and explanation in silence and then said, 'Ah, well, I fear it can only mean that you've got the clerking side coming in.'

Laurence viewed the dismantling and reconstruction of his company with as much composure as he could summon. Gerry Taylor insisted that if he was to modernise the *Guardian*'s advertisement department he would run his office in the hospitable way he had done at Ogilvy and Mather. He therefore had McMillan's drinks cabinet replenished on a more adequate scale. The *Guardian* traditionally disfavoured the whiff of alcohol. Reporters and subs would of course go out for their nightly pints. Fay and Hope-Wallace were part of the El Vino establishment. Monkhouse would occasionally slip out at night for a half of Guinness. The Thatched House pub next to the Manchester office had a special licence to cater for the *MEN* compositors during the daytime as well as for the *Guardian*'s at night. A bit further back in time the chief sub-editor, F.S. Attenborough, would hide his sherry bottle when Crozier entered the room. But alcohol was not part of the *Guardian*'s culture. Laurence rarely drank, probably never in the office, and on visits to London his lunch was a sandwich in the train. Hetherington's abstentions were famous. He had been known to refuse cream with fruit salad at lunch because he was duty editing that night and needed to keep a clear head.

Laurence arrived from Manchester to pay his inaugural visit to the new regime just as the delivery men were loading the spirits and cases of mixers into Gerry Taylor's office. The two had scarcely met, and Laurence could but raise an eyebrow. Several years later, when at the end of the day Taylor called in at Gibbings's room for a drink, Hetherington would occasionally put his head round the door. The managing and advertisement directors would instinctively look serious and lower their glasses to the floor. On his retirement in 1973 Laurence wrote to Gibbings:

> I believe that I was quite a good manager of a provincial newspaper, but when the *Guardian* went national I was neither inclined nor equipped to play a part on the Fleet Street stage, nor did I realise at first the managerial changes that had to go with the change of scale . . . I think also that I was conditioned by the years of hard going, in my time and before, and I found it hard to spend money on entertaining, on charities, on general promotion in the way that is required if one is to be effective in London. It was a mistake. Don't let the *Guardian*'s penury get you down . . .

The *Guardian* had now more or less decided in what direction it should try to move, but not before there had been an open season for argument, some of it vituperative. Much of it hinged round what was called 'the Rosselli solution' referred to in Chapter 5. Although he had left in 1964 Rosselli kept in close contact with the paper and in January 1967, as soon as the *Times* venture had been abandoned, he put his ideas to Laurence:

> In each field the pressure of national competition has caused a number of papers to imitate the 'leader' in the hope of sharing the leader's success. Thus the *Observer* has imitated *The Sunday Times*, the *Mail* has gone back to imitating the *Express*, the *Guardian* in the past six or eight years has, for the sake of reaching 300,000-plus circulation, imitated the potential monopolist in its field, the *Telegraph*. Last year *The Times* began to do the same thing for much the same reasons.
>
> The *Guardian* has shown greater integrity than most papers in its situation; it has kept more of its character. That it has imitated can't, I think, be doubted. The search for more and shorter stories, the emphasis on home news, the attempts to catch the eye of the plain man on the Epsom commuter train, all amount to a measure of Telegraphication.

Rosselli argued that the only way a Telegraphication policy could work would be by injecting vast capital resources into beating the leader at his own game. The right policy for the *Guardian* was to get out of the *Telegraph*-dominated field, jump over the head of *The Times*, and become the highest-quality paper in the country.

> One remembers all too well the *News Chronicle* – first a little smaller and duller, then a little smaller and duller yet . . . What is needed, to my mind, is for the paper to achieve very quickly several areas of surpassing excellence. It needs to be the best in, say, coverage of Vietnam, incomes policy, international currency questions, the arts (these are examples merely). It is already good in many things and very good in a few things. It needs to be so extraordinarily good in some things that people will curse themselves for having missed an issue . . .

Le Monde, Rosselli reminded Laurence, had doubled its circulation in the past twelve years. He might have added that it spent nothing on promotion, carried no pictures, and gave only a slight nod in the direction of crime, cave rescues, and other items of hard but implication-free news. Laurence in reply said they could not decide whether to imitate the leader or try something different, 'but I think the one clear fact is that we have got to decide between them and must not try to do a bit of both, which is what is happening at the present time'. He circulated Rosselli's document to managers and trustees and attributed it to 'A reader', but everyone knew who it was. Hetherington took the Rosselli option seriously but in the end rejected it:

> On the vexed question of 'whether to be thorough on a few things or snippety on many' I take a middle course. It's a matter that divides the editorial staff more than most things. We must remember that weekday newspapers are often read under trying conditions. Even the sublime *Guardian* (I speak ironically, not complacently) is often read by straphangers in tubes or tycoons in traffic jams. Also it's read by liverish people who've just got out of bed (me, for

example) and haven't yet concentrated their attention for the day. Therefore it
must contain some variety and some small items, especially on the front and
back pages.

Kenneth Searle joined in this open house (or perhaps that exaggerates: he was,
after all, now managerially responsible for the *Guardian*) with a note to
Hetherington entitled 'Forbidden Territory' which is on file but may not have
been sent. It observes 'that many a potential new reader . . . regards many of
our leading articles as a form of pontificating from Mount Olympus' and asks
whether 'a light touch and witty approach cannot sometimes be used'.
Moreover 'we are still accused of mixing unpredictably news and feature
material to the extent that facts and comment occasionally become a little bit
difficult to separate'. He followed up this probe with a broadside three months
later objecting to editorial criticism of the advertisement department: this
was 'possibly justified but most certainly inexpedient'. The department now
felt like the black sheep of the family; the collapse of business after the latest
economic freeze had lowered morale to crisis point. About the editorial
department he simply noted that 'Surely the most significant fact in this
context is that it is now permissible for this very subject to be included in
what is essentially a commercial report.' The urgent need was for a new cost
control system, an editorial organisation chart, an assistant editor in charge of
admin, and a production editor responsible for editorial control at night.

Searle was a clear-sighted manager, and he got all these things. Previously
they had not been necessary. In the *Guardian*'s new competitive situation they
were. So indeed, whether old hands liked it or not, was a new marketing
department recommended by both PA Management Consultants and Roland
Smith, at that time Joe Hyman Professor of Marketing at UMIST (University
of Manchester Institute of Science and Technology), later, as Sir Roland,
chairman of British Aerospace. It was Roland Smith also who, in a letter to
Searle on 8 April 1969, recommended the idea of an annual award for the
Young Businessman of the Year, an event which took the *Guardian*'s senior
staff into unfamiliar territory at the Mansion House in the City, flanked by the
financial and commercial establishment, in the presence of the Lord Mayor,
and called to attention by a toastmaster.

The most influential in the long run of all the conflicting pieces of advice
thrown at the editor and the management was a letter from Peter Gibbings
written before he had formally joined the staff. It put an end to any Rosselli-
type notions. First, circulation must be increased. They must set realistic
circulation targets and achieve them.

> Some people may believe that by broadening its appeal in the way it has done
> and thus gaining large numbers of new readers *The Times* will soon move into a
> different market. All the *Guardian* has to do, runs the argument, is to maintain
> its present position and with *The Times* selling 500,000 copies in due course the
> *Guardian* will find itself with a special market all on its own. This argument

always assumes that the special market foreseen will be profitable or at least provide a sheltered retreat. In my view, this is wishful thinking at its worst.

They must aim to cross 300,000 in the first half of 1968. (In fact July–December 1968 was only 268,000; the first half year on 300,000 was January–June 1970.)

Gibbings was in a strong position, having been brought in by Hetherington himself, to comment on the editorial content, even 'at the risk of trespass, and with deference to the quality of the paper'. In the retrospect of retirement he remarked, with slight and pardonable exaggeration, that the paper he joined was a 12–14-page political broadsheet, terribly weak on sport and finance. What he said at the time was that the two basic necessities for a quality daily newspaper which aimed to increase its circulation at a reasonable speed were 'accessibility' and good coverage of the news, particularly home news. Accessibility meant an inviting appearance so that people were not put off before they started – as, by implication, they were by the paper as it stood. *Guardian* readers were not being given the news. 'Personally I doubt if the *Guardian* can do a proper job at any size under 16 pp . . . Our Advertisement Department must approach the problem in this way, asking "How do we get enough advertising to justify reasonable sizes" rather than selling as much as they can at a fixed rate and then deciding the size'.

In advertising, apart from special features, the field of appointments could and should be developed. The readership was already strong among scientists, technologists and engineers. This area of advertising had to be developed, and 'I want to try very hard with the City office's help to break into unit trust advertising'. In promotion Gibbings strongly believed in the hard sell, not the image advertising ('Lively minds like the *Guardian*') previously indulged in. 'Slogans by themselves do not sell newspapers.'

The editorial pages had not been stagnant all this time. Some of the important changes had predated the management crisis. Hetherington made two appointments which influenced, perhaps determined, the direction the paper took for years to come. The first was that of John Cole to be news editor, succeeding Nesta Roberts in 1963. Cole was born in 1927 in North Belfast and brought up there. His father died young; consequently he did not go to university but he did take a London external degree, reading for it in the time he could spare from being a reporter and then specialist writer on the *Belfast Telegraph*. He joined the *Guardian* as a reporter in Manchester in 1956. One of the first people to make him welcome was Brian Redhead, with whom he shared an interest in industry and trade unions, but some of the others were by no means as warm, and Redhead explained to him why. The editor's secretary had left around a copy of the letter appointing him at a salary of £16.10s. All the others were getting fifteen guineas and they said to one another, 'Here are we with our firsts from Oxford or Cambridge, or in Bill Webb's case Trinity,

Dublin, and this guy from Ireland is getting fifteen shillings a week more!' Cole was not put out. He retorted that he had spent eleven years as industrial correspondent and political correspondent and was coming for a lot less money than he had been earning in Belfast.

Cole made an instant impression on the paper and was there for only about a year before he became labour correspondent, traditionally since the time of G.D.H. Cole and Wadsworth one of the prime appointments, in succession to Mark Arnold-Forster who was going to join ITN. Cole spent six years in that office, during which he firmly committed the paper to a George Woodcock trade unionism in which the unions are an estate of the realm, taking part in economic decision-making, reforming their own structures, and deriving their authority from full employment rather than from shop-floor militancy. In this regime there is no long-term place for codes enforced by law.*

In 1963 Hetherington made Cole news editor, a post in which he saw as among his main tasks those of giving the *Guardian*'s reporting a cutting edge of its own and of encouraging specialists to dig for stories and ensuring the subs did not ditch them late at night. In many newspaper offices at the time the practice was for the news editor as day man to hand over to the night editor as night man and then go home. Cole stayed until late hours. He also brought the job of news assessment further forward into the day. Hitherto not much had happened in the office before mid-afternoon when the editor arrived (which is not to say he had been idle: he would have worked at home on correspondence and in any case would be in the office – sometimes in the Commons press gallery – until nearly midnight). Under Cole the news operation acquired a professionalism it had not had before. He loved argument, and could make an opponent feel personally to blame for the heat-death of the universe.

The other editorial change which signalled the emergence of a new newspaper, though its significance may not have been recognised at the time, took place three years later. After nearly a century the London Letter was dropped. It had started in 1868 when the *Guardian* rented two London–Manchester private wires from the Post Office, opened a London office, and started parliamentary reports from its own man in the Press Gallery. In recent historical times the London Letter had been in the hands of James Bone, CH, London editor from 1912 to 1946; John Beavan (sometime editor of the *MEN*, later Lord Ardwick), 1946 to 1955; and latterly Gerard Fay. Those who wished to disparage it said that its strength lay in the 'well-turned paragraph'. That it was well written was never in doubt and its subject matter was weighted towards the arts and entertainment.† But without being a paper

---

* For a less truncated exposition of Woodcock's policy as General Secretary of the TUC from 1960 to 1969, in which post and later he strongly influenced the *Guardian*, see Cole's entry about him in the *Dictionary of National Biography*. Woodcock died in 1979.
† For samples of coverage, see the end of this chapter.

within a paper it had been the preserve and prerogative of successive London editors.

London Letter by that name in a London newspaper was now thought to be an anachronism. Since the whole *Guardian* enterprise was coming to be scoffed at by Fleet Street as an anachronism this was a sacrifice Hetherington felt it important, even if painful, to make. Fay's London Letter gave way to Peter Preston's Miscellany at Large. This made Fay's position in the office untenable. Hetherington, anxious to keep smooth the transition, offered him a new foreign posting in Tokyo. The stringer there, Hessell Tiltman, had for years been advising that Japan needed much closer attention. No one disputed this (though there was a feeling that Latin America would have to take priority as a *Guardian* story), but there had not been the money for it. Hetherington found the money but Fay declined the offer. That was a pity which became a tragedy. Fay, though a director of the company, was the first editorial man to opt for 'voluntary redundancy' in the crisis at the end of 1966. The post of London editor, to which he had been so well suited, and in which he had invested so much knowledge particularly of the theatre, had clearly been undercut when the editor himself was in London. Needlessly or not, Fay had then lost the essential quality of self-esteem. He drank unwisely and died in March 1968 at the age of fifty-five.

Miscellany was a *Guardian* name, and a column so called was for many years until 1945 edited by Gordon Phillips, an innocent little collection of reveries which reflected a lovable world. (An even earlier editor had been John Masefield.) It was set in a type-size called 'leaded minion', or 7 point on an 8-point body, contained four or five items of passing interest but little global importance, and would have been the daily reading, one imagines, of the Rev. Eli Jenkins in *Under Milk Wood*. After Phillips's death Miscellany had become one of the things newcomers to the Corridor were called on to handle, along with letters to the editor, obituaries and the occasional leader about Celtic languages or the ports of the Hanseatic League. Then in 1960 it had given way to a brand new column by Michael Frayn in which, for example, the PR consultants for a firm selling meths under the Johnny Friendly label offered financial backing to a campaign in schools to keep it out of children's hands – 'provided the theme is reasonably objective. The sort of slogans we should be prepared to approve would be ones like "Not for Children – Meths is a Real Man's Drink!" or "X for Meths – the Sexciting, Sexsational Thrill for Over-16s Only!" Something in that line, we feel, would best serve the interests of all concerned.'

Frayn was hugely popular with readers between 1960 and 1962, but he did not stay any longer. Now on 27 April 1966 Miscellany at Large was revived on the leader page with a quite different purpose, and readership, in mind from Phillips's or Frayn's.

Peter Preston started the new column, at a day's notice and single-handed. Preston's career had no parallel in journalism. He was born in 1938 near

Barrow upon Stoar in Leicestershire. When he was ten his father, who was deputy manager to a wholesale greengrocer in Loughborough, contracted polio and died within four days. Peter himself then got the same disease (of which there was an epidemic) and spent periods of nine and then six months at an orthopaedic hospital near Mansfield. For some of the time he was in an iron lung; if he got out of it he found his limbs were lifeless. When he recovered it was with severe disablement to his limbs which he tried to conceal and which he would rarely allow anyone in his company to alleviate by offering help. When typing or driving a car he had to place one hand over the other to guide it into position.

After eighteen months he regained enough control of his limbs to return to Loughborough grammar school where, having lost time, he had a difficult three or four years. His headmaster suggested he should leave at fifteen and become a jewel-cutter: a surprisingly specific proposition but one which would lead to a sedentary job making no great mental demands. Instead Preston caught up lost time, went into the sixth form, and made his way to St John's College, Oxford. At school he did some writing for the local paper and for the magazine run by the local Magic Circle; he did some stage conjuring himself, earning the odd £10 at children's parties. At Oxford he gave up conjuring and took up Liberal politics, though he might not put it that way, and after a year became increasingly involved with *Cherwell*. In the distant past it had been sport; now it was writing which he enjoyed and was good at; he joined the training scheme run by the *Liverpool Daily Post*. Future colleagues were on the paper or had been there as staff men or trainees: Stanley Reynolds, feature writer and TV critic, Christopher Driver, Peter Eckersley, a *Guardian* writer who died young, Peter Fiddick, later to become a famous name in the media at large, and Derek Brown, who when he joined the *Guardian* had just had a spell on the *Post* scheme as editor of its offshoot, the *Southport Visiter*.

When the traineeship was over Preston applied to the *Guardian*, which had been the family paper at home (unusually, in the Midlands of the late 1940s and 1950s) and almost immediately got into political reporting. Hetherington sent him to Cyprus to relieve Michael Wall on that then boiling civil war story, and to Pakistan to cover the war with India. He valued these assignments: it was important, he thought, for a journalist to know at first hand what war was like. Then he became education correspondent: a job in which he retained a permanent interest.

Miscellany at Large quickly became essential reading in journalism and politics. It established itself as one of Harold Wilson's minor obsessions, not least because it could not be penetrated by his counter-espionage network. (Richard Crossman told Hetherington in January 1968 that one of his jobs was to act as Intelligence agent for Wilson and keep his ear close to the ground.) This was because although Preston did much of his own digging he also depended, as does every diary editor, on contributions from others. Thus a minister might drop something to Ian Aitken or Patrick Keatley but if they passed it on and it appeared in Miscellany, rewritten in Preston's idiosyncratic style, Wilson had no means of knowing who had been talking to whom. Thus on 6 November 1967 he complained to Hetherington at their meeting:

> He loved the *Guardian* but he couldn't stand the persistent character assassination that was going on through Miscellany. It was totally untrue that he was preparing a sell-out to Smith [in Rhodesia]. There was absolutely no substance to it. Neither Pat Keatley nor anyone else had a shred of evidence . . . Miscellany nevertheless went on and on about his preparations for a sell-out* . . . He said Pat Keatley was in Kaunda's pocket and in Arnold Smith's [Secretary-General of the Commonwealth]. He also talked to Canadians at too low a level . . .

In his note of a meeting a month later (13 December 1967) Hetherington says:

> He reverted briefly to the question of Miscellany. He said he'd got hold of Mark [Arnold-Forster] last week because I was away in Exeter. He had been incensed by another piece of 'character assassination' over the allegation that Roy Jenkins wasn't his first choice for the Chancellor. He said that Roy Jenkins was his first choice. It was Jim Callaghan who had, in effect, offered the Chancellorship to Tony Crosland. Wilson himself had never done so. He added that the denial carried by Miscellany as a result of his intercession with Mark was even worse than the original story. He didn't altogether blame Mark or Miscellany for that. Indeed, he didn't blame either of them. The fault lay with the people from whom the information reached Miscellany in the first place. (By implication, though not quite clearly, Tony Crosland himself.)

On no topic could Wilson consider himself immune. On 15 July 1968, when the appointment of a general secretary to the Labour party was due, he complained again:

> He himself had not taken an active part in it, nor had he intervened to try to get Wedgwood Benn or anyone else. He said that Wedgwood Benn had read the paragraph in Miscellany about Wilson wanting him to be General Secretary and, like some other people, had believed it . . . Wilson had told him it was quite untrue.

---

* Lord Alport, who had been British High Commissioner to the Federation of Rhodesia and Nyasaland in the early sixties, visited Salisbury at Wilson's behest in June and July, 1967. He reported on return that he had found little solid prospect of an agreement satisfactory to both Britain and Rhodesia. A few days after Wilson's complaint to Hetherington, from 8 to 10 November, the British Commonwealth Secretary, George Thompson, held talks with Ian Smith in Salisbury. On return he reported to the Commons that 'the differences between our position and Mr Smith's proved even greater than earlier discussions had indicated'.

Wilson was allowed an occasional break. On 16 September 1968:

> He was thoroughly relaxed and made no cracks or criticisms of the *Guardian* directly or indirectly. He also forebore from the kind of rather thin flattery of the *Guardian* which has often preceded one of his outbursts. On the other hand, during forty minutes of conversation, he told me almost nothing.

Others in the Cabinet, with which the *Guardian* at that time lived to some extent in symbiosis, also turned to Miscellany early in the morning. It was the occasion for a joke of a somewhat laboured kind as retailed by Tony Benn. In his diary for 22 November 1968 he relates:

> I passed a note to Jim Callaghan which he appreciated enormously, saying 'The real issue is whether John Harris (Roy Jenkins's press adviser) can persuade the Germans to revalue, the French to devalue, and the Americans to deflate, and we shall have to wait till tomorrow's Miscellany column in the *Guardian* to find out.' Jim killed himself with laughter when he saw that and passed it round.

Wilson, of course, prided himself that he worked the system as well as anyone. On 4 November 1968 he told Hetherington he was thoroughly sick of all the praise Sir Alec Douglas-Home had been getting for a speech about Czechoslovakia.

> How much would Miscellany pay for a paragraph? I said not more than £1. He said he wouldn't sniff at £1. Would I like to know that on the morning of the Czech invasion [August 20], when he had tried to get in touch with Alec about the recall of Parliament – Heath being out of the country – Alec had been out on his grouse moor shooting with Willie Whitelaw? He had refused to come back to take the PM's call and he and Whitelaw had evidently agreed between them that there was no need to recall Parliament. Harold, however, not waiting for them to get back from the butts, had got in touch with Maudling, who was rather pleased, and had agreed to the recall of Parliament. So it had been recalled. I asked how he knew that Alec and Whitelaw had decided that Parliament didn't need to be recalled. Through Maudling on another occasion, he said, but we mustn't on any account use that.

Wilson, of course, not only enjoyed Miscellany paragraphs about the Tories but caused them to be supplied. On 12 March 1970 he said what a splendid Miscellany paragraph there had been the day before about Heath's sending a private emissary to Rhodesia. Had it, Hetherington asked, come from Wilson?

> Oh no, he said, he never gave anything to people like Miscellany. He went on to say that they'd tried it on *The Sunday Times*, but for some reason or other they hadn't felt able to use it. They'd then fed it – 'horses for courses' – to Pat

Keatley rather than Ian Aitken. Pat had come up with a beautiful paragraph, worded just right.

By that time, though, Preston had ceased to run Miscellany. He had succeeded Christopher Driver as features editor in September 1968 and begun another revolution by starting a news feature page opposite the leader page, the biggest and most beneficial change in presentation and content which the paper had undergone in recent years.

Not simply the Miscellany of Peter Preston's creation but the very notion of a gossip column, and its conduct under successive diary editors, had an important influence on the evolution of the paper as a whole. It was not subject to inherited restraints. Rather it was a free-standing and self-governing entity in the same way as the City editor's column was, but devoted to quite different ends. It was there to inform, certainly, but so was the paper at large. It therefore had to have another purpose, and what was that? To amuse and entertain? That too could happen in the news, feature and leader columns. Many milestones marked the track along which the bier of the old collegiate *Guardian* was carried. This was one of them.

On successive days taken at random in April 1964 the London Letter, which normally had four or five paragraphs of about 200 words each day, covered:

(1) A professorial appointment at Imperial College; an unusual GLC election candidate (Christian Independent); an exhibition at Central Hall, Westminster, devoted to Thomas the Tank-engine; and conservation work in Snowdonia and the Midlands by students at King's College, London;

(2) Neville Cardus's birthday plans (to listen to Mahler); train-spotters at King's Cross and Finsbury Park; the future of the television periodical *Contrast*; and a festival of film music, organised by Colin Mason, at the National Film Theatre;

(3) Sir John Rothenstein's retirement from the Tate Gallery; GLC elections; a demonstration of the then novel stereo radio; rugby played by ten-year-olds at a block of London flats; and an exhibition of dolls' houses at Bethnal Green Museum;

(4) the GLC elections; the advent of the new ILEA; a rebuttal in the *City Press* of criticism in the *Guardian* of the commercial station Radio Caroline; an afternoon conference on Samuel Beckett at the Criterion Theatre; and methods of attracting youngsters to London Zoo;

(5) Mrs Judith Hart's row with the immigration service over the procedures at London Airport; the GLC elections (two pars); rents and other expenses for GPs in central London;

(6) Enoch Powell on *Panorama*; a tidal-flow traffic system for Albert Bridge; a new daily newspaper planned by members of Natsopa; Professor Box and Professor Cox to address the Royal Statistical Society;

(7) Allegedly inept publicity put out by London theatres; Mr Geoffrey Rippon to be a trustee of the International Freedom Academy; a new painting and sculpture gallery at Copthall Court in the City; and Sir Harry Pilkington lays the corner stone of London University's main student building.

CHAPTER 12

Back to the Paddock

NOT long after he became editor Alastair Hetherington began to wonder aloud about what to do with Saturday's paper. He wrote to Laurence Scott in June 1957 pointing out that the *Guardian* was getting thinner on Saturdays — it was then 10 pages — while the quality Sundays were getting thicker. The *Sunday Times*, indeed, had now risen to 26 pages a week!

He suggested that the *Guardian* should carry a Week in Review section like that in the *New York Times*, though on the somewhat diminished scale of a four-page insert. Alongside a digest of the week's events this would carry a foreign commentary. Max Freedman in Washington had lately been writing a special piece for the *MG Weekly*, he said, which was variable in quality but in a good week one of the best things he wrote. Hetherington would like it in the daily but could not find room for it. Similarly there ought to be a place for a diplomatic commentary by Richard Scott and a political one by Francis Boyd. Thirdly he would like a cultural page with Gerard Fay and James Monahan, the ballet critic,* though he, along with others, thought Neville Cardus was 'getting too stodgy to be borne'. Fourthly there would be an 'outdoor, academic and theological' section. He estimated the editorial costs at £200 a week (cover price 3d; postage 3d) including the services of one senior man.

If the idea was approved then Hetherington thought a start should be made as soon as possible before *The Times* or *Telegraph* jumped in. But the idea was not approved. Laurence wrote back saying that the annual cost of four pages every Saturday would be: newsprint, £14,600; distribution £3,000; and editorial, say, £10,400, making £28,000 in all. Any improvement must help circulation, and this project would undoubtedly be a notable improvement, but he was not optimistic enough to expect a large or immediate response in sales. There was no reason to believe a better Saturday paper would avoid the dip caused by readers having their papers delivered to their place of work. (Laurence's comment here carried the assumption that the *Guardian* was still

---

* Director of Programmes, BBC External Services; occasionally wrote as James Kennedy.

and would remain a businessman's newspaper.) The Saturday section might damage the sale of the *Weekly* a little in this country, though not of course abroad, and in advertising it would be hopeless to think that the *Guardian* could buck the national trend away from Saturday. In short, the paper couldn't afford it and in any case there was no need for concern. 'Since I am convinced the project would be financially unsound, at least for several years, I doubt whether another newspaper will leap in to try it.'

Laurence suggested a quite different approach:

> The Saturday issues of all daily papers have gone downhill for years. All the dailies have suffered and I don't think your comparison with the Sundays is valid. Would we not be wiser to write off Saturday just as we have written off August? If we were prepared to spend £25,000 a year, which at present I am not, would it not be better to spend the money on things which would improve the paper daily?

It took another twenty years for Hetherington's ideas to be adopted; then, in the mid- to late-1970s, the *Guardian* began to set out its stall with an identifiable weekend section. Later still, of course, gigantism spread from the Sunday papers to Saturday, but Laurence lived to see only the beginning of the process in which advertisers' expectations of the weekend readership were so radically changed.

What neither he nor Hetherington paid much attention to at the time was the needs of sport, which became so obviously and inseparably part of a Saturday paper. A fair example of a Saturday sports page – there would be only one – would be 4 May 1957, shortly before Hetherington made his unsuccessful démarche. It was still a seven-column page (the change to eight columns came about in April 1963) and accommodated more than 1½ columns of ads, including the weekend concerts and some display classified. In this space the sports editor of the day, Larry Montague, managed to find room for a long prelim on that day's cup final between Manchester United and Aston Villa (Villa won 2–1) with a diagram of all the matches since the third round; another long prelim by David Gray on the final of the Bournemouth lawn tennis championships; Pat Ward-Thomas on the English golf championship at Hoylake; MCC v. Surrey at Lord's; a prelim to the Rugby League championship between Hull and Barrow (which, Tony Goodridge reported on Monday, Hull won by 11 tries and 6 goals to 3 tries and 1 goal); the complete English and Scottish FA league tables for the season then coming to an end; miscellaneous athletics; the weekend's sports programme; and a modest little piece by Montague himself with the shoulder-head Tennis and the headline 'Bentley and Mather go Forward'. The reason why Bentley and Mather were able to go forward was that they were skilled in the chase and the kill under the grille at the Manchester Tennis and Racquet Club. It was the other game that was qualified by the word 'lawn', not the ancient game which was qualified as 'real'.

In all this there was no mention of the Turf. For some eighty years the *Manchester Guardian* had treated horse racing as distasteful when it was not actually improper. Historians of the period have not thrown much light on the reason why the paper's undoubted expertise on the subject in the nineteenth century should have been abandoned. They probably took Scott family susceptibilities into account, though the clear implication is that the free-church lobby used its muscle. Haslam Mills reports that one day in 1873 John Edward Taylor, the proprietor, gave the order that henceforth racing tips were not to appear. No announcement was made: they simply stopped. Perhaps Taylor became aware of the anomaly recorded by Ayerst in which, in the 1860s, the paper was spending much more on its racing service than on covering the American Civil War.

Before Taylor pronounced his anathema the *MG* had had a racing correspondent writing under the name of Rataplan, taken from the winner of the Manchester Cup at Castle Irwell in the mid-1860s. (Rataplan is the name of a drum-roll; the winner in question went on to sire a Derby winner called Kettledrum.) Even though the *Guardian* gave up racing the *MEN* did not and the nom-de-plume Rataplan was transferred from the one to the other and was still being used by the *MEN* racing editor, Ian Clarke, until the mid-1970s.

There were, however, ways and means of getting round Taylor's, and subsequently C.P. Scott's, prohibition. E.J. Phillips retired in 1940 after forty years in various capacities, including the first editorship of the *Weekly* and the custodianship of the chess feature. But he had also written prelims on the big races in which he tipped, though discreetly, his idea of the winner. He was so successful that one of the London papers reprinted his selection as the 'M.G. tip'. But this subterfuge could not last: a deputation of worthies accordingly recommended C.P. Scott to end the practice, which he did.

Phillips's successor in the deft art of reporting racing and offering tips without appearing to do so was Norman Dixon, chief sub-editor and then night editor in Manchester when the terminology began to be upgraded. Dixon wrote to Hetherington on 2 May 1957 saying that since racing was a subject of discussion, it might be worth recording how the subject had been handled for the last thirty-odd years.

Meetings at Manchester and Haydock Park were covered (invariably, though he did not say so, by Dixon himself) but reports were 'kept deliberately light and non-technical'. It was assumed that the Grand National and the Derby interested people who did not normally follow racing, and so an attempt was made 'to assess the chances of the horses – and with the sensational exception of the Grand National of 1955* and of the Derby of 1949† the assessments usually are quite wrong'.

Of the classics 'the Two Thousand Guineas and One Thousand Guineas

* Quare Times, Pat Taaffe; †Nimbus, Charlie Elliott.

have almost always had a par, with a 10-pt head putting the result on record. A longer par if something of "news" interest has happened – e.g. a royal victory.' The Oaks was given a paragraph and the St Leger at Doncaster in September was regarded as a reporter's job – i.e. one where description, mood and sociological observation were more important than the form of the runners or the cash changing hands. Royal Ascot in June was 'treated largely as a social event (which it is) and a fashion show (for which I used to commission a woman reporter)'. At the Royal Hunt Cup and the Gold Cup, as at Goodwood in July, 'nothing [is] given about the actual racing'. Dixon concludes:

> That, I think, exhausts our interest in the Turf, but there is a case to be stated in favour of the National Hunt Festival meeting at Cheltenham in March . . . I make only one comment. The idea that a league soccer match is as 'clean' as the school sports and that a race meeting is just a gamblers' den is complete nonsense. Gambling (in smaller amounts) on football is much more wide-spread. But a pool sounds so much nicer than a bookmaker!

Dixon assumed that the ethical argument was still important, and doubtless it was, but the financial argument weighed more heavily. Laurence put round a note on 8 July 1957 discussing the expected closure of the *News Chronicle*, though in fact that did not come about until October 1960. 'The *News Chronicle*,' he said, 'has always had a good reputation in racing circles and they have a following among ardent race-goers. These people are not for us . . . ' – but that may have been because he did not want to disturb the established readership pattern in the North or spend money on racing which could be used elsewhere. A few years later, in February 1961, Hetherington wrote to the Scott Trust, of which Laurence was the dominant member, asking for an opinion whether the *Guardian* should report racing. 'It was agreed that the trustees had no strong objections in principle, but considered that the general balance of the paper might be upset by the inclusion at present of racing and that any extra space could be used to better advantage in expanding the existing news coverage.'

The turf then faded from view for another six years or so – in fact until Peter Gibbings arrived. There is no mention of racing in the prospectus he sent to Hetherington shortly before he took office, but it cannot have been far from the front of his mind that a newspaper purporting to compete with *The Times*, and to be in the same league as the *Telegraph*, could no longer afford the luxury of its nonconformist detachment. At all events Gibbings, a keen race-goer himself, joined the company on 26 June and by 18 July Hetherington had taken soundings from some of his editorial people about the introduction of a 'racing commentary', and circulated the results.

David Gray, the sports editor, wanted racing to be a full part of the sports service. A daily column might be a great ornament, but people who wanted race cards would still regard the *Guardian* as only a second paper. Peter

Jenkins, who combined an intimate knowledge of Transport House with an equally intimate knowledge of Epsom, Newmarket, and the *Sporting Life*, submitted a balanced assessment in favour of a regular racing column but giving warning against the pitfalls. The best racing columns, he said, were those which combined a knowledgeable interest in the sport with a service for people who bet.

> There are very few racing people who don't bet, and the literate racing man is more interested in betting information – handicapping, form and stable information – than the man who sticks pins in the *Daily Mirror*. One special problem for us, perhaps, is that racing in the north and racing in the south tend a lot of the time to be two different worlds. All the papers which provide racing services keep northern correspondents and editionalise a lot. Good racing writers are hard to come by. They make a lot of money and lead very expensive lives. It would be quite useless to have somebody who couldn't afford to go to the races. The *FT* and some of the Sunday papers employ journalists who work for the bloodstock magazines, which lessens the expense. Richard Baerlein of the *Observer* is in my judgment – along with Dare Wigan (*FT*) – the best of these.

Bill Taylor, then night editor in Manchester and a former sports editor, thought a daily column would be worse than useless. It would satisfy nobody. The paper must have a full racing service or nothing. The night editor in London, John Putz, had priorities of his own, having gone home weary in the small hours for six years because of production delays in the composing room. He told the editor:

> The only possible benefit I can see in this racing commentary proposal is that it might win us a little (but only a little) free publicity. If we once start a daily column the pressure for the whole caboodle will be immense and in a short time well nigh irresistible. If there is a prospect of funds becoming available on this scale, should not priority be given to restoring strength to some of our depleted staff, editorial and production?

John Samuel, who had joined the sports department from the *Observer*, said results were as necessary to racing as Stock Exchange prices to the City pages. They were the essential news element and should be the first priority. To start racing at half cock would be disastrous and would even suggest a lack of realism reflecting on the whole paper. Finally Derek Malcolm, better known later as film critic but until then (and for some time to come) the regular racing writer, said that much as he would like to write and/or organise a column a day of literate racing commentary, such a compromise was simply not on.

> Two better ideas would be to cover the day's main meeting (comments plus card), or raise our present coverage (about six races a year) to all the year's major

races (about 40, again with card and details). Either of these alternatives would prove satisfactory for those who take the *Guardian* and would like to read about, and bet on, horses occasionally.

Ineffectual compromise or not, the paper began a regular racing commentary – by the Richard Baerlein of Peter Jenkins's memo, there being no conflict with his Sunday slot in the *Observer*. Baerlein would discuss the field beforehand and offer tips. Derek Malcolm would then often cover the meeting. Gradually the notion that the *Guardian* disdained the turf was overcome. Baerlein was one of the great names of the sport and undoubtedly brought readers with him. Word got around.

All the same, the service was a compromise which served its time but could not be expected to last. In 1968 David Gray decided to give his whole time to tennis, on the administration as well as the playing of which he had for several years been a powerful influence. (When he left the paper in 1975, bearing the award of Sports Writer of the Year, it was to become secretary of the International Tennis Federation.) John Samuel, who succeeded him as sports editor* (the post he had previously held at the *Observer*), had known Peter Gibbings from of old and the two of them set about a pincer movement, part editorial, part managerial, against the bastions of what were seen as ancient and anomalous prejudice.

The resistance, however, was financial rather than doctrinaire. In August 1969 Hetherington put out a gloomy note to his heads of department (called Men, Metal, and Horses) arguing that the news service was what mattered most and that it was still thin compared with *The Times* and *Telegraph*. The high proportion of advertising to editorial matter meant (a) that stuff was being cut to get into the first edition and (b) that the few page changes that could be made during the night were inadequate to keep up with developing news. Specialists and reporters were becoming demoralised and were giving up hope of writing a well-rounded story, with all the inquiry that entailed, unless it could be guaranteed a place on Peter Preston's news-feature page – second leader, as it was sometimes called, facing page, or what American papers call the op-ed. But worse was to come. The paper was gearing up to take preprint colour (that is, colour pages inserted into the paper while it was being run off the London and Manchester presses). Papers would take longer to print, and deadlines would have to be that much earlier. Another snag visible downstream was that the Manchester end of the operation was due to move into a new building, where press times would have to be fifteen minutes earlier. (There was no obvious reason why that should be so; it was simply the received wisdom, after the cumulative changes that had taken place, that any new system was bound to take longer to operate.) 'And racing, if introduced,'

---

* The succession of sports editors was: Montague, W.R. Taylor (1957), Gray (1961), Samuel (1968), Michael Averis (1986).

Hetherington went on, 'will double the damage . . . On many days the effect will be to reduce the working news space by between 2 and 4 columns. On top of existing difficulties, this could be the last straw.'

Samuel had been prepared for these arguments. It was obvious to him that a racing service without the card was like a cricket report without the scores, but he realised also that cost would determine the outcome and that nobody had any firm idea what that would be. He therefore asked Fred Hedley, the industrious and much-loved production manager who had been seconded from Manchester to London, to add to his many burdens a series of calculations of time and manpower. The racing lobby did not hide from itself that the cost was going to be heavy. A race card is one of the most difficult pieces of setting that can be asked of a newspaper compositor, and the 'literals' (misprints) which had made the *Grauniad* famous in *Private Eye* would cost the paper credibility – and the readers money – if they turned up in the summary of a horse's or jockey's form. The figure arrived at was £50,000 a year (cover price 6d; postage 5d); everyone was aware that for such a sum the depleted foreign service could be expanded and a correspondent appointed to fill the biggest gap, that in Moscow.

The board was not of one mind. Peter Gibbings argued strongly in favour of a racing service, and so did the production director, Harvey Thompson. Hetherington also called an editorial lunch to hear the views of his departmental heads; John Cole, in an undated note, says 'all of us' are convinced a full racing service would help to make a complete paper, but 'sadly and unanimously we think it wrong to introduce it now because the prime emphasis must be on news'.

The racing service began nevertheless in January 1970, gently at first with cards for the few races due to be televised, but picking up and drawing level with the competition when the flat season opened. The venture was greatly aided by two things. One was a successful TV campaign in which two jockeys, jumping side by side at a National Hunt meeting, forgot about their mounts and discussed the *Guardian*'s new racing service instead. The second was the firm understanding that if the paper was going in for racing it would do the job properly. Harry Haymer, another name well known in the sport, lately of the *Daily Herald* which had become the *Sun*, was appointed racing editor in London, bringing with him David Hadert from the same stable. Because of the *Guardian*'s dicephalous operation the subbing and setting had all to be duplicated in Manchester, where Tom Kelly from the *Sporting Chronicle* was joined by Jimmy Holland from the Manchester sports desk. So complete was the reversal since 1873 that by the mid-1980s the *Guardian* was sponsoring a classic trial which produced five Derby winners.

CHAPTER 13

Forever Ireland

The impossible has happened, and the Irish controversy, the oldest and deepest quarrel disturbing the peace and the politics of the country, is to all intents and purposes settled . . . Let us thank Heaven that that chapter of our history is closed and that a new one opens today.

— *Manchester Guardian*, 7 December 1921

Ireland presents difficulties over and above those of other subjects in this narrative. Since Ireland is a running story it would be premature to assess what contribution the *Guardian* has made to its unfolding during recent years. Secondly, the present author wrote most of the leader comment about Ireland for twelve years or so until 1988 and cannot therefore claim detachment.

It is safe to recall, though, in mitigation of C.P. Scott's enthusiastic outburst that Margaret Thatcher, fairly new in the post of Prime Minister, met Charles Haughey, Taoiseach, in Dublin in December 1980. They agreed to examine 'the totality of relationships within these islands', and the *Guardian* was very happy with the pronouncement. It had argued for some years that Dublin was not simply the injured party, that not only the relations between Belfast and Dublin, or Belfast and London, were wrong, but that all three sides of the lopsided triangle created in 1921 needed to be straightened. This would require political and perhaps constitutional sacrifices by the Irish Republic as well as by the other parties to the conflict. The other important event of that winter was that an IRA hunger strike in the Maze prison collapsed, in something approaching ignominy, and it seemed psychologically impossible that it could be wound up again. It was therefore proposed to run an editorial, albeit of low velocity, saying that the IRA was in slack water and that the worst of the troubles might possibly be over.

It happened that Derek Brown, lately a staff man in Belfast who had known his full share of the tumult and shouting and was recalled to join the political staff in London, was in the office; the proposition was put to him before the editorial appeared. Were the Troubles effectively ending? Brown was a tubby and jocose man. He was also a better judge of the situation than the observer from the British mainland. 'Are you serious?' he said. 'Excuse me while I sit down for a moment. Will somebody bring me a glass of water?'

The editorial appeared[1] but the IRA did not do what was required of it. Instead it performed the tremendous feat of reorganising the hunger strikes, of which David Beresford, one of the next *Guardian* correspondents in Northern Ireland, became the chronicler in the paper and in his book *Ten Men Dead* (Grafton, 1986).

The *Guardian* under Scott, both in its strong advocacy of Home Rule and in its detailed reporting (by, among others, its future editor Wadsworth) of the earlier Troubles, had been closely and emotionally involved with Ireland. Scott was a close friend of the Nationalist leader John Dillon, who even so would mercilessly argue with him about any supposed tactical error in the pursuit of their agreed goal of home rule. He had been estranged from another friend and collaborator, the Prime Minister Lloyd George, largely on account of Irish policy.

The early years of Scott's editorship were not marked by any special radicalism.[2] That was the preserve of the rival paper, the *Examiner*. He was temperamentally cautious on most of the topics requiring comment — extension of the franchise, votes for women, disestablishment of the Welsh church — and his conversion to Home Rule for Ireland did not come about until 1886, during Gladstone's second administration, when he was forty and had been editor for fourteen years. But once he had accepted the verdict of his admired contributor, E.A. Freeman, that 'either Ireland must be free or else she must be more thoroughly conquered than ever'[3] he threw himself almost passionately into the cause and promoted various schemes to bring it about in such a way as to satisfy, or pacify, the Unionist opposition. These included Lord Loreburn's plan for Ulster (as the nine-county province, not the six counties to which the name came to be loosely applied) to have Home Rule within Home Rule – i.e. for its members in an all-Ireland parliament to have a constitutional veto over the application to Ulster of laws they did not like. When this idea ran into both Nationalist and Unionist objections, Scott dropped it and supported instead that of excluding Northern Ireland from Home Rule altogether and leaving it to be administered from Westminster.

This scheme was exhaustively studied at a conference at Buckingham Palace in July 1914, but it failed, in the words of Scott's biographer, Hammond,[4]

not because the problem was too difficult, but because the passions that had been excited had deprived the leaders of their independence. Ultimately the Conference broke down over a question that seemed a trifle – how to place a few parishes in Tyrone and Fermanagh, which were one year more green than yellow, and another more yellow than green. But neither Redmond [the Nationalist leader] nor Carson [the Unionist] could afford, or thought he could afford, to surrender a few square miles, or rather neither of them thought he could afford to ask his party to concede that trifle.

Thereafter events took their terrifying and well-known toll in Ireland, culminating in the tragic British response to the Easter Rising and the oppressive use of military and police force. In the 1918 Westminster election the parliamentary Irish Nationalist party won 6 seats and the Unionists 26. Sinn Fein, the new force in Irish politics under Eamon de Valera and Arthur Griffith, which was pledged not to take its seats, won 73 seats. Scott wrote on 30 December 1918:

> The constitutional party in Ireland is dead; more than any man, Mr Lloyd George has helped to kill it. Now he is faced with a dire problem. By the ordinary law Ireland is now ungovernable, and, unless by some supreme act of statesmanship aid be forthcoming, she is like to remain permanently and increasingly ungovernable. But from Mr George, it is to be feared, we can look for no such act. Nothing in his career suggests the remotest hope of it. What then?

But as the evidence of Ireland's ungovernability mounted Lloyd George made a complete volte-face and decided in favour of Home Rule after all – though with a parliament for the North at Stormont as well as for the South in Dublin. Scott then acted as an intermediary in the final small hours of the 'settlement', on 5/6 December 1921, between Austen Chamberlain and Lord Birkenhead on the English side and Arthur Griffith and Michael Collins on the Irish. The *Guardian* of the next few days duly chronicled the distaste of the Belfast *News Letter* and the *Northern Whig* for the document signed at Westminster, as well as the ominous comment of Lord Carson that 'I never thought I should live to see a day of such abject humiliation for Great Britain'. It was nevertheless the occasion for the deep feeling of merciful release expressed in the *MG*'s leader (quoted at the opening of this chapter).

The treaty between Britain and Ireland was signed in December 1921. The divisions reflected in its narrow acceptance by Dail Eireann in January 1922 precipitated the Irish civil war and all that has flowed therefrom.

What with setting up the Balfour Declaration and partitioning Ireland C.P. Scott had been having a busy time. But so bold an assertion as that quoted at the head of this chapter can rarely go unqualified. The same leader, after discussing the options open to the North, ended:

> These are, no doubt, considerations which will weigh heavily with the North in the decision, which shortly she will have to take, whether to make terms with her fellow-countrymen or to treat them, as she hitherto has done, as enemies. For her own sake, as well as for Ireland's, it is to be hoped she will choose the better part. Whether she does or not, the Ireland of the future is secure. It is certain that it will in due course include the whole of Irish territory.

Northern Ireland was edgy in the early months of 1966, the fiftieth anniversary of the Rising. The Rev. Ian Paisley was incensed that a new bridge across the Lagan was to be named after the Queen and not after Lord Carson as originally proposed. In this he sensed a sop to republicans. He and his followers mounted street demonstrations and he was sentenced to three months' imprisonment. Eric Lubbock, a Liberal MP (later Lord Avebury), urged Harold Wilson in the Commons to call off the Queen's visit to open the bridge, but it went ahead amid some tension and with concrete thrown by a seventeen-year-old youth at her car, an attack dismissed by the Royal Ulster Constabulary as non-political. Brian MacArthur reported for the *Guardian* the response of Mr Paisley's demonstrators and gave warning that 'if Mr Paisley has his way there could well – and this is no exaggeration – be a religious war here quite soon'.

Hetherington in his memoirs blames himself and the paper for not keeping a closer eye on Northern Ireland thereafter, but in themselves the events had an almost ceremonial appearance, like the sporadic IRA raids of the 1950s and early 1960s which had seemed to demonstrate the organisation's out-of-touchness and weakness rather than its relevance and strength. Monkhouse in the leader columns was one of the few people to inform himself about Ireland and had from time to time kept readers abreast of developments North and South. (Leaders were often used at that time to catch up on long-running subjects which, because they had no focus in single immediate events, had not made the news columns: it was one of their most valuable functions.) Elections, and the low-key but unprecedented exchange of visits between Terence O'Neill and Sean Lemass, prime ministers of the North and the Republic, were routinely reported. And so matters continued until suddenly, in June 1968, the tensions of half a century snapped at the village of Caledon in a Unionist-controlled area of County Tyrone. A nineteen-year-old unmarried Protestant woman, secretary to a Unionist politician, was allocated a house against the claims of Catholic families with children. With the occupation of the house by a group of Catholics including Austin Currie, a Stormont MP, and his subsequent eviction, the Troubles resumed. From that summer onwards the *Guardian* gave, it is fair to say, the closest attention of any national daily to Northern Ireland, posting there a succession of reporters who at the time and later became distinguished in their trade.

In the early years the Irish reporting was dominated by Harold Jackson, Simon Winchester and Simon Hoggart, and since they set the tone for several years ahead their own attitudes were important. Each had his sympathies and antipathies. Jackson's view was that Ireland, all of it, was a foreign country; as long as there was an English presence there would never be a settlement.* To that extent he was a Troops Out man – or would have been except that the troops had not yet been sent in. He was too professional to let this judgment

---

* Jackson recalled hiring a car at Aldergrove airport, Belfast, and instinctively driving on the right.

colour his reporting, and for much of the early period he was effectively news editing the work of visiting reporters as well as writing his own, insisting always on minute and verifiable detail in names and places. He conspicuously refrained from offering formulas for he was among those journalists – a growing number on the paper including Gott and Ian Wright at a senior level – who believed a newspaper's prime duty began and ended when it had reported the facts. What interpretation was put on them, what policies should be followed, were matters of individual judgment rather than for corporate pronouncement through the leader columns. Simon Winchester had no hestitation in setting down his instincts in the paper (19 November 1971):

> From the journalist's point of view the war which is being fought out so painfully on the streets of Belfast and Londonderry is unique and satisfying. Satisfying, that is, in the purely professional sense, because for the first time that most reporters can recall, both sides taking part in combat are freely available to us to put their point of view . . .
>
> But there is a growing feeling, expressed volubly on the Tory back benches and probably to a greater extent in suburban sitting-rooms across England, that this is a quite unsatisfactory situation. MPs like Julian Critchley will opine that it is wrong for reporters to be able to promulgate the views of men like Rory Brady and John Stevenson.[5] Neutrality, they say, is an invidious position – worse, an immoral position – from which to report a war in which British troops and British police, men of our own flesh and blood, are being slaughtered. We would never have given space in our papers in 1941 to Dr Goebbels, the argument runs, so why should we do a similar thing now.
>
> Our own position on the *Guardian* staff is that this view is as incorrect and unjustifiable today as it was back in 1969, when neutrality, vis-à-vis the Ulster situation, was an easier option to maintain but one which in fact commended itself to few of the journalists working here.
>
> In those days nearly all of us felt strongly that the Unionists were guilty of injustice and that the Catholics against whom these injustices had been perpetrated were a people to be supported. Yet in most cases we attempted to put forward both points of view and allowed the leader writers to state the viewpoint of the paper . . .
>
> In 1969 neutrality was not too difficult a position for reporters working in Ulster to adopt. One was blamed more than enough for the editorial position of one's newspaper, and to this day we are the 'Manchester Bloody Guardian' on the Shankill Road for the views which the leader columns expressed in the months from October 1968 until the terrorist campaign began in April 1970.

He described the menacing phone calls – 'We've got your home address, you bastard' – and other pressures to which he and others were subject, including the suggestion from the Army that he had a duty to betray IRA informants. A reporter in these conditions needs constant back-up. Recalling his return to Belfast after a short leave Winchester wrote:

The television coverage was patchy in the extreme; and the radio coverage, while better, was often ruinously superficial. It was up to us to try to change British attitudes. Harry Whewell, the Northern news editor and architect of the *Guardian*'s Ulster coverage, said as much when I telephoned from a Belfast coin-box once I was back. 'I don't care if the readers think it *is* boring. You report it all, every day, and we'll get through to them in time – it's a duty now. We have to see it through . . .'[6]

The reporters on the spot and the commentators at home were not the only members of staff to take an interest in Northern Ireland. In the report of his inquiry into the disturbances which had followed the episode at Caledon Mr Justice (later Lord) Scarman said:

> The agitation which started over this case caught the imagination of the non-Unionist minority in the Province and greatly increased the standing and influence of the Northern Ireland Civil Rights Association [NICRA]. Events elsewhere in the world, particularly perhaps the student riots in France in the early summer of that year, encouraged the belief that a policy of street demonstrations at critical places and times would achieve results, if only because they would attract the attention of the mass media.[7]

Even disregarding the reference to the role of the media, Lord Scarman's comment was highly pertinent to the situation in the *Guardian* office.

The nature of the paper gave it a high proportion of politically articulate people. They, as well as NICRA, had drunk the summer wine exported that year from Europe – from Prague as well as the Sorbonne. They had witnessed the civil-rights sit-ins in the American South. They had read Alistair Cooke's tumultuous account of the day Mayor Daley's Chicago police went berserk, clubbing peaceniks and hippies at the Democrats' nominating convention in September 1968, and with Joshua Nkomo and the black opposition to UDI in Rhodesia. They had been stirred, or some of them had, by the unrest which spread from one university to another in Britain. Now they (by whom is meant not only the Left-wing phalanx of Hetherington's earlier wistfulness but others including John O'Callaghan, a pugnacious Irish reporter who was also an NUJ activist) found what seemed a cut-and-dried civil-rights issue within arm's reach. By and large the staff would have liked the *Guardian* to adopt reunion as its policy, perhaps even to treat the North as it was treated in Articles 2 and 3 of the Irish Constitution, i.e. a part of the Republic where for the time being Dublin's writ is prevented from running. The paper at no time within the scope of this survey adopted Irish unity *tout court*. Of course it acknowledged that if Ireland were freely united by consent of its people that would constitute a happy issue. But the short cut – no.

The chief exponent of no-short-cut was John Cole, who knew more about the province than anyone on the staff, having been born, educated and launched into his career there. The very fact of this intimate acquaintance could be turned against him, much in the way than an opinion about tribalism in Rhodesia would have been discredited if coming from a white settler. In fact Cole was more aware than anyone of the stultifying influence of Orange tribalism (and its Green counterpart) and had early – long before the resumption of the Troubles – determined to leave Northern Ireland to escape it. While living there he had been a supporter of the Northern Ireland Labour Party (NILP) in which he had been a colleague of David Bleakley (sometime Minister of Community Relations at Stormont and later head of the Irish Council of Churches). The NILP was and remained a sad small group which strove to bring non-sectarian politics to the province. It was ultimately disowned for these pains by the British Labour Party and its members were no longer accepted as fraternal delegates at Brighton or Blackpool.

Cole's first substantial leader on Northern Ireland appeared after the Derry disturbances of October 1968 (Friday 18 October) and was pegged to a forthcoming meeting between the British and Northern Ireland prime ministers. He complimented Terence O'Neill on the interest he had shown in Catholic schools and in allowing celebrations of the Easter Rising anniversary, but he went on:

> Ulster, of course, needs all the development it can get and this should be the goal of any Prime Minister. But Mr O'Neill has not demonstrated that he really intends to shift the present imbalance between Catholic and Protestant in Northern Ireland. For this is the crux. Are Catholics to be given a fairer share in the electoral system, in housing, in the allocation of Government jobs or not? Economic development by itself will not solve a problem of civil rights. Mr O'Neill has so far done little to improve the relative position of the Catholic minority.

Those do not read like the words of a closet Orangeman, nor did Cole's suggestion of a royal commission (for Wilson was in power and that would have been the method) to examine what degree of equal opportunity existed and how it could be widened. 'Five years after Mr O'Neill came to power, it is clear that his programme is too slow. Mr Wilson must ginger up the pace.'

Support for O'Neill remained the criterion by which any prospect of escape from tribalism remained. In a signed article about the election to the Stormont parliament in February 1969, Cole described it as the most complex but also the most important since the state was founded in 1921.

> It will decide whether Ulster is to begin the evolution of normal politics, in place of the sterile Orange–Green counting of heads which has survived for more than half a century.
>
> It is more than a coincidence that the Republic of Ireland appears, simultaneously, to be tiring of the division between Fianna Fail and Fine Gael which has offered electors a choice without a distinction since the Civil War of the

twenties. Irish politics, at last, may be reaching some kind of maturity, spurred on by increasing impatience among younger voters.

But the central issue of the election would be the battle for the soul of the Unionist party between the supporters of O'Neill liberalism and its opponents, first among Unionists in the Nationalist strongholds west of the river Bann and second among those in working-class Belfast. Cole quoted Keir Hardie as saying that when Belfast went red it would go redder than the Clyde, and commented: 'Industrially, the shipyard and engineering workers of the Shankill Road are militant and Left-wing enough, but it seems improbable that the proletarian revolution will begin there.'

The result of the poll was a clear defeat for reform within Unionism, even though the pro-O'Neill element in the party gained more seats than its rivals. O'Neill retained his seat at Bannside, for which he had previously been returned unopposed, on a minority vote in a three-cornered contest: 7,745 against 6,331 for his Protestant Unionist challenger, Ian Paisley. Harold Jackson reported on 25 February that this 'disastrous showing' cast serious doubt on O'Neill's ability to retain the premiership for long. In a depressed editorial Cole wrote that the result was as complete and sad a stalemate as anyone could imagine. O'Neill and his friends had aroused expectations of reform, without creating the grass-roots support to achieve it, yet it was the only hope of maintaining both the Union and civilised living in Ulster.

Catholics, by and large, had not shifted either. Conservative Catholic farmers in Bannside, Cole wrote, had voted for a far-Left candidate from the People's Democracy movement, who happened to be of a Catholic family, rather than support Mr O'Neill against Mr Paisley. The likeliest outcome was that O'Neill

> will struggle on for a few months with an increasingly rebellious Unionist Party behind him; that he will eventually be replaced by a lowest common denominator figure (and in Ulster politics, that is plumbing the depths indeed); that a period of inertia will follow at Stormont, with the Cabinet unable or unwilling to give a lead on reform; and that the initiative will therefore return to the streets.

That is what happened. O'Neill resigned on 28 April to be succeeded first by Major Chichester-Clark and then by Brian Faulkner.

The biggest event of the epoch was the introduction of internment on 9 August 1971. Cole was absent on holiday and Hetherington wrote the leader (which he might have done in any case):

> Internment without trial is hateful, repressive, and undemocratic. In the existing Irish situation, most regrettably, it is also inevitable. Shooting, bombing, and burning now occur every day. The men responsible generally

disappear, unidentified . . . To remove the ringleaders, in the hope that the
atmosphere may calm down, is a step to which there is no obvious alternative.

With that touch of world-weariness from which comment on Ireland has not
always been free, he added: 'If Orangemen could parade without trying to rub
Catholic noses in the mire, life would be easier. If Catholics could acknowledge that a united Ireland is being pushed further and further away by the
methods of terror, then that too would help.'

In the paper of 12 August, B.L. Meek of Croydon wrote applauding 'your
extremely rational leader'. Paul Foot from NW6 wrote in a different sense:

> More than 12 years ago a Conservative Government declared a state of
> emergency in Nyasaland, and rounded up some 30 nationalists in the early
> morning using the pretext that the rebels had been plotting to murder various
> important people in that colony. The men were interned without trial. A
> torrent of indignation poured from the British liberal press.

In Northern Ireland, Foot wrote, most of those arrested were not 'gunmen' or
even suspect 'gunmen'. They included Michael Farrell, a founder of People's
Democracy, a Socialist organisation 'which has always warned the Irish
workers of the dangers of sectarian in-fighting' and 'Official' IRA men who
had also sought to direct the Republican movement towards a political
solution.

> All these men have been arrested, interned and beaten up without trial or
> charge because of their political views . . . What is the response? The
> *Guardian*, keeper of the British liberal conscience, applauds the decision to
> intern on the grounds that 'there is no other alternative'. The violence caused by
> 50 years' oppression can be solved, according to the new liberal doctrine, by
> still further oppression.

The manner in which internment was introduced was quickly turned by the
IRA to its advantage. An escapade with which Simon Winchester, perhaps
unwisely, decided to taunt the readers was his 'pleasant and civilised' lunch
with the IRA leadership, the account of which appeared on 20 December
1971 in the middle of a period of deadly violence. He wrote that in spite of
setbacks the Provisionals were 'approaching the year-end in a mood of
undiluted euphoria'.

> The British Army GOC, Lieutenant-General Sir Harry Tuzo, will present his
> assessment – presumably an optimistic one – of the military situation at a
> special press conference this morning. But on the evidence of meetings I had
> yesterday with three leading officers [not named: one of them was suspected to
> be David O'Connell, Chief of Staff] and a number of volunteers from the Belfast
> provisionals, the British Army still has a confident, capable, and cheerful
> enemy with which to reckon.
> 'The army believe they will have us on the run by March, or at least that they

will reduce the level of violence to manageable proportions,' one of the three officers said yesterday. 'Their forecast is just pathetic. We can and will step up the campaign as and when we like. Recruits are coming in all the time. Only one of our major Belfast dumps has been found since internment began. It is fair to say that our staff organisation has been hit, but it is still intact and is functioning well.

'Above all, the morale of the men is higher than ever before. The British haven't hit us nearly as hard as even we expected. Internment has done us far less damage than we might have thought.'

The men, each of whom echoed these views, were relaxed and cheerful as they talked over a pleasant and civilised lunch yesterday. Two of the officers were in their twenties, the other was middle-aged; all were hoping to spend a peaceful Christmas with their wives and children . . .

The actual manner in which the 1972 campaign will be stepped up was not discussed in detail either over the asparagus soup, the roast chicken, or the apple pie. The suggestion was in the air, though, that bigger and better weapons would be used against British troops in future . . .

A week or two before (Thursday 9 December) Winchester had reported the killing of a UDR man (a Catholic) and the wounding of his ten-year-old daughter as they watched TV at home on the New Barnsley estate.

The terrorists have really moved back into Belfast in force, reducing the city to a state of confusion it has not experienced since the days just following internment. Hundreds of thousands of pounds worth of damage was caused by a series of bombs which were planted in a filling station, a paper bag factory, a hotel, an engineering works, a boat showroom, and the premises of a removal firm.

The day after the account of the lunch more than a dozen targets, including a hotel, shops, a clothing factory and other public buildings, were destroyed or badly damaged. An outraged letter appeared from Capt. John W. Brooke, Stormont MP. On Christmas Eve four people from Clitheroe Royal Grammar School wrote strongly objecting to the *Guardian*'s being taken in by this 'simple and obvious propaganda trick'; a Catholic priest from Solihull announced he was giving up the paper because of its pro-Establishment and anti-nationalist bias.

In the long-running controversy about where the duty of the media lies in covering a topic like Northern Ireland (not that there are many like topics) the *Guardian* took the view that the duty is not automatically to be an arm of the State against terrorism but to inform the readership as fully as may be about the motivations of everyone in the conflict. Winchester's lunch was one of the first occasions for this principle to be put into practice; the somewhat lofty eccentricity lay in the manner of the piece, not the substance. Winchester's

manner was entirely his own. He was equally at home in discussion with
General Tuzo as at the IRA's lunch table.

Bloody Sunday was on 30 January 1972. The leader, at about 2,500 words,
almost outshone the news reports in length. This was an occasion which, of
course, demanded comment, though it has often seemed that an event cannot
be said to have truly taken place unless it has had a leader written about it.
The bulk had been written in advance as Hetherington's definitive Irish
manifesto and it needed only topping and tailing to bring it up to date. It
reflects the operational and administrative mind which he invariably brought
to his topics. He rejected Troops Out or the simple release of internees,
mentioned a couple of ways by which Catholics could be brought into
government, and put the proposition:

> Why should not the Westminster and Stormont Governments make an explicit
> offer, tied to the progress of the talks and the ending of violence? They could say
> that a proportion (perhaps one third) of the internees will be released as a
> gesture of good faith as soon as the talks begin. They could say that a further
> third will be released after three months free of violence. That would leave the
> final batch –the hardest core – to be released only after all-round agreement in
> the talks.

Cole in a signed piece (11 February) said that The Orange Order no longer
represented the main body of Protestant opinion, if it ever had done, and that
the link with Britain and the restoration of peace were all that now mattered
to the main body of Protestant opinion. Protestants would not necessarily
object strongly to direct rule, he said, provided it were not seen as part of a
slide towards an eventual sell-out.

In response to Hetherington's leader, so predictably that it could almost
have been written as pastiche, came an example of that ponderous sarcasm for
which *Guardian* readers had become renowned throughout the newspaper
world. Herbert McCabe of Blackfriars, Oxford, wrote (2 February):

> Sir, – The *Guardian*'s admirable plan for phasing out internment (one third
> freed when the talks open; one third after three months free of violence and one
> third when agreement is reached) will surely commend itself to all right-
> thinking men. A certain extension of the plan is however necessary if we are to
> avoid the grossly unjust charge of using the internees as hostages to put pressure
> on one side at the conference table. It will merely be necessary for the SDLP and
> the IRA to select 600 men from among the paratroopers, Special Branch men,
> prominent Unionists, British leader-writers and a scattering of the namesakes
> of these people who might easily be mistaken for them.
>
> These men could then be confined in a camp in some suitable place (Tory
> Island off Bloody Foreland suggests itself). There would, of course, have to be
> guarantees that they would only be ill-treated; there would have to be no
> question of brutality, and interrogation in depth could be confined to a mere

dozen or so, with the object of identifying the men who actually committed the murders in Derry. After a few months the talks could begin and there could be a phased release of these captives coinciding with the release of the men in Long Kesh and elsewhere. Thinking men, I am sure, will recognise this plan as exactly twice as admirable as the original one. – Yours sincerely.

People on the paper could be forgiven for asking themselves: is it worth the effort?

Power-sharing in Northern Ireland had no stronger advocate than Cole; his original approach to the politics of the province had been based on the need to overcome its tribalism or at least channel it into more productive directions. He and the paper thus greeted with enthusiasm William Whitelaw's power-sharing proposals in March 1973, which led to the creation of an executive in Northern Ireland headed by Brian Faulkner, with Gerry Fitt of the SDLP as his deputy and John Hume, also SDLP, among its members.[8] The response to the Sunningdale Agreement of December 1973, though again welcoming, was more apprehensive, mainly because the Council of Ireland had been tried before, in the 1920s, and become an historical footnote, and because the old grievance about the refusal of the Republic's courts to extradite 'political' offenders (i.e. members of the Provisional IRA) was left unresolved.

[Liam Cosgrave's, the Taoiseach's] refusal of a firm promise to repeal the clause in the Republic's constitution claiming sovereignty over the whole island is a measure of the strength of Nationalist sentiment in the South. Will juries in the South, who must be assumed to share that sentiment, really convict people for IRA offences in the North? . . . By such practical results the Irish dimension will succeed or fail. Sunningdale accepted a sensible ambiguity on the conflicting national aspirations of the two communities in Ulster. The Council of Ireland could be a great force for peace and cooperation. But unless the men of courage who have created that Council can show even more courage and defeat the men of violence, the Council will wither away.

It did not wither away. It was destroyed along with the power-sharing executive by the Ulster workers' strike five months later. Sunningdale had taken place while most British people's attention was on the combined effects of a miners' work-to-rule, a huge increase in oil prices, with the then familiar 'panic at the pumps', and industrial disruption on the railways. Heath, who, in support of Whitelaw, had given Ireland its best hope since the resumption of the Troubles, did not have the chance to show whether he could have sustained it. He was defeated at the general election on 28 February 1974; Wilson talked loudly to the Ulstermen in a broadcast but visibly did not carry a big stick.

From 1968 onwards the *Guardian* was never without a staff correspondent in Belfast, resident first at the Royal Avenue, then at the Belfast Europa, and then, because the Europa was a good communications centre but not much

Northern Ireland Secretary William Whitelaw succeeded in setting up a power-sharing Executive. In December 1973 London, Belfast and Dublin agreed to a Council of Ireland to consider common problems. However, the Northern Ireland Executive was made unworkable and it resigned after a seven-day general strike. This Les Gibbard cartoon appeared on 21 May 1974. Those looking on are Liam Cosgrave and Harold Wilson, the Irish and British prime ministers. Copyright © Les Gibbard, 1974.

like home, at flats rented by the paper for the incumbent. The posting was unique to British journalism in that the men and women on the job were effectively foreign correspondents reporting a home news story. The techniques – mastery of an unfamiliar history, building up of contacts in the political parties and paramilitaries, sending of copy by phone or telex – were those of Johannesburg or Beirut; but the paper was on every contact's breakfast table next day and the impact on the reporter was as personal and direct as though the copy had been written for the evening paper in Manchester or Leeds. (But time passes, and technology catches up. Some twenty years later Viv Richards, the West Indies Test captain, would storm into the press box in Trinidad or Antigua bearing faxes of that morning's London papers.)

In his early days there Simon Hoggart was one of those who found the split-personality aspect of the job difficult to cope with and he relied heavily on the support he got daily by telephone and occasionally on a visit from Whewell in Manchester. In the end Hoggart stuck at the post for five years, two of them in residence, and acquired a balanced understanding of the situation he was reporting which did something to counteract the simplistic notions then current in the *Guardian*'s London office. In a valedictory piece at the end of his stint he observed that 'I'm not sure any more that there is a solution. It could be that, like a misprinted newspaper puzzle, the answer can never be found.' He had discovered, as did most of his colleagues, that 'the people who live in Northern Ireland are without doubt the friendliest I have ever met or lived among. They are open, frank, hospitable, and without, for the most part, any pretension or self-importance.' Yet these qualities did not point towards a settlement:

For a start, the Protestants . . . don't appreciate that Catholics don't hate them. A few of the Provisionals do (an Official who had just been released from Long Kesh told me last week that the most sickening thing he had seen was a small group of Provos cheering when they heard that a Protestant child had been killed by one of their bombs), but overwhelmingly Catholics have nothing against Protestants as such.

But the same does not work in reverse and perhaps this might be pointed out in Dublin. It was about a year and a half ago that politicians and civil servants in the South began to talk about 'our fellow Irishmen' in the North, as if the Protestants felt some kind of national identity. They feel nothing of the kind; instead they feel anything from resentment to hatred, and it will take much more than tinkering with the constitution and the occasional arrest of IRA men to change that.

For example, not one IRA member has been extradited from the South since the troubles began. There are valid and genuine legal reasons for this, but the fact remains that society in the South will not extradite terrorists to the North and, as long as this kind of circumstance exists, Protestants see no reason whatever to join in a united Ireland.[9]

One of Hoggart's distinctions was his ear for the nuances of tribal and military argot in Northern Ireland and he would enliven his copy with specimens. An example was his quote in the piece above from an army colonel at Newry: 'My unit does not need special devices for detecting explosives. We rely on human eyeball mark I, and the natural suspicion of T. Atkins, Esq.'

During the hunger strikes the *Guardian* did not try to influence opinion against the government's handling of the situation. It adopted towards the settlement of that conflict the same utilitarian attitude it had begun to adopt to Northern Ireland as a whole: the best policy is the one which works. The others, though perhaps theoretically preferable, are worthless if they don't.

Although Ireland ceased to be the divisive topic in the office that it had been when the Troubles began, Troops Out would surface frequently on the Agenda page, in letters to the editor, and of course in reports of Labour party conferences. Anne McHardy did an important stint in Belfast from 1977 to 1980 during which she had personal experience of the surveillance of reporters. At a dinner party one evening a Northern Ireland government (as opposed to Northern Ireland Office) press officer jestingly and impertinently referred to a private telephone call she had made from her flat a day or two before. In 1981[10] she wrote a short series about Troops Out. The series also re-examined the still fairly new idea which had taken root under Andy Tyrie's sponsorship, that Northern Ireland should aim for independence rather than a continuance of the Union. The mainstream of Protestants, however, remained solidly Unionist whatever the feelings in Britain might be, prompting McHardy to write:

> The Unionist refusal to even consider a future outside the United Kingdom may perhaps be the strongest argument for Britain to at least indicate that it wants to leave. At present the guarantee can be paraphrased as 'We would not object to going if the majority wanted us to'. Perhaps, after 12 years of stalemate, it is time to say 'We really would like to get out. How can we help you to survive without us?' If Britain did make such a declaration it would then throw the ball into the Irish court. Britain would have said it was ready to abandon some sovereignty to end the problem. Dublin would have to respond.

That was indeed much the course that events took. Editorially the paper had continued to argue that the distortions which led to conflict in the North were not confined to the province but could be seen in several anomalies between the two islands. This view, along with Anne McHardy's formula, had a sympathetic hearing in Dublin and in the SDLP. Thus the paper reflected the ideas which led to the New Ireland Forum and then to the Hillsborough Agreement (November 1985) setting up the Anglo-Irish Conference. The paper supported the agreement. John Cole, then several years at the BBC, did not, but in other respects the *Guardian* had reoccupied much of the disputed ground for which he had fought while on the paper. Its policy towards Ireland gradually acquired a closer understanding of the basic insistence of Unionists that they would not be stampeded or beguiled into partnership with a state whose ideas and ideals they could not share.

The boldest Irish enterprise which the *Guardian* launched was to send a team of reporters, columnists and specialist writers to spend a week in the North early in 1980, writing about every aspect of the province's life as well as its relations with Britain and the Republic. The week's reporting, which occupied more space than the paper had previously given to a single topic in so short a time, was a corrective both to the 'God-what-a-bloody-awful-country' school of observation attributed to Reginald Maudling and to the vestiges of the 'ditch-them-and-see' school which had been so powerful in the office in the early days.

To mark out the field for the political writing of the week the Agenda page on Monday 18 February 1980 carried pieces by Enoch Powell, the apostle of integration with Britain; Andy Tyrie, supreme commander of the paramilitary Ulster Defence Association, whose banner was that of independence for the province; John Hume, leader of the SDLP; Ruairi O Bradaigh, leader of Provisional Sinn Fein, and Ian Paisley. Except for Paisley's these contributions were written for the occasion; his was lifted from a constitutional document he had previously prepared. These were impressive contributions, and if one is singled out here it is because the *Guardian* editorially found itself in those critical years in sympathy with Hume. Referring to the guarantees given to the Unionist population in 1920, and reaffirmed by successive governments, that Northern Ireland's status would not be changed without their consent, he wrote:

> There are grounds for arguing strongly that rather than producing the basis for an agreement, these British guarantees to the Unionists operate as a barrier to a real and lasting settlement which can only come when political representatives of both sects sit down and hammer out an agreement among themselves. That would appear self-evident yet, as long as Great Britain continues her present policy, there is absolutely no incentive for the Unionist political leadership to talk to anyone.
>
> The real security of the Unionist population rests not on an act by the British parliament but on their own strength of numbers and their own distinctive traditions . . .
>
> In short we are not asking that Great Britain pull out and leave us to it but that she should join the ranks of those who would persuade the Unionists that their future lies in a stable and firm political association with the rest of Ireland, and that she should use all her power and influence in that persuasion . . .

The government and parties of the Republic must now spell out what they mean by unity and what sort of Ireland they envisage. It is essential that it be made clear that the Ireland we seek is not the united Ireland of old dominated by one tradition but is in effect an agreed Ireland, the essential unity of whose people would have evolved over the years and whose institutions of government would reflect both its unity, its diversity, and its respect for difference.

It was one of Hume's oft-repeated themes that the only Irish unity which counted was a unity based on the absence of domination by one part of the community over the other. The *Guardian* liked this formulation: where it placed its emphasis differently from Hume was in arguing that the relations between Britain and the Republic had been artificial since the severance of 1921 and that this artificiality was in large part responsible for the failure to reach agreement in the North. But every view had an airing, usually a persuasive one, that week. Not the least persuasive was Richard Gott's that 'Northern Ireland is neither like the Republic nor yet like Britain. It is a separate, foreign country.'

The team which took up lodgment at the Europa Hotel was formidable by any journalistic standards. Hugh Hebert wrote about the tensions of Army life in Belfast and officers' appeals for more power against terrorists. It was headed 'Why the weary major believes in selective assassination'. John Carvel wrote about the huge British subventions to the province ('The dimensions of Northern Ireland's reliance on outside help are staggering') and Jane McLoughlin about that costly relic of Roy Mason's well-intentioned years as Northern Ireland Secretary, the De Lorean sports car company which eventually collapsed. Polly Toynbee wrote about the slums and Michael Billington about the theatre – in which he included the Sunday night service at Paisley's Martyrs' Memorial Free Presbyterian Church. Malcolm Dean wrote about the social policy of a benign bureaucracy and Peter Fiddick on the strengths and weaknesses of Ulster broadcasting: the vital part it plays in informing the province about itself and the world-weary boredom of the British networks. Jill Tweedie spent time with Republicans, sympathising with their view of the colonial police force, and with the crèches run by Sinn Fein ('The acceptable face of terrorism' her piece was called). John Fairhall looked at the schools, David Ward at the farmers, Brenda Polan at the fashions, Anne McHardy at the so-called Diplock courts (i.e. those without juries), Harold Jackson at the twenty million Irish-Americans, and John Palmer at the sectarian truce between Hume and Paisley in the European parliament. Northern Ireland had a galleries column (Waldemar Januszczak), a sports section (John Roberts), an industry page (Jane McLoughlin again), even a cookery column (Tatie farls and crusties: Hilary Rodwell). At the end of the week Bryan McAllister summed it all up with a front-page pocket cartoon in which a soldier contemplated some new Belfast graffiti: Troops In, *Guardian* Out.

The autumn of 1974 saw one of the IRA's fiercest bombing campaigns in Britain. On 5 October 5 people, including 4 young Army lads, were killed and 65 injured in IRA explosions at two pubs in Guildford. On 22 October a bomb exploded at Brooks's Club, across the street from where Edward Heath was dining. On 28 October the wife and son of Denis Howell, Sports Minister, escaped when a booby-trap bomb exploded under his car outside the family's home in Birmingham. A few weeks later James McDaid, an IRA man, blew himself up planting a bomb in Coventry and Sinn Fein said it would 'publicly honour' his memory. Accordingly on 19 November Roy Jenkins, Home Secretary, announced that he would support police measures to prevent the glorification of McDaid, and a ban was imposed on marches by IRA sympathisers through parts of Birmingham and Coventry when the body left for Dublin.

All that was preliminary to the evening of 22 November when 21 people were killed and more than 120 injured by bombs at two Birmingham pubs. Public fury was at its height. Hoggart (by now on the political staff) reported next day that Jenkins was facing vigorous calls for a return to the death penalty and the banning of the IRA in Britain. The same morning papers carried the story of James McDaid's body arriving in Dublin. The *Guardian* carried a leader written in the heat of the moment which was less cautious than it might have been, saying *inter alia*:

A liberal society cannot let its freedom, and its concern for the rights of the individual, be abused in order that it shall be torn to pieces. From now on anybody who complains that he is being harassed by the police bomb squad will find a less sympathetic audience. Our society is suffering murder and mutilation and it must protect itself . . . Birmingham was an obvious target last night, at the end of Sinn Fein's day of glory, but somehow the bombers eluded the individual vigilance (for the police cannot look under every bar counter) which must have been applied in the pubs in the city centre. Only by greater watchfulness, and public forbearance if the police question the wrong man, can this vicious assault on British tolerance be overcome. The police must question. Only the courts can convict. That cannot be said of the people condemned to die in Birmingham last night at the whim of mock-heroic criminals.

On the following day, after five men had been picked up on the Heysham ferry on suspicion of the murders, the paper held to its tough line:

The rights of the individual are being abused in an attempt to destroy the society that gave rise to them, and this cannot be allowed. The police bomb squad must be allowed to be less fastidious in its inquiries among those suspected of guilty knowledge [i.e. of harbouring terrorists in Britain] . . . The country may have to agree to at least a theoretical infringement of its civil liberties. The infringement will never be more than a fraction of that suffered by the scores of dead and mutilated at the hands of the IRA on Thursday . . .

The IRA must be defeated, even at a cost in civil liberties which has hitherto seemed too high.

Charges were brought during the weekend against the Heysham five and another Irishman from Birmingham, collectively to become the Birmingham Six, and on Monday 25 November four letters to the editor appeared, all expressing degrees of outrage and none dissenting from the editorial line. Tuesday 26 November had reports of explosions the previous night at three pillar boxes near main-line London stations and the lead story recalled the 'declaration of war' made on TV the previous week by David O'Connell, IRA Chief of Staff. The report of Jenkins's statement in the House spoke of his 'Draconian' powers to restrict the IRA and placate public opinion. Of the three letters to the editor the first was from five Irish priests working in London expressing their horror, appealing against a backlash, and asking Irish people in Britain to speak out against the terrorists. The first significant word of caution came in a letter from A. Ramsay of Leeds:

> However, in the inevitable debate over the call for its [the death penalty's] reintroduction, we would do well to remember that our concept of justice demands that our judgment should not be made in a state of anger. Our first impulse to meet violence with violence must be restrained and, however difficult it might seem, we must somehow find a way of viewing events such as these dispassionately. There is a very fine dividing line between justice and revenge and the ability to distinguish between the two is a prerequisite of any society which calls itself civilised.

On Wednesday 27 November the letters included one from Patricia Hewitt, acting general secretary of the National Council for Civil Liberties, criticising the *Guardian*'s line and Jenkins's hastily assembled bill which became the Prevention of Terrorism Act:

> Parliamentary debates have so far indicated a depressing willingness among our elected representatives to accept emergency measures without any rational discussion of their likely effects. Consideration of Mr Jenkins's Bill must include informed discussion of why emergency legislation has failed to combat terrorism in Northern Ireland and whether it can reasonably be expected to succeed in the rest of the United Kingdom.

The paper's most original and important break in the story came on 19 December when it ran the first of several reports by Peter Chippindale about allegations, first of all by another prisoner, of beatings of the Birmingham Six while on remand at Winson Green prison. The men were made to run the gauntlet of groups of prison warders. They were pushed or thrown down one flight of metal and one of stone steps, put in a bath and beaten back to their cells and then made to stand for twelve hours.

> The *Guardian*'s informant claims that his statement is based partly on what he

saw, partly on what he heard but could not see, and partly on subsequent conversations with other prisoners.

There is no doubt that the men were injured between their two court appearances. When they next appeared in court, three days later on Thursday the 28th, five of them bore the marks of new injuries. At the previous hearing on the Monday, only one had shown signs of injury.

One had a black left eye on Monday but on Thursday he had acquired a cut on the nose. The others, who had appeared uninjured previously, had variously a black eye and cuts to the face; a cut nose; two black eyes, a grazed forehead, swollen lips and a bruised jaw; and the last a bruise over the eye. It is understood that the sixth was also bruised, although his injuries did not show in court.

Chippindale referred to an earlier report of attacks on the men on which the Home Office had refused to comment. On the day his new story appeared Jenkins announced an independent police inquiry into how the men were injured. The men were tried and found guilty. Seventeen years later they were released on the grounds of wrongful conviction.

CHAPTER 14

Bread Winners

A TRICKY part of the grand transition was to attract new advertising before the old disappeared. In its Manchester days the *Guardian* was a businessman's paper whose political stance was seen as an eccentricity. It could rely almost as of right on revenue from the domestic and commercial property market and the advertising of jobs in the North-west. Its crises in the 1960s arose from doubt whether it could appeal fast enough to a market of its own outside that limited area. How could a Left-wing or at least Left-of-centre paper join the same scramble as *The Times* and the *Daily Telegraph* with their built-in political advantage?

G.P. Taylor, when he joined the paper as advertisement director in 1967, put the question another way. How far should the paper try to join the scramble? He knew about Laurence Scott's old complaint that *Guardian* journalists were unsympathetic to the City, and most of the business people he met disliked the *Guardian*. But he regarded that as the price the paper had to pay for being what it was. Put at its simplest, Taylor's philosophy was that if the *Guardian* attracted a *Times* reader by acting contrary to its nature, that reader was not worth advertising to. Instead of trying to win advertising where it was weakest, the paper should advertise to its strengths, which lay in what came to be called the caring professions. Eleven per cent of *Guardian* readers were teachers.

The interplay between advertising revenue and circulation can be subtle, and Laurence had been tormented by the fear that the *Guardian* might get the equation wrong, as the *News Chronicle* had done. The *Chronicle*'s tragedy was that it folded in 1960 with a circulation of more than 1,100,000 and a readership nearly three times as large. But as the *Guardian* pointed out at the time,[1] 'The *News Chronicle*'s readers may have been exceptionally loyal and exceptionally liberal, but they were not exceptionally well-endowed with the characteristics that the researchers use in measuring "socio-economic status".' The *News Chronicle* was at the quality end of the popular market and had a higher advertising rate than any of its direct competitors; it also had the lowest proportion of any of the nationals of readers under thirty-five; and its proportion of AB readers was only 17 per cent, compared with 50 per cent each for *The Times* and *Telegraph*, 45 per cent for the *Guardian* and 21 per cent for the *Mail*.

The *Guardian*'s rates had not been uncompetitive; nor were they in 1967. For 1,000 AB readers they were higher (at 5.06d per column-inch) than the *Telegraph*'s (3.68d) but lower than *The Times*'s (5.83d). But *The Times*, under its new Thomson management, was juggling with its rates by reducing its format from a seven- to an eight-column page (something the *Guardian* had done in April 1963).

Taylor knew at once that the *Guardian* would stand or fall as a classified, not a display paper. The distinction is not precise and the *Guardian* of course continued to attract display, but except at times of takeover bids or other City excitements its corporate advertising became generally lower in volume than that appearing in its immediate competitors. During the week City advertising became thinner, in proportion to the size of the paper, with the years; it was at weekends, with the family finance pages originally introduced by William Davis, that the City pages looked healthiest. That alone said much about the nature of the readership. In advertising to decision-making tycoons, the *Guardian* had gradually, since moving south, fallen further behind its competitors; in advertising to people with individual cash to spend or invest it kept well abreast of them.

Another guide to the health of a quality paper is the size of its youthful readership. The Institute of Practitioners in Advertising cited the under-35 figures as 'good advertiser bait but . . . in serious publications, at least, they are a pretty good index of editorial vitality'.[2] In 1964 the *Guardian* had fewer than 40 per cent of readers under thirty-five, though it was still a few percentage points ahead of *The Times* and well ahead of the *Telegraph*. The proportion grew to more than 53 per cent in 1981 and thereafter fell a little but it was still 47 per cent in 1988 compared with *The Times*'s 37 per cent and a distinctly low 25 per cent for the *Telegraph*. The proportion of ABC1 readers remained constant for thirty years at between 75 and 79 per cent, except during the year's stoppage at *The Times* in 1978–9 when it rose to 84 per cent.

Newspapers are usually cautious about how they present these statistics. Groups A and B are straightforward. The first refers to the upper-middle class and higher managerial, administrative or professional orders; the second covers intermediate administrative and professional people, the middle class, in other words, of slightly less exalted attainment. Group C1 covers a multitude of possibilities from young and, for the time being, impecunious men and women who will eventually join the AB ranks, to those for whom the voyage of their life will be bound in shallows, if not necessarily miseries. Corporate advertisers prefer ABs to C1s, so that the ratio of the first group to the second is emphasised or not according to whether it tells in the advertisement and marketing departments' favour. Since there are normally between 1½ and 2 times as many C1s in the population as ABs the interpretation of ABC1 statistics needs almost actuarial skills. In all the quality papers the number of AB readers was, in the period under review, consistently higher than the C1s; only in the mid-1970s did the *Guardian*'s share of both dip seriously, and recovery came before long. (Detailed figures for age and social grouping are given at the end of this chapter.)

Within the classified segment the *Guardian* had to be a recruitment newspaper. Taylor would not claim that the idea of advertising to the paper's strengths was a revelation vouchsafed to him alone. His predecessor McMillan had appointed Alec Pendry in Manchester to look after classified, and Dorothy Cumpstey had already set up an embryonic classified department in London. But the embryo was a fairly slow developer until Taylor pumped hormones into it. The ad department felt it was spending big money when it had six or seven sales staff, but then Gerry Taylor would look at *The Times* with a whole personal page every day and compare it with the little double-column on page 2 of the *Guardian*. It is true that the nature of the ads had started to reflect the onward and upward march of society and newspaper. Gaskell's Baths in Manchester were still there, though now with the addition of a sauna, but Veeraswamy's restaurant in Regent Street, London, was also taking space, and on a Tuesday taken at random on 5 March 1968, out of 13 small classified personals of a few lines each, 4 were for pregnancy tests and 1 for a book on homosexuality. The pattern was repeated throughout the week. But page 2 was a live news page and if personal ads were allowed to take up any more space the subs would start to complain that the news was being crowded out. If they were not, the paper would never pay its way. The only way to resolve this dilemma – and it took a long time, until 1975, to do so – was for personal ads to have a page of their own, and that in turn meant offering heavy discounts to advertisers.

The change of direction in the advertisement department in John Street was of a piece with the other changes brought in after the paper's crisis. Some of those were immediate, some slow. Some were not designed to be noticed by the readership and would not have an immediate effect on it; others were deliberately planned to stimulate circulation and revenue. Internally the editorial staff were introduced to departmental budgets, a novelty on a paper which had previously been run, at least in theory, as a unitary state rather than a federation. When Stanley Porter, down from the Manchester finance department, made his first soundings towards budgets he got a chilly reception from the editor who asked, only half in jest, if Porter was trying to tell him how to run the newspaper. But the necessity for tighter control on departmental spending was glaringly obvious and was in any case part of the price which Hetherington, with the almost unanimous consent of his staff, had offered to pay for maintaining the *Guardian*'s independence. His remedy was to appoint John Palmer, who was already familiar with the workings of the editorial departments, as his administrative assistant in charge of the new star chamber. Since Palmer's financial competence was acknowledged by everyone and people found him easy to deal with, the budgetary idea started well.

The most obvious outward and visible signs of the new regime were the redesign of the paper in February 1969 and the start of a full racing service (see Chapter 12) in 1970. The redesign was a management, not an editorial, initiative. The paper had for several years been joining in the still fairly novel routine of advertising its special series on television. Towards the end of 1968 the circulation director, Michael Jack, had lunch with Robert Bellamy, creative director of the advertising agency Garland Compton, to talk about a new series and how to sell it. When the talk broadened out they found themselves saying aloud what had hitherto been muffled: that the content of the paper was good but they would have to do something about its presentation, which was generally regarded outside the editorial departments as forbidding. Peter Gibbings had made the same observation more obliquely shortly before he joined. The result was that Bellamy should go away and, without altering the content and keeping the same number of words to a page, secretly produce a new design. Bellamy's colleague as art director, John Mainwaring, set about devising a new layout. What emerged from the two men was a large masthead in an entirely new typeface of faintly Egyptian appearance, a more methodical grouping of sections – Home News, Overseas News, Sport etc., many of them echoing the masthead in a smaller size of the new title type as in Guardian Women and Arts Guardian – larger headlines, and more pictures on page one.

Shortly before Christmas Bellamy presented his commercials for the spring to Peter Gibbings and Gerry Taylor, as well as Michael Jack, and added afterwards that, by the way, although his brief was not to interfere with the paper, he just wondered whether they might be interested to see how the *Guardian* could look by relocating the material in sections. The management team were impressed but there remained the problem, as more than one said later, of 'selling it to Alastair'. They need not have worried. They showed it first to Brian Jones, production editor, who was enthusiastic, and eventually they took up courage to present it to the editor. Some recall that his enthusiasm was restrained ('Look what they're doing to our paper'), and if so that was probably because he was surprised not to have been consulted earlier on by 'the management'. For all that he was a member of the parent board and joint chairman of the *Guardian* board, Hetherington frequently spoke of 'the management' as though it were a different entity. The management disliked this distinction; journalists liked it because they saw in it an assertion of their primacy (and also, perhaps, because it placed them above the slightly sordid necessity of earning money). In this case Hetherington was surely entitled to his surprise, but he would not let personal considerations of that kind cloud his judgment.

In the upshot a party of three from Garland Compton and the *Guardian* – Bellamy, Taylor and a TV director – set off to New York so that Alistair

Cooke could make a commercial for the new design. Why didn't Cooke come to London, which would have been a lot cheaper? The answer seems to be that everyone was in awe of Cooke and expected him to regard the making of a commercial as beneath his dignity. In fact the only thing beneath his dignity was to be presented with a script for thirty seconds on screen. Cooke of all people did not need to be tutored in speaking to screen. He ignored the script, turned up at the agreed venue, and extemporised his own, thus disappointing the TV crew who had been looking forward to three or four days of rehearsals and found that the job was over in a couple of hours. Cooke's visitors then, like all since, had two other abiding memories of the meeting: the entirely crimson furnishings of the drawing room in his top-floor apartment, too big to be called a penthouse, on Fifth Avenue overlooking Central Park, and the size of his whisky goblets which was matched by the quantity of their contents.

The new paper appeared on 3 February 1969, with a fractionally smaller masthead for the Manchester print to take account of the greater degree of conservatism which was deemed to become evident with increasing distance from London. The effect on circulation was, by the standards of the industry, small but by the *Guardian*'s standards it was decisive. *The Times* under its Thomson management and with its undisguised appeal to a more popular readership, had risen from 290,000 in the six months to December 1966 to 415,000 in December 1968, and the *Guardian* had slumped in that time from 280,000 to 268,000. But sales began to expand with the new design and continued in that direction for several years. The figures are:

6 MONTHS TO	GUARDIAN	TIMES
Jun. 66	282,709	273,148
Dec. 66	280,077	290,485
Jun. 67	288,862	334,142
Dec. 67	280,158	364,193
Jun. 68	280,868	401,314
Dec. 68	268,399	415,286
Jun. 69	292,602	437,250
Dec. 69	290,018	426,164
Jun. 70	303,332	401,756
Dec. 70	304,102	375,055
Jun. 71	327,897	341,242
Dec. 71	335,548	338,653
Jun. 72	341,075	345,016
Dec. 72	337,080	335,559

The figures illustrate among other things that the *Guardian*'s decline had begun before the Thomson takeover, and that *The Times* reached a peak in 1969 before taking a deliberate decision to modify its 'qualipop' policy.

Ever since Manchester the *Guardian* had been heavily dependent for revenue on special reports on countries, industries or other isolated topics. It was not alone in this. *The Times* and the *FT* (though not the *Telegraph*) used them too: indeed it was probably *The Times* which began them in 1900 in a report entitled The British Empire. The *Guardian*'s reports were normally carried as pull-outs in the centre of the paper and pulled out they frequently were. On survey days the waste bins of underground stations would be littered with special reports on distant foreign parts.

The *Guardian*'s often differed in substance from those in competing papers in that they would focus on a consumer topic like tapes and cassettes, or sleep, or shaving material as well as on Whither Nigeria? But Gerry Taylor was anxious to scale them down in favour of run-of-paper advertising. His objections were partly shared by people in the editorial departments, but not wholly so because the special reports did allow a complicated or unfashionable subject or country to be written about in detail and at a length which would otherwise be impracticable. The misgivings were that although there were strict rules within the office to govern editorial freedom and prevent interference from overseas advertisers it was never possible to prove a negative and show readers that editorial policy had not been influenced. In the second place the special reports distorted the strictly news-gathering and commentary functions of the newspaper by covering subjects disproportionately to their worth. And in the third place, some of the countries which were keenest to have their manifold attractions made known to *Guardian* readers were the least prompt in paying for the ads. Gerry Taylor determined to ease the paper out of this market. He never succeeded entirely, and even to reduce the number of them took much longer than he would have liked.

In any case the paper could not afford to be excessively dainty about where its ads came from. It carried several whole-page declarations of unreadably turgid prose by the North Korean dictator Kim Il Sung, complete with picture, until it was forced to concede that the purpose of the ads was that the controlled press in Pyongyang should quote them as the spontaneous opinion of that prestige-laden independent newspaper, the *Manchester Guardian*. In no way suspect, but equally bizarre, were frequent ads for the Rosicrucians (a cobwebbed chest with such wording as 'Secrets given only to a few') and a surprising series of front-page double-column ads for the Donkey Sanctuary. In the free-for-all epoch of the late 1960s and early 1970s there also appeared a sexy series of ads by the American carrier National Airlines until on 14 December 1972 a report appeared across the bottom of page 1 from Jane Rosen in New York headed 'Hostesses fly into a tizzy':

A group of airline stewardesses, tired of being portrayed as what they called 'sex objects', held a press conference here yesterday and announced the formation of a Stewardess Anti-Defamation Defence League.

The league intends to fight what it claims are a whole series of discriminatory attitudes towards air hostesses. They made it plain they were incensed about advertising campaigns such as 'I'm Linda, fly me!' and 'She'll serve you – all the way'.

'We all know what "fly me" really means,' said Mrs Joanna Chaplin, who has been organising the league while on maternity leave from an airline which she declined to name for fear of losing her job. 'What we want to get across is that stewardesses are dedicated, hard-working girls who resent being labelled as anything else.'

Mrs Toby Gelband, aged 26, was a leader of another new group represented at the press conference, Stewardesses for Women's Rights. She said she was protesting against 'annoying and degrading treatment' by the airlines as well as by advertisers and the public.

'We can be "written up" for employers for telling some drunk to take his hands off and shut up,' said Mrs Gelband, who has flown for six years. 'The airlines back the customer every time. He's paying.'

For all the doubts about special reports they provided a bit of fun in 1977. Philip Davies, the special reports manager, was casting around for a new subject when he fastened on the idea of an imaginary country. Within minutes everything had clicked into place, at least in his mind. He put the idea to Peter Preston that on 1 April, not in the centre spread but in a lowly position at the back of the paper, there would be several pages of special report on a country called San Serriffe. The beauty of the joke was that it would pay for itself because the ad agencies would certainly join in. Geoffrey Taylor was put in charge of the editorial side of the project. Articles were commissioned, photographs distorted, charts drawn, a history of the territory invented, and a realistic survey of seven pages produced, covering everything the *Guardian* would normally write about on such occasions. San Serriffe (the name of the country was based on the typeface and its other place and personal names used types and other printing terms) was originally to be a pair of islands shaped like a semicolon off the north-west coast of Africa, possibly suggesting Tenerife, and maps were drawn locating it there. Two days before publication, however, a serious air crash happened on Tenerife and the San Serriffe islands had to be rapidly relocated in the Indian Ocean and their history rewritten. After that episode the notion of a spoof on 1 April was taken up by large parts of the press. Papers were scoured for the hidden jollity. Not the least virtue of San Serriffe was that it came as a surprise.

Whether or not, and if so to what extent, advertisers try to influence editorial content is one of the first questions people outside the business tend to ask. Even inside the business it is often assumed that stiff resistance to persuasion has to be offered. In March 1973 Adam Raphael completed a long and detailed inquiry into the payment of starvation wages to black employees by British companies in South Africa. His findings were published as the lead story on 12 March 1973 and were indeed sensational. They were followed up day by day and week by week, naming the companies involved, with at least some of which the paper found itself spending large sums in legal fees. For a long time thereafter Raphael would remark at public gatherings that the paper had let him go on writing even though it was losing thousands of pounds in advertising. Yet although it would be impossible to show that advertisers left the *Guardian* out of their schedules the advertisement department had no evidence that that was happening. Similarly Laurence Scott in evidence to a professional body[3] was asked whether he experienced political discrimination after Suez. He replied that Suez produced very little effect and that the *Guardian* lost 'a very insignificant amount' of advertising. After the June War of 1967 Marks and Spencer withdrew advertising support for a special report on the fiftieth anniversary of the Balfour Declaration. It could be argued, though, that such a report would hardly have been appropriate in any case at such a time.

Not surprisingly the Middle East was a constant source of acrimony between the paper and would-be advertisers. For example, in March 1971 E.S. (Solly) Sachs wanted to publish an advertisement called An Open letter to the Jews of Israel and the Western World. Hetherington refused to accept it, saying to Sachs:

> Our policy on advertisements of a political character is that they ought not to be censored if that can be avoided. At the same time we have always said that we shall not knowingly carry incorrect or misleading information. When your document said that the Govt of Israel had 'on every possible occasion' sought to heap humiliation on the Arabs and when it said that that Government constituted a 'dire threat to world peace' we thought you had gone over the line.[4]

A similar ad did appear in *The Times*. It compared the governments of Israel and South Africa and said 'the policies of both governments constitute a dire threat to world peace'. One of three sentences to which Hetherington objected said of the Israeli government: 'It has also behaved like the arrogant conqueror heaping humiliation upon the proud Arab people on every possible occasion, filling the prisons with courageous, desperate Arab men and women . . .' In *The Times* version the words 'on every possible occasion' were omitted. Sachs said he would report the matter to the Press Council, but if he did it did not become a cause célèbre.

On 11 January 1974 Vic Bowden, a circulation man in Manchester, sent in a copy of the *Jewish Gazette* of that date, describing itself as the oldest established Jewish newspaper in the North, with the lead headline 'Boycott *Guardian* call by Degroot', who apparently was chairman of the Zionist Central Council Political Committee, claiming that the *Guardian* had deteriorated since the days of C.P. Scott and urging Jews to change to the *Daily Telegraph*. Then on 10 December 1974 the Committee for Justice in the Middle East, PO Box 295, London N13, submitted an ad. John Ryan, executive editor in charge of legal matters and liaison between departments, wrote to Hetherington saying he had rejected the copy and saying the amended copy was, surprisingly, appearing in *The Times* the next day. 'That doesn't worry me greatly. I think they are wrong to carry it.' Hetherington replied: 'The Arab ad: quite right to keep it out, though in itself it contains no evident inaccuracies. We ought to keep a log of these that we are refusing.'

What applied to the Middle East applied equally to South Africa, where pressure from readers to refuse advertisements by the South African Embassy continued from year to year and was invariably resisted by Hetherington and Peter Preston for the reasons set out by Hetherington to Sachs.

An important advance in the paper's advertisement policy, perhaps in the long run the most important, began with a note from a member of the department, James Abbiss, to Gerry Taylor on 27 September 1971. Abbiss proposed that the education advertising then spread out during the week should be bulked into Tuesday's paper and that for every page of ads there should be 1½ columns of editorial. He estimated that 75 per cent of education advertising would be attracted to Tuesday and that the project would generate 15 per cent new volume.

In putting the idea to Hetherington and Gibbings, Taylor said he had been sceptical but was now convinced. It would bring in some extra revenue; it would safeguard the *Guardian*'s special relationship with teachers against attacks from elsewhere, especially *The Times*; and he agreed with Michael Jack (circulation) that this was 'yet another very good way of increasing our sale'.

Education Guardian came into being on 1 February 1972, with Maureen O'Connor as its first editor. By 1976 education accounted for 30 per cent of the *Guardian*'s job advertising and the paper took nearly 43 per cent of the quality newspaper advertising in that market. Other papers had their niches – the *Daily Telegraph* as always in sales and marketing, *The Times* in legal and clerical, the *FT* in management and finance – and in total the *Telegraph* remained ahead with 52 per cent of the market. But operating in a more restricted market the *Guardian* kept its hold on the teaching and health and welfare groups with the Society Tomorrow pages started under Malcolm Dean in 1978.

At the same time it was on the lookout for new professional disciplines to embrace. It developed its science and technology pages, under first Anthony Tucker and then Tim Radford, with the title Futures. It started a weekly computer section under Jack Schofield. It had long had a special relationship with its own trade of journalism, including broadcasting, and this encouraged it to start the media page under Peter Fiddick and later Georgina Henry. Having resumed its law reports, dropped during an earlier financial crisis, the paper even began to receive ads in the law. In most of these topics – all indeed except the law – advertising demand preceded editorial supply, in the sense that editorial was not originally concentrated on one day of the week.

These later and highly successful developments were carried out under one of the most successful of Fleet Street advertisement directors, Caroline Marland, who joined from *The Times*, and earlier the *Yorkshire Post*, in 1976 as telephone sales manager. She immediately protested to Gerry Taylor that he was selling advertising at a shilling a mile. To promote his whole page of personal classified he had offered cut rates for publishing, for example, a stock display classified notice for Independent Radio News programmes which padded out the ads and made the page look good. The paper then had eleven people selling classified and had 8 per cent of the recruitment market compared with the *Telegraph*'s 50 per cent. A little over a decade later it had eighty people selling classified, and 30 per cent of the market compared with the *Telegraph*'s 20 per cent. Extra office space was taken in London with forty-two people working in it; another thirty-seven worked from Manchester under Suzanne Francis. The ad department had to adopt what under previous regimes would have seemed an uncharacteristically aggressive campaign manner. Each of the tele-ads sales staff made 65 calls a day and between 28 and 32 of these would result in a 'sales conversation'. Staff came under strong inducement to cross to the *Independent* when that paper came to realise on its launch in 1986 that it had a weakness in classified advertising. Not all resisted; some who did wore badges saying 'I've refused a job on the Independent'. Some qualified twice.

Any slight annoyance Hetherington may have felt about the 'management's' intrusion into an editorial prerogative like the design of the paper (and it would be wrong to make much of it: his colleagues on the board were probably more fearsome than they needed to be) was more than equalled by sensitivity on the management side. Two illustrations of this came fairly close together. In January 1970 Laurence, no longer wielding the power he had done in the Scott Trust, took soundings on whether Hetherington should be made a member – an exceptionally long time, fourteen years, after he became editor. The trustees agreed that Laurence 'should endeavour in conversation with Mr Peter Gibbings to resolve the problems which might be caused on the commercial side of the *Guardian* by the appointment of Mr Hetherington'.

That the Trust was clearly not exaggerating the problem is shown by an exchange between its chairman, Richard Scott, and Peter Gibbings in the summer of 1970. Richard wrote from Washington on 18 June arguing that 'the trustees must have a special concern for the character and journalistic traditions of the paper – for the area over which the Editor is primarily responsible. That is a major reason why, in my view, Alastair rather than yourself should be on the Trust.' Gibbings replied on 8 July 1970. His doubts about the editor's becoming a Trustee had 'nothing to do with Alastair personally or my relationship with him which in general I think is very good'. But he believed it was wrong for any top editorial or commercial executive, himself included, to be a trustee, partly because of the working pressures on them but also because in areas of potential conflict the trustees were a court of appeal, before which any future dispute between the editorial and management departments would have to be settled. But the most important reason for opposing Hetherington's membership was as follows:

> There is a feeling – and I can assure you it is quite a strong feeling – that historically the *Guardian* has tended to treat the commercial side as second class citizens and there is a body of opinion which would be happy to see that continued. It may be that in the past the justification for this was that the commercial side was made up of second class people. It is certainly no longer so. I am reasonably confident that today the *Guardian* has a good management team which compares favourably with almost any in Fleet Street – and is half the size! The people concerned are intelligent people who believe in the *Guardian* as much as anyone. They also wish like everyone else today to participate fully in helping to shape its future and in my view they are right. A full equal partnership – and nothing less – is essential for the *Guardian*'s survival . . . This partnership also finds expression in the fact that Alastair and I are co-chairmen of Guardian Newspapers Limited. However if the Editor is in addition to be made a Trustee then that partnership will clearly be seen to be unequal. This can only be bad . . .

Other members of the management team may also have had worries. The paper had undoubtedly been turned round since the mid-1960s, and early in 1971 Hetherington was named Journalist of the Year in the National Press Awards, an honour which, he made clear, he shared with the rest of the staff. On 5 May, the day when a large part of the political and press establishment was to celebrate the *Guardian*'s 150th anniversary at a banquet at the Dorchester, Gibbings wrote to one of his management colleagues:

> It is only natural that at a time like this the glare of publicity should be on the Editorial. I know that for those who have worked very hard in the shadows it is sometimes a little irritating to be overlooked. However I think you will agree all the management has been done very handsomely in the Supplement today and I understand that Alastair will be referring to us in his speech tonight.
>
>   I do not know what future *Guardian* historians will say about the last few years. However of one thing I am fairly certain. They will never really be able to

find out how so much of what we have done and changed has been achieved. Such things are never documented which is probably just as well.

An historian must concur.

PERCENTAGE OF READERS UNDER 35						
	1964	1969	1974	1981	1984	1988
Guardian	39	43	50	52	47	45
Times	36	48	43	45	41	37
Telegraph	29	34	34	32	26	25
Independent	–	–	–	–	–	48

NATIONAL QUALITY DAILY CIRCULATIONS (000S)								
	1937	1947	1962	1966	1973	1979	1986	1990
Telegraph	560	1,020	1,261	1,352	1,419	1,493	1,160	1,110
Times	191	268	254	290	345	–	470	432
Guardian	48	126	263	280	346	388	520	430
FT	37	71	137	148	194	204	250	281
Independent	–	–	–	–	–	–	–	408
Total	836	1,485	1,915	2,070	2,304	2,085	2,400	2,661

SOCIO-ECONOMIC GROUPS (000S OF READERS)									
	1964		1971		1975		1981		1984	
	AB	C1	AB	C1	AB	C1	AB	C1	AB	C1
Guardian	474	283	488	350	402	397	661	400	735	440
Times	433	216	524	294	554	324	476	236	669	284
FT	345	133	336	213	346	236	356	182	375	193
Telegraph	1,427	1,066	1,628	1,130	1,610	1,217	1,643	1,072	1,595	781

	SOCIO-ECONOMIC GROUPS (% OF READERS)									
	1964		1971		1975		1981		1984	
	AB	CI	AB	CI	AB	CI	AB	CI	AB	CI
Guardian	49	29	44	32	39	22	50	31	48	29
Times	47	24	49	28	51	30	55	27	59	25
FT	62	24	50	31	46	31	56	28	56	29
Telegraph	42	32	45	32	44	34	49	32	53	26

CHAPTER 15

Post-Imperial

READERS are not generally concerned with how their newspaper is produced as long as it is legible, relatively free of irritating mistakes, printed with ink that does not blacken the hands, and delivered on time. For some years the *Guardian* failed to meet all those requirements, and on many days it met none. It was not alone, yet it was still the *Grauniad*, even when there were almost as many literals in the *Telegraph* and *Times*. The fact that it was grappling with inadequate printing plant at both ends of the operation doubled the anxiety.

The London print especially had become grubby. Picture reproduction was a disgrace to the skills of the lithographer and stereotyper and brought anguish to the photographers. This was all the sadder because at one time the *Guardian* had been able to pride itself on the physical quality of its product. When printed only at Cross Street its small circulation allowed it the luxury of heavy newsprint, and the sparing use of photographs meant that extra care could be taken with those that did appear. If a zinc block was not good enough it would be thrown away and new ones would be made until the head of the department (the 'process' as it was called) was satisfied. Such niceties were lost in the years of the paper's expansion. It was not until 1987–8 when first with satellite printing plants and then its own new equipment in docklands, that the *Guardian* could again claim technical mastery.

The disappointment of the interim years was illustrated by a piece of industrial archaeology. Among the small management staff was a major-domo figure in the person of George Tucker who, wearing a bowler hat and accompanied three deferential paces behind by a workman in overalls, was a familiar sight in the streets of Central Manchester as he went on small purchasing missions to ensure that the office was kept shipshape. It was Tucker who from 1930 to 1967 caused every month's issues of the *Guardian* to be bound in cardboard, with tapes to secure them, and sent to the works plumber who sealed them in zinc boxes. The several hundred boxes were sent to the John Rylands Library at Manchester University under an arrangement made by the company secretary, Allen Clarke, for the preservation of the company's records. These, not even being available for consultation, became an embarrassment to the university and the company was asked to take them away. They were therefore placed in care with the manager of the *Manchester Evening News* garage at Broughton Lane, Salford, where they added to the jumble of generations in his loft. When a box was opened in 1988 to see how its contents had withstood the years the *Manchester Guardians* of August 1935 were found to be in mint condition, and much superior in appearance to anything the company had produced for many years. Some people read them with a bit of a twang because in quality of reproduction they resembled the *Independent*, which had recently made serious inroads into the *Guardian*'s circulation.

It is therefore pleasant to suppose that quality control was behind the argument when, first in Manchester in 1970 and then six years later in London, the *Guardian* moved into new offices and took on new printing arrangements – though only partly new in London, which was a misfortune. Although the motives were in fact economic they were obviously concerned first of all with the quality of the finished product on which the economics depended.

The paper had occupied a substantial building in the centre of Manchester since 1841, and the *Manchester Evening News* had joined it there in 1879. As recently as the 1940s the *Guardian*'s engineer, Charles Markwick, and its consultant architect, P.G. Fairhurst, had performed a notable technical achievement in shifting the weight of the Cross Street building from one set of pillars to another to accommodate more presses. They could do that with some assurance of safety because Fairhurst's father, who built an extension to the *Guardian* building in 1929, had gone down forty-five feet below street level and had there encountered red rock. Without the earlier knowledge of this rock stratum the Fairhurst of 1945 could not have tackled the job and the company's housing problems would have arisen sooner than they did.

Thus a good deal of history, of more than one kind, had been built into the old place, and the romantics could and did make much of it. Indeed by the time the paper actually left, the deep and sorrowful reminiscences about the leader-writers' Corridor and the reporters' Room had become a little cloying for some tastes, agreeable though it was to recall the reporters' fireplace where W.A. Shovelton would have roasted his chestnuts, or the windowsill on which C.P. Scott would have placed his hard-boiled egg against the preparation of a 'long' on Marshal Pilsudski. The building was in the centre of the city. During the daytime, when the evening paper needed rapid access to its publishing room, the delivery vans could scarcely make their way through the growing traffic. The *MEN* badly needed new premises, and the *MEN* was not simply the life-support system for the *Guardian* but a regional newspaper to which readers throughout the Greater Manchester area were devoted.

Other pressures were being applied. The Crabtree presses were getting old. Several of the units were well beyond their safe working life and the manufacturers were reluctant to forecast how long they could keep such high-mileage museum pieces going. Secondly there was an almost immediate need for colour in both papers – in the *Guardian*'s case because of threatened colour competition from *The Times*. The existing presses were not of standard size (in technical terms they had a page-length cut-off of 25¼ inches compared to the shorter industry standard, and the reels mounted on them were 68 inches wide compared with the 62 inches which came to be in common use). They could not therefore – or at least could only with tedious and costly technical difficulty – be adapted to accept pre-printed colour reels from the company's plant at Leigh in Lancashire for insertion into the paper during the run. To clinch matters the City Council threatened a compulsory purchase order to turn the site occupied by MGEN into part of an Arndale shopping centre and was deterred only when the company's counsel put forward the case that the paper could not move without somewhere else to go but would voluntarily find a new site and sell at a negotiated price. Thus although the buildings where the *Manchester Guardian* had had its solid being did indeed give way to nondescript commercial development they funded the move of both the papers to more modest but more efficient premises.

The crisis of 1966-7 had caused work on the new building to be suspended, but it was revived under A.M. Harvie, head of the company's development division and later managing director of the *MEN*. Sites were explored on an old railway goods yard and other bits of waste ground in Manchester and Salford, but when it came to the point the company had to decide whether, in the light of continued losses on the *Guardian*, it could afford the luxury of a brand-new building and presses. That could have been seen as a wanton extravagance when the prime consideration was the editorial quality of the finished product. The *Guardian* had over-economised. It needed to reinvest in developing the paper. Unquestionably, therefore, the best option was to share housing and printing plant with Associated Newspapers, publishers of the *Daily Mail*, and extend and adapt Associated's premises half a mile away in Deansgate – another main thoroughfare but one with easier access for the vans. Northprint Ltd, the company set up to manage the building and print the papers, was jointly owned by MGEN and Associated.

Kenneth Searle, the company's chief executive, pointed out another good reason for going in with Associated. The papers needed newer presses but not necessarily new ones. Of the two types the traditional letterpress machine, which prints direct from the plates on to the paper, had been used for high-speed printing of evening and mass-circulation morning newspapers. (Each of the Manchester presses – sometimes two, sometimes three – would be run at about 40,000 copies an hour.) The other type, known as web-offset, transfers the impression from the printing plate to a roller and thence to the paper. This normally results in a better quality print, especially of pictures and even more especially of colour, but national newspaper experience in handling it at that time was limited and it was known to be both extravagant in the number of replates needed during a print run and wasteful in 'spoils' – i.e. unusable copies which come at the beginning of the run. Searle pointed out, however, on the basis of technical assessments, that rapid developments were being made in offset machines and it would be foolish to invest in new letterpress machines with a 20–25-year depreciation period when in half that time the method might be superseded. What was needed was access to older but reasonably low-mileage presses which could be replaced by new machines in due course.[1] The time scale differed somewhat from what he envisaged but in the event the result was similar. The *Guardian* and *MEN* stuck with their Northprint presses at Deansgate until 1990, when they left central Manchester altogether and fled to the *Daily Telegraph*'s printing centre near the motorway network outside town.

In transferring from one office to another the *Guardian* took with it all the dreaded paraphernalia of its teletypesetting (TTS) printing system. Nearly half the paper still originated in the Manchester office. The foreign department was located there under Ian Wright and Campbell Page. Much of the industrial and other regional coverage was organised from Harry Whewell's Manchester news room. The Manchester features department under John Course made up all but a few of the features pages and originated a good deal of the material. It was responsible for the edge which the *Guardian* kept over its competitors in arts coverage in the regions. The senior editorial production staff, first under W.R. Taylor, then his successor Joseph Minogue, and the chief sub, Eric Knott, kept better press times than London was able to keep. By using late-night slip pages (i.e. papers with fewer changes than would justify their being called separate editions) the night production team and the Manchester news room still maintained something of the *Guardian*'s Northwest coverage and the vestige of its association with Manchester. Perhaps most importantly for the wellbeing of the Manchester office, the coverage of Northern Ireland was (see Chapter 13) organised from there by Whewell and his deputy George Hawthorne.

When MGEN joined the *Mail* in forming Northprint, so that all three titles could be printed economically from the same press room, a new wing was built alongside Northcliffe House and structural changes made to house extra machinery. A contract to print *The People* on Saturday nights further spread the overheads. The resulting building was unelaborate but comfortable and functional, and spaciously sited near the new law courts and next door to the old John Rylands Library, the original red sandstone building which had come to share its name with the university library some miles away in Rusholme, and where Wadsworth had spent many hours as scholar and governor.

The old building was a neighbour of the Cross Street Unitarian chapel, with which the *Guardian* of the rapidly receding past had been closely allied in outlook. There is even a tradition among Manchester Unitarians that the *Manchester Guardian* was founded in an upper room of the chapel; Richard Cobden, the anti-Corn Law campaigner, held meetings there which were in

Emissaries abroad. TOP: Campbell Page, sometime foreign editor and captain of the cricket XI, introduces J. C. Markwick, later managing director, to the Vice-President of India, Dr G. S. Pathak, during the team's tour in 1974. The tour was under the joint patronage of the Maharajah of Baroda and Sir Neville Cardus.

MIDDLE: Gareth Parry, the *Guardian*'s man in the Falkland Islands during the conflict with Argentina.

BOTTOM: Richard Gott – among other things leader writer, parliamentary candidate, features editor, and literary editor – seen here in his capacity as admirer of Fidel Castro's Cuban revolution.

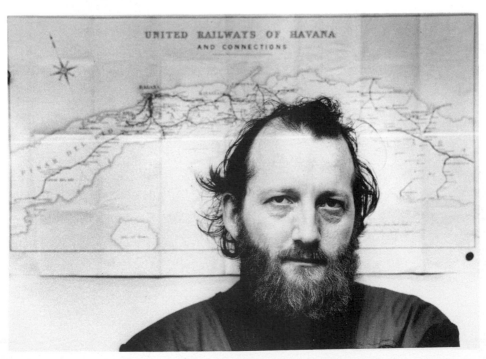

John Anderson, who as yachting editor struck up a close rapport with readers. He is seen here before setting sail from Scarborough in 1966 in an attempt to simulate the oceanic journeys of the early Norsemen to America.

Anderson's successors in August 1989 took part in the Fastnet Race in *Guardian Extra*. Crew lining the deck left to right are: Peter Rodgers, David Fairhall (skipper), Philippa King, Michael White, Sarah Adie, David Sharrock and Stephen Cook. The able seaman missing is Ben Laurance.

The *Guardian* did not entirely give up scenic pictures though they did not appear with the regularity of the *Manchester Guardian* days. Denis Thorpe waited most of a day for the right conditions for his photograph of Hebden Bridge, Yorks, in 1978. By 1978 the sad state of the London presses, along with the loss of quality during wire transmission, meant that he and his Manchester colleague Don McPhee rarely saw a picture in the paper that did them justice.

Joe Minogue, night editor in
Manchester, pictured by
Don McPhee, at work with
a printer on a 'stone'.

Brian Jones, when produc-
tion editor in London,
receiving awards for the
design of the paper in 1971.

W. R. Taylor, Minogue's predecessor on the night desk.

Alastair Hetherington on Saddleback in the Lake District. After editing the paper on Monday, 5 October 1970, he and Harford Thomas, then managing editor, took the sleeper to Manchester, borrowed an office car and drove to the Lakes. They climbed the mountain on Tuesday, spent the night in Hetherington's *dacha* near Kendal and drove to the Conservative party conference in Blackpool early on Wednesday morning. Hetherington then left for Manchester to be duty editor of his paper for Wednesday night, returning to the Conservatives on Thursday. Picture: Harford Thomas.

THE GUARDIAN

37,607   Thursday June 8 1967   Price 5d

CLEAN AT ONE STROKE

Strait of Tiran seized: tanks near Suez Canal: Jericho falls

Israel ready to stop if Arabs will

New Soviet warning

THE SECURITY COUNCIL last night issued a demand to the Israelis and Arabs to cease fire by 9 p.m. Early this morning there was no indication whether either side had done so. The previous day's resolution calling for a ceasefire had been accepted only by Jordan, although Israel announced last night that it would stop fighting if the Arabs did.

RUSSIA, which sponsored the new demand, sent a note to Israel saying that if the ceasefire were not obeyed diplomatic relations would be broken and Russia would "implement other necessary measures stemming from Israel's aggressive policies." The Russian initiatives are seen as an attempt to secure the best possible ceasefire terms for the Arabs and thus regain some lost credit in the Arab world.

IN SINAI after three days of desert warfare Israeli tanks were only a few miles from the Suez Canal. The three groups of their drive were aimed at Qantara in the north, Ismalia in the centre, and Fort Taufiq in the south. The Israeli Chief of Staff, General Rabin, said the main body of the Egyptian army in Sinai had been defeated. The Egyptian Supreme Command admitted that its first defence lines had been evacuated and said fierce fighting was taking place along the second defence lines.

SHARM EL SHEIK was captured to give the Israelis command over the Strait of Tiran. In Jordan, Israeli forces took the cities of Jericho and Nablus and thus established control over almost all the territory to the west of the River Jordan. No comment was available in Tel-Aviv on a Syrian claim to have swept across the Plain of Huleh, north of Lake Tiberias, in the direction of Nazareth.

IN CAIRO, the semi-official newspaper " Al Ahram " repeated the claim that Britain and the United States had given military help to Israel and said that unmarked American aircraft had raided the Suez Canal area on Tuesday.

BRITAIN officially notified the United Nations to send an investigating team to British carriers in the Mediterranean and to the Cyprus and Malta bases to disprove the charge of British air support. But as a result of this charge the Lebanon is withdrawing its ambassadors from Britain and the US, and Saudi Arabia has announced that oil supplies will be interrupted.

MR BROWN told the Commons yesterday that " urgent steps are being taken to readjust the pattern of oil supplies to this country. While there may well be temporary inconveniences for us, there should be no insuperable problem."

PRESIDENT NASSER received the Soviet Ambassador to discuss the ceasefire resolution. He also received a message from the Chinese Prime Minister, Mr Chou En-lai, at a meeting with the Chinese Ambassador.

Russia carries the day at UN

From ALISTAIR COOKE

United Nations (N.Y.), June 7

Tel-Aviv will seek coexistence settlement

By TERENCE PRITTIE

THE Israeli Government has already begun thinking very seriously about peace terms which it will seek when the present war against the Arab States ends.

Israelis in walled city—to stay

Jerusalem, June 7

Israeli tanks and infantry today captured the old walled city of Jerusalem after completely encircling the defending Jordanian troops.

Hussein flying to London?

By our Diplomatic Staff

King Hussein of Jordan, whose country has suffered severe losses of Israeli bombs, was unofficially reported last night to be on his way to London.

Egypt trying to save armour

By HUGH HANNING

Israel says she fired first

By IAN AITKEN

On back page

'Torture' trial verdicts

THE AUTUMN HARVEST

HOW GOOD IS THE YIELD?

Face the future with PEARL assurance

SYRIAN ATTACK
ISRAELI ADVANCES
Roads
Tracks
0 Miles 40

The front page of the London edition during the Six-Day War in June 1967 and, OPPOSITE, after the redesign in 1969. Armstrong's moon landing appeared only in the Manchester edition. Production worries in London prevented so late a page-change.

THE GUARDIAN

Manchester   Monday July 21 1969   6d

Armstrong and Aldrin steer Eagle to a perfect touchdown

Neil Armstrong steps from the lunar module lander to become the first man on the moon.

3 56 am : man steps on to the moon

By ANTHONY TUCKER

Men are on the moon. At 3 56 this morning Armstrong stepped from the lunar module and set foot on lunar ground. It was the fulfilment of a dream which men have shared since the beginning of recorded history. Aldrin followed his commander down the steps of the lander—already named Tranquillity Base—19 minutes later.

Armstrong reported that the surface seemed to be a very fine powder into which his feet sank about one-eighth of an inch. He could see his footprints clearly.

Armstrong's first words on the moon were: "That's one small step for man. One giant leap for mankind." The first television view millions on earth saw was Armstrong's foot descending slowly. Then there was his full figure.

"It's a very soft surface, but here and there where I poke with the sample collector I run into a very hard surface," he said. "It appears to be the same material." The moon "has a harsh beauty all its own," Aldrin reported. "It looks like the desert of the United States, but it is very beautiful."

Aldrin experimented with movement in the low gravity, and remarked that a moonwalker had to be careful to lean in the direction he wanted to go or he would lurch around "like someone slightly inebriated." When they started to examine their surroundings Aldrin reported finding a purple rock.

The decision to walk early was made three hours after the lunar module Eagle had made a perfect landing at 9.17 pm four miles downrange from the chosen site. The spacecraft was steered manually to clear a boulder-strewn crater "the size of a football field." It was a moment of extraordinary tension and silence. The lunar module curved gently down over the Sea of Tranquillity, its drama heightened by the calm, almost casual voices of the astronauts and the mission controller at Houston.

The landing was perfect and the descent rate only 3ft a second. The spacecraft seemed to pause and rock as Armstrong searched the wider area for the landing.

With a permitted touchdown 17 degrees about the horizontal a tilt of 4 degrees in any direction would be supported was seen in the again the search for a landing area had to be a knowledgeable and as perfect as could make it. A few minutes later, although time seemed to

have slowed down, we know that it had been quiet. The tilt in any degrees is known, minute must have worked.

Eventually Armstrong and Aldrin transferred from the command module codenamed Columbia to the lunar module Eagle — leaving Collins alone in the seventh orbit Collins, the third astronaut at Houston, told the world that all spacecraft systems were " operating just fine."

'Now part of our world'

" Because of what you have done, the heavens have become part of man's world.

" For every American this has to be the proudest day of our lives,"—President Nixon to the astronauts this morning.

Install SERVOWARM NOW

MONEY OFF!

HURRY! OFFER CLOSES JULY 31st.

Yes, now is the time for you to install Servowarm, because now giving a big discount the Marvellous Servowarm system for even greater value than ever!

● Over Servowarm has the finest silver, a boiler and burner combined in one slim unit. It keeps the room airy to set up so eight radiators all around the home. And it gets used anywhere.

● Servowarm is a flexible system. Three night other radiators can be in any of eleven different sizes. Your central heating will be tailor-made to meet your requirements.

● Servowarm's skilled engineers can instantly install a complete in 3-5 days with the absolute minimum of disturbance to your home.

Our regular price is £198

Send for Discount Voucher

£198

NOW THERE'S A
BONUS—SAVE MONEY
IN OUR 1969 SUMMER
OFFER!

'A step for a man—a leap for mankind'

Neil Armstrong, the Apollo 11 commander, crawled backwards out of the lunar module's hatch shortly before 4 a.m. today and clambered down a ladder to become the first man to set foot on the moon.

At Houston, 1 am on the 21st he said at 3.56 a.m. as he edged down to to the lunar module, extending leg. He described the moon as a dark powdery charcoal and said that he made word in with about an eighth-of-an-inch.

This is one small step for a man he said as he stepped from the lunar module on to the moon. "one and giant leap for mankind."

He reported feeling no difficulty in moving about in the moon's low gravity, one-sixth of that on earth. half way down the ladder area

Neil Armstrong

From ADAM RAPHAEL at the Space Centre, Houston, July 21

here The Eagle has landed," said Armstrong, a man with a just republican for saying little.

The astronauts were out certain where they had come down because their landmark tracking in the final approach was interrupted by alarms in the lunar module's cabin. Ground tracking stations initially estimated their position at Houston as 4 miles North and 6 East, near the lunar landing well as can be assumed this area

HELP TOOK

Mr Gene Kranz flight director, said last night that the alarms were caused by computers in the lunar module becoming overloaded. It was said not known, he said why Eagle had steered the target area by four miles.

Armstrong described the scene out of his small triangular window shortly after landing. It seems to be a relatively level plain with a fairly large number of craters of the 5 to 50ft variety and some ridges, mostly small but some

In the control-room at Houston there was electric tension as controllers anxiously monitored the displays in front of them.

Step by step the sensational moves of ground control transmitted centre to Eagle and back came equally calm responses. Shortly before 9 p.m. Eagle was told: "You are go for DOI thousand orbit insertion." Back came the single syllable answer from the spacecraft through a maze of static: "Roger." Eight minutes later, at 8.56 p.m. the

The engine fired on 10 per cent throttle for the first 15 seconds, gradually increasing to 40 per cent, putting Eagle into a highly elliptical orbit with a

low point of only 50,000 feet above the moon's surface.

Then, with Aldrin and Armstrong standing side by side in the lunar module the descent engine was refired by computer demands, breaking the orbital speed for the final 230 miles on a slanting course to the moon.

Eight minutes after the descent engine fired Eagle was nearly 7,000 feet above the surface, and it then swung to a nearly vertical position to allow the astronauts to peer out of the triangular windows in front of them at the approaching Sea of Tranquillity.

Ninety seconds later, with the spacecraft flying at about 45 mph forward and 10 mph downward, Aldrin took over manual control from Eagle's computer. For the last 150 feet he held the lunar module in a hovering position directly above the landing

until the probes touched the moon surface. There was a delay of one second. The blue then Houston confirmed the first indication of the first touchdown on the moon.

By our Science Correspondent

Russia's Luna 15 kept everyone guessing right up to the last moment yesterday. As the Apollo craft prepared to separate, Jodrell Bank reported that the unmanned Russian craft had gone into a new orbit, taking it to within 10 miles of the moon's surface at its closest approach, and bringing its track closer to the Sea of Tranquillity.

But not before the American news communication plan to Moscow were broken. They were restored 10 minutes later. At that time Moscow radio carried the first announcement of the American landing.

Luna keeps secret

Soil collected

Using his balance, Armstrong's first action was to a soil with a large scoop. Before he could be put to make a rapid return to lunar module Eagle.

Strictly after this he was joined on the surface by Aldrin. As Aldrin backed out of the lunar module the direction from the Armstrong, his partner, who was making contact and to back down the ground down from Columbia, told the dust how to jump for the moon seemed to Jump he the moon with gravity " feel instrumented up and down.

The first and white television pictures of the lunar surface, as Aldrin and Armstrong walked the pictures, down to make the contact the moon's surface moved down hand "I can't hang duty " in the more, say.

Jumping, the lunar module itself rose by a wide Aldrin moving about the surface now. His feet broke down away from the Sea of Tranquillity to the

Pause for thanks

Nearly three hours after touchdown, Aldrin sent a special message to Houston.

"This is the LM pilot," he said. "I'd like to take this opportunity to ask every person listening in, whoever and wherever they may be, to pause for a moment and contemplate the events of the past few hours, and to give thanks in his or her own way."

Aldrin is an elder and lay-preacher at a Presbyterian church at Webster, Texas.

20ft, to 60ft high, and liberally threatened at little off, and 20, both craters around the area.

We put some angular blocks would hundred feet in front of us that are perhaps 2ft in size and have angular edges.

At various and the rocks were macadam gray in colour but Aldrin second of which is we greys cooked." There is about 15ft and he said "The colour depends on which way you look but there doesn't appear to be much of a general colour at all.

The landing manoeuvre began shortly after 4.08 a.m. (BST), when the lunar Armstrong, standing on the left of Aldrin in the lunar module, reduced the docking latches and Eagle backed slowly away from Columbia, the command module.

Collins, the command module pilot, then took a close look from about forty feet at the lunar module as it reversed slowly rotation that its landing gear was in a " flying position " before this dismounting on inspection. Columbia thrust away for 2,300

The Apollo 11 landing site (ringed) on the southern border of the Sea of Tranquillity close to the lunar equator. This area is one of seven chosen because of their comparative absence of obstacles. The other landing sites, some of which would bring men close to earlier unmanned lunar landing spacecraft, will be used in later Apollo missions.
Map by National Geographic Society

Motor as brake

From this moment, with the tension mounting second by second and with the minimum of interruption from earth, or from the orbiting Collins the lunar module belly Armstrong and Aldrin downward, using its motor as a brake and slowly to low for landing.

On and down and "high pace" at 7,000 feet the brake ing glance console and the spacecraft pulled so that its surface faced forward—the point at which the final approach began.

Still onward and down, no more than now the spacecraft moved with the astronauts checking, checking and checking again that all systems were "go."

Visual approach, but still ready, automatic control began at 500ft by with the spacecraft still moving slowly, forward. At that with all forward motion stilled

How far *will* the *Guardian* go? After the redesign in 1969 the marketing department gave the paper a new prospectus with advertisements in *Punch*, the *Observer* and the trade press.

close harmony with what the *MG* set out to achieve. The new building was alongside the Wood Street Mission, a sanctuary for down-and-outs, on which a carved inscription says that it was founded as the Manchester and Salford Children's Mission, Boys' Home, and Working Men's Church in 1869, enlarged in 1896, and extended and rebuilt in 1905. Alistair Cooke's father Samuel, an iron-fitter and Methodist lay preacher, had been one of the pillars of this mission at the time of its enlargement. It stood, still in the narrow lane called Wood Street, to remind the *Guardian* staff of the society they once served. It also came to remind them of the society they served in more recent times. Part of the Wood Street Mission was taken over by the group's glossy listings and pop magazine, *City Life*.

The work of finding a new home was under the control of Harvie but the impetus came, as did so much of the forward thinking for the company, from Laurence Scott, whose brainchild it was. But although the proceeds of the Cross Street site brought in £2.2m. gross, £1.13m. net to MGEN, that was not enough and a bank loan was needed. The firm was in capital crisis rather than trading crisis when it moved to Deansgate: that is to say the papers were selling well, but one of the customary credit squeezes of that epoch was in force and ad revenue had not caught up with sales. The company was ankle deep in trouble with its wastrel subsidiary at Lowton St Mary. A company known as Lancashire Colour Printers Ltd was incorporated on 19 September 1968 to carry on the work previously done there by Comet Newspapers (Manchester) Ltd, which nevertheless had to continue trading for tax reasons. Another £28,000 (*Guardian* cover price 6d; postage 5d) was shovelled in Comet/LCP's direction.

To add to these misfortunes the finance department succeeded in counting the value of the Cross Street property twice, once as part of the cash-flow forecast and again as security for a loan. When this piece of creative accountancy was discovered and a shamefaced deputation went to Williams Deacon's Bank in St Ann Street, Manchester, to explain it the bank was not amused and refused to lend the money. The error was sad as well as embarrassing because Williams Deacon's had been the company's bankers for 149 years. But the firm had a happy knack of finding the right man at the right time, having lately invited a City banker, John Clay, to join its board. Clay took the company to National Westminster, which lent £2m.; and Hambros, of which he was a director, provided another £½m. The unfortunate author of the accountancy double left the company before long. The papers moved house on August bank holiday, 1970, with closure of streets and much knocking down of walls to hoist 58 2-ton typesetting machines and a 9-ton moulding press, among 600 tons of machinery in all, from one building to the other. The loan was repaid by 1973, not without difficult interim meetings with the steel-rimmed bankers of which, fortunately, the editorial staff remained in ignorance. The old Crabtree machines were sold for scrap.

In the end GMEN did well out of the deal. A large and traffic-free area off Deansgate was redeveloped and the trees, which at that time often grew only on PR handouts before the JCBs started work, were planted and flourished. Heather gardens grew. The company took in the rest of the new department, including what became the education department's offices, as a commercial investment. In May 1971, belatedly marking the 100th anniversary of the *Manchester Evening News* three years earlier, the Scott Trust gave the paper a stainless steel sculpture by Keith Godwin.* It was placed in the Deansgate forecourt called Spinningfield and, to a fanfare by William Walton played by trumpeters of the Duke of Edinburgh's Royal Regiment, was unveiled by Sir William Haley, a former editor of the *MEN*. The handsome piece, commonly called 'the thing outside', was properly entitled Vigilance.

It was in the Deansgate building that the *Manchester Evening News* and the *Guardian* had their first taste of the 'new' technology in the form of text produced by photo-composition. In a study for the Royal Commission on the Press, 1974–7 (the McGregor Commission),[2] Rex Winsbury reported that 1,774 US daily newspaper titles, 84 per cent of the total, were by early 1975 wholly or largely composed in cold type, that is, used photo-composition and some or all of its various electronic adjuncts, having abandoned, wholly or largely, traditional hot-metal systems. As he pointed out, the figure is less impressive when measured in terms of circulation rather than number of titles because the big metropolitan papers in centres like New York and Washington were the last to take the road to photo-composition. When he wrote (1975) only just over half of the US total daily circulation was photo-composed. The British industry as a whole was thus not as laggardly as has sometimes been assumed, and when ACAS reported[3] in 1976, 43 per cent of its sample of newspaper titles in Britain were using photo-composition and 36 per cent computer typesetting. In Winsbury's view, American standards of newspaper production were on the whole lower than British standards. 'The US attitude has largely been that newspapers are a throw-away product, and notions of quality have reflected this attitude . . . In the highly competitive British national press in particular, few if any newspapers could get away with the sort of shoddy reproduction that characterises many US papers, who are often in monopoly sites, and may simply not need anything better.'

Even so, it had been several years since any hot-metal machines were manufactured in the US. 'If needed, they are imported from Britain which seems now to be the centre of world manufacture and trade in these obsolescent items. Old Linotype, Intertype and other hot metal machines are worth only their scrap metal value in the US these days. That, perhaps, is the most telling measure of how far the Americans have got!'

---

* Keith Godwin was head of the School of Sculpture in the Manchester Polytechnic Faculty of Art and Design.

In the traditional hot-metal method of printing, a molten alloy of lead, tin and antimony was (and in odd corners, still continued to be) pressed into a mould on the typesetting machine, which produced a line of type. The machine collected the lines of type, called slugs, which were then assembled into columns on trays ('galleys'). For speed of assembly a newspaper article of more than a paragraph or two would normally be split into several takes, which were given to different compositors and put together when they had all been set. The contents of the galley were next transferred to the chase, which was a metal frame the shape and size of a page. Headlines were cast on a separate machine capable of handling large type and commonly known by its proprietorial name, the Ludlow. The chase containing all the metal for a page, in which each slug of metal was nearly an inch high, was a bulky and extremely heavy assembly which rested on a metal table called the stone. At this stage all the metal was in reverse form, i.e. 'mirror-writing' which a printer, and before long a journalist working with him, would read as naturally as a positive. When it was complete the page went under a high-pressure moulding press which produced a papier-mâché matrix (or mat, or flong) which was positive and could be read like an ordinary newspaper page. The mat then underwent another high-pressure moulding process to produce from it a curved metal plate (reverse again) to fit on the rotary press.

The work that went on in a newspaper's production departments was almost certainly the most highly skilled in manufacturing industry. That was true not only in the composing room but in the 'process', where blocks were made for illustrations, and in the stereotypers' foundry. Compositors had to be familiar not only with the material they were working with but with the visual niceties which made a finished product satisfying to the reader. Until the *Guardian* put news on the front page in 1952 the make-up of the inside pages, apart from the page lead and perhaps another important item, was left almost entirely to the compositors. With the increasing emphasis on design which had long been familiar on 'popular' papers came a new rigour based on the sub-editors' written 'scheme' which the compositor or stone-hand making up the page would follow. But there was a world of difference between simply following a design and making a readable page. In an article marking the twenty-fifth anniversary[4] of London printing Brian Jones described the Manchester composing room of the early 1960s:

There was a fierce pride about the paper. Frank Hall, a seasoned compositor making up page one, ostensibly under the instruction of a recently-arrived young sub-editor, let him have his way for a few minutes, observed the resulting mess, and said 'Are you going to be here regularly from now on?'
'Yes, why?'
'Well, let's get one thing straight. This is the Manchester bleedin' Guardian, not the Comic effing Cuts. Right? Now this is how we do it.' And the

paper was safe once again from being sullied by a novice who had not yet been fully admitted to the club.

In an earlier composing room the chief maker-up of pages, Harry Bailey, would put the slugs of type in a vice rather than ask the sub-editor to make a small cut which might involve resetting and thus delay the page.

That was the old technology, based on the Linotype of 1886 and the more versatile Monotype of 1897 and still owing many of its skills and craft exclusiveness to Gutenberg's introduction of movable type in 1455. The *Guardian* began serious use of the new technology in 1973–4, through the good offices of the *Manchester Evening News*, and was the first national paper to do so.

The *MEN* was without question the senior partner in the Manchester enterprise, which had to gear itself to the exacting demands of an evening paper. It had reached its maximum pagination of 40 broadsheet pages on five days a week (though with only 32 on Saturdays). It carried a heavy volume of display classified advertising – 20 pages a day – and in addition its composing room set all the display classified for the *Guardian*, which was cast in plates for the Manchester presses and sent by train in mat form to London. The result was a very large quantity of advertisement and editorial matter lying in metal galleys waiting to be used for which there was no longer storage capacity. Newspapers always kept a certain amount of metal on hand for use in emergency, for when a big story collapsed or an advertisement failed to turn up, or as obituaries of celebrities. (In the case of the monarch, for example, the obituary standing ready would run to several pages.) Two stages were needed in resolving this difficulty, which entailed major changes in traditional work handling.

The first stage was to cut out the hot-metal setting of the classified display by the use of photo-composition, thus increasing the production capacity and solving the problem of metal storage. In this process keyboards produced perforated tape which was fed into a computerised Whitacker's ACM 9000 Photosetter, which in turn produced a bromide print-out of what had been typed, in appearance similar to a large photographic slide. The second stage was to make a metal block from the bromide so that the normal production processes could continue from there. Zinc had been the traditional material for etching blocks but to etch a full page on zinc took half an hour. The *MEN* might have twenty pages to produce. It was therefore decided to switch from zinc to magnesium, which could be etched in five minutes or ten at the most. But magnesium is tricky stuff to handle. It is highly reactive with the acid and during etching the plates have to be kept in baths cooled by ice-cold coils. That was the easy part. The coating used on zinc plate had posed no special hazards but the coating on the magnesium, trichlorethylene, was developed by an unfamiliar substance to the men who had to handle it and requiring strict control standards. To be on the safe side the *MEN* bought a Swedish machine, the Mavom, for the magnesium process, which had a large extractor system built into it to remove the fumes from boiling trichlorethylene and conformed to the Swedish health and safety regulations. Those standards were deemed to be so renowned for their severity that the machine was bought with a view to removing any hazards (and to impress the men operating the machine).

When the time came to convert to the new system all the old zinc equipment was destroyed so that there could be no question of reverting to it. The team arrived to operate the machine under instruction. But one had remembered his experience during military service days and had taken a library book the previous day. From this he had gained the impression, rightly or wrongly, that in certain conditions trichlorethylene, such as when inhaled through a lighted cigarette, could produce phosgene gas. In the light of this alarming suggestion the only escape was to call in a factories inspector, although it was Sunday afternoon, and after examining the machine from all angles he pronounced it safe to use provided nobody knelt against a certain valve at floor level smoking a cigarette!

With this assurance the blocks were finally made. With no other method remaining of making the blocks the production of both papers would have been at least seriously interrupted. This was only the half-way stage to full photo-composition, in which bromide would be used almost from start to finish, but the new technology had been introduced by the seat of the production manager's pants, in this case M. J. Smith's. In place of the slow and hot-metal-intensive method which had been used before, all the ads for the *MEN* were made on the morning of publication and the plates thrown away once a moulding had been taken to print from. Only the bromides were kept on file. *Guardian* ads were made during the day for that night's publication.

The *Guardian*'s night stereotypers in Manchester thought they should have the sole rights to moulding *Guardian* pages, as indeed they always had had. But the industry had evolved ways of handling problems of that kind into which it was rarely advisable to inquire. Matrices of pages for the *Guardian* made from bromide and magnesium began to arrive at Euston station as regularly as they had from hot metal and zinc.

With the move to Deansgate on the August bank holiday weekend of 1970 there began, partly because the group was in financial straits again, a period of acute managerial instability which lasted for three years. Kenneth Searle had taken over from Laurence as managing director and chief executive (he employed both terms) when Laurence was relieved of his executive responsibilities by resolution of the board after the 1966–7 crisis. Under him was a network of interlocking limited companies, some of more substance than others, which in addition to Guardian Newspapers Ltd and the Manchester Evening News Ltd included North News Ltd, Comet Newspapers

(Manchester) Ltd, Lancashire Colour Printers Ltd, Colourpix Studios Ltd, Guardian Business Services Ltd, Post Publications Ltd, Guardian Publications Ltd, Manchester News Centre Ltd, Manchester Exhibition Halls Ltd, Manchester's Radio Voice Ltd, Northprint Manchester Ltd, and Manchester Guardian Inc. (USA). What Nesta Roberts had called 'the clerking side' was in its element among all the directorships in these concerns, and with Laurence's removal from power the scene became reminiscent of that in a colonial territory with the departure of the imperial power. Brian Redhead, editor of the *MEN* and therefore a director of the parent company, wanted to get rid of all the proliferating boards and go back to being a simple unit as of old, but Hetherington disagreed, not least on the stated ground that it would cause such pain and loss of status to the dislodged directors.

There are good reasons for not entering in detail into the manoeuvrings which took place. First, they did not differ in any marked particular from what happened and happens in other industrial groups. Secondly they did not impinge noticeably on the conduct of the two newspapers. And thirdly some of the participants are still active at the time of writing and it would be a rash person who presumed to know all the facts which went into the managerial in-fighting. Even so, a few happenings can hardly be ignored.

Milbury no longer played the disruptive part it had played in the 1960s but the Comet division of the group, now more or less subsumed under Lancashire Colour Printers, was still there. For the twelve months to March 1970 the group loss before tax was £185,000. In July 1970 Searle reported that the Comet division was in urgent need of its own full-time managing director. Further losses were likely to be sustained on Post Publications* (which then included at least eighteen titles) and its general manager had been dismissed. In August Laurence reported to the Scott Trust that the Comet division was now losing about £100,000 a year.

In October G.P. Taylor, dissatisfied with the conduct of Comet, resigned from the brief directorship of it which he had held. By November Searle, as chairman of Comet, was reporting a potential loss on that company for the year of £218,000, which he regarded as 'quite unacceptable'. 'In present circumstances, with Group resources stretched to the limit by the Deansgate project, there remains no time for further debate before immediate and drastic corrective action is taken within the Comet Division.'

Matters were becoming urgent, but Searle decided not to cancel a visit to Chicago which he was due to make as part of a freebie for businessmen. Since becoming chief executive he had immersed himself fully and with a certain grandeur in the ceremonial duties attaching to the post. On his return from Chicago he circulated among the directors on 10 November a four-page memorandum praising the hospitality afforded by the British Consul-General in the windy city (who, he pointed out, was the senior British consular

* See Chapter 23.

representative in the whole of the United States!) and suggesting that any director wishing to visit Chicago would be ensured of a warm welcome if prior notification were given to the consulate through him, Searle. On the same day, however, Searle was asked by the board to produce a report outlining what his plans were for the future conduct of Lancashire Colour Printers so that they could be reviewed by the company's finance committee as a matter of urgency.

Whether or not alternative proposals were put forward is not recorded, but after a meeting of the parent board on 17 November the resignation of Mr Searle was announced. It fell once again to Richard Scott, present at the meeting in his capacity as chairman of the Trust, to inform Searle about the feeling of his fellow directors, and to Laurence to negotiate terms for the severance.

Few people outside the company knew it at the time, and not many inside it who were not immediately concerned, but in 1970–1 MGEN underwent a re-run of 1966, with Laurence Scott, who was still chairman though not chief executive, strongly advocating a merger with *The Times* and his colleagues trying to persuade him not to get excited. On paper the financial situation was worse than it had been in 1966. There were difficult pay negotiations with the NUJ chapel of the *MEN*, the *Guardian's* cover price went up from 6d to 8d in February, and the financial report for the twelve months to March 1970 showed a *Guardian* loss of £1,115,000 (£76,000 more than budget), a North News profit of £1,066,000 (£306,000 below budget), a loss on Lancashire Colour Printers of £142,000 and on Post Publications of £71,000. The group loss before tax was £185,000. One cause was rising production costs: £10,000 overspent in Manchester and £38,000 in London (almost negligible figures by the standards of other newspapers or by the *Guardian's* own twenty years later) but another, ironically, was the *Guardian's* success. Its circulation from January to June was a record 303,000 (compared with 401,000 on *The Times*, which represented a fall of 35,000). Extra sales meant extra expenditure on paper and ink until such time as a steady figure could enable the advertisement department to put its rates up. The immediate financial effect of a circulation increase is almost always bad.

It was about this time, the summer of 1970, that arguments broke out between Peter Gibbings and Richard Scott about the desirability of Hetherington's becoming a trustee, and Laurence Scott had become more anti-Hetherington than ever.

On 14 July Laurence sent another of his memos to the Trust, this time entitled The Future, in which he said:

> It is common knowledge that *The Times* is making a large annual loss, probably well over £2m . . . It is widely rumoured that Roy Thomson is sick of it and is

seeking a way to let go the tail of his tiger. In these circumstances the possibility of a merger between *The Times* and the *Guardian* once more raises its head – and it might well be a merger on our terms, if I rightly interpret what our terms would be . . .

His main requirement was that the Scott Trust should maintain in existence the *Guardian* 'or something like it', and that the trustees should directly or indirectly control the appointment of the editor. To have the editor appointed by one person or organisation and the managing director by another would be a certain recipe for trouble, and possibly disaster, and therefore in practice 'we' (i.e. the Trust) should appoint both. Negotiations should be conducted by Richard Scott, Laurence Scott, Hetherington, Gibbings and John Clay.

The Trust agreed to form the working party proposed by Laurence. But evidently Richard had again said something to upset Laurence's calculations because on 31 July Laurence wrote to him about 'the danger that the editor of the T-G could be prevented (or inhibited) from taking a political line that offended advertisers or readers by the refusal of our partners to provide the necessary finances'. Laurence went on:

> As I see it, if the trustees press this to the extent of demanding that the editor of the *Guardian* has the right to be supported by every penny that the joint group possesses then a joint deal is not possible and the only course open to us is to sit and wait for the *Times* or ourselves to fold. The trustees have the right to take this view, but it would not be mine . . . As we stand today, with the profits of the *MEN* fully committed, an editorial line by Alastair that cost us a significant loss of advertisers or of readers would bankrupt the group within months, unless we closed the *Guardian* first. And I see little prospect of this situation changing much within my lifetime . . .
>
> Looking at our national newspapers from outside it really does seem inevitable that presently there will be fewer of them with larger circulations, and most of all inevitable that it will not be possible for both a *Times* and a *Guardian* to survive. (I know that our newspapers are incredibly tenacious of life, but this only means that somebody is prepared to subsidise them and one cannot expect this to go on for ever. I admit also that if I had foreseen all this I might never have advocated taking the *Guardian* to London, but that is spilt milk.) It is quite clear to me that within measurable time, which might be as little as two years and is unlikely to be as much as ten years, there will only be one quality morning paper where now there are two.

These depressing broodings fortunately had little effect on Peter Gibbings, who although still fairly new to the scene, had early grasped the conflict of ideas and personalities. On 25 August he wrote a paper on the alternatives facing the *Guardian*, all of which, he said, would mark a retreat from the present position and therefore inevitably produce an inferior paper. The three possible courses were: (1) to print only in Manchester. To print only in London would save considerably less. Within five years, possibly less, the savings made by abandoning London would probably be balanced by lost revenue. If this happened the next step would be (2) to print a specialist political daily. This could be done by web offset outside Manchester or London. It would by definition be small and expensive and would be bought as a second paper. Such a truncated *Guardian* might find it very difficult to recruit and hold the outstanding writers on which it depends. The final step would be (3) a *Weekly Guardian*. This, Gibbings said, was undoubtedly feasible, and the loss could be kept below half a million. But it would soon be in a life and death struggle with the *New Statesman*, and two left-of-centre weeklies would be one too many. The one remaining option was that David Astor might be willing to sell control of the *Observer*, which could then be run as the *Observer and Sunday Guardian*. He believed the *Observer* lost money in most years but not more than about £250,000. Gibbings concluded:

> To sum up, all the possibilities mentioned in this paper entail a greater or lesser reduction in the influence of the *Guardian* and in the number of jobs available for existing employees. Further, only the last two ideas – the *Guardian Weekly* and the *Observer/Sunday Guardian* – appear to provide the basis for a long term future. They are all much inferior to what we are doing at present.

Second time round it was Gibbings who took the initiative in saving the paper.

Nevertheless there was less than unanimity at the top of the GMEN group, with Andy Harvie, then managing director of the *MEN* and with a different set of priorities, arguing strongly that the *Guardian* should abandon London printing altogether, print at the LCP plant at Leigh, and distribute by aeroplane or helicopter. Whatever happened, Harvie insisted, the *Guardian* must cut its losses by half. Hetherington had to remind him that the *Guardian* was the prime reason for the company's existence.[5] But Harvie saw far enough ahead to propose that the *Guardian* should develop itself as a European newspaper, flying negatives after photo-composition or using facsimile to a number of European centres. Something of the sort did come about, in Frankfurt and Marseilles, but not for nearly twenty years.

The merger proposition was taken seriously enough for Laurence to discuss it with Lord Thomson over dinner at the Gleneagles Hotel during a meeting of the Commonwealth Press Union in October, and for Thomson to express interest and ask (according to Laurence's report) whether the editor of the *Guardian* would be any good. Hetherington meanwhile dutifully dusted off the 1966 prospectus which Laurence had got him to prepare ('A newspaper of the highest quality . . . drawing on the best traditions of both *The Times* and the *Guardian* . . . well informed . . . vigorous comment . . . strong social conscience . . . as proud of their recent attainments as of their past history . . . ').

One of the few editorial people on the *Guardian* to know about these moves was Brian Jones, then production editor. He wrote an uncompromising note to Hetherington opposing the notion. Jones had copies of the merger papers in his briefcase as he drove home at the end of the week's work to his house near Bath. On the way he had a crash. His first thought on waking up in hospital was what had become of the papers: had somebody picked them up from the wreckage and handed them to *Private Eye*? Journalists least of all enjoy exposure in the media.

The figures had not improved much by mid-1971. At the end of the financial year in April the *Guardian* showed a loss of £1,190,000, the *MEN* a profit of £1,438,000 and Comet a loss of £293,000. The group trading loss was £45,000 and the total loss £265,000. Strikes which were then plaguing the industry cost the two papers £225,000 altogether. It was not until 1973 that Anthony Barber's budget, which created the 'Barber boom' designed to return the Conservatives to office, put the company back in funds – the same boom which, by giving rise to the heavy job advertising on the *MEN*, led to the technological innovations already referred to.

The next significant figure to go was Harvie, managing director of the *MEN*, in April 1973. He and Peter Gibbings, who was joint chairman of the *Guardian* board as well as deputy chairman of the group, were potentially and often in fact on opposite sides of any argument. More to the point was that Laurence was clearly not going to continue in office for much longer and indeed suddenly announced his retirement in June 1973. Gibbings was designated his successor as chairman. Laurence formally retired in November of that year and the *Guardian* carried a most affectionate and appreciative farewell by Hetherington. But the long saga was not over. Laurence started legal proceedings to secure the pension he understood he had been promised. The company sought counsel's opinion which went in Laurence's favour, in that an undertaking given in April 1972 that the pension should rise in line with the Retail Prices Index was deemed to be legally enforceable. It might have been disagreeable to have Scott of the *Guardian* giving evidence in court against the successor regime. Laurence received his pension. He died in 1983.

By 1975 the group had managed to put behind it all the theoretical notions about whether the *Guardian* should continue and if so in what form, but the question of where to print in London had became pressing. The effects of the boom began to be dissipated. There was £4m. in the bank with which to move house, but the national economy was once again in crisis, and GMEN would have to look sharp if it was not to be forced either into an uneconomic dependence on another contract printer or into new arrangements on its own which might turn out to be profligate. The contract with Thomson was not due to expire until 1976 but his purchase of *The Times*, and his plan to consolidate the printing of both that paper and the *Sunday Times* at Gray's Inn Road, had complicated matters. In the first place there was the obvious discomfiture of running two rival newspapers from the same offices and plant.

But more to the point the printing unions began to get agitated about the loss of jobs at Printing House Square, owned by the *Observer*, if *The Times* stopped printing there and only one night's work a week remained. They insisted that the *Guardian* negotiate terms with the *Observer* for printing on its presses.

As early as 1972 Peter Gibbings had started talks with his former *Observer* colleagues and found that they were not particularly amenable to what he had in mind. In the first place the *Observer* itself wanted to move. Even if it stayed at Printing House Square, it maintained there was no room to spare for the *Guardian*. Gibbings reckoned there was ample room (25,000 square feet, compared with the 14,000 the paper had at Gray's Inn Road) though it would cost something to prepare and furnish it. He therefore proposed a joint company to own the factory block at PHS, each paper owning half. This was a similar deal to the one struck with Associated Newspapers in Manchester. The *Observer* would not look at it and instead offered a twenty-one-year lease 'with very onerous terms particularly in relation to termination'.[6]

However, there did not appear to be much choice. Marmaduke Hussey, the executive in charge at *The Times*, had originally said the paper could stay at Gray's Inn Road after the contract expired but changed his mind during the year as the complications became apparent. Gibbings thought the unions might make him change again, but even so the added cost to the *Guardian* would be about £500,000 (selling price 5p; postage 3p). Associated were not interested in printing the *Guardian* because if the *Daily Mail*'s circulation fell much further they might decide to pull out of Manchester and do all their printing in London. The only other way which Gibbings saw at the time would be to keep the editorial headquarters in London and do all the composing for the *Guardian* in Manchester, sending the pages by fax to London for printing and distribution. A more diabolically accident-prone system would be hard to imagine, and it is tempting to think that Gibbings had tongue in cheek. Nevertheless John Sinclair, one of the group's technical advisers, was asked to look into the prospect. But it was too daunting to be taken seriously and Gibbings advised that the best thing was to try to wear down the *Observer*.

It didn't work, and over a period of eighteen months joint managerial and editorial committees looked at all the options again. It was at this time that Harry Roche, who in 1988 was to become chairman of the whole enterprise, had his first direct contact with the *Guardian* in London rather than with the two papers jointly in Manchester. After the George Mitchell School in London Harry Roche had started work as an apprentice in the stereo department of the *Daily Mirror* in London. He did further training at the Watford College of Technology and the London College of Printing and became successively foundry overseer and deputy production controller at the *Mirror* before moving to Manchester as the Mirror Group's northern production executive. From there he joined the *Manchester Evening News* first as deputy production manager, then as production director, then as managing director and from

1985 managing director of the *Guardian*. Among the others in the team was Peter Preston, who was already interesting himself in new production techniques and who spent a hectic fortnight in the United States looking at how things were organised on papers as diverse as the *Miami Herald*, the *St Louis Post-Dispatch*, the *South Bend Tribune*, and the *Wall Street Journal*.

They could not get away from the fact that Thomson was subsidising the *Guardian* heavily by taking the £1.28 a square foot for office space agreed in Laurence Scott's day and charging less than the going rate for production staff employed by Times Newspapers Ltd but engaged on *Guardian* work. Whatever they did they were going to have to find large sums of money.

Thomson's people had been too preoccupied with their own move from Printing House Square to Gray's Inn Road to bother themselves much about the *Guardian*, but in so far as they were willing to discuss terms it was obvious that the *Guardian* would have to pay a more realistic £10 a square foot after September 1976 and also guarantee Times Newspapers a profit of 10 per cent on all its outlay on wages and so forth on the *Guardian*'s behalf. In any case *Guardian* people believed that the space they were occupying in Thomson House was needed for Thomson's new-technology direct input terminals. The *Observer*, the paper which had always seemed to be the natural partner, offered even stiffer terms under which the *Guardian* would pay £1m. a year in addition to the cost of materials and maintenance labour.

But the paper then had one of its lucky breaks. Less than half a mile away from Gray's Inn Road, and well within the Fleet Street ambit to which it was then important for a paper to belong, a new building was going up in Farringdon Road where the *Guardian* could have as much office space as it needed for £3 a square foot, where the departments of Trade and Environment had agreed to grant an industrial development certificate allowing it to be used for the first stages of newspaper production, and where a lease of thirty-five years could immediately be obtained. Instead of looking for offices only the paper could have everything needed to produce the first copy – writing centre, composing room, stereo moulding presses – under one roof. Only (a big only) the printing centre remained to be found.

At first it looked as though the *Guardian* would again link up with Associated Newspapers and print on the (London) *Evening News* presses at Carmelite House, but Harvey Thompson, twice in the past a *Guardian* man (having been apprenticed under Charles Markwick in Manchester and later serving as production director) was now production director at Times Newspapers. He still had spare capacity and offered the use of it. That would save a good deal of upheaval and in the event that is where the *Guardian* decided to carry on printing. J.C. Markwick (Jim Markwick, director, future managing director, and son of the Charles who performed the engineering feat in Manchester) scoured the country for second-hand machinery to put in Farringdon Road. He bought foundry equipment for £200 from HM Stationery Office and two moulding presses which had been put to store in an aircraft hangar in a field near Thetford. With refurbishment they cost £11,000 for the two whereas to have bought new ones would have cost £80,000. Pennies still had to be pinched. The paper sent its finished pages by van on their short journey to Gray's Inn Road. The printing contract was again secured on highly beneficial terms because it included a clause saying the *Guardian* could pull out if *The Times* were acquired by anybody else, as it was by Murdoch in 1981, but could not be expelled.

The discovery of Farringdon Road was to change the nature of the paper once again, as it had been changed by the move to London in 1961. It both secured the paper's economic wellbeing, although that was not known at the time, and first reduced and then virtually eliminated the influence of the Manchester office. But before any of this could happen there was another matter to be attended to. Senior staff were informed of the forthcoming upheaval at the end of January 1975. Six weeks later Hetherington announced that he was resigning the editorship to become Controller of BBC Scotland.

CHAPTER 16

The Charing Cross Hotel

THUS ended a radical and challenging editorship which must be seen as the editorship needed for those times. It had called into question not only old assumptions – that can be relatively easy – but new ones too. It had not espoused the unilateralism which some of Hetherington's senior colleagues found so natural yet had made Britain aware of the contribution it could make to curbing the spread of nuclear weapons. It had not entered into a simplistic anti-Americanism, especially over Vietnam, which would have endeared it to the Left. It had encouraged the women's movement. It had shown an impatience with the remaining white role in central and southern Africa, though perhaps more from instinct than analysis. At home it had not voted a straight ticket on any of the political platforms. It had supported Labour, been generous to the Tories and reasserted a *Guardian* respect for the Liberals which had been allowed to dwindle. It had started the debate back in the 1950s and early 1960s about how to share the growing affluence of the South of Britain with the declining North. It had promoted the care of the natural environment, which was a cause close to Hetherington's heart long before it became the consumer-oriented fashion of the late 1980s.

Doubtless there were things Hetherington regretted he had not done; he envied the role of the *Sunday Times* in bringing the thalidomide scandal to a satisfactory end through its long and litigious campaign. Except for Adam Raphael's investigations showing where British companies were paying wages in South Africa which were well below the poverty line, it did less campaigning than he would probably have liked – and less than his foot-in-door news editor, Jean Stead, was inclined to undertake. But the obverse of that particular penny is that the *Guardian*'s role under Hetherington was not simply to reflect political events but to mould them under his definition of its role, which was 'government in the widest sense'. That had been the natural assumption of the paper and the people writing for it: when John Cole was in Washington in the summer of 1966, for example, and was invited to see Dean Rusk, the Secretary of State, Rusk had on his desk a whole file of *Guardian* leaders on Vietnam and quizzed him closely about 'Why is your paper saying these things?'

Hetherington was given a good send-off. The Trust thanked him warmly for 'the single-minded devotion with which he has served the *Guardian*' and noted that during his nineteen years, 'a period of acute difficulty for the newspaper industry', the circulation of the paper had more than doubled. And that again conceals an important role for it could have been more than doubled if Hetherington had been willing to make the concessions of style and content which management had urged upon him but which he believed could have destroyed the character of the paper. Two of his closest colleagues[1] spoke almost identically, some fifteen years after the event, of the steely determination which had made him 'a great editor'. The company gave him a farewell party on board HMS *Belfast*, moored in the Thames. Except perhaps for a couple of investigative reporters, who sat in a corner wearing black leather, tinted lenses and expressions of distaste, everyone seemed to enjoy it.

Hetherington was fifty-five when he decided to leave. Under a rule introduced not long before, directors (on grounds of executive strain which others were deemed not to feel) were not only entitled but required to retire at sixty: too young for a man of vigour but too old, perhaps, for another demanding post. But the demanding new post was now on offer. His notice to the staff said he had for some time been interested in returning to Scotland, and that the BBC's offer coincided with major changes in Scottish affairs and a new vitality in Scottish life. The first Scottish assembly would probably be elected in 1977, with greater governmental authority devolved from Westminster to Edinburgh. The BBC had said it would give greater autonomy to Scotland. 'The opportunity to share in these developments and to help in shaping them – both within the BBC and in Scottish affairs – is one that I most warmly welcome.'*

Newspaper editors are normally appointed by the proprietor, as Hetherington had been. The *Guardian* no longer had a single proprietor, but even though Laurence had been emphatically relieved of an executive role at the end of 1967 he had remained chairman until 1973 and his spirit continued to move upon the face of the waters. As early as January 1970 he had circulated a

---

* He got it wrong of course, though in passing he could have been well satisfied with the way his successors at the *Guardian* handled the question. David McKie took over editorial responsibility for Scotland, and shortly before the referendum in March 1979 he wrote in a signed article (14 February): 'Seen from London as ever, the case for calling off the whole fraught and contentious exercise seems very strong. But from my own occasional samplings of Scotland over this past five years I find it hard to believe the mood has gone away. It exists; it ought to be recognised by a democratic government. And the devolution settlement – though sadly flawed by the Government's failure to recognise valid objections on the system of financing, the method of election, and much more – is the only presently available route to recognising it.'

document to the Scott Trust noting the alleged friction between Hetherington and Peter Gibbings. He wrote:

> The *Guardian* is run by two people, Alastair and Peter Gibbings, with equal
> status. The *Guardian* is going through a very difficult time, when its existence
> could be threatened if it does not manage its affairs skilfully. Success depends
> on a fruitful partnership between Alastair and Peter, between editor and
> manager. At the moment the partnership works reasonably well and is
> successful. But it works with a lot of friction, and there is a possibility that this
> friction could one day develop into an open row between the two men. If this
> happens, and I do really fear that it could happen, either one of them will resign
> in a huff, which could be disastrous for the paper, or else the dispute will land
> straight in the lap of the Trust.

Laurence had frequently used his communications to the Trust almost as a
form of transcendental meditation; in this case, since neither Gibbings nor
Hetherington was a member of the Trust and would therefore not receive a
copy of the document, he could have been justly accused of stirring the pot.

But since there was no single proprietor, new machinery had to be devised.
In fact it had been put in place two years earlier when it became known that
Hetherington had considered taking the offer of a vice-chancellorship but
declined. It was decided in February 1973 that the people who needed to be
consulted were the trustees, the group directors, the *Guardian* operating
board directors, senior members of the editorial staff, and the NUJ chapel (the
singular was used in the document, although there were separate chapels in
London and Manchester). From this formula there emerged a sort of electoral
college to represent the various interests. It would have seven members: the
Trust chairman, possibly a second trustee, the group chairman and deputy
chairman, the retiring editor, the managing director of the *Guardian* and one
senior member of the *Guardian* editorial staff who would be 'ostensibly
nominated by the Trust and Board, but because of time in practice probably
selected by the other members of the committee'. (In law the board would
have the responsibility, acting with the agreement of the Trust.) In principle
that remained the system but the composition of the college had to be hastily
revised when Hetherington announced his resignation on 13 March 1975.

The Father of the London NUJ chapel, M.J. Downing, was first instructed
by his committee to ask whether elected representatives of the two chapels
could join, and was told by Hetherington that they could not because there
was not time: it would mean reconvening the board and the Trust to vary the
agreement they had reached two years earlier. The Trust then met on Friday
14 March and agreed on the composition of what came to be called the
Advisory Group. Jo Grimond and David Ayerst were asked to serve as
additional Trust members, and John Fairhall to double as an extra trustee and
representative of the London editorial staff. The body was, however, not yet
complete. Downing and his Manchester counterpart, Robert Armstrong,

persisted in their argument that chapel representatives should be included. This was not a request which, given the character of the paper and a recent dialogue about 'participation', could be unceremoniously dismissed. Whatever was decided had, moreover, to be decided quickly.

In the event each chapel was asked to put forward a list of names for the advisory group with one or more names 'starred' to indicate a preference. (This was not unlike the device adopted some years later by James Callaghan and the General Synod of the Church of England for the appointment of bishops!) The chapel fathers' conversations, face to face in London and by telephone from Manchester, were with Hetherington, who in turn was in touch with the Trust chairman. An understanding had long ago been reached among trustees that in matters affecting the control and management of the company and its papers they should not concede representation as of right to the chapels or allow them to mandate any of their members who might find themselves in executive positions. Some people remained anxious about confidentiality: were the NUJ men there as representatives or delegates? There had, however, grown up over the years a tradition of consultation, albeit informal, between editor and staff which could hardly be set aside on such an occasion as this. But the management was not happy at the introduction of a new editorial element, and both Gibbings and Taylor expressed annoyance at having neither been invited to attend the Friday Trust meeting nor been consulted about the discussion with the NUJ fathers.

The London chapel put forward a list of eight nominees, with the name of David McKie starred. Robert Armstrong was unable to call a chapel meeting but after consulting his committee put forward the names of David Bridgeman and Peter Hildrew. On Saturday the Advisory Group co-opted McKie and Bridgeman. With the additional trustee already nominated it now numbered ten instead of seven, which could have led to an embarrassing tied vote, and in fact came as near to doing so as was mathematically possible. The ten were: Richard Scott, chairman of the Trust; Peter Gibbings, chairman of the company; Gerry Taylor, managing director of the *Guardian*; Jo Grimond, trustee and parent board director; David Ayerst, trustee; John Fairhall and Dennis Johnson, nominated by the Trust to represent the London and Manchester staffs respectively (though Fairhall was also a trustee); David McKie, chosen by the London editorial staff; Dai Bridgeman, chosen by the Manchester staff; and Alastair Hetherington, outgoing editor. The group met on Monday morning and by instantly agreeing that all proceedings were to remain permanently confidential placed an apparently insuperable obstacle in the way of any future discussion of the matter. For present purposes that pledge of confidentiality will be taken to apply to the protection of the interests of the candidates. The formal procedure for finding a new editor lasted about a week, from 13 to 21 March, though those involved say it seemed like a couple of months.

Anyone of the rank of assistant editor or above on either of the company's papers was entitled to a hearing. Of the *Guardian*'s four assistant editors, Brian Jones and Geoffrey Taylor decided not to stand. Peter Preston (production editor), Jean Stead (news editor), Harry Jackson (features editor, a post considered as of equal rank with the others) and Peter Jenkins, columnist, joined John Cole, deputy editor since 1969, among the candidates. Hella Pick was nominated by Lord Kennet (Wayland Young) and Michael Foot by the Warden of Nuffield College, Oxford, Sir Norman Chester.

The first job was to write down the long list of everybody who had applied to either Richard Scott or Hetherington. This ran to two dozen names, including two strong outside candidates. One of these was David Watt of the *Financial Times*, later Director of the Royal Institute of International Affairs, who made a strong favourable impression on the interviewers but whose claims did not override those of existing members of the staff. Another strong outsider was on *The Times*. A third, who did not personally apply but was favoured by Hetherington, was Harold Evans of the *Sunday Times*. Evans was eliminated on the ground that the only course would have been to appoint him without further ado: he was too senior in the newspaper world to be made to hang around the Charing Cross Hotel until the room booked for its interviews (for the *Guardian* had a long-standing weakness for railway hotels) should become vacant. The Advisory Group made its own headquarters at the Great Northern Hotel. It appointed Richard Scott and David Ayerst to conduct the interviews, in which Jo Grimond also took some part, sound out other members of the staff, and report back.

The London NUJ chapel sent four representatives to talk to members of the group. They said they wanted an 'insider', whom they defined as a member of the *Guardian* staff. They did not want an Olympian editor or an ideological editor who would lay down a line for every editorial department. They saw in John Cole a man who would fight the editorial corner against the management. The features department, Preston's power base, supported him but nevertheless believed that Cole would make a good editor. The City office, then located in its own premises at London Wall, enjoyed a long-standing private grievance in that none of the candidates, and indeed few others from the land of the living, had ever been seen there. On balance, though, the four from the London chapel agreed that the staff of all editorial departments taken together admired Cole but favoured Preston. Members of the advisory group noted from their own consultations that although that was the case, opinion among most of the paper's heavyweights went the other way: they admired Preston but favoured Cole. Manchester opinion on balance favoured Cole, possibly reflecting the perceived cultural differences between the two centres, though it needed constant emphasis at the time that either man would be fully acceptable.

It became evident in the interviews, as reported to the group, that all the principal candidates realised that the paper was approaching some kind of watershed and that the new editor would be required to lead it in directions which were not yet familiar or even discernible. Much attention was given to the candidates' political stance. The paper had not long emerged from a period of keen political activity and some disagreement which, though friendly, was critical to the direction in which the paper would move.

Two general elections had been held in 1974. Wilson emerged from the February poll with a minority government and from October with an overall majority of three. During the first campaign Hetherington strongly favoured a centrist policy, summed up in his leader headline (27 February 1974): 'Class conflict is not the road for Britain', in which the Liberals under Jeremy Thorpe would hold the balance of power in the Commons. From this position the influence they exercised 'ought to be a healing one and not divisive'. The Liberals' programme included electoral reform, industrial partnership, and parliaments for Scotland and Wales (as well as the ancient mantra recited at Liberal assemblies: the taxation of site values) and Hetherington hoped they would be wise enough to ration their demands rather than thrust the whole platform at whichever party led at the polls. The result, minor parties apart, was:

	VOTES	SEATS
Labour	11,634,726	301
Conservative	11,963,207	296
Liberal	6,063,470	14
S. & W. Nationalists	803,396	9

Labour thus failed to gain an overall majority. Different people read the result in different ways but Hetherington enlarged on the theme of taking a middle road. 'Logically,' he wrote on 4 March, 'the situation points to a Grand Coalition of all three parties, possibly with Mr Thorpe at its head. Although it is unlikely to come about, it would represent the nearest approach to what the public appears to want.' Before Heath had surrendered the keys of Number Ten the *Guardian* argued that 'a Lib–Lab arrangement, with [Scottish and Welsh] Nationalist backing, remains the best way out'. When Heath finally went, the leader columns lamented that a coalition was not to be, but hoped one might come about within the life of the Parliament. Wilson preferred a minority government, though a slightly different version of the *Guardian*'s Lib–Lab formula was adopted by Callaghan later in the decade.

The Hetherington formula was anathema to Cole as it was to Ian Aitken, political puritans both, who regarded parley with the Liberals as idle, possibly sinful, self-indulgence. Cole took the view that when the press, apart from the *Daily Mirror*, was heavily weighted on the Tory side, the *Guardian* had an obvious and simple duty to bear the standard of the Left; he quoted C.P.

Even-handed political cartoons from John Kent on 8 October and 31 December 1973.
Copyright © John Kent, 1973.

Scott's desertion of the Liberals to that end. Certainly, he would argue, Wadsworth had been entitled to say that Labour had run out of wind and that the Tories should be allowed a short time on sufferance, but actually to propose giving power to the party with the fewest votes seemed to him indefensible.

The argument had been several times rehearsed during the winter of 1973–4; it was rehearsed again during the summer of 1974 over Hungarian delicacies at the Gay Hussar restaurant in Greek Street. (Under the influence of Peter Preston and Christopher Driver, who had run a food column under the name of Archestratus, the heads of department were no longer reliant on the midsummer roast beef and Yorkshire pudding of the Great Northern Hotel – or when that was unavailable the Great Eastern at Liverpool Street.) While accepting the virtue of what Cole was saying Hetherington preferred to cleave to the other strand in *Guardian* tradition in which the desirable object is first decided upon and the means to achieving it then worked out. That dialectical process was an enduring characteristic of Hetherington's leaders, and had been of Monkhouse's. What was desirable in this case was the end of the stop–go, Left–Right, public–private ideological uncertainties of post-war British politics, and if the Liberals, reflecting the public mood, were to be the catalysts for turning 'party polemics' into 'conciliation and harmony' then let them be put in a position where they could be of use. This policy was regarded by Cole as perverse, and probably the language used to express it as naïve; consequently the difference between him and Hetherington was not resolved. Hetherington records[2] that Jean Stead and Keith Harper stayed with Labour, as did Harry Jackson and David McKie and probably Brian Jones. Geoffrey Taylor argued that Labour was more irresponsible in opposition than the Conservatives but supported the general Hetherington line; Peter Preston thought Hetherington's leaders were insufficiently critical of Labour. On the way back to the office Hetherington said to Cole that the roll-call had gone 7 to 3 in Cole's favour; Cole claimed half of Preston, making it 7½ to 2½. Hetherington says of Cole:

> John was always a friendly critic, except once or twice over Ireland; and part of his great value to me, in addition to his high qualities as a journalist, was that he gave plain and candid advice. He was important also because he knew more than I did about the way industrial workers lived and about the trade union movement, and he compensated for my more academic background. His criticism was sometimes a grindstone on which to sharpen and polish my opinion; but it was much more than that, for he was one of the major creative forces at work inside the *Guardian* office. Our differences over the 1974 elections were not painful.[3]

It would be fair to add that Peter Preston was regarded in the office as a man of personal rather than of political conviction.

Apart from political stance the other thing the advisory body was interested in was the less tangible quality of flair, about which the management was especially keen and which nobody doubted Preston had in good measure. A year or two earlier, before the luncheon migration from King's Cross to Soho, he had summed up his feelings about the *Guardian* by saying what it lacked was zing.

By Thursday 20 March the short list had been reduced to two – John Cole and Peter Preston – who were invited to state their case before the Advisory Group as a whole. That privilege was not given to Brian Redhead, at the time editor of the *Manchester Evening News*, though he was formally interviewed (at the Midland Hotel, naturally). There is no doubt that Redhead considered himself well qualified for the post; in his time on the *Guardian* he had never hesitated to make that clear. He was the editor of one of the group's newspapers and a member of the group's board. His incisiveness as well as versatility became well known later at the BBC. But his chances were never seriously considered by the working party and it must be supposed that the most senior management and editorial opinions were not in his favour. When the group took its vote, Preston won by a tennis score, and three of Cole's votes came from the four editorial members of the group. In a note for posterity written a year afterwards Hetherington said he thought the procedure had worked well and that John Cole was satisfied he had had fair consideration. The *Guardian* had avoided the mistake later made by the *Observer* of demanding that all candidates should declare themselves publicly. 'Such a course,' Hetherington says, 'would have made still less feasible the consideration of an established national newspaper editor', from which it must be inferred that he still wished closer attention had been given to Harold Evans.

Jo Grimond read a different lesson from the procedure. Two or three years before, when the college was still a theoretical exercise, he had argued in favour of advertising the vacancy. Peter Jenkins, he said, who had been with him in Germany when Hetherington resigned, had expected that applications for the post would be invited and had put his own name forward only when Grimond had suggested he should (and although he might have done so in any case, Grimond says, he might by then have been too late). The decision of the *Observer* to advertise the post did not mean that all candidates must declare themselves in public.

For the future Grimond was concerned lest it should be almost impossible to appoint outsiders.[4]

> The general agreement seemed to me that an outsider must have an outstanding advantage over those within the paper. But I believe there is a danger that papers, like all other organisations, may become ingrown. Further, for the general good of the country and industry a certain amount of cross-posting may be desirable. With the composition of the committee I have a feeling it may be difficult.

Grimond's last word on the procedure was to raise another doubt:

There is also the question as to whether the outgoing editor should play such an active role in choosing his successor. In this case it worked well. No doubt he should be consulted. But it did occur to me in discussing with various candidates how they would operate if they got the editor's chair that they might be somewhat inhibited in criticising the present editorial direction to members of the Board who were going to report back to a committee including the editor.

Given the narrowness of the vote Grimond may have feared a situation in which the outgoing editor was also chairman of the Trust (as Wadsworth had been) and thus would have a casting vote on his successor.

On 21 March 1975, when the white smoke rose from Gray's Inn Road, Preston's peers in Fleet Street were happy to send their congratulations. John Cole left soon afterwards for the *Observer* and then the BBC. David McKie became deputy editor, a rank he shared with Brian Jones. William Rees-Mogg offered a piece of avuncular advice which was probably more disinterested than might at first seem. Never be afraid, the editor of *The Times* told the editor of the *Guardian*, to appear boring.

This method of choosing an editor was seen as a success and was adapted for the *Manchester Evening News* soon afterwards when Redhead, feeling rebuffed by the *Guardian*, had a row with management and left. The main change was that with only one NUJ chapel only two journalists were co-opted instead of four. When Redhead's successor, Douglas Emmett, retired in 1984 the procedure was used again, but this time it did not work. The NUJ put forward four names to the Trust, which selected two. Candidates were again promised confidentiality, but one of them, already an evening paper editor elsewhere who was well thought of for the post, found that his own NUJ chapel had been asked from Manchester what they thought of him, and whether he was the sort of man who was likely to be friendly to the union.

Michael Unger, who was appointed from the *Liverpool Echo*, had the edge in experience of the North-west and effusive apologies had to be offered to his rival. The Trust resolved to be more cautious about NUJ representation in future. The formula has nevertheless been open to the criticism that it is excessively punctilious. A trustee with wide experience of the intellectual world outside the newspaper business said some years after these events that he never ceased to be astonished by the secretiveness of journalists. In any other activity, he said, you applied for a job, people knew you applied for a job, and if you failed to get it that was just hard luck. Only in Fleet Street was a job application regarded as a token of betrayal.

CHAPTER 17

Libera Me

Why did these discontented wives ever embark on matrimony in the first place? They were obviously of sufficient intelligence to appreciate the so-called limitations of the daily round of a housewife. May I remind them that owing to financial limitations, many wives are compelled to engage in full-time employment outside the home. How many of these women would be only too happy to be merely housewives and so be able to give their families and homes the time and attention needed for full comfort and happiness?

> — Letter from 'Contented Housewife', Women's page,
> 6 July 1956

Feminists to-day face a dilemma which may be insoluble. On the one hand, they themselves continue to make claims and forward proposals to further equality between the sexes. On the other hand, the public, and in particular feminine, interest in their activities seems not only negligible but declining. To some extent feminists are accustomed to being a minority group, but to-day their organisations are recruiting little idealism or even membership from the type of educated woman who might reasonably be expected to be interested in matters of equality; while the uneducated woman remains almost completely untouched by the whole movement for equality.

> — Thelma A Hunter, The Decline of Feminism,
> *Guardian*, 22 March 1957

To be young, female and a hackette when the Women's Movement was getting into high gear was very heaven, the icing on the Sixties cake which, for all its excitements, hadn't done much more for women than shove us into bed with a lot of stoned hippies playing rotten guitar.

> — Jill Tweedie on her time with the *Guardian*, from the
> *Observer*, 17 February 1991

Mary Stott was editor of the women's page from 1957 to 1972, performing a far longer stint than any of her successors. Her retirement was only the beginning of a new career in which she invigorated any number of feminist causes and organisations, including Women in Media and the Fawcett

Society, the repository of the women's suffrage movement, and wrote under the Virago imprint. It might therefore be supposed that she acted as spokesperson for all the souls who felt themselves newly liberated by the 1960s, and that the reputation the *Guardian* acquired in that decade and after, among friends as pathfinder of women's lib and among opponents as brazen hussy, would belong to her.

That would be both an oversimplification and an injustice. (She would probably have disowned the term spokesperson, because she would not allow feminist convictions, to which of course she held, to distort the language, which she could use to great effect.) Mary Stott did establish a close partnership with her readers such as only a handful of journalists have achieved. But they were not necessarily the readers the paper as a whole was looking for, certainly not those the advertisement and marketing departments wanted.

One of Mary Stott's first innovations was a series called Women Talking, which not only encouraged readers to air what was on their minds but led to the creation of several important social organisations. One of the prime examples came in a letter to the women's page on 26 February 1960 from Maureen Nicol at Eastham in Cheshire saying: 'Perhaps housebound housewives with liberal interests and a desire to remain individuals could form a national register, so that whenever one moves one can contact like-minded friends.' This drew an avalanche of letters – 400 in one week – to the home of the astonished Mrs Nicol and she set up a network of regional organisers of what came to be called the National Housewives' Register. Betty Jerman reported in the paper two and a half years later:

> Now the number of members is unknown, since Mrs Nicol gave up counting and only guesses at four or five thousand. She had two young children under three, a three-bedroomed house and no help . . . she was often several pounds in debt for writing paper, envelopes and duplicating ink. In her two years as organiser she was anxious about money, overworked and, she admits, probably very irritable at times. But she still does not regret writing that letter. Housewives working together, she feels, can tackle and in many cases partially solve their own particular troubles.

By similar publicity and the involvement of readers the *Guardian* helped to set up the Pre-School Playgroups Association, Invalids at Home, the National Association for the Welfare of Children in Hospital, the National Council for the Single Woman and her Dependants, which became the National Council for Carers and their Elderly Dependents with London headquarters in Chilworth Street, Paddington, and the Disablement Income Group. Not so much the Swinging Sixties, Mary Stott commented, more the D-I-Y decade. By definition, however, the housebound women of Mrs Nicol's initiative were not the big spenders. The Mainly for Women pages did not necessarily attract to the paper's readership the younger women who were. Brian Redhead, the former features editor who was appointed planning correspondent on his return from a brief spell at the BBC, took into his portfolio the planning of the paper, and wrote to the editor on 20 January 1964: ' . . . There is something seriously wrong with the women's pages. All those jokes about Mainly for Unmarried Graduate Mothers are not far from the truth. There is something tatty, foolish, and out of date about the women's pages. I shrank from clashing head on over this when I was features editor.'

The remedy, he said, was to develop the New Lines consumer feature so that it occupied most of Monday's woman's page, and to 'get rid of those "women talking" columns and other nattering pieces and produce a really first-class consumer advice page and service'. Hetherington himself from time to time needled Stott for a different kind of page. On 24 July 1962:

> Perhaps we ought to exercise some caution over future contributions from Judith Cooke [properly Cook, a nuclear disarmer who wrote frequently, and to the letters column also, from Ding-Dong Cottage in Cornwall]. I'm told by people who know better that although her movement began on completely honest and straightforward lines it's partly getting into the hands of *Daily Worker* fans.

He wrote on 20 May 1964 complaining, perhaps not without reason, about the conjunction in the Mainly for Women page of that day's paper of articles by Jacqueline Warren and Lyn Davies. He calls it Mainly for Mournful Women. Warren starts 'My world is that of the educated, tidy, fairly conventional middle-aged . . . ' and goes on to describe her daughter's marriage before graduation and the general squalor of her marital home when the baby arrives. Davies is about a day in the life of a harassed mother, with much commonplace incident (which would, of course, strike chords with all the other harassed women who at that time made up a fair slice of the readership). Harford Thomas, the deputy editor, wrote to Stott on 7 July complaining that 'writers as negatively destructive as Gerda Cohen leave a disagreeable flavour'.

There then came a suggestion that contributors' pictures should appear. Mary Stott replied to Hetherington on 6 June 1966: 'So far I've always resisted suggestions from readers that they would like to see our faces in the paper. It seemed un-*Guardian*.' Hetherington replied mildly in favour of occasional pictures for the Women Talking feature. (It is wrong to suppose that all writers like pictures, or even by-lines. In her early days on the paper Nesta Roberts found that her name appeared on a fashion piece which Norman Dixon, then acting as women's page editor, had asked her to write, though it never appeared on her serious social and political pieces. When she remonstrated Dixon said it was intended to be more friendly. 'But I don't want to be friendly,' Nesta replied.)

Gradually it became more and more difficult to distinguish what were women's interests from what were the interests of the readership at large – a problem which the *Guardian* wrestled with for years and did not entirely solve. Somehow feminism modulated into the other libertarian 'isms' of the day. Contributors to the features pages began to fidget with the idea of drugs. The paper itself pronounced on the question on 2 July 1967 after Mick Jagger and Keith Richards of the Rolling Stones were given prison sentences (quashed on appeal) on drugs charges. Clearly it did not quite know what to say:

> The sentences in the Chichester drugs case have produced a public reaction which may confuse two matters that are better kept separate. One is the issues of whether Mr Jagger and Mr Richard were justly dealt with, which is now to be the subject of an appeal. It is not surprising that there has been strong criticism of the imposition of prison sentences for first offences, and the suspicion that the authorities, in the way in which they prosecuted the case, were attempting to make examples of young men who if they are unduly idolised in one age group are most certainly the subject of a quite ludicrous and unnecessary dislike in others. These are proper subjects of discussion in the Rolling Stones case.
>
> They are, however, almost totally irrelevant to our legal and social attitudes to drug-taking. If the Chichester case, with its excessive accompaniments of adulation and handcuffing, reduced the public discussion over drugs to the level of Swingers versus Squares this will be a memorial to the maladroitness of the authorities, but also a sizeable tragedy. There is no Straight Progressive Ticket for people to vote on the issue of drug-taking, and it is a serious enough social problem not to be dealt with at the level of a late night Saturday show on the BBC. To see the issues as an attack on middle-class values (and therefore good) or the dethroning of pop singers (and therefore good) is so much simplistic and dangerous nonsense.
>
> What is now needed is a rapid accumulation of as much scientific information as can be got on the physical, mental and social effects of different drugs. As a report in Saturday's *Guardian* showed, medical views on marijuana differ sharply . . .

On hard drugs, the leader referred to their 'frightful' effect and went on:

> There is no God-given principle, and no principle of liberal thought to support a man's right to damage or destroy himself. The law on drugs, like all our social legislation from the Factory Acts onward, must have regard to the rights of the individual, but also to the Biblical injunction against placing stumbling blocks in the way of the weak.

As its autumn promotion for 1967 the paper put its imprint on the 1960s in a 'roving exploration' into 'The Permissive Society' with contributions from, among others, Margaret Drabble, Adrian Mitchell, someone from *Private Eye*, Jonathan Miller, Richard Hoggart, Edward Boyle (then a Conservative MP who became Vice-Chancellor of York University), and the Bishop of Woolwich, Dr J.A.T. Robinson. The series began with Mary Quant talking to Alison Adburgham in a piece filling most of the leader page. 'But I *love* vulgarity,' the piece began. 'Good taste is death, vulgarity is life.' 'And attitudes to permissiveness?' she was asked. 'Do you in fact agree that this is a permissive society?'

> No, I don't. Or at least I would say it has only reached a reasonable level. And of course in some ways it is less permissive. We are less permissive to authority. The young won't be told now, they insist on thinking for themselves, they don't just accept things. This is more hopeful. And we are less permissive to violence. In the last war conscientious objectors were out on a limb of their own. Now America has produced a million or more people who have refused to go and kill. If there were a war in Europe tomorrow, there would be millions of European conscientious objectors. The Beautiful People are non-violent anarchists, constructive anarchists. They are the real breakthrough . . .

Alison Adburgham asked about fashion and whether, just as there was a new brutalism in architecture, painting, the theatre and music, there was an element of brutalism in fashion, and particularly in fashion photography. 'The intention is to shock, although the possibilities of shocking our present society without being pornographic must soon be exhausted.'
'Pornography is great if it's good,' Mary Quant replied.
'What is good pornography?'
'Good pornography is erotic but pleasing. Only ugliness is obscene. Yes, I'm for pornography if it's good, against if it's ugly.' Alison Adburgham went on:

> Earlier we had looked at some of the photographs in a glossy magazine and paused at one of a model girl in knickerbockers lying on her back with her legs straddled up in the air. 'You see,' Mary had said, 'this is a tremendously sexy picture, but in actual fact the girl is more inaccessible than she would be in any other period of fashion. Just look – she's got those thick tweed knickerbockers buckled tight under the knee, and she'll have stocking tights underneath and perhaps a pantie girdle as well. That's the thing about today's fashions – they're sexy to look at but more puritan than they've ever been. In European countries where they ban mini-skirts in the streets and say they're an invitation to rape, they don't understand about stocking tights underneath . . .
> 'The crutch. This is a very balanced generation, and the crutch is the most natural erogenous zone. Clothes are designed to lead the eye to it. The way girls model clothes, the way they sit, sprawl, or stand is all doing the same thing. It's not "come hither" but it's provocative. She's standing there defiantly with her legs apart saying "I'm very sexy. I enjoy sex. I feel provocative, but you're going to have a job to get me. You've got to excite me and you've got to be jolly marvellous to attract me. I can't be bought, but if I want you I'll have you."

Now that there is the pill, women are the sex in charge. They, and only they, can decide to conceive.'

Adrian Mitchell's piece in the series, a whole-page Guide to the Underground, began with his biographical list of 'the priests and prophets of permissiveness' – a long list which included Blake, Freud, Lenny Bruce, Alex Comfort, Bertrand Russell, Benjamin Spock, Allen Ginsberg, Bob Dylan, the Beatles, John Arden, and Fidel Castro, 'the nearest man on earth to being a politician in power who is at all respected by the Underground', whose revolution was '*merciful*'. Mitchell tackled censorship – *Fanny Hill* available only in an expensive edition; the BBC film *The War Game* shown only to an audience of defence correspondents, not TV critics – and drugs.

Mention the Underground and most of us are conditioned to think of drugs. Certainly cannabis is becoming easier and easier to obtain and pot-smokers are becoming more discreet in their smoking habits. Nobody in the Underground doubts that pot will become legal. On the other hand hardly anyone in the Underground believes that heroin is anything but a particularly horrific way of suicide.

LSD is different. There are evangelists around who won't trust anyone who hasn't been on an acid trip. There are plenty of others who believe that a man should be in control of his own visions. After all, runs the argument, everyone has visions, but most people dismiss them as daydreams and so they don't work on them or develop them.

The reference to Castro gave rise to some small-scale internecine warfare when the readers' letters started appearing. David Holden, foreign correspondent, did not think Castro was a merciful revolutionary at all. His executions had continued until at least 1966, nearly eight years after he came to power, and the total must now run well into four figures. The middle class had been systematically destroyed and elderly people subjected to cruelties and indignities when they were 'mercifully' permitted to join refugee flights to the United States.

Mr Mitchell and the Underground may believe that Castro is genuine in his beliefs, that the revolution is good for Cuba, or that – as your correspondent Mr Richard Gott seems to imply in his overwrought dispatches from Bolivia – it should be exported forthwith to the rest of Latin America. These are all tenable views. What is not tenable is that Castro is significantly merciful.

Hetherington asks in his memoirs:

Did moral standards . . . decline in the sixties? And did the *Guardian*, as some critics alleged, contribute to the decline? Personally, I do not believe that morality suffered, and there was a great gain in the sixties through the dissolving of Victorian hypocrisies, the reform of laws on obscenity, censorship,

divorce, abortion, and homosexuality, and the growth of artistic freedom . . .
If the *Guardian* provided some stimulus to social change, so much the better.[1]

It would be silly to argue with that judgment. The fact remains that the
Guardian entered the 1970s as a very different paper from the one Wadsworth
had edited in the 1950s or which Hetherington had guided into the 1960s. It
was subsequently identified with everything, good and bad, constructive and
destructive, that happened in that decade.

On 7 October 1967, the day the Permissive Society series was announced,
Hetherington wrote to Mary Stott about his anxieties.

> I said once again [at a page planning conference in the London office] that you
> must have your proper measure and was told with considerable heat . . . that
> the material coming forward simply wasn't worth putting in the paper and it
> was ridiculous to waste space on it.
>
> I myself haven't any substantial complaints . . .
>
> I am aware also, as no doubt you are, that there is quite a strong feeling both
> in the Features Dept and in some other quarters that we are still too stringently
> bluestocking and don't care enough for the younger readers (men and women)
> in the women's pages. The undergraduate brother of one of our own staff was
> reported as having said that he was fed up with the *Guardian* because it was
> completely out of touch. I don't really know why he was fed up and so asked for
> elucidation. But perhaps it's symptomatic.
>
> Anyway . . . I have encountered a disconcerting amount of resistance to
> giving the women's page what it is supposed now to have in the way of space.

Mary Stott's reply a few days later, after dealing with a few procedural
matters, said:

> . . . 4. Under the influence of CPD [Christopher Driver, features editor] we are
> moving to a more 'professional' women's page, covering various interests
> (eating out, wine, fashion, household, design) rather more fully, more effi-
> ciently and more decoratively . . . Only you can decide if this *is* what the
> *Guardian* needs, and whether we should now finally abandon the old image of
> the women's page which depended mainly on warmth, sincerity, and personal
> involvement . . .
>
> 5. This is the most difficult thing I have to say, and I do ask you to bear with
> me as a colleague for more than ten years. Suspended, as it were, between
> London and Manchester, I am very unhappily aware of a deep difference of
> opinion on what today's *Guardian* ought to be. I believe I am right in saying
> that many of us, perhaps most, in the north, feel that we know our people and
> what they want, and that what they want is different from what our colleagues
> in London think our more sophisticated metropolitan readers want. It almost
> seems as if there are sometimes two warring *Guardians*. It must be possible to
> weld them into one, but I don't believe we have succeeded yet.

As if to illustrate the clash of cultures, on the day of Adrian Mitchell's piece the paper carried a by-election study by Joseph Minogue entitled (in the Manchester edition) 'The three faces of Gorton' with an evocative picture by Tom Stuttard of old folk against their back-to-back houses.

The barrage was fairly unremitting. Hetherington wrote to Mary Stott again on 15 November 1967 asking for a new picture of Gillian Tindall, a regular writer on the page, 'which makes her look less austere or less Victorian'. In August 1968 Gerry Taylor, having had a complaint from his women's sales executive, which he said was 'emotional in the extreme', about the difficulty of attracting ads to the women's page, had an analysis made for Hetherington and Peter Gibbings of the proportion of advertising and editorial in the *Guardian* and its competitors. The total of column-inches devoted to women's page topics in the previous months had been roughly the same for all three papers but the proportion of advertising was *Guardian* 9 per cent, *Times* 39 per cent, *Telegraph* 44 per cent.

Taylor noted two possible reasons for the lack of advertising:

> Our women's readership figures are uncompetitive or low compared with *The Times* or *Telegraph* or . . . the content was not attractive to advertisers . . . The largest volume of editorial space in the *Guardian* covers subjects of sociological and general interest and this has much to do with the fact that the women's pages tend to carry more advertising than other newspapers for products which have no specific women's appeal.

His analysis showed the editorial content of the qualities' women's page to be (in percentages):

	FASHION ETC.	HOME, DESIGN	BEAUTY	COOKERY	SOCIO-LOGICAL	GEN. INT.
Guardian	13.4	12.6	2.1	7.6	34.2	30.1
Times	27.6	18.5	0.7	8.7	13.9	30.6
Telegraph	34.8	13.1	1.2	21.2	11.1	18.6
All three	25.5	14.7	1.3	12.7	19.5	26.2

At the point in Gerry Taylor's memo where his sales executive said there was too much emphasis on the sociological problems of old age, the pill, abortion, etc., Hetherington wrote an emphatic 'No' in the margin. Where she wanted more attention to clothes, beauty and good fashion photographs he wrote an emphatic 'Yes'. Mary replied to the criticisms:

> I expect we are now all agreed that the *Guardian* seems to have reached the limit in readers who like it as it now is and that as increased circulation is vital we

must try the effect of some changes in its content, appearance and personality
. . . But it must have its own strong, effective personality *right through*. If we
changed the pattern of the women's page to give a preponderance of fashion,
furnishings, food, beauty care and so on we should certainly lose some of
our faithfuls to *The Times*, which still has a lot of serious women's page
content . . .'[2]

Several months later, in February 1969, Mary Stott quoted Lady Simon to the
editor as having been told that the *Guardian* had lost 20,000 women readers
to *The Times*. Hetherington replied next day saying the figure was far worse
than that. According to the National Readership Survey for 1967 the
Guardian lost 50,000 of its 374,000 women readers between the first and
second halves of 1967. Gerry Taylor advised that this figure should be treated
with caution because it was unduly severe and might be the result of a
sampling error. Nevertheless, he said, that was the figure the industry relied
on and there was no doubt *The Times*'s changes to its women's pages had made
their impact.

Just as the change in design in 1969 came about as a management initiative,
so it could be argued that further moves in the libertarian direction were
marketing-led. After the design change, ads appeared in the trade press,
Punch and elsewhere extolling the new *Guardian* and asking 'How far will the
Guardian go?' They were as much fun as anything in the paper, for example
the ads postulating an agony aunt for a feature called Your Guardian Angel
Advises:

> Dear Guardian Angel, Can you help me? I have just started going out with boys
> but I'm very ignorant of the facts of life which embarrasses me. I can't talk these
> things over with my parents. Please, what is Dialectical Materialism? –
> 'Perplexed', Preston.

> I am sending you privately a list of books to read on this subject but there is a
> good general guide entitled *Das Kapital*.

> Dear Auntie Guardian, I'm one of your male readers – one of your devoted male
> readers. The sympathetic advice you give every week has convinced me that you
> and I are soulmates. Will you marry me? – 'Hopeful', Hatfield.

> You've got a problem – I'm a feller.

The series had a *Guardian* spot-the-ball contest from a girls' lacrosse match,
the entries to be judged by Neville Cardus and John Arlott. It had a horoscope
(e.g. Cancer: Assert yourself. Join the Parent Teachers Association or appeal
against the rent; Taurus: A disturbing influence from overseas. Romantic Leo
types should be reminded of their responsibilities towards the au pair girl;

Scorpio: A good week for political activity – Monday, Wednesday and Friday are favourable for sit-ins). It had a *Playboy*-type centre fold – '. . . a new layout which makes Britain's best-written daily paper easier on the eye. Take a peek tomorrow.'

Another series for the trade press asked 'Why don't you advertise in the *Guardian?*', and produced some answers: 'Because the Editor is a Russian Spy planning to blow up the IPA [Institute of Practitioners in Advertising]', 'Because Harry Shaw of the Forty-Fourth always blamed it for the loss of India', 'Because Aunt Emily put her back out laughing at Papas'.

Whether or not it was designed that way (almost certainly it was) this amounted to a management prospectus for the editorial department to follow, which it did, though sometimes the liberationism had a touch of solemnity. In September 1971 the paper ran another 'permissiveness' series based on the obscenity trial of the underground magazine *OZ*, in which the three editors were given gaol sentences, later quashed by the Court of Appeal. The first piece was by Richard Neville, chief of the magazine's three editors, and its references to Lord Longford are to the 'commission' which he set up to study pornography in Britain and abroad. It was a joyless piece, 2,000 words long, in which Neville wrote:

> The Angry Brigade are catapulted to public enemy number one and have not killed a soul. Because the national press is so cowardly of sub judice over questions, we cannot here inquire fully into some of the extraordinary methods used by police in pursuing this chimeric quarry, but the most banal civil liberties of subjects have been trampled upon with relish and it is left to *Time Out*, with comparatively minuscule circulation, to bring police atrocities to its readers' attention. Sadly, bombing buildings (not people) is becoming increasingly accepted as a tactic within the underground to convince backroom bureaucrats that revolution is not rhetorical and that generalised State violence must sometimes be answered in kind. This is not to justify the foolhardy exploits of exasperated powder monkeys, but to question the criteria by which the perpetrators of social outrage are rated. A bomb hurled at an inanimate symbol of oppression is called violence. Because of a cost-cutting design, a bridge collapses killing scores of workers and is called an accident . . .
>
>   . . . A sexual ethic designed by the superstitious to be imposed on the ignorant has not the mildest relevance in the seventies. If you have no wish to preserve the inheritance of property, why preserve the family? If you have no wish to preserve the family, of what use is even lip service monogamy? If aggression has outlived its usefulness, what better substitute than exhilarating exploration of our sexuality in word, deed, and fantasy?
>
> My visit to Copenhagen preceded Lord Longford's last by 21 months. Who knows in what sexual climate were reared those who favoured whips and pigs, but the audience looked more like the products of British public schools than potential readers of *OZ*. It all seemed old-fashioned, rather than particularly

squalid. My visit took place on Christmas Eve. At the end of the performance, the sweating naked cast began singing carols, with the audience joining in, while brightly wrapped presents were distributed to us all (a generous selection of porno books) proving that Sin City believes in Santa Claus.

With the redesign the women's page underwent one of its many metamorphoses. It first became Woman's Guardian, which was a less accurate description than the previous Mainly for Women but conformed to the new style of labelling the sections and putting the word Guardian on each to derive as much advantage as possible from its display in public places. After Mary Stott's retirement the page was edited by men from the features department, principally Peter Fiddick. Then in March 1973 Linda Christmas, who had been working on the page, took control of it and in October of that year changed its title again. As she explained to readers: 'The page still discusses topics which might be regarded as primarily of interest to women, but it also contains a great deal which is aimed at anyone who takes a caring and lively interest in the complexities of our society.' The paper, she said, had for years been 'hermaphrodite in its corporate attitude'. The women's page had been edited by men, two of the news editors (Nesta Roberts and Jean Stead) had been women, and 'the coverage of such arcane topics as the European community, domestic politics, NATO, the war in Vietnam and the vagaries of world economics' had been handled by whichever man or woman was felt best qualified at the time. That was true, and on the foreign beat the best-qualified person had often turned out to be Hella Pick, who had handled several of the topics Linda Christmas listed, and Africa, the UN and Washington as well. The ghetto-word was therefore done away with and the page renamed Guardian Miscellany. Its first appearance under that title gave an idea of how it would be run: two long complementary pieces by John Grigg and Jean Stead about the place of ritual in our lives. Guardian Miscellany ran Adam Raphael's consumer column, John Arlott's wine and Harold Wilshaw's food. The Monday page also continued to house Varoomshka, John Kent's long-running cartoon creation in which the delectable girl of that name, dressed in hot-pants or negligée, asked innocent questions which floored the politicians of the day. Kent put the leader-writers to shame: he could often say more in one cartoon, and certainly say it more memorably, than they could say in a thousand words. But most famously the page housed Jill Tweedie.

When the *Guardian* sent almost its entire features staff and several specialists to write about their topics from Belfast (it later did the same in Moscow and South Africa) Jill Tweedie was among them. An astonished Northern Ireland spectator described her as a one-woman torchlight procession, and that is how she blazed her way through the women's page during the 1970s and for much of the 1980s. When she hit the paper in 1969 she stood in relation to what had gone before as heavy metal to Handel. More than anyone else she personified not only the liberated Guardian Woman but the young, emancipated, agnostic, and for the most part profoundly worried clientele of both sexes who had taken over the baton of radicalism from the Manchester branch of the United Nations Association. Another paper wrote of her: 'Tweedie represents far more than the liberal angst of the traditional old *Guardian* reader. She was the doyenne of feminist journalists, bringing the hottest bulletins from the frontline of the sex war.'[3]

But not only the sex war. Every cause she could get to grips with.

> The sun beats down on Dorset – green meadows spread under blue skies and, in a pleat of a hill, one grey church steeple. A perfect summer's day and what more traditional a way to pass a perfect summer's day than watching, say, an otter being torn to pieces?

A youth from the saboteurs confronts a hunt follower.

> Doggedly, the youth continues. Are otters pests? No, says the lady. Well, do they taste good when you cook them? The lady's eyes, glazed until then, clear. She regards her kibitzer with warm amusement. My dear boy, you don't *eat* otters. Oh ho ho ho *no*. Really? says the youth in his thick way. They're not pests and they can't be eaten. What do you kill them for, then please? The lady's smile sets and she gazes with consuming interest at the horizon. Beside her the Major – a fine specimen of an Englishman with a curling moustache and a florid complexion – gazes with her. They are not related but they could be twins, two C. Aubrey Smiths, incredibly noble, with faces made for the quelling of natives or felling lions at a glance. They don't make 'em like that any more.[4]

And that, with an address at the bottom for anti-blood sports donations, was another interest group added to the *Guardian*'s list. Her politics were of a piece with her feminism, as she showed at what most others on the paper thought was a disastrous Labour party conference in 1980.

> In my time I have myself marched and protested and signed petitions for troops out of Ireland, more aid to the Third World, more industrial democracy, and equal rights for women, black people and gays. I have also marched or protested against nuclear weapons, the Common Market, private education, and the House of Lords. Some of you must have been there, too, because there was ever such a crowd.
>
> We thought, then, that They were listening. The Labour Party, that is, because most of us were loyal Labour voters. The kind that Mrs Shirley Williams praised at her Blackpool mini-conference last week, and how we all loved Mrs Williams. But at Blackpool we learnt – if we had our ears open – that They had never been listening. They had only patted our heads and made agreeing noises and said comforting things about freedom and democracy and righting wrongs while they got on with the real business of the Party, which is to make it look as much like the Tories as possible without actually losing our

votes. Because, though I, for one, have always marked my cross for Labour, what I was really doing was all they allowed me to do – vote *against* the Tories.

Indeed, I had more or less forgotten there was any more positive way to vote Labour until Tony Benn stood up at Blackpool and actually gave voice – on a real platform and in front of real politicians – to all my beliefs and principles. Well, you would have thought the skies had fallen in. Not only did the Centre not hold, it broke cover and ran in small circles, frothing at the mouth. How *disgraceful* of Benn to blow the gaff. How contemptible to air such views in *public* where the voters could hear. Argument, anger, conflict? It's not right to worry our pretty little heads with such things. I tell you, sir, the man's no gentleman.

But it was dispatches from the sexual battlefront which made her famous, even though they often described a different sort of war from the one her readers were expecting. As for instance when she watched a TV film of animals copulating and suddenly realised they were not enjoying it, that the female gorilla preferred her banana leaf and 'the bull got it over within two seconds flat'.

Pity the poor marriage counsellors, the sex advisers who continually grapple with people's sexual problems based on high expectation for a mundane activity. In come the couples who, after years of marriage, say the lust has gone out their union. Do they say 'naturally', or 'of course it has, you twits'? Not at all. Brainwashed as the rest, they scratch their dedicated heads and recommend sex clinics, advise grotesque positions, hand out illustrated booklets in full colour, advocate peculiar undies. Why not, they say, have sex in the middle of a field for a change? Or buy some technological gadgets for an extra frisson? Or do it on the bonnet of your car or in a plastic dustbin? Or ask a friend to join you for a wee touch of the voyeurs? . . . Next time you feel the glories of sex are passing you by, take a look at the faces of a couple of mating gorillas. It'll cheer you up no end.[5]

On 21 February 1971 Tweedie wrote one of her most influential pieces about the battering of women. It took up half a page and quoted harrowing evidence. 'Mum and us kids,' a seventeen-year-old girl told her, 'we've spent our lives dreading him coming home. One day when I was 14, I came home and found him hanging in the kitchen. Oh, we were glad.' This piece was in large part responsible for Erim Pizzey's decision to set up the first Shelter for Battered Wives and their Children at Chiswick later that year. Years later Jill Tweedie asked over a dinner table how it was that Alastair Hetherington had always appeared to be uneasy when she went to see him. Why did he squirm in his chair? Surely a liberated man like the editor of the *Guardian* should not be embarrassed in the presence of his women writers? 'It's the same with Peter Preston,' she said. Could Jill Tweedie really be so innocent? Her subject was sex, her speciality within it was male domination, and everything she wrote, she wrote with ten-tenths vigour. How could any man fail to be terrified at her approach?

Peter Preston became editor. As features editor he had been in at the end of the *ancien régime* but had been night editor during Linda Christmas's tenure of the page. He thought a reversion to straightforward women's interests was due, and Guardian Women came into existence. Suzanne Lowry, at that time No. 2 to Michael White on the diary, took over, edited the page with distinct flair, and then left. Preston was contemplating the succession yet again when David McKie recommended Liz Forgan, a leader-writer on the *Evening Standard* whom he had met at party conferences. Preston met her and concluded that she was the person to make the points that still needed to be made about the expanding nature of women's opportunities. She became women's page editor in February 1978 and she too was much admired in the trade and outside. But she made the mistake, from the paper's point of view, of interviewing and writing a profile of Jeremy Isaacs who was in process of setting up Channel Four TV. He was so taken with the piece that he offered her a job as a commissioning editor and she left in April 1980. She later became the first woman to join the Scott Trust.

It had been part of the paper's way of operating that all the incumbents on the page had not been women journalists but journalists who were women. Frances Cairncross was the economics leader-writer, columnist, and member of one of the husband and wife teams which the *Guardian* seemed to attract. (Others were Stanley and Gillian Reynolds and Mark and Val Arnold-Forster.) Cairncross's husband was Hamish McRae, the City editor. Whether her slightly un-*Guardian* and proto-Thatcherite economic views played a part in her transfer is not known but she was the next to put an imprint on the page. She was, however, a writer and an innovator. The women's page had always attracted to itself a large and faithful body of people who were more than readers, almost a fan club. The task of coping with the masses of mail, much of it passionate and intense, was one that daunted most women's page editors at the time. At all events, Frances Cairncross joined the *Economist* early in 1984. Her first successor was Jane McLoughlin from the City office, who wore black leather trousers and wrote a weekly column which was almost heavy rock in words. She held office for rather more than a year before returning to the City office as industrial relations correspondent and was in turn succeeded by the much-liked fashion editor, Brenda Polan, who was the first woman's editor to have joined the paper from 'women's' journalism, i.e. *Woman* magazine.

In the late 1970s and 1980s, when women's page editors would come and go, the character of the page was determined by its contributors. Polly Toynbee wrote alternately with Jill Tweedie: less excitable, more cerebral, but still appealing to roughly the same readership. Andrew Veitch pulled together every week an embarrassingly funny collection of sexist quotations from other

Posy Simmonds began her series of cartoons for the Guardian *in 1979. This one appeared on 26 November 1979. Copyright © Posy Simmonds, 1979.*

papers (occasionally the *Guardian* itself), public notices, and other sources under the heading Naked Ape. But asked to name what most cheered them up on a Monday morning most readers of the paper, men as well as women, would probably say Posy Simmonds. Posy, whose drawings were full of minute detail and whose words were full of anxiety, guilt and torn social conscience, chronicled the lives of an archetypal *Guardian*-reading family, the Webers, who lived in North London and occasionally escaped to be ripped off by the pseudo-locals, pseudo-yokels at the Cornish village of Tresodit. George Weber lectured in jargon-ridden sociology at a polytechnic. Wendy tried to instil liberal values into her awful progeny. Those were some of the women's page happiest days, for the consumer if not the producer.

Not strictly a women's feature, more a men's, but appearing in that part of the paper when it changed its nature slightly on a Saturday was Boston on Beer. Richard Boston started his intermittent freelance writing for the *Guardian* in 1965 but in 1973 was commissioned by an airline to write a guide to London pubs for use as promotional reading. He became aware not only that small classic pubs were being vandalised by the brewers but that the beer was no longer the hand-drawn and living beverage it was supposed to be but was beer delivered to the bar by air pressure in the kegs. Small breweries were being closed and variety was diminishing. A correspondence about these trends began in the *Guardian* and a reader wrote asking why the novice beer-drinker could not have the sort of guidance which Arlott gave to novices in wine. Boston discussed it with Michael McNay, then deputy features editor, and they launched a column which, though nominally and for the most part actually about beer, gradually took in the world at large.

The myth grew up that Boston's column led to the setting up of Camra, the campaign for real ale. That was inaccurate. Camra already existed when he started the column but he had not heard of it. When he first mentioned it, applications for membership flowed in, but Boston himself never became a member and could not therefore be accused by the brewers of being Camra's creature. Eventually he found himself being typecast and went on to other things. If he wanted a drink he would go to a Watney pub because only there was he safe from being buttonholed by beer-bores.

Food, like most other aspects of life in the 1980s, became open to the charge that the treatment of it was sexist. After Ambrose Heath Harold Wilshaw the paper had Prue Leith and Colin Spencer to look after food, but women's page editors began to complain that cookery gave the wrong image to their page. Accordingly the subject was hived off into a small department of its own and a wheel came full circle.

During the financial crises of the mid-1960s an edict was issued requiring departmental heads to stop using freelance contributions as far as possible and make fuller use of their own staff. Christopher Driver, features editor at the time, set the example by starting a food column. It was not a list of recipes, though there were some of those, so much as an exploration into food

18 June 1979. Copyright © Posy Simmonds, 1979.

including interviews with restaurateurs, competitions, and books. Driver wrote under the name Archestratus. Some of those on the staff who did not know who Archestratus was were embarrassed to ask, for the feeling half-persisted that some knowledge of the classics was desirable in people purporting to serve an intellectual readership. (Seyffert's *Dictionary of Classical Antiquities* (translated from the German) says of him: 'Archestratus, of Gela in Sicily, flourished about 318 BC and composed the humorous didactic poem Hedypatheia (= good cheer), supposed to describe a gastronomic tour round the then known world, with playful echoes of Homer and the dogmatic philosophers. The numerous fragments display much talent and wit.') Driver turned such an elegant and well-informed comment that Raymond Postgate recommended him as his successor as editor of the *Good Food Guide*. They exchanged courtesies in Greek. But although Driver was not for several years *on* the *Guardian* he was always *of* it and was the natural person to take charge of the weekly food page of the mid-1980s (no longer the monthly column of old time) and relieve the women's page editor of that chauvinistic and anachronistic burden.

CHAPTER 18

Islas Malvinas?

A FORCE from Argentina invaded the Falkland Islands on Friday 2 April 1982. In an emergency debate in the Commons the next day Dr David Owen said the government had to explain why no action had been taken a month earlier to counter the threat; there had been ample warnings.

That was true. Dr Owen quoted the *Guardian* of 25 February with the headline 'Falklands raid hint by Argentine Army'. But the paper had interested itself in the islands and wondered what to do about them for many more months than that. On 15 January 1976 a leader comment began:

> Within a few years, if Argentina plays its cards right, the British Falkland Islands will have become the Argentine Islas Malvinas. This bleak archipelago in the South Atlantic was seized by Britain in the nineteenth century and peopled with tough and sturdy British settlers. In those days we thought we needed it for strategic reasons. But it was over-valued even then, and we certainly don't want it now. It may be rich in exotic plankton, there may even be oil, but the time has long since passed when Britain could hang on to obscure pieces of territory marked pink on the other side of the globe.

The leader was written by Richard Gott, who had begun his lonely campaign as long ago as November 1968. He was living at the time in Santiago, during of period of absence from the paper, when the Queen arrived for a state visit to Brazil and Chile, though not, on Foreign Office advice, Argentina. She was accompanied by Lord Chalfont, the Foreign Office minister responsible for Latin America, and by a small press corps from *The Times, Telegraph, Mail* and *Express*. It emerged that Chalfont had arranged to visit the Falklands, taking the visiting pressmen with him, and Gott asked the *Guardian* foreign desk in Manchester to intercede with the Admiralty for him to go too. Thus in a most pleasant South Atlantic summer they sailed four days out from Montevideo in the ice-patrol vessel HMS *Endurance. The Times* and *Telegraph* were given officer accommodation; the *Guardian, Mail* and *Express* were given lesser quarters appropriate to their station. The entire party joined Lord Chalfont for poker each evening in the officers' mess.

After arrival in Port Stanley, Gott soon came to hear about a document which Chalfont was hawking around, and about the meetings he was holding with the islands' notables. Accordingly the *Guardian* of 27 November 1968 carried a startling cable from Gott about the British government's intentions:

> The terms of a draft agreement that would cede the Falkland Islands to Argentina have been the subject of prolonged and heated discussion here between Lord Chalfont and the islands' Executive Council . . .
>
> The Executive Council was sworn to secrecy. But I understand that it feels it will have to agree to Lord Chalfont's document although, as one member put it, 'We will have to put in a lot more safeguards than he was originally prepared to.'
>
> Lord Chalfont . . . has allowed the Council to believe that he is bending a little under their pressure, but basically he has forced them to accept not only that negotiations with Argentina were necessary but also that things could get worse if they were to collapse.

A few days later Gott wrote a feature about the islands, beginning with the service at Christ Church Cathedral on 'stir-up Sunday' the week before. Maybe, he mused, the vicar, in choosing the hymn 'The day thou gavest, Lord, is ended', had thought that his tiny flock would be comforted by the words of the last verse:

> So be it, Lord, thy throne shall never
> Like earth's proud empires pass away.

For the fact was that Lord Chalfont had come to tell them that the proud empire that had sustained them for so long was in the process of following the western sun beneath the horizon.

> The islanders loved him. So palpably honest, so dashing and debonair, he melted the suspicion from all hearts. Even the terrible old gang of sheepowners who have misruled the colony for years had to admit that they had more than met their match, prompting the irreverent thought that if they are going to be sold down the river the islanders would prefer it to be done by a lord . . .
>
> Rummaging through some old parish magazines I found that lack of concern in Britain appears to have been a constant complaint throughout the colony's history. Even in 1914, when it was in its heyday, at the time of the battle of the Falklands when Churchill packed off a fleet of ships to avenge the defeat at Coronel,* the islanders found it hard to excuse the ignorance of the outside world . . .
>
> The present highly unsatisfactory situation in which emigration has caused

---

* The engagement in November 1914 in which a naval squadron under Admiral von Spee inflicted a serious defeat on a British force off the Chilean coast which was avenged a month later by the sinking of the German cruisers *Scharnhorst* and *Gneisenau*.

an absolute decline in population is not without parallel in the past. I found, talking to young people in Stanley, that most of the brighter ones were already making plans to leave, not because of British equivocations but simply because they did not see an economic future for the islands.

The paper's editorial reaction was a good deal less far-sighted than Gott's story or Chalfont's document. No doubt it was influenced by the paper's general support of 'self-determination' but the leader pointed only to the weakness, not the strength, of the government's position. 'Repeatedly this year Ministers have said, in the Lords and the Commons (a) that the Falklands will not be handed over to Argentina without the consent of the people; (b) that the overwhelming wish of the people is to remain a British colony; and (c) that talks are being held with Argentina on the question of sovereignty. The syllogism is nonsensical.'

So much for the 1960s and 70s. In early 1982 Latin America was one of the main preoccupations of the foreign news pages, though the focus was not so much on Argentina as on the intervention, actual and threatened, of the United States in the civil strife of Nicaragua and El Salvador. Then on 3 March Jeremy Morgan reported from Buenos Aires:

> The Argentine Government has warned that it will 'put an end' to negotiations with Britain over the disputed sovereignty of the Falkland Islands and feel free to take other action unless a quick solution of the issue is found.
>
> In a strongly-worded statement which reflected exasperation at what is seen as British foot-dragging, the Foreign Ministry said yesterday that unless there was progress, Argentina would consider itself free to choose 'a procedure which better suited its interests'.
>
> Argentina has negotiated with Britain 'with patience, fidelity and in good faith' for more than 15 years under the terms of United Nations resolutions over its claim to the Falkland Islands, the Ministry added.

This phraseology, Morgan said, contrasted strongly with the polite tone of a joint statement by both countries after negotiations in New York the previous week, which it described as 'cordial and positive'. But it was not the first indication that the Argentinians might be losing their patience. 'Public opinion over the islands . . . is also starting to run high. The suspected presence of oil . . . has done little to keep tempers cool.' The fundamental difference at the talks was that Britain did not see them as necessarily leading to the transfer of sovereignty to Argentina, whereas that was exactly how Buenos Aires saw the purpose of holding negotiations in the first place.

A leader a few days later (Monday 8 March) enlarged on this theme. It noted that the talks had been going on since 1977 and that in the past the phrase 'cordial and positive' had meant that, while both sides had gone through the motions of asserting and rejecting claims to the sovereignty of the islands, in practice both would have been extremely grateful for any suggestions as to how the Falkland Islanders might be brought to accept Argentinian claims. The islands were indefensible against a serious Argentinian invasion. The only naval vessel on regular patrol in the area, *Endurance*, was about to be withdrawn as part of the 'penny-pinching' by the Defence Secretary, John Nott, to pay for Trident nuclear missiles. But

> as Mr Luce [Richard Luce, Minister of State] repeated in the House of Commons last Wednesday, it is inconceivable that any British government could now lend its name to a deal with Argentina without obtaining in some form the approval of both the islanders themselves and of the House of Commons. On this basis, the problem of the Falkland Islands is likely to be with us and souring Anglo-Argentinian relations for some time to come.

Minor diplomatic movement occurred in the next week or two and then, on Tuesday 23 March, the front page carried a mock-solemn piece by Patrick Keatley, the diplomatic editor, about the far-distant defence of British interests:

> British sovereignty has been defended in the Antarctic, national honour has triumphed, and a bumptious band of Argentinian scrap metal merchants have been sent packing by four brave Britons . . .
>   Sadly, this comic opera episode, so soothing to British pride, is certainly not the end of the story. The Argentinians came away from recent talks with Britain on the future of the islands saying that they reserved the right to take 'other measures' if swift progress in negotiations was not apparent. Buenos Aires certainly has the capacity to do far more than stage a half-baked flag raising ceremony on the remotest bit of an already remote group of islands.

David Fairhall, defence correspondent, confirmed that the scrap merchants were there under contract to dismantle some derelict buildings owned by the South Georgia Whaling Company. (Neither he nor anyone else on the *Guardian* recalled or possibly knew that GMEN had once before had reason to follow the fortunes of the South Georgia Whaling Company.)* By 31 March, when British government concern about the increasing Argentinian belliger-ence had for the first time become the lead story, the day's third leader commented:

> That the situation has many ludicrous aspects is clear. But this alone does not help those in charge to decide what, if anything, to do about it in the short-term. The right answer is probably little or nothing, beyond making protests for the record and waiting for the oncoming winter to persuade the Steptoes of the south that the point has been made and the time come to go home. The reported presence of units of the Argentine navy does not, in practice, much affect the position; any more than would the surprise arrival of a Polaris

---

* See Chapter 6, p. 74.

submarine on the British side. There will be many more such symbolic pinpricks in the future. Given the poor cards dealt to our side, it seems best that we rapidly develop a pretty laid back style of play for the future.

Gareth Parry's voyage to the Falklands in 1982 was a good deal less relaxed than Richard Gott's fourteen years earlier. The naval task force began to be assembled as soon as the Argentinian invasion, and the surrender of the tiny garrison of Royal Marines, were known about. The Ministry of Defence and its permanent secretary, Sir Frank Cooper, had only one object: to win the war and regain the islands. It was not their job to provide copy for newspapers or pictures for television. This irreconcilable distinction was immediately made clear in the regulations issued to reporters in the ships: 'The essence of successful warfare is secrecy. The essence of successful journalism is publicity.' It is therefore unsurprising that arrangements for the conveyance and convenience of the press and television were given a low naval priority.

The original intention of the MoD had been to fly correspondents to Ascension Island and let them join the ships there. The Navy overruled this seemingly sensible arrangement and insisted that everyone must be on board when the fleet sailed. It was offering ten places, of which five went to television, so that the MoD press officer telephoned the director of the Newspaper Publishers' Association, John Le Page, at home during lunch on Sunday 4 April, asking him to allocate the remaining five [1] There was no equitable means of selection so he drew the names of newspapers out of a hat, or rather his wife did. She picked, among others, the *Daily Telegraph*, but not the *Guardian* or *The Times*, the *Daily Mirror* but not the *Sun*. When the losers in this lottery raised hell Bernard Ingham, the Prime Minister's press secretary, made one of his more helpful interventions and almost every national newspaper was given a place either with the Royal Navy in the carriers *Invincible* and *Hermes* or in *Canberra*, converted to a troopship. Fortunately for the paper, though not, as it turned out, for him, Parry was at home on Sunday evening when the *Guardian* learned that it could send a man. The office telephoned him at 9.30 p.m. and he had to be in Portsmouth by midnight to board *Invincible*. The last train left at 10.15, so that he had only minutes in which to assemble some totally inadequate kit – mainly a sweater, a raincoat, and a paperback to read in the train. At that stage, of course, the voyage had some of the elements of a jaunt. It would not have been credible to suppose that several weeks and 8,000 miles later he would spend four days of winter under constant air attack in an ammunition ship in San Carlos Bay.

Parry, a Welsh-speaker from Anglesey who was both very tough and very gentle, had joined the paper in 1974 after covering wars in the Middle East, Cyprus and Vietnam, where he spent two years for the *Daily Express*, and acting as a foreign 'fireman' for the *Daily Mail*. He was thus one of the most experienced correspondents with the Task Force. He and the other four pressmen in *Invincible** were given an MoD minder who was the first of three links in the chain of censorship, the others being the censor on board ship and the duty officer at the MoD in London. Neither Parry nor his editor objected to the principle of censorship: both accepted that of course naval or military security was the overriding need. But Parry was 'devastated' when he eventually returned to England to find what had happened to his copy. At the start of the voyage out the paper received almost daily reports but as the ships went south much of the copy, from routine reports on the voyage to important eye-witness material about the fighting on the islands, had never reached the office at all. Other pieces had been blue-pencilled or even altered.

Some of the censorship seemed merely perverse, some more subtly motivated. Britain that spring was bathed in sunshine, which Parry believed might be having a psychological effect on the gusto with which the war was treated. He thought it important to correct such exultation by describing the very heavy seas and mists the ships were meeting as they went deeper into winter. The censors did not agree and removed all mention of the weather, ostensibly because it might betray a position, although it was pointed out to them that with satellite surveillance anyone can now find out where anything is.

Throughout the campaign Parry made contact with the office only three times and the office with him not at all. On one occasion the office had been given a direct line to a warship but found it had been disconnected. Copies of British newspapers were being dropped by Hercules aircraft from Ascension, along with the mail, but they were two or three weeks out of date. All he really knew of what the British papers were saying came in reviews from the BBC World Service. That was how he learned of the *Sun*'s celebrated headline 'Gotcha' on the sinking of the *General Belgrano*, and that his shipmate Tony Snow had signed a missile on behalf of *Sun* readers with the words 'Up yours, Galtieri!' The only exception to the telegraphic silence imposed on outgoing messages to Parry was a strange SG (service message) he received from the *Mail on Sunday* asking him to supply a colour piece about our lads going in because that paper did not have a man of its own. The surmise, and it can be no more, is that the MoD thought the *Mail on Sunday* more deserving than the *Guardian*.

In spite of these handicaps Parry filed daily until almost the end, though much of his most important work was wasted. His daily accounts of the air attacks on shipping in San Carlos Bay (where he and his four colleagues were incarcerated in the ammunition ship *Resource*) failed to reach the paper. The MoD minder attached to them had found a better hole – which they would have done if they had had the means to leave. Under questioning after the

* Alfred McIlroy, *Daily Telegraph*; Michael Seamark, *Daily Star*; Tony Snow, *Sun*; John Witherow, *The Times*; plus Roger Goodwin as minder.

fighting by the Commons Defence Committee[2] Parry remarked that 'four days on a fully-laden ammunition ship under air attack almost by the hour is enough to prompt you into a good idea of where you should be and where you should not be and – I am not being facetious – it really is the wrong place to be.' Asked why he and the others from *Invincible* had been put on an ammunition ship Parry replied 'I have no idea. I would not like to read too much into that.'

The result of the minder's disappearance was that no one was on board to vet their copy before it was sent. *Resource* had its own Marisat (marine satellite) equipment and they knew the operator was filing their copy. Similarly Parry, when nominally attached to the Welsh Guards, witnessed the awful air attack on that regiment on board *Sir Galahad* but not a word appeared. (Michael Seamark of the *Star*, who had been on the other side of the bay, filed a story which reached his paper only after several days.) In the end, a few days before the assault on Port Stanley, Parry's lack of equipment got the better of him. He took a helicopter flight to the main depot ship *Fearless* and then to the carrier and flagship *Hermes*, but neither could offer him much in the way of winter clothing. On the virtually shelterless land he relied on the Marks and Spencer raincoat with which he had left Waterloo and waterproofing which he had been able to scrounge, but the moisture content inside it went very cold at night. His sleeping bag (and these deprivations applied to other members of the *Invincible* team also) was not of the Arctic variety and therefore was not effective in a Falklands winter. The only act of insubordination in face of these discomforts to which he has confessed was to take a Royal Navy fork from *Fearless*, which had been refused to him, to eat his reconstituted rations, though he had been warned that the offence would be treated as theft.

The last piece to get into the paper with Parry's by-line was a pooled account on 7 June of the funeral of Argentinian soldiers, with military honours from both sides on a hillside overlooking Darwin and Goose Green. His last important piece not to get in was taken from an overheard military radio on board a BP tanker of the engagement at Goose Green in which the Paratroop commander, Colonel 'H' Jones, was killed. The *Guardian* had to take the details of that from Jeremy Hands of ITN.

For most of the time afloat Parry was under Captain Jeremy Black of *Invincible*. His action station during air attacks, when the range of the incoming Super Etendards with their Exocet missiles was being counted down on the Tannoy – 'twenty-five kilometres, twenty kilometres, missile launched: Jesus!' – was six decks below the water line. When they emerged they had to pester Black for permission to send their messages. 'He had a capital ship with a thousand people on board and probably some nuclear devices as well. All we could bother him about was that it would be inequitable not to get our stories out. Black was our only court of appeal. He was very pleased when we went.' Some of the press fell out with Black. Parry liked him. Thereafter the two of them met for an annual lunch.

Back at the *Guardian*'s office Admiral Preston took personal control of the helm, though not before Hugh Stephenson had performed a delicate and important act of pilotage. Stephenson was spending a year as a leader-writer with the paper after resigning from *The Times*, where he had been editor of the Business News section, on the takeover by Rupert Murdoch. He did not in fact write many leaders but the one he wrote on the morrow of the Argentinian invasion set the tone for much that was to come. If he was unduly sceptical about the prospects of repossessing the islands, that was a fault he shared with many others inside and outside the paper. The leader, with Preston's headline 'Far away, forgotten and now filched', referred to the 'confusion if not concealment' of the previous day, with conflicting statements in the Commons about whether or not the islands had been invaded, when it soon became clear that the government had known all along that they had. It went on:

> From the start the Falkland Islands affair has had heavy comic opera overtones. Before spurious national sentiment here is whipped up to match the considerably more real Argentinian feelings that the Islas Malvinas are part of the motherland, it is worth taking stock of the facts. Reality number one is that, if the Argentinians have once established themselves by force in the islands, there is likely to be little the British Government can in fact do to dislodge them. Reality number two is that the Falkland Islands do not represent any strategic or commercial British interest worth fighting over (unless one believes reports of crude oil under its off-shore waters). And reality number three is that, in taking military action, the Argentine forces are in clear and flagrant breach of international law and guilty of wholly unprovoked aggression . . .
>
> The present British Government comes extremely badly out of the affair, which it has presented as an issue of sovereignty on which there should be no compromise, thus raising a whole variety of expectations. The reality is that in practice the life of the islands has long been significantly compromised in the direction of Argentina. The islands' communications are through Argentina. There are significant Argentinian commercial interests in the islands. The first major runway was constructed by Argentina. Even, in a touch of pure farce in the midst of the affair of the illegal scrap merchants on South Georgia, it has been revealed that 50 Argentinian 'military scientists' have been sitting on South Thule illegally since 1976, without anyone seeing fit to make a fuss.

The leader ended by reverting to a familiar *Guardian* theme. If the Royal Navy turned out to be no help to Port Stanley, in what conceivable realistic circumstances could a Trident missile strengthen the hand of a future British prime minister?

Preston resumed the bridge on Monday 5 April and stayed there day after day until the campaign ended on 14 June. It was a formidable performance. He wrote as few people had written in the paper's history – Hetherington at the height of Suez, perhaps, and Wadsworth during the immediate post-war crises domestic and foreign – and he carried the staff with him throughout.

The task he set himself was all the trickier, and his success in it the greater, because of the conflicting emotions which the Falklands crisis aroused. Argentina *had* carried out unprovoked aggression. That country *was* under an odious military regime. The Falklands were *not* Suez all over again. The US *did* (eventually) come down on Britain's side despite the best endeavours of its UN ambassador Mrs Jeanne Kirkpatrick, and the Security Council *had* ordered Argentina to withdraw its forces in Resolution 502, passed on the day after the invasion.

Yet the unwanted remnant of empire with its 1,800 luckless kelpers had to be put into an international perspective of which so many politicians (and journalists) quickly lost sight, and the possible cost in lives and money of liberating them and keeping them liberated could not be ignored in the spasm of national indignation. Moreover Resolution 502, for which Britain's friends had voted, had also told the two sides to seek a diplomatic solution.

For ten weeks the *Guardian* had to balance these considerations. The voices in the Commons dissenting from the use of force, notably that of Ray Whitney, the Tory member for Wycombe, were drowned in the high tide of emotion which swept through the debate on 3 April. After a day to reflect, the *Guardian* on Monday did not oppose the dispatch of the Task Force and distanced its response to the Falklands from its response to Suez. Not every point in the leader was totally clear at first reading but the final impression was one not of opposition so much as of distaste. The purpose of the fleet was to force Argentina to negotiate.

> . . . And, perhaps, the first fine fury of a Parliament speaking in full flood for a nation betrayed will slowly abate to echo the doubts that already seep from diplomats and military men, concerned at the enormity of recapturing – and holding at huge cost – that which has been so cheaply cast away . . .
>
> But the Falklands issue is not Suez. The background is not one of grandiose plotting, but of Whitehall ineptitude – or grotesque malfortune. The fleet sails now in restitution. The cause, this time, is a just one; but the dangers are immense and the prospect of a simple, happy outcome deeply shallower. To say as much is not to wish General Galtieri anything but his bloody nose, but nor is it to increase pressure on a government that presently feels its only escape, politically and emotionally, lies in potentially horrendous military gambles, with Falkland as well as military lives at risk.
>
> We have, perhaps, two or three weeks to think as the crisis unrolls. Some of these thoughts and possibilities may today seem profoundly unpalatable. But time stretches. Parliament, having had its hour, should now turn down the heat and give Mrs Thatcher and Lord Carrington their time to think as well as to react.

That set the tone of much subsequent comment. On 7 April the paper insisted that Michael Foot's Commons speech (when the Tory side had praised him for 'speaking for Britain') had not given the government a blank cheque for when the Task Force arrived.

> The Government has previously been willing to compromise with Argentina, but failed to convince the Falklanders. Would not some Falklanders prefer peace under Argentinian rule or money and a settlement in NZ, Scotland or Wales?
>
> . . . It is critical, as the wait lengthens, that all politicians, from Number 10 down, do not heedlessly allow raw emotion to undercut the possibility of realistic compromise. Why does the word 'compromise' in such circumstances sound so dirty when politicians otherwise (returning from Brussels, ending a strike) would embrace it eagerly? There is the chance of compromise. The careful formulas preserve it. They must be underlined and sustained.

Alexander Haig, the US Secretary of State, began a wearying shuttle between London, Buenos Aires and Washington which for a while held out hope that the Argentinian military rulers could unite behind a peace formula. They didn't, at least during Haig's mission, but the *Guardian* invested heavily in that mission. In a leader of 13 April:

> There are no facile paths to complete triumph in the South Atlantic. But there is now a clear possibility of peace. If we are to push it to the limit, those who have publicly sought a Falklands' rapprochement with Argentina for two decades and who now tacitly anticipate just such a deal around the corner will have to say so frankly. That perception is reality. Once we grasp it, then the unrealities that clutter the road will be thrown into stark relief.

And on 14 April:

> . . . (1) Time is not inevitably running out. There remains a week or more before the fleet arrives anywhere useful . . .
> (2) That 9,000 Argentinians on the islands are shiftable, if at all, only at high risk to life and limb on all sides . . .
> (3) There remains a premium on negotiation. America has not chosen between the British case and the Argentinian case, and rigorously refuses to choose. Yet such a full-hearted choice is the best hope of making General Galtieri crawl down the couple of pegs necessary for damage limitation with honour; and, remember, it is Galtieri who is constructing the impediments to that now . . .

Peter Preston's leaders, since before he became editor, had never needed to be signed to be identified. This one ended:

> Mr Haig has delivered all the hours and exhaustion we could wish. But he has not yet delivered the unflinching support, over a chunk of rock and a principle, that Mrs Thatcher might have expected of our oldest ally and supplier of two billion dollar deterrents. If he can deliver, and there is an alpha for effort, then damage limitation with tolerable honour can follow. If he cannot, then

Downing Street is in its tightest corner, and Britain will have much – besides 'new ideas' and consultations with Mr Reagan – to ponder in the South Atlantic and beyond.

On succeeding days Preston nagged at and berated the American indecision, which continued for the rest of April until on 1 May he sighed with relief, for American support gave legitimacy to the British expedition which had been so conspicuously lacking at Suez: 'Once mediation had run into the sands, then a decision had to be made . . . It must be said that the decision [to impose American economic sanctions] seems both generous and wholehearted.'

Throughout the campaign Preston continued to remind the war party of the wasted opportunities for negotiation over the Falklands and of the efforts, sometimes overt, sometimes more clandestine, of successive governments to come to terms with Argentina. The paper denounced the war fever of the Saturday-night crowds in Leicester Square, written before the first news of the attack on the cruiser *General Belgrano* had become the lead story.

> In Covent Garden on Saturday night (only a few hundred yards from the deep leather armchairs of the Garrick Club, where Mr Peregrine Worsthorne habitually taps the heartbeat of the British nation) one might have observed a gaggle of youths, fresh from the terraces, roaming and singing a new version of the Clementine of the Kop. 'Shoot the bastards, shoot the bastards, shoot the bastards . . . right now.' And so on. War is not all clean limbed professional-ism and right principles and soaring opinion poll ratings. The exultation of the banner headlines – 'Navy hits them all to blazes' – is echoed on Port Stanley airfield only by the maimed or dismembered carcases of 18-year-old conscripts whose lives, this summer, might otherwise have been devoted to surrogate World Cup battles. Bash a Paki, shoot a Dago, with the arm-chair generals and retired rear-admirals playing Lawrie McMenemy and Brian Clough, leaves some rancid taste amid the euphoria.[3]

The paper asked in effect whether the British public was prepared for the consequences of either a long siege or an invasion. 'Public opinion, in so far as it is known and relevant, will not accept such casualties easily, having correctly deduced that victory, when it comes, will be one of principle and not, in the end, of practicality. We are still seeking to regain the Falklands by force in order to give them away by negotiation.' It analysed the erosion of international support which began to be evident ('Mrs Thatcher does not want to go back to the UN because the second time would not yield the overwhelming vote of the first') and called attention to the arithmetic.

> The generals, in choosing their beachheads, will be giving some estimate of casualties: X to land on East Falkland, Y to take the hinterland, Z to storm Port Stanley . . . Would 50 British dead and wounded be more acceptable? Would 500 or a thousand be more acceptable? How many sunk ships and downed

planes are acceptable? Are one, two or three dozen Falklanders winged by strafings and ricochets acceptable?

The front page of 4 May carried reports of the huge casualty figure likely in the sinking of the *Belgrano* alongside a deep three-column picture of a 'relaxed' and clearly exuberant Mrs Thatcher returning to Downing Street from Chequers, which may have been frank rather than fair. Then on Monday 10 May came another clear call to the government to pause for one last try.

> Invasion, in sum, is a foolish gamble. Mr Nott's blockade would be better. A short ceasefire in order to see how the junta of disarray reacts to the pressures of peace would be a useful break with a strategy that has so far got us nowhere. Blockade and qualified ceasefire can sit together. That, amongst other things, would offer a moment of evacuation to the people who weeks ago we sailed to protect.

As May advanced the difficulties of making editorial policy for a nation at war became more intense. They were well put on Wednesday 19 May: 'Mrs Thatcher will stand or fall by what our troops achieve in the South Atlantic. We hope, on those terms, that she stands. But that cannot, now, hide the acute unease which attaches to so close an identification of political and military fortunes. Our efforts for peace have perceptibly become mere formalities this week.' Mrs Thatcher, a leader observed on 1 June, 'likes to win 20 goals to nil'. When the bit was between her teeth, then there was an awesome refusal to compromise. 'That can be shaking and stirring; people who have supped their fill of fudge and mudge cannot be too dismissive. But it also betokens a deeply unmagnanimous concentration on simple victory today at the expense of endless trouble tomorrow.'

Peter Jenkins, columnist, had helped at the outset to establish the *Guardian*'s anti-war reputation. On Wednesday 7 April he wrote:

> One has to keep pinching oneself . . . I could hardly believe my ears listening to the Commons debate last Saturday. Nearly everyone seemed to have taken leave of his senses. By what gigantic lack of proportion was the loss of the Falkland Islands to be seen as a major national humiliation? . . . Lives are being risked, vast sums expended, everything else dropped and forgotten – all for 1,800 islanders and their 600,000 sheep. Why?
>
> Chiefly, one suspects, because the ghosts of Munich still haunt the British establishment. One does not appease dictators. A sound principle, no doubt, but one elevated out of all proportion when applied to a Latin American dictator seizing hold of a territory the size of Wales . . . Another explanation, one fears, is wounded national pride. A 'tin pot' dictator provides the chance to avenge the loss of empire, the true 'humiliation' of Suez and the long slide in power and influence. A traditional naval expedition, a task force sailing out of

Portsmouth, all hands lining the ship – a wonderful, nostalgic sight, as good as a Royal Wedding or Trooping the Colour . . .

He kept it up until the war ended, sparing Opposition no more than government. For the Labour party:

Until now[4] Mr Foot has trodden a skilful path through the Falklands crisis, an inveterate peacemonger wrapped in the Union Jack. But he and Mr Healey had carefully prepared a bolt-hole for themselves in that warren of lost causes, the United Nations. Yesterday, as Mrs Thatcher showed signs of abandoning diplomacy for war, they showed signs of abandoning her.

For the government:[5]

There is already entering an unpleasant note of cultural superiority as the 'Argies', the 'gauchos' or – in the lexicon of some Tory backbenchers – the 'dagoes' show a less than Anglo-Saxon love of battle. Perhaps the First World team will always beat the Third World team at modern warfare but technological advantage is no guarantee of moral superiority. We should have no wish to become the Israelis of Western Europe.

Along with the *Mirror* the *Guardian* was the anti-war paper: a position decided for it not only by the formulations of the leader column but by readers, contributors – and cartoonists.

On the Monday opinion pages labelled Agenda, which for several years had been given over to outside contributors, attacks flowed fiercely on the government's past miscalculations and present attitudes as well as on the jingoism encouraged by sections of the press. James Cameron in his weekly column blew a few raspberries. On Tuesday 6 April he quoted the governess who advised her girls: 'When rape is inevitable, settle down and enjoy it,' and went on: 'Why then do I appear in a merry mood when I think about the Falklands? Partly because I hardly ever think about the Falklands, any more than John Nott thinks about them, or Mrs Thatcher, or Lord Carrington or Edward du Cann or the rest of the mouthing Tories who give a moment's thought to the Falkland Islands about once every blue moon.' Unlike Cameron at his best this was perhaps too easy to write and not challenging enough to read.

On 12 April Lord Chalfont, who in most other respects had become an international hardliner, wrote that sovereignty was negotiable. The standard response that the wishes of the islanders were paramount was a precarious basis on which to construct foreign policy. 'Even as the military phase of the British response develops Mrs Thatcher should therefore be insisting that her colleagues at the Foreign Office are already formulating a realistic policy for the negotiations which must inevitably follow.' On the same page the *Guardian* reprinted a speech by Tony Benn calling for the Task Force to be withdrawn.

A week later the Agenda page followed up with a piece by Cecilio Morales, an Argentinian 'Washington policy analyst', headed 'Why we all hate Britannia so' and urging Americans not to 'try to rescue Albion's empire from the dustbin of history where it belongs'.

A long-standing friend of, or at least sympathiser with, the *Guardian* was Brigadier Michael Harbottle, general secretary of the World Disarmament Campaign and former Chief of Staff of the UN peacekeeping force in Cyprus. He wrote on 26 April proposing that the UN should assume temporary administrative responsibility for the Falklands, which was an idea already canvassed by several readers in the letters column in the days soon after the invasion.

Another ally, Bishop John Robinson, author of the theological best-seller *Honest to God* and at that time Dean of Chapel at Trinity College, Cambridge, wrote (3 May) under the heading: 'War is not an instrument of peace' that four successive Lambeth conferences had declared that 'war as a method of settling international disputes is incompatible with the teaching of our Lord Jesus Christ'. He went on: 'I do not know with what gems from the Bible General Galtieri studs his speeches, but I do remember Mrs Thatcher using on the day she came to power Saint Francis's prayer, "Lord, make me an instrument of Thy peace". I felt at the time that here was mere prostitution, if not blasphemy.'

Alone of the 'popular' dailies the *Daily Mirror* had courageously challenged its readers to reflect on their own mood. In a leader on the Monday after the emotional Commons debate it had said:

> Many men, including some Falkland Islanders, may die. There will be other consequences as well, political and economic. World reaction, sympathetic today, can change when the shooting starts. Suez taught us that. The Government's determination seems designed to disguise its bungling of the past few weeks. It wants to recover its reputation as much as it does the Falklands . . . The islanders are now under the control of one of the most odious governments in South America – which is saying a lot. Our incompetence put them there. It is our responsibility to rescue them from it. But that doesn't require counter-invasion. The islands don't matter. The people do. We should offer each of them the chance to settle here or anywhere else they choose and we should pay for it.

The cumulative heresy appearing in the *Mirror*, the *Guardian* and (it alleged) from Peter Snow on the BBC's *Newsnight* programme, was too much for the *Sun* which had whipped itself into a frenzy against 'the Argies'. On Friday 7 May its leader began:

> There are traitors in our midst. Margaret Thatcher talked about them in the House of Commons yesterday. She referred to those newspapers and commentators on radio and TV who are not properly conveying Britain's case over the

Steve Bell became famous for his Falklands cartoons, as bitingly satirical of the journalists covering the war as of the generals and politicians. This one appeared on 6 May 1982. Copyright © Steve Bell, 1982.

Falklands, and who are treating this country as if she and the Argentines had an equal claim to justice, consideration and loyalty. The Prime Minister did not speak of treason. The *Sun* does not hesitate to use the word . . .

It attacked Peter Snow. It attacked Les Gibbard, the *Guardian*'s cartoonist, who, after the sinking of HMS *Sheffield*, had adapted one of the most famous Second World War cartoons by Phil Zec in the *Mirror*. In the new version the shipwrecked sailor on the raft bore the caption 'The price of sovereignty has been increased – official'. The *Sun* attacked the *Mirror* 'which again and again demonstrates it has no faith in its country and no respect for her people'. Peter Preston called it 'sad and despicable'.

But at least this prepared the ground for Tom Baistow, a veteran foreign editor of the *News Chronicle* and commentator on the press, to cite the 'Yobspeak' headlines of the *Sun* and the *Star*,[6] those Fleet Street warriors who turn from bingo to jingo in the battle of sagging sales. 'The *Sun*, owned by an Australian and edited by an Australian, naturally is out to show the decadent Poms how to write a war.'

On Tuesday 11 May the *Guardian*, exceptionally at that time, gave the second leader page to an outside contributor for an edited version of Henry Kissinger's speech the day before to the Royal Institute of International Affairs. It was mainly a disquisition about where British and American foreign policies diverged and converged but included several compliments appropriate to the occasion including one, reflected in the headline, that those who cherish the values of Western civilisation must be willing to defend them. 'In the Falklands crisis Britain is reminding us all that certain basic principles, such as honour, justice, and patriotism, remain valid and must be sustained by more than words.'

Another approach with which the paper was sympathetic came from Mary Kaldor, of the Science Policy Research Unit, University of Sussex, in the paper of 17 May. She attacked the export of arms made necessary to sustain large defence forces at home. 'Our own dependence on the export of arms, together with that of other developed countries, is directly responsible for the combination of distorted industrial development, extreme inequality and militaristic repression that creates the circumstances in which wars start. The Argentinian invasion was not a chance event . . . ' Almost the only contributed article unreservedly supporting the government's view, by the chairman of the Conservative party Cecil Parkinson, appeared on the Agenda page on 14 June, the day the Argentinians surrendered.

A year later the paper seized in its leader columns on the only occasion during the general election campaign of 1983 when Mrs Thatcher appeared to be rattled. In a BBC phone-in programme she was asked by Mrs Diana Gould of Bristol about the sinking of the *Belgrano*. 'A keen student,' the *Guardian* hazarded of Mrs Gould, 'of the collected works of Mr Tam Dalyell.' Why, she had asked, had the war cabinet ordered the sinking of the *Belgrano*, with huge loss of life, when the ship was steering away from the battle zone? Was it a terrible coincidence, or more, 'that the Belgrano took to the bottom with it the fabled Peruvian peace plan which might (nay, would) have resolved the Falklands crisis without blood or continuing heavy cost?' Mrs Thatcher's reply was muddled, and the *Guardian* commented:

> The episode provokes a number of thoughts. One is a sad reflection on the quality of our Parliamentary process. Mr Dalyell has been banging away at Westminster month in and month out. He has never managed to put the Prime Minister, the head of the war cabinet, on such a spot.[7]

Dalyell's campaign to have an investigation into the sinking was reported and supported in extenso in the news columns by Richard Norton-Taylor, but it did not become an election issue. The *Guardian* in its leaders thought that 'the whole business smells a little' but did not mount a campaign.

Les Gibbard, attacked by the *Sun* for subversion, had a good war, but the unforeseen rise to fame was that of Steve Bell, the *Guardian*'s punk cartoonist as admirers and opponents both described him. His parodies of politicians he disliked were and for years afterwards remained grotesque. For Falklands purposes he had a naval vessel of his own with its funny and thoroughly offensive caricatures of commander and padre. The only sane people on board HMS *Incredible* were the insubordinate AB Kipling and his adopted penguin. For years afterwards, when the editor had to decline invitations to speak to meetings of *Guardian* devotees, they wrote back asking for Steve Bell instead.

At a frivolous level there is some similarity between the *Sun*'s onslaught against the 'traitors' in the Falklands conflict and the action of the *Manchester Courier* during the Boer War when it is reputed to have hired a brass band to march round the *Manchester Guardian*'s offices playing the Dead March from *Saul*.[8] More serious comparisons can be drawn between the paper's attitudes

Steve Bell, 29 April 1982. Copyright © Steve Bell, 1982.

on the two occasions, though in one respect the results were dissimilar. Between 1898 and 1902 the circulation of the *MG* fell from 48,000 to 40,000, a loss of more than 16 per cent. From March to September 1981 the average sale of the *Guardian* was, in round figures, 388,200; for the same six months of 1982 it was 421,700, a rise of more than 8 per cent. This was a better figure than those for the other two quality dailies which showed an increase (*The Times* from 290,300 to 303,300 and the *FT* from 199,400 to 199,700), and the *Telegraph* lost sales during the period, from 1,379,000 to 1,313,000. An obvious conclusion can be drawn about the growth in the *Guardian*'s constituency.

In two other respects the coverage of the Sudan and Boer wars and that in the Falklands show striking similarities, allowing for the changes in technology and in readers' expectations which had taken place during eighty years. Mr Paul Bernard Carney wrote in 1989 a master's thesis* for Leeds University in which he studied attitudes and methods of *The Times* and the *Manchester Guardian* during the Sudan and South African campaigns. The present writer is grateful to Mr Carney for permission to quote from this unpublished work.

Both at the turn of the century and in 1982 the *Guardian* relied heavily on outside sources rather than its own staff correspondents at the scene. In the two earlier wars the *MG* bought a service from Reuters and the *Daily Telegraph*, with reprints from *The Times* and the *Daily News*, partly because 'this approach . . . suited its financial position'[9] and also because the *MG* 'set most store by its interpretation, and not its reportage of events'. During the Falklands it was not penury or a disinclination to get involved in day-to-day reporting which gave rise to the *Guardian*'s dependence on other sources but the hazard of having its own reporter in certain places at certain times. Pooled dispatches and notes taken from radio and TV provided much of the news

* War Correspondence and War Correspondents. An analysis of two newspapers, 1898–1902.

from the islands and their seas. The political response to the two imperial episodes showed, however, a striking similarity.

The *MG* was opposed to British involvement in both the Sudan (and Egypt) and South Africa . . . Significantly, the *MG* applied its anti-war attitudes to campaigns and crises other than those involving Britain . . . Prior to and during the Russo-Japanese War in 1905, the *MG* stood out for a diplomatic solution up until the day war was declared. Throughout the war it raised objections to armed conflict, expressing the view that the crisis could easily have been settled through negotiation. This severely tests theories alleging that the *MG* took an anti-war position between 1898 and 1902, simply to spite the Tory Government. Had it shown a lack of concern about the Russo-Japanese War, such a theory might have had substance. The fact that the *MG* was consistently anti-war in its outlook adds to the credibility of its position during the Sudan and Anglo-Boer Campaigns. It did not restrict its attitude to political targets in Britain.

The interpretation of news from the Sudan has a direct relevance to C.P. Scott's personal politics. Being essentially Gladstonian, they could be expected to present the Sudan campaign as something distasteful, increasingly so the longer it went on . . . The actual campaign vindicated *MG* policy. Kitchener's reconquest of the Sudan and his defeat of Mahdism was total. The battles of Atbara and Omdurman were sweeping British successes, involving large numbers of enemy casualties, small numbers of British losses and stirring incidents of British heroism. The *MG* did these victories full credit in its war columns . . . The news that awoke *MG* interest in the campaign was that Britain was to remain in occupation of the Sudan, the news that the tomb of the Mahdi had been desecrated immediately after the Battle of Omdurman and, most significantly of all, the allegations of atrocities levelled first at British auxiliaries and then at British troops during and after the battle . . . There was something crusade-like, and hence quite Gladstonian, in the way [Scott] seemed to feel it his and the *MG*'s duty to make 'the facts' known to the general public.[10]*

On Monday 6 September 1898 the *MG* printed its first news of the battle of Omdurman and it dealt with the British victory in its editorial columns. This was the first time that news from the Sudan had merited the attention of the editorial pages. In accordance with the assessment of Scott's sense of priorities for the paper, no news came from the *MG* correspondent. The largest proportion of the coverage was from the *Daily Telegraph*'s reporter. Opposed though C.P. Scott and the *MG* might have been in principle to British involvement in Egypt and the Sudan, neither were obtuse enough to actually

---

* 'By hook or by crook,' Scott wrote to Hobhouse, his leader-writer on Sudan and South Africa, 'the whole rotten policy must be challenged. It would be political crime to allow the country to be led on blindfold.' (Undated, but before February 1899.)

condemn or even fail to acknowledge the sweeping success of British arms. The [leading] article that appeared congratulated British troops on a fine display of military discipline and gave every indication of being proud of the army.

There was a marked tendency, Carney writes, immediately before and in the early stages of the Boer War for *MG* editorials only rarely to deal with the fighting. It reserved the bulk of its editorials for the issues it felt surrounded the outbreak of war; issues that the government were failing to reveal. Boers in the Transvaal had offered British settlers (Uitlanders) the vote on condition that they had lived there for seven years. The paper thus depicted any potential war as something of a farce.

> In early March [1900], *MG* editorials clarified several issues. It did not believe the war was being fought for the voting rights of Uitlander settlers but for financial reasons. The *MG* challenged the Government to deny the charge [and] referred its readers again to the official explanations of why the war was being fought. It used these explanations to urge a speedy end to the war, remarking that if franchise for the Uitlanders was genuinely the aim of the fighting, the Boers ought to be told, so that the fighting could end.[11]

The paper reassured readers of its allegiance to the army by criticising other papers for failing to give due credit to the British troops who had held out during the siege of Ladysmith. After the relief of Mafeking it wrote: 'In a quarter of an hour the sound of cheering had swollen into one vast volume of continuous sound, in half an hour the city was crowded and at midnight, some two hours after the arrival of the first news, there was such a spectacle of public rejoicing as that can seldom have been seen in central Manchester.'[12]

But the *MG* put the war in perspective by pointing out that the British empire was fighting a state with a population equivalent to that of Salford. 'Correspondents have told us how men bowed with age have been seen following with difficulty the line of retreat, how boys of fourteen have been taken, and how women have been found dead in the trenches. These are inevitable incidents of a war of conquest. The conqueror makes a desert and calls it peace.'[13]

Carney's conclusions at the end of his lengthy survey are that in Sudan, in line with its opposition to British involvement there and in Egypt, the *MG* interpreted the victory at Omdurman as a chance to withdraw from both areas. In South Africa:

> During the Anglo-Boer War, the *MG*'s editorial attitude towards the origins of the war, the conduct of the war's later stages, and Britain's involvement in South Africa were kept separate from the actual campaign. The . . . paper has not been given credit for its patriotic coverage of the actual events that took place during the war. Once war was declared the *MG* stated openly that Britain was bound to fight, and win, the war. It qualified its support for the war with the condition that it should be won quickly and not result in territorial

acquisition for Britain. The *MG* used its position of support against the Government by stating that if Britain were to gain anything from the war, the war was not being fought upon the grounds the Government had originally stated. Thus, the *MG* was not 'pacific' in its attitude towards the campaign. Nor can it be stated that it was pro-Boer in its editorial coverage. There is no evidence within *MG* columns throughout the war that substantiated any charge of treachery. At no stage did the *MG* discourage British troops or treat news of British victories with scepticism. The paper's treatment of the news of the relief of the siege of Mafeking, for example, was distinctly patriotic. *MG* editorials that dealt with the fighting in South Africa were always kept separate from editorials that dealt with the origins of, and political issues behind, the war. The *MG* might be interpreted as having been anti-British for its opposition to the Conservative Government. From before the outbreak of war, the *MG* claimed that the Government was being led, and were in turn leading Britain, into an iniquitous war. It confined its criticism to the lack of justification for the war and consistently argued that any differences between Britain and the Boer Republics ought to be settled by diplomacy. The outbreak of war foresaw a continuation of the paper's political assault, not only on the Government but on those parties it regarded as having a vested interest in the war. The force of the *MG*'s political attack upon the origins of the war, and not its interpretation of battle correspondence, nor the battle correspondence itself, formed the crux of the paper's coverage of the war.

This heavy concentration on editorial analysis marked the main *Guardian* departure from the model established by William Howard Russell of *The Times*, during the Crimean and American civil wars, of battle reporting from the front. 'Moreover,' says Carney, 'it seems to have resulted in the creation of a myth that the *MG* opposed Britain itself during the Anglo-Boer War. This was never the case.'

CHAPTER 19

Process of Law

IN the autumn of 1987 the law firm of Lovell, White & King gave a lunch at the Garrick Club to mark the opening of their 1,000th *Guardian* file. The introduction had been made thirty years earlier in a way characteristic of the informality of that time. It was not the least of the many and varied services for the paper by one of its best-loved people, Mark Arnold-Forster.

Mark was nineteen on the outbreak of the Second World War. Before he joined the *Guardian* to become variously German correspondent, labour correspondent, confidant of and performer of special assignments for three editors, chief leader-writer and finally diplomatic editor, he had an outstanding naval career as the commander of a motor torpedo boat, patrolling the Channel against such mighty German warships as the *Scharnhorst* and *Gneisenau* on their escape from Brest. He emerged from the war with a DSO, a DSC, three mentions in dispatches, and the down of his youth still on his chin. His own laconic ship-to-shore signals became legendary: after one engagement he could find no means of returning to base undetected and therefore signalled 'Am proceeding bearing so-and-so in formation with [German] E-boats'.* Mark was senior officer of the 13th MTB flotilla; one of his commanding officers in MTB 210 was P.R. Everett. Their friendship continued after the war when Mark joined the *Guardian* under Wadsworth and Everett was a partner in Lovell, White & King. The *Guardian*'s offices in Fleet Street were almost next door to LWK's at Serjeant's Inn, so that in 1957 when Gerard Fay, London editor and Mark's immediate superior, needed some legal advice Everett's was the firm they turned to. Two names became well known and valued in the editorial offices: John Notcutt, who was the first adviser on defamation questions, and his successor, Geoffrey Grimes. MGEN had its own solicitors, Tatham Worthington, in Manchester, but with the move

---

* There were few things to which he could not turn a hand. Tony Benn reports in his diaries (*Office without Power, 1968–72*) an occasion in 1968: 'Mark Arnold-Forster had just come from seeing Melina Mercouri, who had come over for the big Trafalgar Square rally tomorrow, and he had to go away early to write her speech.'

south LWK grew in importance as advisers to management as well as editorial staff. Hence the 1,000 files.

For much of the time during Hetherington's editorship the paper took out libel insurance. This was a tricky undertaking not only because the paper had to prove due care and attention, etc., but because once a plaintiff had brought an action it had to be conducted in the way prescribed by the insurers, not by the paper. In one libel case which ran for several years, and which cannot be named here because part of the settlement out of court stipulated that it should not be, the plaintiffs entirely withdrew their very substantial claim for damages and paid all the *Guardian*'s costs, which amounted to many thousands, or tens of thousands by later reckoning. The case could have been settled years earlier and much wasted editorial time spared, had not the insurers insisted on getting back every penny of the money they had already laid out.

Gibbings was a lawyer and probably sensed the weakness of this system, especially at a time when the paper was being much more adventurous and investigative than it had been. Both Hetherington and Jean Stead, news editor, had a keen eye for scandals which they wanted to have exposed. Insurance premiums mounted and eventually Hetherington and Gibbings decided to take the risks unaided. When Preston came to the throne he brought the *Guardian* into line with everyone else in Fleet Street by employing night lawyers to vet copy before publication. They saved their salaries in legal costs and lifted a burden from the night editor and duty editor. They were concerned about legality, not taste, though sometimes they could not suppress an opinion about syntax. Taste was a matter for the Press Council, which occupied a lot of time but cost a lot less money.

Kenneth Morgan, Director of the Press Council and one of the more amiable adornments of the journalistic profession, was commonly asked on public occasions about the snubs which the council received from the *Sun* and other tabloid newspapers. He replied that the first comprehensive snub came not from Kelvin MacKenzie, editor of the *Sun*, but from Alastair Hetherington. He could have been referring to the *Lady Chatterley* case, where the *Guardian* had had a public row with the unreconstructed Press Council under George Murray in February 1961 for using four-letter words (see Chapter 5, pp. 55–7) but in fact he was talking of a yet more splendid act of defiance against the council under Lord Devlin in September 1968.

On 28 March of that year the *Guardian* had printed the result of a detailed inquiry by Ann Shearer, welfare correspondent, into the treatment of forty children in a ward at Harperbury in Hertfordshire, described in the article as 'one of the leading hospitals for the mentally subnormal in the country'. The article brought to light some horrific conditions which became the subject of a government inquiry and some action to remedy staff shortages. Here is a sample:

These then are the mad children. They are locked in the dining room, with either one or two very young Asian nurses. The dining room is not large and there must be a dozen children in it. A window is open a crack, the central heating is full on. The stench when the door is opened reaches right into your stomach. It is impossible not to turn away . . .

These are the dirty children. They are incontinent. The floor shines with urine and piles of excrement are walked in, smeared about and eaten. One of the young Malayan nurses makes a distasteful gesture towards wiping up a pile: this is not a battle she wants to fight any more . . .

The children are filthy. They have matted hair, their pants are wet and dirty, their jerseys smeared with excrement . . . They don't call it the dining room out of any coy instincts. That is what it is. Three times a day some of the children from outside go in there, into that stench, and they wolf their food . . . A visitor who comes very often to the ward says this scene is not unusual. It is better in the summer because the children are outside. But in over a year of visiting, the conditions have been much the same as they were this afternoon.

And so on for several hundred more words.

The Verulam (St Albans) group hospital management committee complained, saying that although Miss Shearer visited the hospital by appointment to make her research, 'this followed a private visit she had made, apparently without knowledge and authority. At that time the ward was in isolation because of dysentery.' After a full investigation the management committee had passed a vote of confidence in its medical and nursing staffs. The Press Council conceded that the subject was one which the press had a right to deal with, but 'it must be careful to do so with the utmost objectivity and accuracy'. It concluded: 'The article in the *Guardian* does not conform to those standards. This complaint is therefore upheld.'

Hetherington was not having this, especially as the judgment did not say where the article had allegedly gone wrong. He published the council's judgment in full across six columns, but underneath he republished the original article (the whole occupying more space than before) and left readers to judge. In a page of letters a few days later the chairman of the North-West Regional Hospital Board, the Professor of Human Genetics at London University, and a parent of one of the patients denounced him for his insensitivity and the harm said to have been done to staff recruitment; the Director of the Spastics Society and the secretary of a London branch of the Society for Mentally Handicapped Children were sympathetic; several readers were highly complimentary. In the mixed bag of opinions which always comes on such occasions the consensus to emerge was that the staff were well intentioned, hard-working, and badly underfunded.

The most frequent complainant to the *Guardian*, and probably to the Press Council, was one L.E. Weidberg, of Templewood Avenue, Hampstead, NW3. His most original complaint, however, was made under the assumed name of S. Gomez of Bridge Lane, NW11. On 2 June 1975 snow several inches thick interrupted Derbyshire's county cricket match at Buxton. John Arlott, covering the Middlesex v. Surrey match at Lord's, reported next day that although Lord's could not compete with Buxton 'During the afternoon play, snow fell. Howarth [the Surrey opener] clearly did not trust the pitch nor relish the conditions. In fairly steady snow he played with all his instinctive wrist aggression.' Mr Weidberg/Gomez wrote to complain that he had been at the match and that no snow had fallen, only rain. When the *Guardian* failed to publish his letter he wrote to the Press Council, which invited the *Guardian*'s comments. The paper submitted a four-page reply saying it believed Mr Arlott. Against Mr Gomez's contention that no snow fell it relied on the well-known philosophical argument about swans. The belief that all swans are white can be upset by the sighting of one black swan. Similarly the proposition that no snow fell could be falsified by the observation of a single flake, and was so falsified by Mr Arlott. The Press Council accepted the *Guardian*'s stand that Mr Gomez was not entitled to use its columns to say that no snow fell but only to say that he saw none. His original letter was therefore misconceived. Five months after Middlesex met Surrey the council rejected Mr Gomez's complaint and acquitted the *Guardian*.

In its campaigns against doubtful ethical practices the Press Council generally had the *Guardian*'s support. There was one occasion, however, when scarcely a single newspaper behaved with strict propriety and that was the arrest of Peter Sutcliffe, the 'Yorkshire Ripper', in January 1981. Several of the tabloids were later condemned by the council for their conduct towards Sutcliffe's wife and family but that was not the immediate concern of the *Guardian* or, one dares say, its broadsheet competitors. The point here was the simple one of prejudice to a fair trial. Between 1975 and 1981 some twenty women were attacked in similar circumstances, almost all of them in Yorkshire, and thirteen were killed. The West Yorkshire police had mounted an exhaustive hunt and were at their wits' end. Sutcliffe was arrested by chance in Sheffield on Friday 2 January and a press conference was called by exultant policemen on Sunday. They left no doubt that they believed they had caught the Ripper.

Every paper then had to decide what background to give to the story and the acting night editor of the *Guardian*, Roger Alton, splashed pictures of the Ripper's thirteen dead victims across the top of the page with the headline 'Man held in hunt for Ripper'. Alton was absolutely right to do this but it was a decision that needed some courage. The law still could and in theory still should have borne heavily on a newspaper which prejudiced a person's trial. (Sylvester Bolam, editor of the *Daily Mirror*, was sent to gaol for three months and his paper fined £10,000 for contempt of court when the *Mirror* prematurely identified a villain, the 'acid bath murderer' John Haigh, before his trial in 1949.) The *Guardian* did not name Sutcliffe on the Monday, though the *Yorkshire Post* and some others did. But that was a detail. What accounted for the difference between 1949 and 1981?

In a leader two days later the *Guardian* agreed that a fair trial, before a jury which would subject the evidence to impartial scrutiny, was now difficult to visualise. 'From the moment the West Yorkshire police held their euphoric press conference, it was inevitable that the media would hardly feel obliged to confine themselves to the spartan, and now largely discredited, requirements of the law of contempt.' The law had been ignored and the concern of the Solicitor-General aroused, but 'the Law Officers should ensure that the police, too, uphold those principles of justice which they rightly upbraid the media for ignoring'. When the Press Council carried out its own inquiry into media coverage of the arrest it invited editors to comment. Preston was able to cite this as an example of the way in which British law and decencies had been eroded from Northern Ireland. He wrote:

Did I, as an editor, feel entirely happy about the tone of the Yorkshire press conference or the immediate spate of television and radio coverage that it generated on that night? Of course not: that was the point of the editorial you refer to and ask about.

Our objections to that police performance were laid out in the editorial. But it is important, I feel sure, for the complaints committee to get chronology right and to remember the law of contempt as it applied at the time that Mr Sutcliffe was taken in for questioning . . . We feel, and have said explicitly, that the laws of contempt have fallen into a certain degree of disarray under the pressure of events in Northern Ireland. We have cited the way in which Gerard Tuite was named as a perilous terrorist by the police after his escape from Brixton Prison and before his imminent trial. If there is one law for citizens of England and another law, bent by the political authorities and the police, for alleged terrorists from Northern Ireland, then the law itself becomes extremely difficult for newspapers to attempt to operate . . .

Had one taken the *Guardian*'s front page of Monday 5 January completely in isolation one might have said that it ran a risk of prejudicing Mr Sutcliffe's trial once he had been arrested and charged. But newspapers, alas, do not exist in a vacuum; nor, equally alas, does any one newspaper gain credit either with its readers or with anybody concerned for failing to report facts which are already far more widely available elsewhere. That does not seem to readers a high moral stand; it merely appears a curious aberration. Our treatment of the original questioning was naturally much influenced by the welter of instant publicity surrounding the press conference by Yorkshire Police. Not to have reported that, in the circumstances, would have seemed ridiculous on the morning after. Did we ever have doubts about the tidal wave of publicity? We did and expressed them in the editorial you refer to. It is always easy in the rush of the day to day events to seem hypocritical. In this case there is of course the possibility of the charge of hypocrisy: but we felt — as indeed the Attorney-

General seems to have acknowledged – that the massive reality of press
conference coverage had to be recognised as did the later, separate existence of
legal and moral issues which we felt bound to discuss.

A good deal of anxiety, perhaps a little fun, and much useful investigation are
hidden in the vaults of Lovell, White & King. An early example was a piece by
Geoffrey Moorhouse, whose keen interests included architecture, which was
published on 28 November 1964, with pictures by Neil Libbert, under the
title 'The sack of Worcester' and accurately foretold what was about to happen
all over the country.

If anyone wants to see the fate in store for Old England unless we do something
about it fast he should go to Worcester. It used to be the sort of place that means
bread and butter to the British Travel Association, with a cathedral and row
upon row of tipsy half-timbering and demure Georgiana in the city centre.
Now it looks as if a lot of bombs have been dropped there. The developers have
moved in and the effect is the same . . .

Like Topsy the Worcester we used to know had just growed without
anybody's planning permission. This was its charm. It was full of small visual
excitements – the sudden view of a church off-centre at the end of a curving
street, the gradual appearance of the cathedral where the Georgian High Street
petered out, thoroughfares which might contain only a couple of really
distinguished old buildings but which needed their contemporary surroundings of second-raters to give them a context.

But opposite the cathedral now was an enormous area of devastation, and the
whole destruction had been carried out under at least the 'muddled indecisive-
ness' of the city councillors. 'In Worcester today no one seems much
concerned about the looting that is going on apart from the members of the
five-year-old Civic Society.'

A letter published a day or two later from A.H. Gomme at Keele
University began: 'After one of the "Baedecker raids" the Germans, I believe,
announced with satisfaction: "Exeter was a jewel – we have destroyed it." The
developers of Worcester are in much the same position (and not those of
Worcester only).' On 5 December Arthur Holden wrote from Newcastle upon
Tyne: 'There is indeed a real danger that precious features of England which
are beloved all over the world may be wantonly destroyed by the irresponsibil-
ities of local administration and the rapacious greed of speculators'; on 8
December a letter of support was published from Lord Esher (the architect
Lionel Brett) as Vice-President of the RIBA.

Nobody sued, but in response to the welcome the Worcester piece had
received, and encouraged by Professor W.G. Hoskins, Exeter historian and
authority on landscape, Moorhouse then investigated a dubious planning
matter in Exeter,[1] and it is clear from the reading that the lawyers had crawled

all over it. They decided to limit the libel actions to one, and so all other names were eliminated. The story concerned the city council's decision to redevelop the centre in collaboration with a single developer, who was not named at the time. This turned out to be the Norwich Union Insurance Societies. The person named in the piece was a long-standing member of the city council's planning committee and a local director of the Norwich Union Fire Office. He took out a writ, but months later the record was withdrawn, the court order noting that 'the defendants do not withdraw any averments in their defence'. The *Guardian* won comprehensively.

A choice piece of investigation was carried out in 1971 when Hetherington, the news editor Jean Stead, and a reporter Peter Harvey collaborated to expose malpractices in the handling of private information.[2] Harvey hired a detective agency to gain information about minute details in Hetherington's and Stead's income tax returns, which it did within a few days by deception on the telephone. It also secured information from the Criminal Records Office about a member of staff who was not a criminal but who had passed through police hands as a conscientious objector to military service twenty years earlier. The detective agency knew what the paper was up to and was promised anonymity when the inevitable police inquiry followed publication.

The story developed oddly. Edward Heath, then Prime Minister, first congratulated the *Guardian* in a Commons statement[3] on a 'valuable public service' and later muttered coldly about its having commissioned an illegal act and made itself liable to prosecution. Chief Superintendent John Hensley began the police inquiry with an overbearing caricature of the 'Knacker of the Yard' manner but ended by sending roses to Harvey's mother. (Soften them up?) The *Guardian* agreed to cooperate with the police and did so short of naming the detectives. All documentary evidence it handed over was in transcript or retyped form. Eventually the police found the agency by accident: its offices were searched in a different inquiry and a copy of its invoice to the *Guardian* found. Two of the agency staff were sentenced to imprisonment and two to suspended sentences. The Younger Committee on Privacy was sitting at the time (the paper's labour correspondent, John Torode, was a member) and the material was referred to it. It adopted the *Guardian's* recommendation that detective agencies should be licensed and supervised, but its report suffered the fate of most inquiries and commissions at the time and was largely ignored.

Much would depend on the tenacity of the individual writer, but the *Guardian* tried not to neglect friends in adversity. One of its long-standing friends had been T. Dan Smith, the Labour party's supremo in Newcastle upon Tyne who held, among many other posts, the chairmanship of the Northern Economic Planning Council. He embodied that regional initiative and enterprise which the paper had long tried to foster. At the height of Smith's legal ordeal, though before he had actually been imprisoned for what in law was a corrupt association with the architect John Poulson, John Ardill, the paper's regional affairs correspondent, wrote an affectionate though not uncritical profile of Smith[4] in which some of the ideas have gone out of fashion but the thrust remains:

> He first came to attention as leader of Newcastle city council clearing the Scotswood slums and bringing in [a celebrated planner of the day] as city planning officer to replan the city as the 'Brasilia of the North' . . .
>
> As chairman of the regional planning council . . . he was looking beyond the defined boundaries of his patch to the concept of a region stretching from the Mersey to the Tyne, with universities as its intellectual and technological powerhouse and with a semi-autonomous role to play in a federal European community . . .
>
> The North-east . . . had something to give, he wrote, 'because my people understand the way that communities tick. They know about the arts and leisure and living together . . . Given a ghost of a chance, we could set the world on fire with a qualitative contribution to the well-being of mankind. We could export ideas, and we could provide a pattern for similarly deprived regions and countries.'

The piece was headed: The mouth of the Tyne.

Sometimes, though rarely, the impact of a newspaper story is so startling as to cause a change of law or practice overnight. That happened in February 1979 when Melanie Phillips, social services correspondent, found that intimate gynaecological examinations were being carried out on Asian women arriving at Heathrow to discover whether they were trying to enter the country illegally. If the women were 'bona fide fiancées' they were entitled to enter without lengthy clearance procedures. Otherwise they were not. The story concerned the experience of an Indian school teacher who had arrived the week before, though a consent form published alongside the Phillips story made clear that the examinations were standard practice ('This is to certify that I, Miss — agree to a gynaecological examination which may be vaginal if necessary . . .').

> The clear implication is that if a Hindu woman was found to be a virgin – which in this case she was – she would be believed to be unmarried; and that if she was found to be not a virgin she would be believed to be married.

The woman had signed the consent form, she said, because she was not familiar with British law and was frightened she would be sent back to Delhi. The story went into harrowing detail about the woman's being required to strip for examination by a male doctor – sufficiently harrowing for the Prime Minister, James Callaghan, to express his disquiet to the Commons. Alex Lyon, MP for York who had been a Home Office minister for a few years in the mid-1970s, told Melanie Phillips that examinations had been carried out fairly frequently at Dacca, which was a main point of departure for would-be immigrants, and that he had ordered the practice to be stopped. Apart from anything else it was contrary to English law that anyone should be forced to give evidence against herself through a medical examination to show whether she was lying.

The personal and cultural enormity of the woman's treatment caused outrage among MPs and those ethnic minority organisations which were already a firm part of the *Guardian*'s constituency. The Indian Deputy High Commissioner went to the Foreign Office to protest. Two days after the story appeared the Home Secretary, Merlyn Rees, banned the tests altogether.

The most humiliating ordeal which *Guardian* staff suffered at the hands of the law was in the arrest, trial and imprisonment of Sarah Tisdall. The paper itself was not prosecuted, which made matters worse. Repeated assurances from the bench that it had acted with great propriety were hard to take. Propriety was not the quality required.

The episode began with an exclusive story on 22 October 1983 in which an important part of the *Guardian*'s readership was keenly interested: the date for the arrival of cruise missiles at the US base at Greenham Common, Berkshire. The story also described plans by the Ministry of Defence for handling the public and parliamentary reaction to the event and for extra troops to be on hand to deal if necessary with Greenham women protesters. It was based on photocopies of two documents left anonymously at the *Guardian*'s reception desk by Miss Tisdall, a clerical officer aged twenty-three in the Foreign and Commonwealth Office. David Fairhall, Defence Correspondent, wrote the story, having first confirmed the facts from his own sources. They were good sources. He was one of the best-informed specialists in Fleet Street. This must have been the first story he acquired by such adventitious means.

Miss Tisdall was not a political activist – though she was the very type of reader the *Guardian* set out to reach – but she thought a serious deception was about to be practised and that she should make it known. The *Guardian* was keen on that kind of story. She naturally believed her identity would be protected. But in the end it was the *Guardian*, under threat of action by the courts and after an agony of internal debate, which handed one of the incriminating documents back to the government, thus enabling the source to be traced and landing Miss Tisdall in prison with a sentence of six months. Her appeal against sentence was rejected. Those who thought that the sentence was admonitory were disabused. It was punitive.

The public impact of the story was all the greater because the day it appeared had been set for a large CND demonstration against the siting of the missiles (carrying nuclear warheads) in Britain. Indeed Miss Tisdall later told Granada television (World in Action, 26 March 1984) that she had delivered the papers when she did in order to achieve that impact. When the story appeared, however, there was no immediate and overt government response. No formal inquiries were made by the MoD, although Whitehall agreed that an internal leaks inquiry was under way. But the government then announced that a Commons debate on the missiles would be held within a week,[5] whereupon the *Guardian* decided to publish the full text of the memorandum under the heading 'Heseltine's briefing to Thatcher on cruise timing'.

Text rather than summary put beyond doubt the existence of a source who had handed over a document and not merely given an oral summary of it. Was publication in that form, enclosed in conspicuous quotes, not an unnecessary act of bravado? The stand-first (introduction) to the text even used the much-loved phrase 'A document which has come into the possession of the *Guardian* . . . '. The Prime Minister ordered an immediate inquiry, as she could scarcely fail to do.

The *Guardian* then received a demand from the Treasury Solicitor for the return of the document. Its own solicitors won from him a few days' grace in which to consult counsel, but the cost of doing so was high. In their letter of 11 November they confirmed that the *Guardian* possessed the document and noted, almost as might an archaeologist examining a potsherd, that 'certain markings' appeared at the top and bottom right-hand corners of the first page and on the fourth page, and that an attempt had been made to obliterate some of them before the document was delivered anonymously to the *Guardian* office. The editor took the view, the solicitors said, that these marks might help to identify the source of the information. The letter went on:

> In accordance with the well-established convention of journalism, which now has statutory force by virtue of the Contempt of Court Act 1981, he is not prepared to take any step which might lead to the disclosure of the source of information published in his newspaper. As the editor is concerned only to protect his source I am, without prejudice to any argument as to property in the document, authorised to hand it to you with the three areas of marking excluded from it. This would provide you with the whole of the text.

There followed a discussion of the legal process that might ensue if this course of action was not acceptable, and the letter concluded: 'In the meantime you may take it that the document will be preserved intact.'

This response, which effectively tied the editor's hands and prevented him from destroying the copied memorandum, may well have been less robust than the Treasury Solicitor had expected. But LWK had been engaged by the Guardian and Manchester Evening News Ltd as its lawyers because of the quality of their advice and also because of their high standing in the profession. Under the principle of horses for courses it could be that in a case like this, on the fringes of law and politics, the paper should have hired someone like the Mafia law firm of Prizzi, Prizzi, Johnson and Prizzi. But it didn't. It relied as hitherto on its highly esteemed 'officers of the court'.

The Treasury Solicitor rejected the *Guardian*'s proposed course of action. On 22 November he issued a writ for the return of the document, unmutilated, in the names of the Secretary for Defence and the Attorney-General.

The matter went to court. The *Guardian* retained Lord Rawlinson QC, who had been Solicitor-General under Sir Alec Douglas-Home, Attorney-General in the Heath administration from 1970 to 1974, and chairman of the Bar thereafter. It may have been hoped that in a case involving CND, the women of Greenham Common, and a breach of confidence in Whitehall, those august antecedents would lend additional authority to the defence. If so, the hope was a vain one. The case came before Mr Justice Scott in the High Court on 14 December. The Crown won. An immediate appeal was rejected by the Court of Appeal. After what it would not exaggerate to call a paroxysm of regrets the editor of the *Guardian* handed the document, complete with its distinguishing marks, into the gloved hands of the government's emissary.

Alongside the facts were the arguments. One of these, put forward by the *Observer*, was that the editor of the *Guardian* 'has not betrayed his source unless the source was careless enough in turn to leave incriminating evidence of his identity on the photocopy itself'.[6] But not many copies of the document had been made (the Treasury Solicitor said seven) and if Miss Tisdall had mutilated the distinguishing marks on her copy, several of her colleagues would have fallen under suspicion. Her own honour would then, in all probability, have forced her to confess; but in any case to suppose that the document would be returned for examination begs the question at issue. Again, as *The Times* observed in a leader with the high Timesean title Caveat Talpa,[7] her traffic with the *Guardian* was not of the usual confidential kind:

> . . . the information received by the *Guardian* was in the distinct though growing category of material sent anonymously. The recipient's obligations towards an informant who does not trust him with his identity can hardly be of the same kind as those in a genuine confidential relationship. No explicit or implicit contract exists, and it is almost quixotic to act as if it did.

The arguments of both papers extended sympathy to a beleaguered editor but Preston, perhaps thinking them casuistical, did not seek refuge in them.[8] Instead he acknowledged the initial mistake in hanging on to the document. It had found its way into the maw of the filing system as documents do.

The journalists' rule that sources of information should not be disclosed is not a moral absolute but it is very strongly cherished. The circumstances in which it can be set aside are generally taken, and since 1981 had been recognised by statute,[9] so it was thought, as relating to matters like the prevention of war or serious crime.[10] In the early stages of this affair, before Sarah Tisdall's identity was known, some newspapers did argue that it was vital to the security of the state that the Ministry of Defence 'mole' be found. (E.g., the *Sun*: 'Is there not a danger that out of some twisted political convictions, he is prepared to betray us all to a potential enemy?') The *Guardian*, however, did not argue that it was discharging some public duty higher than that to the ethics of its trade. Its case in court was that the information it had come by was not a threat to the security of the state but only a matter of political embarrassment to the government. The paper relied on that section of the recent Contempt of Court Act which read:

> No court may require a person to disclose, nor is any person guilty of contempt of court for refusing to disclose, the source of information contained in a publication for which he is responsible, unless it be established to the satisfaction of the court that disclosure is necessary in the interests of justice or national security or for the prevention of disorder or crime.

Mr Justice Scott specifically did not reject this argument, but found that the document was Crown property which the Crown was entitled to have back.

At the end of the long and wounding series of court appearances the Law Lords decided, one year after the article had appeared and six months after Miss Tisdall had been convicted, that national security did demand the surrender of the document. Their decision was by a margin of three to two, Lords Scarman and Fraser coming down on the *Guardian*'s side. But in one of those agonising anomalies on which case law is built, the Law Lords as a body rejected the original ground on which Mr Justice Scott, at the first hearing, had found against the *Guardian*, which was the government's property in the document.

The days and weeks after the initial surrender, and then after Sarah Tisdall's conviction, were the most depressing that *Guardian* people could remember, especially for the editor, who received the voluminous hate-mail which attends a public figure in distress. Some papers (notably *The Times* and the *Observer*) made a staunch effort to sympathise and share in his dilemma. The *Economist* commented that the hidden danger in the whole proceedings 'was the wide extent of private censorship created in recent years by skilful abuse of the law on confidence and copyright'. The *New Statesman*'s editorial comment, Hugh Stephenson having taken over the editorship, was less censorious than many of its staff would have liked. He made the point which had already become painfully obvious at the *Guardian* that it should not have entered into correspondence with the Treasury Solicitor or been caught with the document in its possession.

The paper's political staff reported that Cabinet ministers were surprised by the severity of the sentence on Miss Tisdall. Mr Gerald Kaufman, then Shadow Home Secretary, commented:

> I have no doubt that, faced with the choice of surrendering the documents or going to gaol, the editor of the *Guardian*, like journalists on the *Daily Mail* and the editor of the *Daily Mirror*[11] before him, would have chosen gaol. However, he did not have that choice. The new practice of imposing fines of hundreds of thousands of pounds in contempt cases could literally have destroyed the *Guardian*. Such fines can now be turned into the equivalent of banning a dissident newspaper.

Outraged protests against the sentence were expressed by various MPs, civil liberties groups, CND, and the national executive of the National Union of Journalists, which said that the *Guardian*'s editorial management bore a heavy responsibility for what had happened to Miss Tisdall. In the *Guardian*'s own NUJ chapel, where his integrity was better known, Preston's predicament was better understood too. Of special importance, perhaps, was the considered view of James Cameron, not a staff member but a weekly columnist whose steely professionalism (and past condemnation of the managerial 'betrayal' of the *News Chronicle*) had given him added authority in such a crisis. He wrote:

> I, too, believe that the *Guardian* made a mess of it. To its credit the paper did what is unusual and difficult for a serious journal to do, and made a formal and public admission of 'serious errors' . . . To my mind . . . this distressing episode reflects rather more credit on the paper than otherwise . . . Sarah Tisdall betrayed nobody. The *Guardian* betrayed nobody. The only people who were traitors to the true formula of British justice last week were Mr Justice Cantley [the judge at Miss Tisdall's trial] and the British Foreign Office . . .

The most bitter condemnation of the *Guardian* and its editor personally was a tirade of several thousand words in the quarterly *Granta*[12] by David Caute which Paul Johnson,[13] no friend of the *Guardian*, described as 'a collector's piece of Leftist vitriol'. On a wall opposite Farringdon station, which many of the Guardian staff passed on their way to work, appeared a shaming piece of graffito: 'Guardian workers ! Have you no conscience ? Sarah Tisdall is innocent'. The words remained conspicuous for several years. Money raised by the NUJ chapel was used by Miss Tisdall to buy a bike for her new job in London on release from gaol. She received more than 3,000 letters of support from readers.

At no stage was a jury required to pass judgment on Sarah Tisdall or the *Guardian*. Not long afterwards, however, another civil servant, Clive Ponting, leaked in another direction (to Mr Tam Dalyell MP) a Ministry of Defence document containing alleged lies about the sinking of the *Belgrano* during the Falklands campaign. At his trial the jury was left in no doubt that Ponting had done the deed, but on 11 February 1985 it acquitted him none the less. The acquittal was clearly perverse. Equally clearly it was the jury's way of expressing discontent both with the state of the law on secrecy and with its abuse as a political rather than a security device. Ponting became something of a cult hero among radicals in Farringdon Road.

The Tisdall case had barely ended before the Peter Wright case began. Here again, the *Guardian*, mainly in the persons of the editor and the executive editor, Kenneth Dodd, found itself immured in seemingly interminable sessions with the lawyers. It is tempting to speculate that the drubbing the paper received in Tisdall was a powerful motive for the vengeance it exacted in Wright. Having won in the Court of Appeal the *Guardian* (acting this time with the *Observer*) had its victory unanimously confirmed by five law lords and the little matter of its costs, amounting to some £219,000, settled to its satisfaction in that Lovell White Durant, as LWK had then become, achieved 70 per cent recovery, a high rating.

Wright began in the *Guardian* on 17 July 1984 when the paper reported the allegations he had made the previous night on the Granada TV programme *World in Action*. These were mainly about an event in 1955 when MI5, in which Wright had served, had allegedly stolen documents from the flat of a wealthy communist in Mayfair. They gave the first inkling of the much more wide-ranging charges he was to bring in his book *Spycatcher*. When *Spycatcher* had been published in the United States, and the government brought its case in an Australian court to prevent publication elsewhere, Richard Norton-Taylor wrote[14] an account of the more detailed allegations made in the book which were about to be cited by Wright's counsel. The *Observer* carried a similar report. On 27 June 1986 the Attorney General won a temporary injunction preventing publication by either newspaper of any further reports of malpractice arising from that source. These included what soon became a familiar litany of attempts to destabilise the Wilson government in 1974–6, the bugging of the French, West German, Greek and Indonesian embassies and of the Zimbabwe independence conference at Lancaster House, and a supposed plot to assassinate Nasser in 1956. The injunction was confirmed at a full hearing in July, and the *Guardian* and the *Observer* laboured under it until released by the House of Lords on 13 October 1988, by which time the whole thing had become stale. (In 1987 the *Independent* and *The Sunday Times* had published, noisily and perhaps disingenuously, claims from *Spycatcher* on the grounds that the injunction was against other newspapers, not against them. The courts disabused them.)

The Wright case conveniently illustrates, and in a routine rather than abnormally dramatic way, the not infrequent disagreements between the leader columns and the regular signed commentaries appearing opposite the leader page which, under Preston's editorship, came to express an increasingly important part of the opinion which the *Guardian* presented to the world. Such a dichotomy of opinion would have been unusual in Scott's day. Certainly 'The voice of opponents no less than that of friends has a right to be heard', but it was important to know which was which. The news columns flowed with accounts of the Australian and other court proceedings, and the leader columns thundered away – on some forty-nine occasions until 1988 – about the issues of press freedom raised by the Wright case, which indeed were real, as the law lords eventually signalled. For example, when the High Court originally confirmed the temporary injunction:

> It is implicit in the judgment [confirming the injunction forbidding publication in the *Guardian* and the *Observer*], and in the Crown's case, that confidentiality is considered more important than the disclosure of possibly criminal

acts. Although, as Lord Denning stressed in his report on the Profumo affair, the security services must act within the law, just like any ordinary citizen, we must not report allegations of criminal behaviour made by someone in a position to know. No naming of a Blunt, a Hollis or a Philby by Mr Wright could be mentioned in the *Guardian*. No Watergate leaks here if they came from Mr Wright. The secrecy of MI5 is paramount . . . The Government is concerned that his breach of confidentiality might encourage others to write their memoirs. We neither applaud nor condemn such breaches; much information which reaches newspapers represents a breach of confidence by someone . . . We have been told that if we wish to publish some matter of burning importance now covered by the injunction we have only to return to the court to seek permission to do so. It is a curious kind of press freedom (and threatening) which says you might be able to publish, but you'll have to ask the court first.[15]

But the whole Wright episode did raise questions beyond those about the elementary freedom to publish. The *Guardian* itself acknowledged this but with less apparent conviction than did Hugo Young in his column,[16] of which, since it was more than 1,600 words long, only a flavour can be given:

[But] taken in the round, the *Spycatcher* affair no longer seems a great case in the annals of struggle between government and publishers. It is, instead, a generalised disaster from which not a single British institution emerges with status or reputation enhanced: not the Prime Minister, not the Government, not the law officers, not the lower courts (save one judge), not the higher courts (save two), not the civil service (in the person of its chief, Sir Robert Armstrong), and not even, in any ambiguous way, the press . . .

Spycatcher ought never to have been written or published . . . Except in one particular,* a vital but limited one, it does not pass the public interest test which surely has to qualify, in security matters, the overwhelming presumption in favour of publication. No great principle is at issue, such as the protection of sources, or the right to expose government deception, or the defence of openness against concealment . . . It is a riveting book . . . but to achieve this effect it breaks a lot of perfectly sensible rules. It reveals vast quantities of detail about the methods and product of interrogation, surveillance and, the holy of holies, cryptography . . .

The victim of these grand strategic follies has not been one institution but many. The country as a whole has been the loser. The Government has become a global laughing-stock . . . There is, however, another down-side from the press's point of view. Once this insider's allegation about the Wilson years has passed unanswered – indeed, was treated with arrogant indifference by the party of law and order – newspapers had to act as they did. Once the book was available to any importer from the US, they were right to challenge an

* MI5 and the Wilson government.

outrageous attack on press freedom. They ought still to go to court to try and undo the grosser restraints invented by Messrs Donaldson, Ackner and Templeman. But the fact remains that they have been ensnared from the beginning in what is, at bottom, a bad case.

Young received 'a surprisingly large number of approving letters' from other journalists.[17]

The Lords' judgment is not expected to stand as a monument for all time to the freedoms for which Preston was arguing. Jennifer McDermott of Lovell White Durrant wrote in the journal *Administrative Law* (December 1988):

> The majority of the House of Lords in this final appeal following a full trial and with the benefit of hindsight, therefore, effectively found that the Government should not have sought and been granted the June 1986 injunctions against the *Guardian* and the *Observer*. Notwithstanding this finding, it is thought likely that in a future, similar case an interim injunction would still be granted. This is because at the pre-trial stage all that the Government has to show in order to obtain a restraining order is an arguable case that the information is confidential and that the balance of convenience weighs in favour of preserving the 'status quo' until a further trial can take place.

It has always been part of the *Guardian*'s case under its two most recent editors that in legal matters the status quo prevents rather than permits. Defeat in Tisdall, notwithstanding the Lords' eventual judgment, left lasting scars. Victory in Wright can only have been ephemeral.

CHAPTER 20

Trans-European

THE *Guardian* maintained both continuity and authority in its reporting of the Soviet Union and Eastern Europe. It published the first connected account, by David Soskice, of the storming of the Winter Palace in 1917,[1] and Arthur Ransome reported for several years the beginnings of life under Leninism. In 1968 Victor Zorza foresaw 'with astonishing accuracy and against the flow of informed opinion' the Soviet invasion of Czechoslovakia and was named Journalist of the Year, with that citation, by his colleagues in the trade. In 1991 Jonathan Steele, veteran foreign correspondent then serving in Moscow, talked his way on to the aircraft taking the plotters of a coup d'état to Mikhail Gorbachev's villa in the Crimea and secured an exclusive interview with him, though that event is outside the scope of this book.

Starting in 1950, Zorza carried on his minute scrutiny of the Soviet and East European press and broadcast transcripts for almost twenty-five years. At a time when all Moscow correspondence, if not censored, had to be self-censored, his account of happenings in the Soviet bloc, though necessarily confined almost entirely to public affairs, was the best to be had in the Western press. In a profile of Zorza at the time of his award[2] it was noted that one of his repeated themes was the liberalisation of the Soviet system, growing out of its economic development. Did that not mean that he was writing himself out of a job? 'Yes,' Zorza replied. 'The pace of change will be so greatly speeded up that within 15 years we shall see the Communist world adopt many of the political practices we regarded as democratic. The process of decision-making will be observable on the surface. The press will be more free. And my job will be not just harder, but no longer necessary.'

That prediction, though a few years out in time, might have merited the award even more than did his analysis of Czechoslovakia. The Soviet march against Prague was a distinct possibility all that summer, as some of Zorza's colleagues argued with him at the time; the Soviet empire, on the other hand, looked secure for decades to come.

Zorza was a sixteen-year-old Polish refugee at Kuibyshev on the Volga in the winter of 1941–2, living rough, queueing for bread, and then discovering that his literary hero Ilya Ehrenburg was in the city. He sought out Ehrenburg's apartment and went to pay his respects. Ehrenburg was suspicious, and to test Zorza's credentials asked him which of his books he had most liked. Zorza named the book *Julio Jurenito*, written soon after the Revolution in praise of an anarchist leader but banned by Stalin. Ehrenburg could not afford to be reminded of it, but although he immediately changed the subject he took Zorza under his protection, fed him and housed him, and advised him how to go to the West.

Polish prisoners in Russia were being formed into a unit to fight the German Reich. An air contingent was due to go to England, and if Zorza could claim some familiarity with English and with gliding he might be able to join them. He did, and remained in the RAF until 1948. It was when he then joined the BBC monitoring service at Caversham that he began writing for the *Guardian* as 'A Student of Soviet Affairs' – a title invented on the night of his first contribution by Wadsworth, who himself wrote as 'A Student of the Press' – and the BBC sacked Zorza for that reason. He had already become the paper's well-established kremlinologist when he joined the staff in 1956.

It was another literary link which helped to keep the *Guardian* at the centre of East European reporting from shortly before the Prague Spring in 1968 until the collapse of the regimes. Bill Webb, the literary editor from 1959 to 1989, took his degree at Trinity College Dublin and learned on the job by editing a rustic weekly in Ireland. He joined the *Guardian* in 1955, spent eighteen months in the reporters' Room, and went through a familiar process of dogsbodying on the Corridor: writing short leaders, arts notices, Miscellany columns and obituaries, editing letters to the editor, choosing the 'back-pagers' (essays contributed normally by outsiders, which had originally appeared on the back but by then were on an inside page) and doing whatever other tasks the editor found for him. (Stand-in editor of the *Manchester Guardian Weekly* for a week or two was one of the duties thrust on anyone who happened to be around.) Webb introduced the idea of an arts page into the features department: a weekly page of arts news, interviews and celebrations of the kind which years later Nicholas de Jongh provided on a grander scale in both news and features columns.

Webb became literary editor in succession to Anthony Hartley, who had brought with him from *The Spectator* an attachment to the 'angries' of the mid-1950s – Philip Larkin, John Wain, Kingsley Amis, D.J. Enright – which Webb was glad to inherit. But Webb's enthusiasm for Anglo-Irish writing had given him a feeling for books born out of places which, through reading Kafka, he transferred to Prague. Not having enjoyed that editorial perk of the period, the 'freebie' abroad, he asked the travel editor Adrienne Keith-Cohen to keep him in mind. Thus he went to Czechoslovakia in 1966 to write travel copy and got to know some of the writers in Prague who were the powers behind the reform in the Communist party and who were to rise and fall with Dubček (and then, of course, if they survived, rise again). Having established this rare connection, and with the advantage of German learned during national service, Webb found no difficulty in persuading Hetherington that he should go to Prague in the autumn of 1967 to attend the writers' congress. Webb was a writers' editor and spoke in the literary patois of the time. Patois is possibly the wrong allusion: contrary to years of stylistic convention that foreign words should when possible be avoided, Webb made a point of sneaking German nouns into the paper (and not only when writing about those three stalwarts of his pages, Günter Grass, Heinrich Böll and Hermann Hesse).

The signals coming from Prague became more overtly political. Geoffrey Moorhouse was sent to describe the gathering storm early in 1968, when Antonin Novotny was forced out of office first as party secretary and then as state president, and Webb returned for another spell in May. When the invasion burst Hella Pick, who had been on her way there, had the right visa but was in the wrong city (Vienna) but Harry Jackson was dispatched from England on the first flight and managed to find a frontier post which would let him in. He reported from Prague, manning the telex as well as writing the copy, at what was for him, as chief foreign fireman, a frenzied time. Within the space of months he was covering Vietnam, Northern Ireland, the Middle East and the end of the Prague Spring.

Webb in the meantime was also leading a fragmented life. In addition to covering Prague he was also helping to set up the Booker literary prize, of which he was the first chairman of judges, the *Guardian* fiction prize which he had introduced three years earlier having endeared itself to the publishing trade. He nevertheless found a novel excuse for presenting himself at the Czech Embassy to go on another visit almost immediately after the Russians had secured their invasion and carried out their purge.

The Webb family lived in a famous house in Princes Road, Stockport, which had been home to a succession of *Guardian* families.* One of his neighbours was a wine merchant, Richard Godlee, whom he consulted, along with Raymond Postgate, editor of the *Good Food Guide*, about the plausibility of writing a supplement on Czechoslovak wine. Postgate said that the hill of Tokay descended on the northern side into Slovakia and a specious case could therefore be made for saying that the British public were keen to learn more about Slovak Tokays. Godlee wrote a letter of credence expressing a wine merchant's support for such a project which Webb took along to the visa section.

The people at the Czechoslovak Embassy said, roughly speaking, that they recognised this for the load of rubbish it was but added with a wink that, if he really wanted to go, there was an engineering fair at Brno for which he could have a five-day visa. Having dutifully filed his piece about the tractors and

* Fay, Shrapnel, Moorhouse, Webb.

muck-spreaders Webb went to Prague and extended the five days to six weeks. The *Guardian*'s Czechoslovak reporting was thus able to continue, in attenuated form, after the invasion and the unveiling of the Brezhnev doctrine as it had done before.

The silence which then fell over Eastern Europe was never absolute. The ubiquitous Hella Pick, now diplomatic correspondent/editor, reported either from there or from London. She had already acquired a formidable reputation on three continents; her vast experience of events and people, her refusal to be thrown out of her stride once she had started on a story, and her professional accomplishments in commanding English, French and German equally fluently, as well as understanding economics, made her one of the paper's most valuable assets at any period in its history. The story may be apocryphal, but is probably true, of her being overheard telephoning the Elysée Palace to secure an interview with President Giscard d'Estaing. 'Yes, I know the President is busy,' she said (though in French), 'but I am busy too!'

Hella arrived in England in March 1939, a refugee from Vienna who was among the children whose freedom was bought, literally, by representatives of the Jewish community in Palestine from the Nazi authorities in Austria. Her mother secured a permit to leave her comfortable middle-class home on the strength of a promised job as a cook in an English household. Her father died after emigrating to America, her mother's mother in a concentration camp. The cook's job was at the home of the Lakes landscape painter Heaton Cooper who, with his wife Ophelia, proved to be the most important influence on Hella's life. She immersed herself in English language and culture and indeed Anglican worship, casting aside her Austrian origins permanently, her German language until she had mastered English, but her Jewishness only until she felt mature enough in later life to reacknowledge it. But Cooper's influence had a negative aspect too, in that his attachment to Moral Rearmament, which she could not share, gave her a sense of failure which she said she never entirely shed.[3]

Knowing, or so it seemed, everyone in the world who could be the source for a story, she introduced several of them as guests at the editor's Tuesday conferences. They were men as diverse as Robert McNamara, former US Secretary of Defense, and, in the early 1980s, Myecislaw Rakowski, the Deputy Prime Minister, later Prime Minister, of Poland and until shortly before his visit editor of the party's intellectual journal *Polityka*. It was a sign of the changes that had already begun that he spoke freely, if cynically, about Poland's being divided between the rulers and the ruled. Asked what attitude his paper had adopted to the recent Soviet invasion of Afghanistan he said it had ignored the episode. 'To have told lies would have been wrong,' he said, 'but to have told the truth would have been worse.' Hella Pick got Rakowski to write several pieces for the paper. She was also a close friend of Willy Brandt and shared Hetherington's admiration for him as the author of Federal

Germany's Ostpolitik. (It was he 'who finally convinced me that there was moral integrity in post-war Germany'.)[4]

Michael Simmons, who had specialised in Eastern Europe for the *Financial Times*, now did so for the *Guardian* in the Solidarity year of 1981, and John Torode had an early, hectic, and revealing interview with Lech Walesa.[5] Webb was still active on the whole East European scene. This combination of writers and interests gave the paper an especially strong feel for the unfolding of events over the next eight or nine years.

Roy Jenkins, when president of the European Commission, noted in his diary for Monday 8 May 1978 that he had lunched with Peter Preston and 'found him remarkably agreeable; not difficult to talk to as I half-expected, very European, well-informed, and sensible on practically everything'. Very European: the political integration of Europe indeed became one of the *Guardian*'s liveliest concerns. But that is not how it was in the beginning.

One of the early hints of the transformation of Western Europe, which the paper did not seriously pick up at the time, came with the conference of foreign ministers of what was then only the European Coal and Steel Community (ECSC) at Messina, Sicily, in June 1955. The *Guardian*, not having a correspondent to spare in what, after all, was only a 10- or 12-page paper (occasionally, as during the general election of that year, expanding to 16), relied on Reuters and British United Press. The conference was duly noted in the leader columns, but without any unusual urgency. Reuters had interpreted the result as a 'slow motion' programme for the eventual economic unity of Europe, with pooled transport and power resources. In its leader, however, the paper said it was a mistake to dismiss the result in this fashion and that Britain should be 'gratified' that 'the Europeans are going their own way'. There was no discernible expression of regret that Britain was not there, either in the comment on the outcome or during the conference which led up to it. In later years the *Guardian* became an advocate of stronger powers for the European Parliament, but at that stage it was content with things as they were. It agreed with the decision not to give the Common Assembly of the ECSC legislative powers, preferring a method of cautious study which is 'slow and unspectacular but sure'.

If this seems uncharacteristic of the paper as it later became, with Continental typography and satellite presses in Frankfurt and Marseilles, it should be remembered that in 1955 Britain had not yet entered the post-imperial chrysalis in which it underwent so great a change. Britain was still a power East of Suez. *Look Back in Anger* had not yet hit the Royal Court. As late as 1957 strikers on Merseyside, as seen in a *Guardian* picture taken outside a shipyard, still wore belted raincoats and trilby hats, with not a bomber jacket or brazier to be seen.[6] England was still known for its reserve, and haste was deemed incautious.

The Rome treaties were signed on 25 March 1957 and a report of the occasion was carried on an inside page. Much more space had been devoted during the previous week to the meeting between Macmillan and Eisenhower in Bermuda, reflecting the paper's priorities at the time, which were, as they had been under Wadsworth, with the Anglo-American alliance. The leader on Rome was No. 3 after one about an offer of 5 per cent to the railwaymen and another about the Communists in Kerala. Characteristically it was concerned lest the preference given to French colonies in the trade with the Six should redound to the detriment of Commonwealth countries, and argued that 'it would be deplorable if the historic British decision to commit vital economic interests to Western Europe [through the European Free Trade Association, EFTA] were to fizzle out in a vain struggle with complications', which is what it did.

During the 1950s the *Guardian*, in spite of its general support for Labour over several decades, still had a fond affection for the Liberal party, which indeed it never lost. It is illustrated by a letter from Laurence Scott to G.K. Daniels, of the company's Manchester solicitors, Tatham Worthington & Co., on 22 May 1958:

> We have been asked and have agreed to make a small annual subscription to the funds of the Liberal Party. For our own reasons, however, we are most anxious that this should remain anonymous. Will you please send to Mr P. Fothergill, 70 Alexander Crescent, Dewsbury, a subscription of 25 guineas saying it is for the funds of the Liberal Party from an anonymous subscriber. We shall advise you if we want the subscription repeated next year.

It was probably the Liberals' enthusiasm for Europe which confirmed the *Guardian* in its growing support for the new alignment taking hold. (Certainly that support owed nothing to Labour.) Macmillan announced the British application in the Commons on 31 July 1961, but Hetherington was dissatisfied with it. (He was nearly always highly critical of Macmillan, and perhaps did less than justice to him when he rose to the great occasion. The paper dismissed[7] Macmillan's 'wind of change' speech to the South African Parliament in Capetown as 'inadequate'.) On Europe it now commented:

> The plunge is to be taken, but, on yesterday's evidence, by a shivering Government. Mr Macmillan announced that Britain is to apply for full membership of the European Community, but he hedged the announcement with doubts and reservations. While he said that we should 'spare no effort' to reach a satisfactory agreement, he seemed at least as anxious to emphasise that no commitment was being made yet . . .
>
> Most Europeans – even President de Gaulle – want us to join the Common Market. They will be glad to see Britain as an equal partner in the new Western Europe. But they want us to come in wholeheartedly. They see it as the most creative development in Europe for a hundred years . . . Whitehall has never quite believed that the Community would not collapse . . . They are deter-

mined that the British must not undo what they themselves have already achieved . . . After more than a year's hesitation, [Macmillan] still hesitates. Where a warm and unequivocal declaration could have transformed the atmosphere of the negotiations, he has been coldly correct.

Later in the week, when the Commons held a two-day debate on Europe, Macmillan made himself more clear. Norman Shrapnel, parliamentary correspondent, reported in the lead story on Thursday 3 August:

> In marked contrast to his gloomy hesitancy earlier in the week Mr Macmillan looked and sounded yesterday like a man leading a nation into the next stage of its history. It was a vigorous and imaginative speech in which he invited the Commons to endorse the Government's decision on the Common Market . . .
>
> He was sharply taken up on this by Mr Gaitskell, who mentioned an earlier Government prospect, offered by the President of the Board of Trade, of political federation as the likely outcome. The country, Mr Gaitskell was convinced, would not have that at any price . . .
>
> Mr Gaitskell had, of course, put himself in a position in which it was hard to shine. He had to celebrate hesitancy – to erect a statue, as it were, to a man sitting on a fence . . .
>
> The Liberals could be excused from attending very hard. They looked like early Christians being preached to by a bishop who had been converted late . . .

Edward Heath was Britain's negotiator with the Six in Brussels. Leonard Beaton, who had taken over defence for the *Guardian*, volunteered to post himself there and monitor in intricate detail what was stirring on the New Zealand lamb and Indian tea tariff front. Beaton was a Canadian who at least once professed that he would never understand English ways. The occasion was early in his time at the paper's Fleet Street office when he wrote to Patrick Monkhouse, then deputy editor, putting a proposition and addressed the letter 'Dear Mr Monkhouse'. The reply came back 'Dear Beaton, I think we've known each other long enough to drop the Mr . . . ' Usage changed, and surnames did not survive the 1960s.

It was to be assumed that Beaton's sympathies would lie with the Commonwealth, and indeed they largely did, but his doubts about the wisdom of British entry went beyond Commonwealth emotionalism: he had studied the texts as closely as any minister or civil servant and largely under his influence Hetherington became more and more wary about what they entailed. The two were close friends and would discuss the Common Market on their walks in the Lake District, taking a transistor with them so as not to miss the one o'clock news even on the top of Great Gable.

Hetherington was concerned not so much about what the Brussels terms might mean politically for Britain, for he was prepared for a high degree of political integration, but about the economic future of both Britain and the newly independent states of the Commonwealth. He found the Common

Market to be among the most divisive subjects between himself and his lieutenants. Harold Griffiths, the economics leader-writer who had been expected to succeed Fry as City editor when in fact Laurence Scott successfully lobbied for the 'name' of William Davis, was aware of the negotiating snags but strongly supported a continued policy of entry into Europe. Mark Arnold-Forster was among the sceptics and over the next decade kept up a staunch campaign in the leader columns and in signed articles against the extravagance of the Common Agricultural Policy. (It was he who broke the story about the surplus butter being fed back to the cows.) Harford Thomas, then assistant, later deputy editor, whose instincts for the paper were almost always to make it a vehicle of change and advocate of new causes, was strongly pro-European. John Anderson had spent some of his early years in British Guiana and was a Commonwealth man. Monkhouse stuck to the Labour line and would probably have gone along with Gaitskell in his warning against the sacrifice of 1,000 years of history. In the event Gaitskell died within a few days of the French veto and the political landscape underwent a sudden change.

However, other things were happening in the world. Macmillan met Kennedy at Nassau in December 1962 and agreed to buy Polaris missiles from him, thus confirming to the satisfaction of the French their suspicion that the special relationship with the US was more valuable than the link with Europe. Eighteen months after Macmillan's application, on 14 January 1963, President de Gaulle vetoed British membership. Or, as Darsie Gillie more delicately put it in his dispatch from the Elysée palace, 'Hope that French diplomacy might facilitate Britain's entry into the Common Market was reduced to a negligible quantity by President de Gaulle at his press conference today.'

Beaton was puzzled, but probably less downcast than the foreign ministers of France's five partners. He had seen ahead the big snag which Britain had been about to hit.

All those who have studied the economic and tariff issues in the negotiations [he wrote on 30 January after negotiations formally collapsed] consider that the British have taken up a position which is extraordinarily reasonable . . . The technicians of the French delegation have failed to produce convincing evidence to support General de Gaulle's statement about British unwillingness to abandon Commonwealth preference and adapt herself to the requirements of the Rome Treaty. The real battle, however, remained to be fought at home when the terms became known. The lack of frankness in the Government's approach to the British people on this question was bound to bring the most serious political consequences. Just how profound these would have been will never now be known.

Beaton was wrong in the last particular because Britain reapplied, and the whole laborious saga of New Zealand dairy quotas and Caribbean avocados began again.

The first *Guardian* office in Brussels was set up in an Edwardian apartment overlooking a square near the Commission's headquarters. Its occupant was Richard Norton-Taylor, previously a stringer, always an agreeably anarchical person, who joined the staff on 1 January 1973, the day of Britain's entry along with Ireland and Denmark. The Common Market, as it was still generally known, was a hot domestic issue during the Wilson administration because of Labour's initial opposition, the device of renegotiation to cover up splits in the party, and the eventual referendum. As an institutional story it was, and long remained, centred on the CAP (Common Agricultural Policy) which the *Guardian* lost no opportunity of condemning. (In so far as the CAP was designed to keep small French farmers on the land and thus contribute to social and ecological stability, was this opposition, a later and more environ-ment-conscious generation might have asked, always well-founded? Or was it the unintended effects that stuck in the paper's gullet for so many years?) Reflecting on the ten years he had been writing about the topic Norton-Taylor wrote in 1978:[8]

> Many thousands of tonnes of fruit and vegetables have been crushed by EEC bulldozers in that time; thousands of tonnes of butter have been exported at cut price to the Russians or stored in refrigerated ships off the French and Irish coasts; surplus EEC cereals have been stored in rented barns in Czechoslovakia; milk powder has been forced on dairy cows whence it came in the first place . . . the gap between rich and poor Community farmers has increased; . . . the poor in the Third World are as hungry as ever, while food consumption in the West is reaching saturation point . . . Ireland sends as much as 45 per cent of its total beef production into EEC-approved intervention storehouses.

Norton-Taylor pursued the lack of British parliamentary supervision of EEC activity. The paper itself was concerned about the weakness of the European Parliament which it nevertheless appeared to believe was something which would be remedied as member-states adopted a more concerted foreign policy.

Despite earlier doubts the *Guardian* supported Britain's joining in 1973 and remaining in 1975. Under Peter Preston the paper did not, throughout the 1970s and 80s, have any serious hesitations about Britain's belonging to Europe, though he did not carry the whole staff with him. Ian Aitken in particular remained a resolute opponent of closer European union and found common cause there with one of those staunch House of Commons men — Enoch Powell — for whom he had a deep personal regard while standing at the other end of the political spectrum. Others on the staff queried not so much the direction as the pace.

(For many years only two differences of opinion arose between Preston and his deputy, David McKie, at leader-writers' conferences, though it is possible that more delicate decisions were reached in greater privacy. One was Europe,

Anglo-French distrust, the same old story – depicted by Gibbard on 4 May 1971. In 1971 the actors were Heath and Pompidou. Copyright © Les Gibbard, 1971.

about which Preston was impatient of delay. The other was Kerry Packer. Preston had an iconoclastic disregard for the niceties of traditional cricket and welcomed the pyjama game in Australia, or said he did – perhaps he was trying to tease. McKie, voicing the sentiments of most of those in the office who believed the matter important, abhorred it. Preston had a long-running cricketing dispute with another of his deputies, Peter Cole. That concerned the virtues of Boycott as England Test opener, which Cole upheld through all vicissitudes.)

Sandwiched between two stints in Brussels by the European editor, John Palmer, was one by Derek Brown, a most versatile reporter (Ireland, the Lobby, and India). But it was Beaton, Pick, Norton-Taylor and Palmer who upheld the *Guardian* in Brussels. Norton-Taylor was impressed by the way the European agenda never changed: the budget, farm policy and food mountains, the budget again, and the long-running tension between those countries which wanted to press ahead with economic and political union and those, notably Britain, which did not. Palmer made himself an authority on everything produced by the Commission and earned the reluctant admiration – at least sometimes – of Roy Jenkins.

> Lunch with British journalists. I still don't find them an immensely rewarding group, partly because I think – slightly under Palmer's leadership – they always behave so depressingly professionally. They immediately started asking question as though they were at a press conference.[9]

> At 6 o'clock I saw John Palmer of the *Guardian*, who asked curiously desultory questions, but we got on in a reasonably friendly way, which is not least an improvement on a year ago. I had in fact been extremely nice about him (although I have no idea whether he knew that) to Peter Preston ten days before, saying, which is indeed the truth, that he was much the best informed of the British correspondents in Brussels.[10]

> *Guardian* lead story about Commission's financial estimates a total fabrication. Probably malevolent coming from Palmer. I rang up Preston, the editor, and began by saying firmly 'You grossly libelled me this morning'. He sounded absolutely terrified, as though he had been shell-shocked, and we then dictated to him a statement which had to appear on the front page the following morning.[11]

> Malicious little story in the *Gdn* next morning [about Shirley Williams], originating no doubt from Château Palmer.[12]

The Jenkins–Palmer dislike appeared to be mutual. Palmer suspected that it was Jenkins's influence when he was Chancellor of the Exchequer which led to his being dropped from the post of economics leader-writer[13] though there is no doubt that Hetherington was not in sympathy with Palmer's approach and

"Arthur Egbert Miller (Conservative) two votes. I therefore declare that the said Arthur Egbert Miller is duly elected as member of the European Parliament for this constituency."

The turnout of voters for the 1979 European Parliament elections was very low, captured by Bryan McAllister on 12 June 1979. Copyright © Bryan McAllister, 1979.

a less conspiratorial explanation may well be the more persuasive. But if, during his years in Brussels, Jenkins found Palmer writing something of which he approved he would again make a surprised entry in his diary.

Yet the fact is that although the *Guardian* dutifully devoted many hundreds of columns to the minutiae of the Brussels transaction and to the advocacy of this, that, or the other course concerning them, they were wearisome enough to follow at the time and would be even more so in retrospect, had anyone the patience to try. It took years before the 'big idea' about Western Europe – the prospect of political union – engaged the attention of those in Britain to whom the argument was not part of their livelihoods. So much of Brussels was necessarily concerned with the little ideas (the sheep-meat regime was much in vogue at one period) that it was dwarfed by the huge unfolding of events east of the Elbe. And when the time came the spadework done by the paper in Eastern Europe in earlier years (part of which people in those countries had learned about through the BBC World Service) paid unexpected dividends. People had heard of and admired the *Guardian*.

In the mid-1980s the foreign editor, Martin Woollacott, faced the sort of conflict of priorities which is familiar to anyone in that job on any newspaper. He would have liked to resume staff coverage of black Africa for which the *Guardian* had gained a reputation. The weekly pages of the *Third World Review*, first under Michael Simmons and then under Victoria Brittain, had dealt with the long-term philosophy of Third World development and the trade imbalances which had distorted African economies, but they could not pretend to offer a news service. On the other hand, was black Africa any longer a hard news story except for its appalling famines and its repetitive coups? The other claim on Woollacott's attention was Moscow. The *Guardian* had not had an office there since the war, and although, largely through Hella Pick's good offices, it had cultivated relations with the Soviet and East European regimes ('They do have governments as well as dissidents', she once reminded her colleagues), it was having to rely for consistent day-to-day coverage on its syndication partners, the *Los Angeles Times* and *Washington Post*. That was not at all a bad system. They were like-minded newspapers which provided high-class material to the *Guardian* in exchange for what the *Guardian* offered them from other capitals. But they were not staff suppliers, ready for a morning conference at the other end of the telephone. Increasingly that was what the paper needed.

Woollacott's conflict of priorities therefore solved itself, especially when he and Preston started discussing candidates and quickly agreed that the man for Moscow was Martin Walker.

Martin Walker was one of the paper's most valuable acquisitions. He arrived along an exceptional route which had something in common with that taken by *Manchester Guardian* hands in days of yore. It began with a scholarship to Balliol College, Oxford, and a first-class honours degree in modern history and continued with a Harkness fellowship to Harvard. As a fellow of the American Political Science Association Walker joined the campaign team of Senator Ed Muskie who was vice-presidential candidate to Hubert Humphrey in 1968. On the campaign trail Walker came to know Richard Scott, Washington correspondent, who recommended him to Hetherington. The form was for new reporters to start in Manchester and learn their trade from Harry Whewell. Walker was the last to do so (and became eternally grateful to Whewell for his instruction), starting in 1972. For the interview with the northern editor and news editor (something of a nicety, perhaps, with the endorsement of the editor and the chairman of the Trust already in his pocket) Martin turned up in a dark suit. When he began on the staff the next day he had changed into kaftan and beads and carried a shoulder-bag. He had to be told that the Town Clerk of Manchester might not yet be ready for the culture shock.

Walker went to London, reported, did a lively and litigious stint on the diary,* covered the first of the disastrous famines in the Sahel, reported from Idi Amin's Uganda, took a year off to write a book, and soon after returning was offered Moscow. He absorbed the language with his Sony Walkman and arrived in Russia at exactly the right moment, with the last of the Brezhnev–Andropov–Chernenko years dragging themselves out and the emergence of the Soviet leader who transformed the continent. At the May Day parade in 1985 Walker sneaked round a side-street near the Kremlin, bought a bunch of red roses, and pressed through the security apparatus to give them to Raisa Gorbachev with the words 'A happy May Day from the British people'. He thus secured the first interview with her in a Western newspaper. Thereafter his voluminous and first-hand accounts of what everyday life was like in Russia and the other Soviet republics became among the most vivid and sustained exercises in reporting that the paper had enjoyed.

Where Zorza had built up over the years a unique X-ray picture of Soviet society, only the man on the spot, in the new era of glasnost, could supply the flesh and blood. Zorza's life underwent another abrupt change on the death of his young daughter; after a period at Georgetown University he devoted himself to the hospice movement and then went to live the life of an Indian peasant, albeit one with sophisticated access to the outside world, writing a weekly column for the paper about the experience. With the opening up of the Soviet Union he was eventually allowed to visit Moscow freely – on the first occasion to a cordial welcome from the Soviet journalists who had scrutinised (and denounced) his writings in England. The crowning of his work on Anglo-Soviet relations came when he immersed himself in coordinating expertise and fund-raising for hospices in Leningrad with the help of his friend, the pianist Vladimir Ashkenazy. Zorza had resigned innumerable times, telephoned foreign editors at all hours of day and night, and monopolised their attention in the office for the sake of a dropped sentence out of 1,500 words. But now the Soviet politics which had been his life dropped away. 'After all,' he said, 'it was only words.'

---

* Hetherington wrote to Alistair Cooke on 8 January 1973, presumably in a reference to Walker's diary, called Open File: 'Martin Walker is a thorn in the flesh, for me even more than for you, but he is a useful man to have around – very bright, irreverent, critical, but friendly and well in touch with the ideas of younger readers.'

CHAPTER 21

Close-run Things

REPORTERS get into scrapes. The serious scrapes were generally
abroad, including Ireland, and some of the nastiest were in Africa.
John Fairhall was taken at gunpoint to Idi Amin's death camp,
Makindye prison in Uganda. He had worked on the *East African Standard* and
The Nation, Nairobi, before joining the *Guardian*, and was an obvious
candidate for an African story. He was picked up at his hotel in Kampala by
police in September 1972, along with Chris Munnion of the *Daily Telegraph*,
John Harrison of the *Daily Express*, and two Swedish journalists who had not
been in the country for more than six hours. They were thrown on to
mattresses in the prison without knowing what plans Amin's uncontrollable
guards might have for them.

> No shots were ever heard in the prison. African prisoners told me that the
> normal method of execution was by 'tapping' a man's skull with a 20lb.
> hammer. One said he knew of 20 prisoners who died in this way. He said he had
> seen one group made to lie down. Then the first man was forced at gunpoint to
> get up and smash the skull of another prisoner. Each was made to kill the man
> beyond him and a soldier dispatched the last. The prisoner who described this
> was a highly intelligent and articulate man who had seen it happen not long
> previously. He himself seemed to have been arrested quite casually because he
> was not carrying documents.[1]

Fairhall and his colleagues were held for several days, learning the privations
and even greater fears of the African prisoners who had no foreign governments to protect them or press to agitate. British good offices secured their
release and they thankfully drank the captain's champagne on the BOAC
flight from Kampala to London. But their thoughts were still in Makindye
and with the Africans being slaughtered by their fellow-countrymen.

Some years before that episode Walter Schwarz had spent an alarming
thirteen days in gaol in Nigeria —to be precise in the self-styled republic of
Biafra, what had been the eastern region of Nigeria and was then in revolt
against the federal military regime of General Yakubu Gowon. Schwarz had
lived in Nigeria for a few years, as manager of the African University Press,

Lagos, and then as *Guardian* stringer in 1965–6. He was deported as an undesirable by the leader of the last coup but one, Major-General Aguiyi-Ironsi, and joined the paper as a foreign leader-writer in London (like most of Hetherington's other leader-writers of the time, of pronounced Left-wing persuasions) in 1966. He kept up his West African contacts and was assured by Biafran friends that he would be welcome there any time. The friends included Douglas Ngwube, an aide of Colonel Ojukwu, leader of the rebellion, the economist Dr Akigbo, and Chinua Achebe, the novelist. Achebe had dined at Schwarz's house the night before Schwarz left London to put his friends' invitation to the test. But there were no postal, cable or telephone links, and when he took the ferry across the Niger to Onitsha in the first week of July 1967 he was immediately arrested as a Gowon spy and treated as such for the next two weeks. Schwarz wrote:[2]

> Onitsha police station, where I was made to wait five hours for the superinten-
> dent to appear, was my introduction to the underworld of detainees – returned
> Ibos from all over Nigeria who had failed to prove that they were not federal
> spies, non-Ibo minority groups suspected of dissidence, refugees from the
> North whose families had not absorbed them.
>
> There was a girl of about twelve whose father had been killed in one of the
> Northern massacres. Her mother . . . had stayed behind. Her elder sisters had
> apparently been locked in the local leprosarium for the enjoyment of the
> soldiers and, if the story be true, were still there.
>
> They told me 'my case' had to be cleared with Enugu [the eastern capital]. So
> at two in the morning the superintendent drove me there. During the 70 miles
> he fell asleep at the wheel twice. He was one of the least likeable people I had
> met (he confiscated a taxi driver's licence merely for being in his way) but it was
> in my interest to keep up a lively conversation.

Schwarz's succeeding days had the Kafkaesque quality since remarked on by many hapless detainees; at that time, though, it was the exception for a journalist, certainly a British one, to be put in gaol on a diet of cassava and peppery soup. By a ruse he reached the telephone of the Deputy High Commission in Enugu which expressed no surprise at his fate, and indeed could be of no help because the British were no better in Biafran eyes than the federal regime in Lagos. After thirteen days he was put back on the Niger ferry. 'What got me out I still do not know. No doubt the humbled bulldog managed a snarl, or at least a whine. I fancy, also, that my wife may have given visiting Biafrans in London quite a rough time. Perhaps one of my friends finally turned up.'

Schwarz had been one of that generation of Jewish refugees from Germany and Austria not long before the war and had been to Manchester Grammar School before Oxford. After Biafra he became a full member of the *Guardian*'s editorial nomenclatura, serving successively as correspondent in Israel and India (jointly for the *Observer*) and as Paris correspondent, covering Germany at the same time, from 1975 to 1984. In 1985 he became religious affairs correspondent and brought a new vigour to that increasingly stimulating part of the *Guardian*'s features work.

The worst upheavals in Zanzibar during its transition from British protectorate status to independence in unity with Tanganyika came in 1963–4 with the overthrow of the Sultan by the Afro-Shirazi party and the proclamation of a people's republic. Clyde Sanger was one of the press party of about twelve which had some cause for grievance against the *New York Times*. The airport having been closed, they first hired a dhow to take them the twenty-two miles from the old mainland slaving port of Bagamoyo to the island and then seized control of the vessel when the Arab crew of three refused to complete the journey at nightfall. A British survey ship, HMS *Owen*, was in those waters and signalled the dhow alongside. The RN officers entirely agreed with the assessment by the crew of the dhow, which tied up for the night alongside the *Owen*.

Next day the party went ashore and were met by the American Vice-Consul, who started to fill them in on events. When several of them automatically pulled out their notebooks one of the revolutionary guards, dressed in Cuban-style fatigues, seized the press pass of the *New York Times* man. The pass was issued by the Pentagon and the reporter's name was Robert Conley. His surname was given first so that the revolutionary guard read out the Pentagon pass as in the name of Colonel Robert and the group were arrested as spies arriving secretly by dhow and were marched away. They made their escape from the island.

Sanger was in Leopoldville (later Kinshasa) to report the excruciating symbolism when King Baudouin's sword was seized from its scabbard by a man in the crowd as he drove in procession on the eve of the Congo's independence, and in Elisabethville (later Lubumbashi) when it was proclaimed the capital of Katanga during Moise Tshombe's revolt against the hapless regime of Patrice Lumumba. All the foreign press corps there had hairy experiences and tended to hunt in packs for safety's sake. It was when he was on his way to negotiate peace terms with Tshombe that Dag Hammarskjöld, the UN Secretary-General, was killed in a crash as his light aircraft was going in to land at Ndola in Northern Rhodesia. Sanger filed a story based on the presumed arrival and the tasks awaiting him. The paper ran a double column on page 1, saying he had arrived and was locked in talks with Tshombe* when in fact he was dead.[3] This embarrassing error may have been Sanger's or it may have been that of the foreign desk in not waiting to check (on the point of edition time). But it was certainly not Gerard Fay's though it was he, as London editor but without

---

* The courtesies were still observed in 1961 and Tshombe in the headline was M. Tshombe. For a quality paper not to have used a woman's title ('Castle' or 'Thatcher') would have been considered a linguistic outrage.

either control or knowledge of the previous night's events, who was called upon to answer for it on the BBC. After Hammarskjöld's death Katanga became even more unpleasant for non-Belgian foreigners. The *Guardian* sent a cable to Sanger telling him not to go back there because it could no longer afford the life insurance premium. Sanger was miffed by this caution from 5,000 miles away, believing he was the better judge of the situation, but accountants' rules prevailed.

Several of the *Guardian*'s African scrapes were alarming, but the one which lasted longest and seemed at one point most likely to get out of control was the arrest, trial and imprisonment of Peter Niesewand in Rhodesia.

Niesewand had succeeded John Worrall as the *Guardian* stringer when Worrall, in late January 1969, had been bundled out without explanation by the Smith government. Niesewand was a highly professional operator and his methodology was probably unique. He ran a one-man office, with no wire services to depend on, with only an unfriendly government information service as his source for official items, and a network of private and secret contacts for the invariably more important unofficial ones. In addition he was his own librarian, filing clerk and telex operator. The method of clearing copy from Salisbury, after sanctions had been imposed during the Smith rebellion, was to send it by telex to the most famous communications centre in Africa, and certainly the most efficient, the Johannesburg office of 'Fingers' Van Der Merwe. From there 'Fingers' would redirect it instantly to any address in the world. Niesewand was so proficient on the telex – a large, noisy, cumbersome machine in the 1960s and 70s, not easy to use – that he could type on it faster than it could register the result. Instead of preparing a tape beforehand, correcting it for literals, and then feeding it through, as almost anybody else would have had to do, he typed live and faultlessly – or if he did discover a fault he would patch up and correct the tape before it reached the transmitting end at its sixty-six words per minute.

More to the point, however, for the *Guardian*'s foreign department in Manchester, he had a wide range of informants in all sections of Rhodesian life and by their means gave the *Guardian* a thorough and reliable Rhodesian service. It was too thorough and reliable for the regime. Police raided his office on 26 November 1972, as the result of a story he had filed earlier and which appeared on an inside page on 16 November. It said that Frelimo guerrillas in neighbouring Portuguese Mozambique had launched a major new offensive on the railway line from the port of Beira to Tete, the site of the Cabora-Bassa hydro-electric scheme, and that according to Rhodesian intelligence reports, Frelimo bands had crossed the border from Malawi the previous Saturday and laid landmines at about twenty places on the Tete line. They were operating from bases in Malawi, a few miles from the railway; for months the road from Rhodesia to Malawi, also running through Tete, had been

Nesta Roberts (TOP), the first London news editor from 1961. Jean Stead (MIDDLE) had a long stint, 1969–78, and Melanie Phillips (BOTTOM) sandwiched three years as news editor (1984–7) between leader writing and a weekly column.

The *Guardian*'s enduring emphasis was on home politics. From a long and distinguished line of commentators are, from TOP, Francis Boyd, Norman Shrapnel, Julia Langdon, Michael White and Ian Aitken.

John Cole, Mark Arnold-Forster and David McKie carried a multitude of other burdens but politics was their base.

TOP: Peter Gibbings, chairman of the company, shares a table with Mrs Thatcher. BELOW: Peter Preston shares a joke with Neil Kinnock. Photographs: E. Hamilton-West.

A culture shock for the Kremlin. In 1983 the features department sent a team to spend a week in Moscow, each specialist writing about Russian topics as he or she would at home. In Denis Thorpe's picture are, back row: Jonathan Steele, foreign correspondent; Polly Toynbee, columnist; Richard Gott, features editor; Peter Fiddick, media; John Fairhall, education; Alan Rusbridger, diarist. Front row: Waldemar Januszczak, paintings and sculpture; John Carvel, politics; and Tim Radford, science and books.

Three familiar names over long periods were those of Hella Pick, diplomatic editor (right); Jill Tweedie, columnist (below left); and Nikki Knewstub, political writer and, as night news editor, puller together of many loose ends in the newsroom during the small hours (below right).

ABOVE: John Perkin, editor of *Guardian Weekly* from 1969.

LEFT: Three long-serving reporters: Richard Norton-Taylor, Brussels, Whitehall and spies; Martin Walker, Moscow and Washington; and David Hirst, Middle East.

BELOW: John Samuel, sports editor 1968–86.

Some of the Manchester staff *c*. 1965. Standing, left to right: Michael Morris, George Hawthorne, William Taylor, Moira Bye, William Webb, Joe Minogue, Margaret Smith, Mary Walthall, Sonia Erstling, Stephen Daly, William Martin, Fred Armstrong, Imelda Lucas, Ernest Dewhurst. Seated: Kevin Rafferty, Harry Whewell.

Editorial conference in London, early 1980s. Standing, from left, are: Peter Hildrew, Victor Keegan, John Gardner, Richard Gott and Dennis Piggott. Seated, from left, are: Derek Taylor, Philip Osborne, Michael Averis, Peter Preston, Ian Wright and Bernard Jolly.

officially considered 'unsafe', even for convoys travelling at walking pace while troops tested the road for mines.

That much would probably have been unexceptionable, but half way through Niesewand had written:

> Military sources said the Rhodesians are already taking an unofficial part in the Mozambique guerrilla war – including supplying aircraft of the Rhodesian Air Force for specific tasks in the neighbouring territory, and sending patrols of soldiers across on request.
>
> In August, Rhodesia's Minister of Defence, Mr Jack Howman, said that if the Portuguese military authorities asked Rhodesia for help to fight terrorists in the Tete area, this would be granted . . .
>
> Military sources say that although the Rhodesian Government is reluctant to officially admit its forces are already taking an active part in the Mozambique war, the true position is that security forces from this country have been involved for most of this year.

That report both gave away the Rhodesian involvement in the Mozambique war and bespoke good contacts in the Rhodesian armed forces. A detention order against Niesewand was signed on 19 February 1973 (by Desmond Lardner-Burke, Minister of Justice, Law and Order, who was a friend of the family and had been a guest at Peter's wedding to Nonie) and on 1 March Peter heard over BBC World Service while in Gwelo gaol that he had been charged under the Official Secrets Act. He may have thought, as did his colleagues in Britain, that he would be given a cautionary sentence and put on a plane. Not at all. His trial before the regional magistrate began on 19 March. Judgment was set for 30 March and postponed for another week. The magistrate, J.E.T. Hamilton, sentenced him to two years' hard labour, one suspended. A month later, on 27 April, an appeal was heard before three judges headed by Sir Hugh Beadle, Chief Justice, and the conviction was quashed. On 3 May Niesewand flew to London. He had a choice of staff jobs on the *Guardian* and the BBC, for which he had also been stringer. He chose the *Guardian* where he served on the news desk. He left to write thrillers and live in Ireland but died young in 1983.

Except for a fairly short period towards the end of the Rhodesia/Zimbabwe revolution the *Guardian* did not have a staff man in Salisbury/Harare, though in those months James MacManus, based in Johannesburg, spent much time reporting from there. Rhodesia had always been in the hands of stringers. Among the most useful was Nathan Shamuyarira, editor of the *African Daily News*, who as the only regular black stringer for a British paper was able to tap the parts of Rhodesia that other stringers could not reach. His own paper was closed by the regime and he left to teach in Tanzania and involve himself in politics on the Zanu (Mugabe) side. The sequence of events had been his great disillusionment: he had believed that black and white could work together in

The timebomb was the huge debt burden and grotesquely high interest rates being carried by the Third World to the profit of Western banks, here portrayed by Gibbard on 12 October 1980. Copyright © Les Gibbard, 1980.

Rhodesia, as he and others had tried to do in the Capricorn Africa Society based in Salisbury.

The paper then took on John Worrall as stringer in mid-1965 and had one or two differences with him, but only one row, because he thought the paper's line too harsh. He airmailed two LPAs on 1 April 1968 strongly objecting on moral and practical grounds to the paper's new-found wish to use force against the regime. This was very much Hetherington's own *démarche*. His leader-writer on Africa, Geoffrey Taylor, agreed with Worrall that Britain would eventually win but the war would be harder, longer and bloodier than many confidently assumed. It would lead to appalling colonial rule problems, 'a kind of reimposition of the British Raj', as Worrall expressed it. Rhodesians would 'feel themselves justified in taking all possible steps to hit the Zambians'.

Hetherington replied on 9 April saying he would have used the pieces if one month had not elapsed since the leader they referred to, but the subject had now become dormant (which was questionable) and 'as things stand, I do not foresee that we shall return to the subject unless and until there is further cause'.

Worrall was not therefore a zealot looking for the violent overthrow of Ian Smith. But abruptly and without explanation he was ordered to leave Rhodesia in late January 1969. Harold Wilson told Hetherington on 20 March of rumours that he had been deported for working for MI6. Wilson had checked on this and found it wasn't so. Anyway, he said, MI6 wasn't intelligent enough to employ someone like John Worrall.

That might have been a fairly routine journalistic episode had not John Worrall's son Nick become stringer in Harare after Zimbabwe's independence. The Minister of Information was now the selfsame Nathan Shamuyarira with whom the *Guardian* had had a long connection and it was he who expelled the second Worrall. The allegations were directed mainly against Nick Davies, a *Guardian* staff writer who had been covering the nasty suppression by the North Korean troops in Mugabe's service of unrest in the southern province of Matabeleland. Shamuyarira's statement said:

> The catalogue of unfounded allegations in the articles are unworthy of a prestigious paper such as the *Guardian*. As a direct result of the article the accreditation of the local stringer, Mr Nick Worrall, has been withdrawn and he has been declared an undesirable person and an enemy of the people of Zimbabwe.
>
> Mr Worrall has consistently falsified the position of the Government and people of Zimbabwe. On Matabeleland he had gone out of his way to give credence to allegations he knew were unfounded.

David Hirst started writing for the *Guardian* in the mid-1960s. It was almost by accident that he took up an interest in Arab affairs which eventually made him the senior British correspondent in the Middle East.

After national service in Cyprus and reading French and German at Oxford, he went to Lebanon and picked up some Arabic at the American University of Beirut. Having acquired more of a feel for the area he joined the *Middle East Economic Survey*, mainly a specialist oil magazine. He wrote one or two pieces for the *Guardian* and applied to be a stringer, for the paper was then without anyone in Lebanon, and the association thus begun lasted into a third decade.

Hirst was exceptional among *Guardian* foreign correspondents in that he covered one area throughout his career. Others worked in South-East Asia (e.g. Jonathan Steele) as well as the United States, Israel (e.g. Eric Silver) as well as India, Latin America (e.g. John Rettie) and Moscow. Still others split their lives between long spells abroad and work in the London office – Michael White as Washington correspondent and then political editor; Alex Brummer, also in Washington, becoming successively foreign and City editor; Harold Jackson proceeding through such disparate posts as Northern Ireland, the features editorship, Washington, and the new technology office; and Martin Woollacott covering a multiplicity of action stories in South-East Asia and the Middle East before taking over the foreign desk and then amassing a high reputation as chief roving correspondent. But the Middle East of all places offered so intricate a web of interlocking and, to the general reader, usually contradictory political, economic and military themes that the newspaper which could secure continuity of coverage over the decades as well as the years was fortunate.

The *Guardian* was in that position. From his old Ottoman residence overlooking the Corniche in West Beirut (until he was forced by events to move to Cyprus) Hirst built up an intimate knowledge of the Arab world, and if he began as a spectator he was not confined to that role for long. He wrote as an authority in his own right, and the two big ideas which informed his work were the failure of the Arabs collectively to achieve a genuine independence and the gross inequalities within the Arab states – whether monarchies or republics. On one august occasion he could almost have passed as a head of state: at Nasser's funeral in 1970 he was in the official cortège between Emperor Haile Selassie and King Hussein, having wangled a ticket and been placed in alphabetical order. With Nasser's successor he joined the rulers of Syria, Iraq and Saudi Arabia (all of whom banned him from entry at one time or another). Nor did the hostility of the regimes (as opposed to their people, among whom he was popular) stop at the frontiers of the Arab world. In July 1981, during the war between Iran and Iraq, he went briefly to Tehran and on opening his paper next morning he read a story about himself describing him as 'the world's most dangerous spy' and giving the room number of the hotel where he was staying.

Hirst was, of course, an advocate of the Palestinian cause, and his sceptical response to Anwar Sadat's visit to the Knesset in November 1977, and the subsequent peace treaty, made him enemies in the new ruling quarters of Cairo. (Sadat indeed denounced him on the BBC *Jimmy Young Show*.) These were the normal hazards of the trade. What was less normal was to be mistaken for a terrorist by an Israeli tank commander at an almost deserted Shi-ite village in southern Lebanon and, having found a redoubt, to be put under shellfire there.[4] After a second bout of mortar and small-arms fire, and with planes screaming overhead (though by that time they were aiming at another target), Hirst, along with Ned Temko of UPI and Douglas Roberts of Voice of America, sought refuge. In an Arab cottage 'we were given what was perhaps the warmest welcome of our lives – the kind of welcome which only the very poor can give – and all the warmer in that here were strangers who, at least for the night, were sharing in their affliction'. Next day they learned that the tank commander, Captain Uzi Dayan, paratrooper, nephew of General Moshe Dayan, and 'a transparently decent and humane man', had ordered the shelling from 1,200 yards away, thinking that Hirst and companions were guerrillas. 'We thought for sure we had killed you,' he said. Hirst hitched a ride out of the village and into Israeli lines on the back of Dayan's tank. Israel was one country which did not declare Hirst persona non grata.

In the tumult of 1980s Beirut even Hirst, long-time Muslim-sector resident, fluent Arabic speaker, connoisseur of every dodge for getting around the country, was as vulnerable to kidnapping as any other valuable foreigner. He had taken all the right precautions. On 26 September 1986 he was to travel from the Muslim Ein el-Mreisse suburb where he lived to the Christian sector of the city to reach north Lebanon, going by taxi just after dawn with an escort of Druze militiamen in a separate car for the most dangerous part of the crossing. But the taxi had two successive flat tyres, and there being no one about the escorts went to find help. That was when the three gunmen, whose car he had noticed cruising in the opposite direction, arrived alongside and seized him. As soon as he was in the kidnap car they produced guns and ordered him to silence. A black blindfold was placed on him, and when he shouted and resisted 'my neighbour, pistol in my side, hissed half in Arabic, half in broken English: "Shut up, shut up, or I kill you. I kill you now."' He was thinking, at that point, about two other British victims, Leigh Douglas and Philip Padfield, who had been kidnapped shortly before the American raid on Colonel Gadafi's headquarters in Libya and were found murdered shortly after it. They had apparently been 'sold' by just such freelance abductors as Hirst's to a pro-Libyan organisation.

> I thought it was going to be hopeless. But then, or so it seems, my abductors began to cast anxious glances around. Perhaps my yelling was having some effect, and I think I more imagined than saw faces beginning to appear in windows and doorways.
>
> I broke loose and ran 20 yards into an alley. There was little real pursuit, and no pistol shot from the rear. I believed I had made it.

He lost all his money and, far worse, an address book with ten years of phone numbers. Sad to say, *The Times* account of the kidnap, by Robert Fisk, was rather better than the *Guardian*'s by the modest Hirst himself.[5]

Nesta Roberts would not have suggested that the scrapes she was involved in compared with those of her colleagues in the Third World. Even so they were not exactly what she expected when she went to Paris. During the summer's disturbances of 1968 her natural sympathies were with the students. Had they not been so to start with they would swiftly have been pushed in that direction when she found herself repeatedly bolting from the riot police and choking from tear gas over the story she dictated to Ethel Alsoe,* the copytaker in Manchester. Once, after a heavy day at the barricades, she went to 6 o'clock mass at Saint-Germain-des-Prés. (Her persuasion was High Anglican, but in France Rome had to suffice.) She was conscious of noise outside and although M. le Curé administered the mass as usual he hastened out immediately afterwards. He then reappeared on the chancel steps to announce that things outside were a little agitated, and recommend a safe route home for those who had received the sacrament. Outside the church Miss Roberts resumed her reporting role as the paving stones were once again hurled across the boulevard, to be answered once again by the tear gas.

Nesta Roberts was helped during that tumultuous summer by Joe Carroll,

---

* Miss Alsoe was a foreign copytaker of long standing, and her knowledge was encyclopedic. She had learned so much Ugaritic archaeology from the dictation she received that she was the only person who could make bold to correct Darsie Gillie if he got his millennium wrong.

a stringer whom Darsie Gillie had engaged in the last sick days of his work as Paris correspondent, and by Hella Pick who went over from London from time to time. But the *Guardian* had yet another source in Paris. Peter Lennon communicated to the features department, avoiding the foreign news desk, in much the same way that the CIA in Beirut used a back-channel to the US National Security Council, avoiding the ambassador and the State Department. Miss Roberts and Peter Lennon were aware of each other's existence, and indeed Lennon had preceded her and written material for the features pages which she had much admired. They first met when they found themselves competing for the last copy of the *Guardian* at the Deux Magots kiosk in Saint Germain, on the ground that each was writing for it. Lennon was one of a number of overseas writers who used the back-channel to the features department, including W.J. Weatherby in his arts and politics writing from New York and Linda Blandford in the same city. George Armstrong combined both news and features work in Rome.

The scrape from which the Hungarian-born Nick Dallman extracted himself was exceptional in that it came a good twelve years before he joined the paper. It was in the years immediately after the Second World War that opponents of fascism found themselves overnight the opponents of communism and the new security apparatus, the AVO, took over without qualms the headquarters of its Admiral Horty predecessors.

Dallman was offered an escape route from Hungary by an acquaintance posing as a friend. The man betrayed him and after incarceration with other suspects as an enemy of the regime he was sent to the Andrassy prison in Budapest. Dallman was wont to gloss over what happened next but he escaped from the Andrassy in 1948, and fled across the frontier into Austria, though he was still in that country's Soviet zone. He bribed a tram driver to hide him under the seat and reached the Western sectors of Vienna and then Britain. He took a job on a farm, and in a cotton mill in Blackburn. He joined the *Sheffield Telegraph* and moved to the *Guardian* in 1960.

Conditions softened slightly in Hungary in the later stages of his exile; he was able to meet members of his family who had remained behind when the relaxations of the Kadar regime made it possible for them to go on holiday to Italy clutching $30 and as much salami as they could carry – but the police knew where they had been and questioned them about their brother when they returned. In 1989 Dallman was able to report the emancipation of his country forty years on. What makes his story exceptional from a newspaper's point of view is that a foreigner with only a skimpy command of English could so master the language as to become a sub-editor working in it. One of the essentials of good subbing is a command of English both at its most precise and at its most colloquial. Nick Dallman became a foreign sub, then chief foreign sub, and then assistant foreign editor. No one on the paper was held in higher respect and affection. He was not the only Hungarian émigré to make his home on the *Guardian*. In the tumult of 1956 one of those who escaped was Ferenc Szabo, and he again had the immense personal, cultural and linguistic transition to make. In this he was closely helped, like so many other short- and long-term arrivals in London who might have expected a less friendly welcome, by Mark and Val Arnold-Forster, through whose good offices he found his niche in the *Guardian* library.

CHAPTER 22

Quantum Journalism

J.G. CROWTHER was the *Guardian*'s first science correspondent. Indeed he was the first science correspondent to write regularly in the British press. After Cambridge, and some post-graduate work in publishing, he identified the weakness of science reporting in the non-specialist press and in 1929 wrote to the London editor of the *Manchester Guardian*, James Bone, proposing that he should join the staff as science correspondent. The *MG* and other papers had already published occasional pieces by him on subjects as far apart as nuclear structure and the possibility of a deep freeze mausoleum. When he was summoned to the presence of C.P. Scott for interview he was told that the profession of science correspondent did not exist. He replied that in that case he proposed to invent it.[1]

Crowther left journalism for more expansive forms of authorship in the early 1950s. He opposed the West's possession of the bomb as a deterrent to Soviet adventurism in Europe, whereas Wadsworth favoured it; whether that would have been enough to cause a rupture between them is uncertain. It was not long before Wadsworth found his replacement in John Maddox, a lecturer in theoretical physics at Manchester University, who became science correspondent in 1955. In addition to regular reporting for the news columns Maddox, in the new weekly science page, took part in the expansion of the features department which began during the transition from Wadsworth to Hetherington, gathered pace after Redhead was appointed features editor in 1959, continued as sections were added in the middle of the paper, and reached its full efflorescence with the introduction of two sections in 1988. Maddox's science could be either pure or applied: he would write his 2,500 or more words for his Tuesday page on sub-atomic particles, fuel supplies, prospects for planetary exploration, the population explosion, the Dounreay reactor and how it worked, control of the climate, the face of the moon, and the chemistry of artificial diamonds (all of which did in fact appear over a period of eight weeks, arbitrarily selected, in the autumn of 1959). He once promoted a scheme for housing everybody in England south of the Thames, leaving the rest as wilderness, which perhaps seems a better idea today than it did at the time.

In 1962 Maddox and Leonard Beaton, defence correspondent, collaborated on a project much in Hetherington's mind in their book *The Spread of Nuclear Weapons*.[2] The *Guardian*'s nuclear policy was a fairly subtle one. It was not unilateralist but it did not believe in British possession of an independent deterrent. It therefore crystallised round the proposal for a non-nuclear club. Britain would renounce nuclear weapons if all other countries not then possessing them (which so far as was known then meant every country except the United States and the Soviet Union) would refrain from acquiring them. This was one of the great themes of Hetherington's early editorship. He worked in close collaboration with those members of the Establishment including Lord Simon, a former trustee of the paper, Dr William Greer, Bishop of Manchester, and Lord Adrian, a former Vice-Chancellor of Cambridge University, who shared his concern about proliferation.

The Labour party and the TUC jointly accepted the notion of the club in June of 1959. In the meantime Hetherington, along with Maddox and Beaton, also found allies in the Irish Foreign Office where the minister, Frank Aiken, and Conor Cruise O'Brien, then one of his officials, were promoting a similar policy at the United Nations – with some success because no country wanted to offend the neutral, romantic and (it seemed) blameless Ireland.

[At the UN General Assembly in the autumn of 1959] Frank Aiken put his resolution again, and this time it went through the political committee to the full Assembly. Once more he used the known arguments, adding that even if full international control could not be obtained that did not vitiate the scheme. It was the plain self-interest of the Great Powers to keep the weapons to themselves because in parting with them they parted with a measure of their power and influence. He accepted that the French and Chinese might have become nuclear powers by the time the agreement could be negotiated, but held that that also would not vitiate it. This time the vote in the political committee was even better than in 1958: it was sixty-eight to none, with twelve abstentions – the abstainers including the three nuclear powers and France. (The Soviet delegate said the resolution was 'inadequate' and would not stop the supply of US nuclear weapons to NATO.) The Assembly accepted the resolution by acclamation, without a vote, referring it to the Geneva disarmament negotiators.[3]

The club was killed by the election result in September 1959 which returned Macmillan to office. The idea did not die, however, and eventually found expression, first in the partial Test Ban Treaty of 1963 and more substantially, though still in attenuated form, in the Nuclear Non-Proliferation Treaty, 1968.

Maddox left to join the Nuffield Foundation as assistant director, later director, in 1964, and twice became editor of *Nature* (from 1966 to 1973 and again from 1980). The succession from him to P.A. Tucker (Phil to his friends, Anthony in his by-line) was one of those metamorphoses which the *Guardian* seemed exceptionally well able to undertake.

Tucker's first experience of the paper was from the top of a scaffold on the fifth floor of the Cross Street building where he was painting a very large mural in the canteen. One day John Anderson too climbed the scaffold and asked Tucker, who was there by virtue of having come from the Manchester College of Art, whether he knew anyone who could write arts notices. Tucker volunteered himself, favourably impressed Monkhouse, who looked after that among many other disparate sides of the paper, and became a permanent fixture, though not yet a member of the staff. He soon became an editorial odd-job man, regularly writing arts notices, drawing the weather map when the regular man was away, editing pictures, and writing Miscellany, the proto-diary column, in the interregnum between Gordon Phillips and Michael Frayn. In 1958–9 he helped Redhead to redesign the features pages, took on the administration of the arts notices and soon became responsible for editing Maddox's science page. The link between the two spheres of influence was that Tucker had started a degree course in engineering before the war and joined the RAF as a pilot, where the training again involved a good deal of science. After the war he decided to switch tracks and take his degree in fine arts. But when Maddox left abruptly for the Nuffield Foundation, Tucker was chosen as successor; handling Maddox's copy had been a further education course in itself.

From the early 1970s onwards Tucker became the principal thorn in the flesh of the nuclear industry and devoted increasing amounts of time and space (his own as well as the paper's) to exposing its shortcomings and alleged shortcomings. That is not to say that he neglected the sciences in the round. Indeed not, and he won the first national award, the Glaxo award, for science writing. He learned early one of the basic tricks of the trade: that the best time to produce a piece on the permeability of membranes or developments in electron microscopy was Sunday afternoon, when the news editor had time to look at it and the chief sub was anxious for early copy and had space to put it in. But he was strongest on the social aspects of the physical sciences. He was campaigning for lead-free petrol in 1967 (e.g. 27 June) and warning against the destruction of the rain-forest in the Futures page of 6 May 1981. He and Harford Thomas were active in the Club of Rome epoch in the early 1970s, taking up the ideas in the club's 'The Limits to Growth', and those at the Stockholm conference which succeeded it. (Thomas, indeed, continued that valuable enthusiasm well into his retirement in his City page column entitled 'Alternatives'.)

The paper's leader line on nuclear power was not the same as Tucker's; the leaders lamented the 'bad housekeeping' (in the words of the Flowers Commission, 1974) at Windscale, later Sellafield, but did not support Tucker's campaign when it seemed to imply that dangers were being deliberately hidden. Arguments were therefore robust, but Tucker was acknowledged to be the fairest of adversaries, and even in the throes of disagreement would break off into infectious laughter. He was the living rebuttal of C.P. Snow's two-cultures hypothesis. Even so, nuclear matters came so to dominate his attention that the Futures pages were in danger of losing their wider scientific appeal and Tim Radford, another man who bridged arts and science, was appointed to edit them. After becoming, in fact if not at first in title, science correspondent, Radford became literary editor in succession to Webb, but not before he had introduced a succession of important science contributors, including John Gribbin, Paul Davies and Rupert Sheldrake[4] to the *Guardian*'s pages during the early and mid-1980s.

These writers were exploring the frontiers of quantum theory, molecular biology, and in Sheldrake's case the suggestion that not only biological but viral and crystalline behaviour is directly influenced by the experience of similar organisms or molecules distant in time or space. Gribbin and Davies were concerned to bring to intelligent popular awareness the astonishing developments in quantum mechanics which enabled a particle to be sometimes here, sometimes there, and to change its nature in the interim. It is tempting, though of course unforgivably fanciful, to suggest that the *Guardian*'s science and arts writers exemplified this quantum journalism in that they sometimes appeared in one capacity, might disappear for a while, and might then return in new guise.

Edward Greenfield began life on the *Guardian* as a general, then a political, reporter under Wadsworth; he went into the parliamentary Lobby as assistant to Francis Boyd and could well have become the paper's sketch-writer in the Commons gallery, the post which eminently went to Norman Shrapnel. Greenfield dashed for some months until 1964 between concert hall and Commons, but his speciality was recorded music, including later the compact disc about which he became one of the earliest, possibly the earliest, newspaper enthusiast. He became a household name on Radio Three and the BBC World Service, as well as in the *Guardian*, for the sheer ebullience of his love of music, which communicated itself to everyone who read or listened to him.

Ebullience, infectious though it can be, is not the only function of music criticism. A critic of a very different stamp was Gerald Larner in Manchester, who before he made the quantum leap was a lecturer in German at Manchester University. It is probably an over-simplification, but if Greenfield's notices gave the executant the benefit of any doubt, Larner's would go to the composer. He followed the performance with the score on his knee and would scold a misinterpretation of tempo or tone. It therefore appeared to the casual reader that Larner did not enjoy music, but that would be a quite wrong judgment. His concern was that the composer's intentions should be respected, not flouted, and that standards of musical performance could only be enhanced thereby, even if that sometimes earned him the reputation of Leader of the Loyal Opposition to the Hallé Orchestra. One important witness to the value of Larner's work was his counterpart on the *Daily Telegraph* in Manchester, and senior critic in that city, Michael Kennedy. Another was Sir Michael Tippett.[5] It was endearing, but unpredictable, of the *Guardian* to chop between the arts and the sciences; between the texture of the Lachrymosa and the composition of Saturn's rings; exuberant musical experience on the South Bank and adherence to tempo in the Free Trade Hall. In science, Maddox was the purist and Sheldrake (a contributor only, but thoroughly mediated into the paper by Radford) the explorer. It was Sheldrake's book, made popular in the *Guardian*, which Maddox in his different capacity denounced in the columns of *Nature* as a book fit for burning. In music the thrill of the vocal passage was one response; the liberty taken, perhaps permissible but a liberty nonetheless, was another. The yin and the yang?

CHAPTER 23

Expansion Phase

T HE *Guardian* moved into its new London building on 29 August 1976, the day the long drought broke. It was a much more spacious office, decently decorated and well fitted out, than the paper had enjoyed under Lord Thomson's roof: the white-tiled subterranean canteen, which most people had visited once for curiosity's sake but never again, gave way to a room which qualified for the title of staff restaurant and, under Peter Preston's influence, had a table licence for a glass of wine with supper. These, however, were relative trivialities. The move was not painless, and it turned out to have big implications for what became not just the two daily newspapers but the Guardian Group.

The move could be made to finance itself only by the concentration of all production and editorial decision-making, with two important exceptions, in London, and the planned and negotiated redundancy of 135 or so people, including production staff at both ends and some 45 journalists and 10 ancillary editorial staff in Manchester. The terms for editorial redundancies were generally agreed to be as generous as any to have been offered in the industry, and they included a special incentive for the Manchester subbing staff to stay to the end and see off the last issue to be typeset in the home city. Henceforward the technique developed by Charles Markwick and the Muirhead company more than twenty-five years earlier was operated in reverse, and the pages were faxed from London to Manchester rather than the other way about. The exceptions to the total concentration in London were in setting the advertising and in running the Manchester features department. There the same team as of old under John Course continued to produce whole feature pages for use at both printing centres and, which was perhaps even more important, to organise the paper's regional arts coverage. The national paper to look at for the notice of any significant play (Robin Thornber), concert (Gerald Larner) or exhibition in a provincial centre was the *Guardian*. (Regrettably as time went on the place to look for Manchester news was the *Daily Telegraph*.)

But the company had three titles to its name, not two. The *Guardian Weekly* was produced at a variety of printing plants and from a series of editorial offices in the south Manchester area including the home of the editor, John Perkin. It was in 1969 that Perkin took what had hitherto been a heap of interesting selections from the daily and began to transform the *Weekly* into a highly professional periodical with an ever-increasing overseas readership. It had first appeared on 4 July 1919, so that in 1969 the question arose of how its golden jubilee should be celebrated. The answer was that it would be ignored. The paper's most important market was the United States where it continued to sell (and was still doing so at the start of the 1990s) under the title of the *Manchester Guardian Weekly*. Jim Markwick, who had managerial oversight of it, was frequently asked about its origins by inquisitive Americans. His stock reply was that 'The *Manchester Guardian* was first founded as a weekly in 1821'; which was a truth disguising a falsehood. The inquirers were not therefore to be disillusioned with the knowledge that it was only a newcomer. Under Perkin's control the *Weekly* soon expanded to take in sections from *Le Monde* and the *Washington Post*. Technology allowed it to be printed simultaneously in England, Canada and Australia. Yet it remained a bastion of those values with which A.P. Wadsworth and Hetherington, especially in his early years, had imbued their newspaper.

From 1959 onwards Perkin doubled as crossword editor, a more onerous post than an outsider might suppose because the slightest error, normally typographical, would of its nature bring in a flood of protests. Perkin's policy was to provide cryptic puzzles of a varying standard of difficulty rather than the somewhat uniform standard required by the crossword editors of other papers. His senior and most classical compiler was Custos (Alec Robins), his most adventurous Araucaria (John Graham). Possibly his least demanding was Rufus (Roger Squires) who appeared in the *Guinness Book of Records* as the most prolific compiler. One of the great clues of all time was from Crispa (Ruth Crisp): '"Men's my one failing" – Mother of Nine' which yielded Mnemosyne (mother of the Muses).

The crossword was one of the two items in the paper which on no account must be omitted if the mailbag was not to overflow with protests. The other was the Country Diary which had appeared daily, latterly on the leader page, since before the First World War. The most honoured of the diarists were both from the Lake District – Enid J. Wilson, who died in 1988, and even more especially Harry Griffin. He was a north-country journalist appointed as a contributor by Wadsworth in January 1950 and was still writing his evocative pieces forty years later. Wadsworth had told him, 'You can write about anything you like, but for God's sake keep off birds. The others do enough of that.' Martin Wainwright, on 12 January 1991, summed up Griffin's identification with *Guardian* readers in a piece to mark the forty years: 'Harry on skis. Harry on crags. Harry on foot. And Harry on the multiple threats to his beloved Lakes. Harry the eyes, ears and especially thick-socked, stout-booted legs of thousands of proxy climbers on Pillar Rock, Napes Needle or Dow Crag.'

Almost the last in a series of reporters and leader-writers recruited to the *Guardian* in Manchester straight from university was Simon Hoggart. Since before Hetherington's time, indeed since C.P. Scott's, this had been a favoured method of appointment. Monkhouse, as deputy editor, then Hetherington as editor, used to make an annual trawl through the ancient universities to meet likely candidates, and since Harry Whewell as news editor in Manchester would be in charge of the successful candidates, he would usually go too. Some stayed a few years and went elsewhere to become famous names. They included Michael Frayn, Neal Ascherson (though he spent some time working abroad before taking his first journalistic job on the *Guardian*), David Marquand, Richard Bourne, Martin Adeney and Benedict Nightingale. Ann Shearer remained in orbit round the paper for a good number of years, working on the social science pages during the 1980s. One graduate trainee in particular, Victor Keegan, stayed to become a mainstay of the paper in any number of capacities: industrial reporter, financial reporter, economics commentator, leader-writer, duty editor, assistant editor, and a long-serving member of the Scott Trust.* The graduate recruitment scheme had to be abandoned towards the end of the 1960s when the NUJ required that recruits to a national newspaper, whether in London or Manchester, must have had previous experience in a weekly or smaller daily office.

It was not only Whewell but Joseph Minogue, sometime political reporter, briefly foreign editor, later night editor, who helped the new recruits on their way. Minogue was a good example of an accomplished professional at work. He would not spend much time on theories of the higher journalism, but nobody turned in a better factual account of anything he went to cover. He made a shorthand note of everything he heard, or so it seemed, on the radio or telephone. He was a by-word for reliability. As a Roman Catholic of the traditional school he must have disapproved of most of the fashions which came to prevail at the *Guardian*; he simply got on with his own work and let them wash over him.

Harry Whewell was for years the paper's Mr Manchester. In addition to his news editing he wrote a highly regarded weekly column and shortly before his retirement in 1988 became an OBE. The circulation department loved his talents as a raconteur and for several years after he had formally left the paper he was in demand as an after-dinner speaker wherever journalists and other newspapermen met. It is questionable whether he recognised all that was entailed by the move to London in 1961. He would rarely go there himself and looked to the North, and Ireland, as the gathering ground – as indeed it had

---

* On 1 March 1984 Keegan and Hamish McRae, City editor, pulled off the most comprehensive Budget scoop for many decades with their report of Nigel Lawson's intention to scrap tax allowances on new life insurance premiums. Peter Kellner, writing in retrospect in the *Independent* (15 February 1990), commented that 'Shrewd investors rushed to beat the deadline; Mr Keegan's exclusive cost the Treasury tens of millions of pounds.'

to be for the northern news editor. Young reporters, indeed some older ones, found that it was appropriate to join him for a lunch-time drink in one of the many city centre pubs. One who thrived without benefit of such observances was Baden Hickman, who became churches correspondent and bore that office with the manner, gravitas and clerical grey suiting of an archdeacon.* He produced a long succession of off-beat church stories during the 1970s which made the 'basement' on the front page. Both he and his successor Martyn Halsall were well into the ecclesiology of their subject; after Walter Schwarz took over religious affairs in July 1985 the *Guardian* rose to some eminence, within the obvious journalistic limitations, in examining religious and philosophical ideas and experience.

Manchester was contracting but Peter Gibbings, as chairman, with his London housing and printing problems out of the way, could give his whole attention to making the *Guardian*'s and the company's future secure. The modest concern which Laurence Scott took over in 1948 had three titles. Forty years later it had fifty-three, as well as interests in television and show business. No doubt Gibbings and the long-standing finance director, Stanley Porter, were helped in the mid-1980s by the management of the economy at large. But even before Margaret Thatcher came to power they had shown that with the right sort of investment, and by steering clear of adventitious non-publishing interests which had formerly seduced the parent company,† a decent financial base could be built from which the *Guardian* could be operated without constant anxiety. Salvation came from three sources: weekly papers, including 'free-sheets', in Greater Manchester and Surrey; car magazines; and the shareholding in Reuters.

The first flirtation with free-sheets (which became a disparaging term; free newspapers was considered more polite) began in the late 1960s. A.M. Harvie, the chirpy, entertaining and kindly man who had been deputy editor of the *Evening Chronicle* when MGEN took it over in 1960 and acting editor (under the editorship-in-chief of Tom Henry, editor of the *Manchester Evening News*) when the company closed it, was then working for the *Guardian* but gave some spare time to one of the earliest free-sheets, the *Bramhall Post*. Since this publication was well within the *MEN* circulation area Henry asked Harvie to desist, which he did. He had nonetheless inserted the idea of free-

---

* During the selection process for Canterbury, to which Dr Coggan succeeded in 1974, Hickman was retained by bookmakers to advise them on the odds. A few days before the announcement was due they rang him up and asked tentatively: 'Mr Hickman, these bishops – will they know the winner before he's announced? We were thinking, like, that if they did . . .'
† In 1969, a time when offshoot companies were proliferating, the parent board found itself seriously confronted with plans for a subsidiary to be called NATO – Northern Air Tour Operators – on the ground that if Thomson could make a success of package holidays so could MGEN. Fortunately it pulled out before any damage could be done.

sheets into the company's consciousness. He put forward ideas which seemed extravagant at the time but were not greatly different from those on which the company capitalised fifteen or so years later.

In 1969 the company took over nine monthly free-sheets run by Post Publications Ltd at Cheadle, a Manchester suburb, which were reputed to have a total circulation of 100,306. The project had been talked about for eighteen months, but because the papers neither made much money nor offered serious competition to the *MEN* nothing was done about it. Then in Harvie's words[1] the situation changed dramatically when it became known in September that Rupert Murdoch was launching into free-sheets on Merseyside. With the arrival of such a formidable contender on the edge of the *MEN* circulation area, and the danger that he might be tempted into Greater Manchester, Harvie was able to spur the Guardian group into buying Post Publications and to look for similar projects elsewhere. He proposed expanding the Post series from 9 to 42 newspapers and 6 magazines with a total circulation of over half a million, catering for a population of over 1½m. 'Key shopping towns' outside the immediate Manchester area, including Widnes and Runcorn, were selected for the first assault.

The idea was for Lancashire Colour Printers (LCP), the company's subsidiary, to print the papers at the offset plant at Leigh. LCP, however, was going through one of its many rough patches. Its projected losses were a steady item in the group's budget year after year and by November 1970 had reached £218,000 (cover price 9d; postage 5d). Repeated reorganisations did no good; by mid-1972 Laurence was forced to announce, and was happy to announce, that it was being got rid of.

This epoch was not, therefore, especially happy for the company or the *Guardian*. GMEN (as the company had then become) had to assert a toughness which was contrary to its nature. In the autumn of 1973 there was created the Manchester Times Ltd with a share capital of £5,000 of which GMEN held 49 per cent and Messrs O'Callaghan & Rudd and their associates the remaining 51 per cent. GMEN provided another £50,000 as loan stock so that a capital loss could be claimed for tax purposes if the venture failed and the loan was not repaid. Gibbings reported to the board:

> From the group's point of view the operation has two objectives: (1) to make life as difficult as possible for the *Manchester Weekly Advertiser* [a publication recently launched] by siphoning off advertising and so helping to prevent it from establishing itself on a sound financial footing and possibly becoming a serious embarrassment to the *Manchester Evening News*; (2) to find out as much as possible about the potentialities for a major freesheet operation in Greater Manchester by using the services of acknowledged experts in the field.

The *Manchester Times* started in October and appeared in desultory fashion for a few months. By February it had run the *Manchester Weekly Advertiser* out of town and accordingly ceased publication itself, thereby, at least in theory, diminishing by two titles the supposed healthy diversity of a free press. In May 1974 Peter Gibbings reported that there were no free-sheets left in the Manchester area. That did not, however, mean that Harvie's instincts had been wrong. If a Napoleonic march had been started by Murdoch from Liverpool to Manchester it had been given its 1812, and GMEN was left with a clear field for future exploitation.

In the summer of 1974 Porter reconnoitred the *Rochdale Observer*, after the proprietors, G. & A.N. Scott Ltd (no known relation), had suggested that the *Guardian* might be interested in a purchase. Porter recalled to the board that they had often thought, because of the slow but persistent decline in regional evening circulations, that they should broaden the profit base by becoming involved with other newspapers. He could not at first understand why the Scott family of Rochdale wanted to sell, since the concern was healthy enough. In fact, the family wanted to diversify into other interests. The *Rochdale Observer* was a twice-weekly paper, founded in 1856, and almost since the beginning had been run very much in the North-west radical mould. (It had been Wadsworth's training ground before he joined the *MG*.) Porter recommended that negotiations should be opened. An offer of £1.3m. was accepted and the Monopolies Commission satisfied itself that the deal did not jeopardise the Rochdale paper's editorial independence or 'the public interest'.[2] Rochdale carried with it three other nineteenth-century weeklies in those reaches of the Pennines made perhaps forlorn by the bleak redevelopment which began in the 1960s (and about which, it could be argued, the *Guardian* had been insufficiently investigative or critical). Over the next decade and a half the four papers expanded into fourteen, some free, some paid for, some of greater editorial distinction than others, which themselves were part of the Greater Manchester Newspaper Group of thirty-two titles distributing 1,200,000 copies a week.

Thus the *MEN*'s interests in North Manchester were protected, but two years later Gibbings came to hear of a disturbing possibility on the city's southern flank. The *Stockport Advertiser* was another family business, founded in 1822, owned by Swain and Co. Ltd, and controlled by the family of Colonel J.A. Christie-Miller and a charitable trust whose funds were used to support the town's infirmary and grammar school. It had two sister-papers in Macclesfield and Wilmslow and was afraid of running into financial difficulty. The papers appeared healthy enough and had ample property advertising, but the space was all sold to estate agents at a high discount. The danger here was that Swain and Co. were in direct competition with the *Stockport Express* series owned by Thomson's. Thomson's might buy them out and use the resulting base to launch a South Manchester evening newspaper. This would then eat into the profits of the *MEN* and weaken the *Guardian* against *The Times*. At a cost of £100,000 the bargain was not to be resisted and GMEN seized it. Eventually the dangerous deal went the other way. GMEN bought the

Thomson papers, merged them, expanded them with satellite free-sheets, and made itself as nearly impregnable as might be in the Greater Manchester area.

These transactions went through the board without much trouble. That was not the case at the tail end of 1978 when Peter Gibbings came to learn that Ray Tindle, chairman of the *Surrey Advertiser* group of newspapers at Guildford, a man known in the locality for his public spirit and good works, and an admirer of the Guardian group, had been looking for a buyer for 85 per cent of the equity in his company, which originally had been owned by local families but was now dispersed, some of it overseas. Associated Newspapers (the *Daily Mail*) and Thomson's were both interested. However, Mr Tindle and his fellow-directors had settled on the price they were seeking and were attracted by the idea that GMEN was owned by the Scott Trust and that no individual would reap inordinate benefit from the transaction proposed.

Since they were offering the Surrey group at an attractive price they were looking for a quick decision, but Peter Gibbings found he had some persuading to do. Both the *Guardian* and the *Manchester Evening News* had only recently emerged from another round of serious economic difficulties. What money there was in the kitty might be needed to cover unforeseen crises, and the company would have to borrow heavily (a relative term, but heavily for the GMEN of those years). Strong misgivings were expressed by both Peter Preston and Gerry Taylor. They foreshadowed a philosophical debate which was to come to prominence in later years about where the interests of the company – and of the Scott Trust – lay. Should the *Guardian* continue to engage itself with other companies for the sake of financial security, or should it disengage in order to concentrate its whole attention on the production of the one quality newspaper, or at most the three original members of 'the group'? But Gibbings got his way at the board and an exceptional meeting of the Scott Trust was called on 18 December 1978 at which he argued the case all over again. By the deadline of 31 December he had borrowed £2m. towards the cost of purchase from the NatWest Bank.

This was clearly a risk. If things had turned sour elsewhere in the group there would have been no ready money. But the transaction paid better than even Peter Gibbings could have expected. The purchase had paid for itself within less than three years and everything that accrued to the group thereafter was found money.

For a year from November 1978 to 1979 *The Times* was off the streets, closed by one of the longest industrial disputes in newspaper history. During that time the *Guardian*'s sales jumped from 293,000 to what seemed an unrealistic, or at least artificial, 379,000. But it was not artificial, for within a few months of *The Time*'s return, from January to June 1980, the *Guardian* was still selling 375,000 and rising. One important reason for this outcome was that the *Guardian* had resisted the temptation to poach on *The Times* territory by simulating that paper's features, so that when the dispute was over there was no editorial section which had to be shed. In advertising it had profited by the absence of the *Times* supplements, but there again the boost which the *Guardian*'s classified received was long-lasting. It should not be supposed, though, that the editorial staff enjoyed their semi-monopoly position in that segment of the market. On the contrary, journalism is not much fun without competition.

So the question arose for the management of where the *Guardian*'s expansion should stop. In late 1980, when Thomson's had seen their journalists, protected throughout the stoppage, go on strike, they lost the stomach for any more fight and decided either to sell their two main titles or cease publication. Harold Evans, editor of *The Sunday Times*, approached the *Guardian* in its capacity as a sympathetic outsider and Peter Gibbings drew up the suggestion for a consortium to buy that paper. The *Guardian* would hold a little under 25 per cent of the equity (the figure which, under monopolies legislation, would trigger a reference to the Secretary of State) with the rest being held by institutions, trade unions, employees and the public with the Scott Trust perhaps playing some role in the appointment of the editor. Gibbings made clear that he would want to go ahead only if such obstacles as manning and other union agreements appeared surmountable. An alternative would be to put in a bid for the *Times* supplements. The discussions appear to have been intense while they lasted but they did not last very long. In early January 1981 Gibbings reported to the Trust that GMEN had decided not to take part. Evans has written a fairly charged account of the proceedings[3] ('[Gibbings] is in his fifties, as smooth-looking as the racing thoroughbreds he kindly appraised for me in the paddock at Ascot one summer with the head of the Thomson Organisation, Gordon Brunton, an owner with a box . . .') and there is no reason to doubt his accuracy, especially about the gloomy financial forecast for its papers in 1981 which caused the *Guardian* side to change its mind. The *Guardian* side maintained that eternal silence on the topic was vowed at the outset. But since the discussions came to nothing it is scarcely worth pursuing them here.

Nevertheless, from 1982 onwards the Scott Trust found itself presiding not only over the newspapers it had been created to protect, or of the kind which the Trust settlors had envisaged, but over a diversity of interests which had little to do with the editorial direction of the *Guardian* beyond, of course, the small matter of providing the financial freedom in which the *Guardian*'s independence could be exercised. A new division of the group thus came into existence to handle the Auto-trader series of periodicals devoted to car advertisements which later extended its range in the London area to take in consumer durables of all sorts. Profits started with a modest £150,000 from the *North West Automart*, acquired in February 1982 and run as an adjunct of the Manchester free-sheets, and rose with the launch of new regional editions (London, the Midlands, Scotland . . .) to more than £2m. in 1987. Hetherington, who became chairman of the Trust on Richard Scott's retirement in 1984, was a keen supporter of the Auto-trader division, not least because it gave another outlet to the talents of the chairman of the group, who otherwise was a salaried employee with limited financial expectations.

Few of the national newspapers which made a fortune from the public flotation of Reuters had done anything to deserve it. The *Guardian*, late arrival on the national scene though it was, had unwittingly done more than all the others put together.

At least one billion pounds, which at that time still counted as real money and which five years earlier had not been known to exist, was pumped into Fleet Street in the summer of 1984. It was immediately pumped out again to build the electronic newsrooms and automated publishing plant in the London docklands which put the industry through its biggest technical revolution since the invention of movable type and transformed the working expectations of a generation of craftsmen – those, that is, who had failed to see what was in store for them.

The *Guardian*'s editorial department, like everybody else's, was converted from paper and scissors to visual display terminals. Unlike most of the others it stayed where it was in Farringdon Road and watched the changes sweep over it in conditions of some considerable disorder. Not so much the senior common room: more like a limestone quarry. Channels were drilled through concrete floors and holes gouged in breeze block walls to take the cables linking every desk-top terminal with the main-frame computer. No news desk operation had ever been carried on in the conditions Melanie Phillips and her people endured. Next to the editor's own desk, moved to make room for a trestle, a discussion about forthcoming features, or the night's main leader on Poland or sixth-form colleges, was liable to be cut short when a collapsing partition showered the contents of a bag of cement. In training sessions on the top floor the staff learned a new electronic language. New presses, the first the paper had owned in London, were installed in the then almost inaccessible Isle of Dogs. To many of those taking part it scarcely seemed real.

The history of the *Guardian*, and sometimes the *Manchester Evening News*, bumps at odd times and places into the history of Reuters, from the Manchester of the mid-nineteenth century to the chairman's office in Farringdon Road in 1983. It was John Edward Taylor, proprietor, editor and son of the paper's founder, who led the revolt by provincial newspapers against the three telegraph companies of the day which held a monopoly over the distribution of news, charged extortionately for it, and often got it wrong. It was under his chairmanship in Manchester on 1 November 1865[4] that the Press Association Co. Ltd was formed, but it could not operate because the telegraph companies would not do business with it. Taylor therefore led the Scottish and Irish papers, the *Sheffield Telegraph*, *Huddersfield Chronicle*, *Birmingham Daily Post* and several others in negotiations with the Post Office to use the public wires. The first PA message was sent from the head office in London to subscribers all over the British Isles in February 1870, and before long the

London as well as provincial papers were using the service, which became and remained the bedrock source of home news, owned by the British provincial and Irish newspapers.

The Press Association thus took care of home news. In the meantime the world's most famous international agency had already begun its work in April 1849 when Julius de Reuter used carrier pigeons to bridge a gap of about 100 miles, between Aachen and Brussels, in the Berlin–Paris telegraph link. The railway took nine hours over the journey, the pigeons two.[5] As a result of domestic upheavals within Reuters, too distant to be entered into here, its manager in South Africa, Roderick Jones, became sole proprietor in 1919. His tenure is relevant for two reasons. In the first place he struck a deal with the government which some alleged, though he strenuously denied, compromised the independence of the agency during the First World War. In a move to deflect criticism Jones offered, in May 1925, all the shares in Reuters, apart from a small holding which he retained, jointly to the Press Association, representing the provincial press, and the Newspaper Proprietors' Association, representing the nationals. The NPA, then as later a body riven within itself, could not agree on the terms, but the Press Association leapt at the chance. On the last day of 1925 the provincial papers collectively, in the form of the news syndicate created on Taylor's initiative sixty years earlier, became the owners of Reuters.* Not long afterwards Reuters underwent yet another crisis of confidence in which the *Manchester Guardian*, this time personified by *Manchester Evening News*, became involved.

In 1938 Haley, as editor of the *MEN*, became the company's nominee on the board of Reuters. Soon after the fall of France in June 1940, when Reuters began to take over the contracts of the important French news agency Havas, it came to light that the British government had secretly paid £64,000 to Reuters 'for propaganda purposes' over the past year. Haley wrote later:

> To Jones, who had been chief executive and director of propaganda at the 1918 Ministry of Information, such wartime cooperation was natural. One or two directors were uneasy, but the board approved. Jones did not disclose to them that his agreement with the Government also covered far more questionable matters. The Ministry deliberately betrayed him. When Jones's good faith was challenged by one of the directors at a board meeting on 4 February 1941, he resigned.[6]

Haley, a man who at all times wielded his probity like a bludgeon, did not say so, but the director concerned was himself.[7]

---

* It was a committee consisting of Jones, John Russell Scott of the *Guardian*, and Alexander Ewing of the *Glasgow Herald* which in 1935 saw to the building of the Reuters headquarters, designed by Lutyens and paid for by the provincial papers, in Fleet Street, near St Bride's Church. By the end of the Reuters upheaval this handsome remnant was virtually the only newspaper building still to be seen in the street.

Jones was a by-word for imperious behaviour but had been a successful head of the agency. He was forced out of office in a state of great bitterness.[8] The upshot, however, was that the press barons of the NPA, led by Kemsley, were alarmed at the withdrawal of Jones's expertise and the inexperience of the provincial board members. Those men were nominated in rotation and until the arrival of Haley and Ewing of the *Glasgow Herald* had usually been content that Sir Roderick should run things his own way. The Fleet Street proprietors now urgently sought, and were readily granted by PA, the half holding in the Reuters shares which they had refused in 1925.

In the mid-1960s MGEN had three fingers in the Reuters pie. One belonged to the *Guardian* from the days when the PA was founded, one to the *Manchester Evening News*, and one to the *Evening Chronicle*, which the group had bought from Thomson's. Yet a fourth finger came to be inserted when, after moving to London in 1961, the *Guardian* became a member of the NPA. It was then required to pay for a further Reuters shareholding.

No one in Fleet Street, certainly not Laurence Scott in Manchester, thought of Reuters as an investment. It was a supplier of news, which is why the NPA involved itself, but it had no pecuniary value. Indeed part of the 1941 agreement was that the holding should be treated not as an investment but as a trust, a disturbing term which threatened to apply a cold douche to the Fleet Street merry-making of 1984[9] until that obstacle was, as so often happens when a trust is ill-defined, circumvented. Newspaper proprietors had tended to treat the share certificates as eccentric collectors' items, like Tsarist bonds, or at best as membership cards of a club, albeit one which served one of the traditional purposes of a club in passing on useful information. J.C. Markwick, who in the early 1960s had been a young assistant to Laurence Scott, recalled handling the cheque when the *Guardian* was required to assume its portion of the NPA shareholding. It amounted to a little over £3,600. 'These thieves in the NPA,' Laurence commented to Markwick when the cheque was put before him for signature. 'Do they think I'm made of money?'

The Reuters millions of 1984 did not come through reporting foreign wars or resolutions of the UN Security Council. They came from the extension, in the early days of the new information technology, of the service which the pigeon service between Brussels and Aachen had been set up to provide: fast and reliable financial news. It was not mainly newspaper managements but a few executives of Reuters who first realised that the huge scale of the new financial operation brought with it the opportunity for huge wealth, though among newspaper managers one of the first to savour the full delicacy was Peter Gibbings of the *Guardian*. In their account of the Reuters flotation Lawrenson and Barber[10] note that Gibbings, with a seat on both the NPA and the PA, was 'on the inside track' and was 'faster off the mark'. In March 1982 the *Guardian* carried an article by Maggie Brown of the City staff giving the first detailed account of the Reuters windfall. 'It was,' she wrote, 'as if a hidden treasure had been discovered in the loft.' Lawrenson and Barber write:

Reuters' own management watched the machinations inside the NPA council with a mixture of bemusement and frustration. With journalists now alerted to the story of how Fleet Street had discovered oil at the bottom of the garden, it had become impossible to deny that there was indeed a chance of Reuters going public . . .

In the event, it took an outsider to break the deadlock inside the NPA. Peter Gibbings, the self-effacing managing director of the *Guardian*, proposed a series of meetings in his offices where representatives from the NPA and the PA could both iron out their differences and agree on a feasible plan to turn Reuters into a public company.

A large part of Gibbings's difficulty in this star chamber was the long-standing hostility between the Express group, now under Lord Matthews, and Associated Newspapers (the *Daily Mail*) under the third-generation Lord Rothermere. When the shares had been thought valueless they had been stored in fairly random fashion at the NPA offices in Bouverie Street and there was even some uncertainty about which belonged to whom. The *Mail–Express* argument had been made even more intractable by the merger in 1981 of their two London papers, the *Evening Standard* and the *Evening News*. It was under Gibbings's prompting in Farringdon Road that Matthews finally agreed to a formula which allowed the sale to go ahead. By the spring of 1990 the Guardian Group had cashed chips in Reuters worth more than £70,000,000 and had paid off all its debts and mortgages.

CHAPTER 24

In Trust

THE expansion considered in the last chapter had obvious implications for the Scott Trust as owners no longer of a small family concern but of a significant commercial enterprise. Moreover questions which had lain dormant for some years, like worker-participation or the intentions of the Inland Revenue, were at any time liable to pose themselves afresh.

Until the mid-1960s the Trust, as has been seen, was a quiescent body which went through the formality of hearing reports from the company chairman but was neither expected nor disposed to assert itself. The imperative which suddenly arose at the end of 1966 of deciding between the conflicting opinions of Laurence Scott and Hetherington about the future of the paper brought about a permanent change in the nature of the Trust and required members to question themselves and one another about why they were there.

Richard Scott had no doubts about their purpose. In a paper dated 20 January 1967 he said he believed profoundly that 'the prime concern of the Board, and the sole concern of the Trust' must be to sustain and preserve the integrity and independence, spirit and character of the *Guardian*.

> This does not imply . . . that I would subordinate (in the sense of sacrificing) everything to this, which would amount to suicide. It does imply that the MG and EN is not in business for the sake of business; that we are not an ordinary commercial firm animated by ordinary commercial motives; that the Company has to be commercially viable, not in order to make profits, but so that we may continue to publish the *Guardian*.

In a sense this may have begged the question, which was whether the Trust had an active as opposed to a passive role in upholding the *Guardian*'s independence, but Richard was replying to an angry, indeed bitter, memorandum by Laurence which had specifically disagreed with the Richard–Alastair approach. Richard, Laurence wrote,

> appeared to take the view that the main purpose of the organisation was to sustain the *Guardian* and seemed to feel that if necessary everything might have

to be subordinated to this. I cannot agree. Suicide, however good the cause, does not appeal to me. Nor do I think this view acceptable to all those executives in our organisation who work hard and well for commercial success.[1]

But perhaps those on the battlefield had a less clear view of what was happening than did someone at a distance, like F.A. Montague, a son of C.E. Montague, who was appointed to the Trust in that family capacity but as a colonial civil servant was far removed from daily newspaper practice. He wrote:

> If either of these [Laurence's or Richard's] views is accepted, what remains of the function of the Trust? It holds and administers minor funds for charitable purposes and is jointly the owner of the ordinary capital of the Company. But it has sedulously avoided any of the real responsibilities of ownership . . .
>
> The Editor alone could change the character of the paper to a marked degree and in quite a short time – and that, incidentally, without affecting either its integrity or independence. If the Trust were to remonstrate in such a case it would be charged with infringing editorial freedom. If it raised objections to managerial policy which might adversely affect the character of the paper it could equally be charged with interfering in the management of the Company. If the Trust is really to take up the responsibilities initially attributed to it by RFS it must be prepared, in case of need, to intervene in either of these fields, and its right to do so must be recognised. Alternatively it becomes a dummy holder of the Company's capital, free of any of the responsibilities of ownership, and devoting its time solely to the disbursement of charitable funds. I do not see how this gives effect to the basic intentions of the Trust Deed, and I doubt if it is acceptable.
>
> It follows, to my mind, that if the Trust is really and conscientiously to assume the responsibility for the maintenance of the paper's character and spirit it must at least be aware of all that the board is doing, and of the Editor's way of thinking, and be ready in the last resort to intervene.

Francis Boyd reopened the discussion at the end of 1969 with a number of questions about how interventionist the Trust should be. Should it, for example, be asking whether in certain situations it would sell the *Manchester Evening News* as a going concern? This was to become a lively issue some fifteen years later when Peter Preston and Gerry Taylor began to draw up schemes for floating the *Guardian* away from the rest of the group.

When it became clear in 1973 that for the first time since 1905 the management of the company would not be headed by a Scott, David Ayerst, the *Guardian*'s historian and at that time a trustee, wrote a paper which relentlessly pressed home all the practical and philosophical questions which the change of regime would eventually raise. Among the consequences of having had a Scott in managerial control had been a self-limitation by Laurence and his father, based initially on regard for C.P. Scott's wishes, which had ensured for three successive career-editors (Crozier, Wadsworth and Hetherington) an editorial freedom and job security unique in Fleet Street. Similarly, successive editors had accepted a self-limitation to stay within the Scott tradition, but subject to that had been almost as free to formulate editorial opinion as if they were editor-proprietors.

By contrast the chairman was less free than other newspaper proprietors and chairmen. The business head of the group must always be a salaried official; he could not (by this means at any rate) become a millionaire. Then there was the 'nuisance of shareholders' (i.e. trustees) as 'permanent residents and to some extent nosey parkers instead of a fluctuating body of investors who buy and sell as the group's profitability and their economic advantage indicate'. The relationship of the chairman to the editor was exceptional. The editor was both an employee and a subordinate, but also the embodiment of the purpose for which the Trust, the directors and the whole group existed. What were the implications of the influence wielded by the chairman of the board on the political direction of the paper and the choice of a future editor?

> . . . Should we put high among the necessary qualifications for a future chairman the likelihood of his picking 'a real *Guardian* man' as editor? Would this involve insisting on the chairman sharing the *Guardian* outlook on the world? If so, would we be putting unnecessary obstacles in the way of getting the best possible top management? But, chairman and editor once appointed, does their ability to work together necessarily involve the same broad identity of social and political outlook?

Was it not necessary, Ayerst asked, to explore more fully what was meant by editorial freedom, and even editing? Someone had said of a contemporary editor that he was hardly allowed to be a real editor and virtually only looked after the leader pages. 'Before 1914 there was quite often a "political editor" of a paper who dealt with leaders but left the rest of the editing to others – or was forced to do so. We clearly mean more than that. How much more?' Hetherington must have found in this an uncomfortable echo of Laurence's earlier idea of splitting the editorship, with someone else to run everything except the comment pages. In the event the Trust agreed in April 1973 that 'the appointment of a Group chairman was a matter of direct concern to the Trust and that anyone nominated to this position should be broadly in sympathy with the *Guardian* outlook'.

Jo Grimond, in answer to the question about editorial freedom, went further.

> I suspect that most of my fellow trustees would lean very far towards the view that they can exercise very little responsibility for the general running of the paper. I personally would lean more towards intervention. I do not believe that owners of newspapers can divorce themselves from some responsibility for the general tone and indeed particular activities of their paper. I have no respect for

those owners who when faced with some gross breach of taste, invasion of privacy, sensationalism or misrepresentation, shrug their shoulders and say it is a matter for the Editor. Of course, at present we are not faced with any difficulty in this region under the present editorship. Nor do I think any change needs to be made in the personnel or functioning of the Trust. I merely put it on record that I probably lean a little more towards interventionism than some of my colleagues and I feel that the Trust should both keep itself well informed about what goes on on the paper, as it does at present, and should not feel inhibited from expressing views.[2]

The question was not entirely new, though it had never arisen, so far as the records show, during Crozier's or Wadsworth's editorships. As early as 1960 Richard Scott proposed that the Trust should hear occasional reports from the two editors. (Report can be a term of art; in the early stages of the *Guardian* operating board the heads of the advertisement, circulation and other departments submitted reports. The head of the editorial department made a statement. In other words the other departmental heads could be called to account but the editor could not). Alastair Hetherington replied (21 March) that this 'might become the thin end of a troublesome wedge'.

> The dilemma as I see it will be on whether to follow the presentation with a discussion. If you don't do so then each of the Editors may be left in some doubt as to what is really going on in the Trustees' minds. But if you do, where will the discussion end? If I were then to find that the Trustees were not happy about certain future developments that I propose – or, still more seriously, about certain lines of political policy that I have lately followed – I should be in an awkward position. I should either have to modify my approach or resign.

Hetherington added, in his winning way, that inhibitions on an editor's freedom might, of course, be no bad thing. When in April 1962 he himself proposed a meeting with the Trust he drew up a report on everything under the sun: printing problems, size of paper, sales ahead of *The Times*, Zorza's third resignation in nine months, policy towards the Common Market, spread of nuclear weapons, help for Gaitskell in defeating unilateralists, support for Grimond's Liberals, wage restraint, Algeria, the Congo, David Holden in the Caribbean . . . and the fact that the *Guardian* did not pay enough to its editorial staff. He was a bit disconcerted at the end of this recital when, far from offering criticism, scarcely anything was said beyond a polite word of thanks.

A tumultuous decade in the universities and colleges – Essex, Nottingham, Bristol, Lancaster, Cambridge, LSE . . . – had ended with the National Union of Students sitting down with the vice-chancellors and principals to consider university reforms. It was not unexpected as the age of deference waned that the London and Manchester chapels of the NUJ should look for some direct influence on the running of the *Guardian* company. Additional

reasons could be found in the management's maladroit handling of the 1966
crisis, the secrecy which had surrounded its merger proposals, the discovery
that the company was far from bankrupt after all, and the deposition of
Laurence from the post of chief executive; and in the wider world on the
sympathy which under the influence of Grimond and the Bonn correspond-
end, Norman Crossland, the paper had expressed towards *Mitbestimmung*,
or co-partnership, in German industry and even 'auto-gestion', the self-
management of enterprises, then being introduced in Yugoslavia.

In November 1970 the Trust first took cognisance of 'the whole question of
participation; i.e. some share by the employees in the running of the
company', to which Hetherington as editor was not unsympathetic, and gave
a lot of time and attention. The demand came in two forms. The first was for
representation of staff on the board or (or and) the Trust. There was no
objection in principle. Indeed when the first Trust was wound up and the new
one constituted in 1948 one of the possible ways which the family and trustees
considered of achieving the first Trust's intentions was co-operative ownership
of employees.[3] Journalists other than editors had been appointed to the Trust
from the beginning: James Bone and Evelyn Montague (though he was also a
grandson of C.P.) in 1936, Larry Montague (another grandson) in 1948,
Richard Scott himself in 1948, Patrick Monkhouse in 1957, and Francis Boyd
in 1961. These men, however, whatever their merits in the chapels' eyes (and
they were undoubtedly great), were nominees. The chapels wanted direct
input, initially to the board but then to the Trust.

The obstacles were several. The most obvious was the practical one of
confidentiality. Philip Schlesinger, in a monograph about the Scott Trust
commissioned during the chairmanship of Alastair Hetherington, notes:

> The Trust's most crucial objection to repeated requests for representation from
> the NUJ chapels both in the *Guardian* and in the *Manchester Evening News* (but
> particularly the former) has been that a delegated or elected staff member would
> be obliged to report to his constituency. The Trust's worry is that this could
> result in a breach of commercial secrecy or other confidential matter, and that,
> as the trustees are themselves the proprietors of the newspaper, one who acted as
> a delegate for one section of the employees could well find himself with a
> conflict of interests.[4]

In practice, trustees who have been members of the editorial staff – and indeed
some who have not – have made a point of keeping in close touch with day-to-
day opinion in the editorial and other offices. But then, if the *Guardian*
editorial staff were represented at either level, what became of the *Manchester
Evening News*? The question was never better put than by Boyd in the open
discussion after the editor had addressed a staff meeting in November 1970.
Did workers on the *Guardian* regard workers on the *MEN* as colleagues or not?
The *MEN* was giving up the benefits of £1m. a year in order to sustain the
Guardian. 'Us college chaps', Boyd said, would have to be careful how they

treated 'them slum kids'. (The irony here is that although most of Boyd's audience were 'college chaps' Boyd himself often made it known that he was not.) Moreover if the editorial staff had a direct input into management or Trust, should not the production staff also? Here again the *Guardian* staff were being asked to examine their egalitarian principles.

The years 1969–71 were ones of growing militancy among the NUJ chapels; among those most influential was John O'Callaghan, a reporter who had been leader of the opposition to the paper's Irish policy. This militancy was in some sense a reaction to the cosiness of relations between chapel and management in the Manchester – and to some extent early London – days. It took the form of several demands: that the heads of each department – news editor, features editor, chief sub-editor – should be answerable to meetings of their departments every six months at which they would be required to give an account of their conduct and stewardship; and a staff veto over all senior appointments. In practice there was no newspaper on which the give and take of everyday discussion between the editor, his heads of department and the staff was further advanced, but to formalise the arrangement in such a way as to require a vote of confidence in heads of department every so often was unacceptable to the editor.

That particular demand did not long survive O'Callaghan's departure from the staff, and the dialogue about Trust representation was modulated into a lower key when the practicalities of singling out the *Guardian* editorial staff for special treatment became more apparent, and when the values of the system actually in operation came to be more widely appreciated.

To overcome the problem of confidentiality the Manchester chapel at one stage proposed an organisation separate from the NUJ, to be known as a Society of Guardian Journalists, but the idea was opposed by some of those in the London chapel who had given most thought to the topic, including Jonathan Steele whose writing for the paper was as much admired among colleagues as his attachment to its principles. He and others considered the Manchester scheme 'élitist' in the Boydian sense, and the very use of that word was enough to rule out the idea. A short time afterwards Michael Downing, father of the London chapel, and Laurence Dobie, a sub-editor who had worked in both Manchester and London (and was also a playwright), drafted a scheme for the election of two trustees – one elected by editorial staff on the three publications in the group and one by the rest of the company's staffs.

The Trust was not ill-disposed to this idea, but in the meantime Francis Boyd wished to resign his trusteeship. While it was natural to appoint another journalist to take his place some trustees felt there should be a delay in doing so lest the Trust establish a precedent from which it would find it hard to escape. In the event there was no delay: it was decided that the journalist should be a man from the upper ranks of the paper but not a head of department. John Fairhall, education correspondent, was invited to join, on the understanding that the appointment would be for a maximum of seven years (it could be only an understanding because in law a trustee is appointed for life). A few months before John Fairhall was due to retire from the Trust towards the end of 1981, Richard Scott as chairman reverted to the question of Trust composition and membership. He recalled that among the suggestions made were a ten-year limit on membership (which was later agreed, with a seven-year clause in the case of members from the editorial staff), a lower retirement age, and a Trust composed entirely of outsiders, with no staff members. He believed it was wrong for any group to feel that they had a right to an automatic seat on the Trust and therefore favoured not replacing Fairhall for the next year or so. Charles Scott said that when times were easy the Trust largely fulfilled its obligations by being in existence. The only time the trustees were called on to take a very active role was as proprietors if the whole operation showed signs of becoming financially unworkable. They would then need the ability to ask the right questions in order to reach their decisions; that was an argument against having too many staff members on the Trust. Later in the year, however, Richard acknowledged that desirable though it was to allow an interval after Fairhall's departure, in practice the staff would seriously oppose any delay. Victor Keegan, then economics editor, was therefore invited immediately; indeed his contributions were such that he was asked to remain a trustee after the seven years of the gentlemen's agreement had expired.

In the absence of a formal agreement about direct representation on the Trust the system evolved during the 1970s seemed likely to continue; especially since any formal acceptance of the right of a section of the newspapers' staff to representation might be seen as a de facto change in the constitution of the Trust and under legal challenge be found prejudicial.

As vacancies arose during the 1980s among the possible ten members of the Trust the name of John Cole was twice put forward, and an informal approach was made to him. There can be little doubt that the editor, now Peter Preston, was keen to have him, but the suggestion appears to have encountered misgivings of a similar kind to those raised against his succession as editor in 1975. Shortly afterwards trustees were obliged to recognise that unless a new member of the Scott family were chosen to succeed Charles Scott, who was due to retire on account of age, the link would be broken. After Hetherington had become chairman of the Trust in 1984 he felt that the family should be represented by Jonathan, the younger son of Laurence and Constance Scott, but corporately the Trust decided that Martin, the elder son, who had had a productive spell with the company and had been early groomed by his father for a senior appointment, had at least an equal claim. Both men were accordingly appointed in 1988.

Before he left the *Guardian* for BBC Scotland in mid-1975 Hetherington had an extremely nervous few months during which it seemed that the Wilson government, with Denis Healey as Chancellor, had set a juggernaut in motion which they could not stop and which was inadvertently, but inexorably, going to crush the *Guardian*. An extensive account of the resulting meetings with the lawyers, with the Inland Revenue at Somerset House and with the Treasury in Whitehall, forms the concluding section of Hetherington's *Guardian Years*, and since the outcome was eventually satisfactory it is not proposed to repeat the detail here. The resolution of the problem represented Hetherington's last act, a very valuable one, as a member of the staff.

In a nutshell what happened was that Healey's Finance Bill in 1975, foreshadowed by a white paper in August 1974, introduced a Capital Transfer Tax, including provision for periodic levies on trusts which did not distribute their income. It was apparent to Stanley Porter, the GMEN finance director, that the Scott Trust would fall within this category and would be liable at intervals of seven, ten or fifteen years, starting within a few years, to charges of £2 million or more, and he alerted his colleagues on the board to the danger. Moreover a proposed Wealth Tax, about which a green paper had also been issued in 1974, would treat the trustees, in whom all the assets of GMEN were vested, as beneficiary owners of those assets and hence as very rich men.

The peaks of anxiety which the company was going to have to scale became apparent at a meeting with one of HM Commissioners of Inland Revenue, Mr Barry Johnson, at Somerset House on 23 December 1974. Hetherington was using 1978 as the year on which a demand for £2 million could be forthcoming, but the Commissioner said he had been examining the file and that the date would probably be 1976 and the figure as much as £3 million. In answer to the arguments which Hetherington was able to deploy about the origins and purpose of the Scott Trust, its inability in law to accumulate funds, and the requirement that profits be ploughed back into the business Mr Johnson could say only that as far as he knew the Chancellor had considered the matter and did not intend to make special provision for newspaper trusts. 'To do so would be too difficult and too dangerous because of the risk of opening new loopholes which others would use for tax avoidance.'[5]

Ironically the *Guardian* supported editorially the more equitable distribution of wealth which was the principle behind both the Capital Transfer Tax and the Wealth Tax, but such an argument cut no ice with a commissioner whose duty was clear to interpret the law as it stood, or was about to stand. It was only when Hetherington, as a last resort, said he might have to brief Mrs Thatcher, Leader of the Opposition, on the threat posed to the existence of the *Guardian* that a Treasury official present at the meeting intervened to say he hoped nothing would be said to the Opposition until the Chancellor had had an opportunity to write him. The corner was turned. Wilson was due to attend lunch at the office, and although he said he was not going to put the *Guardian* out of business the means of keeping it in business had still to be devised and given clearance by the Treasury and the Revenue. Again Hetherington, Porter and the lawyers, Lovell, White & King, drafted a document of which a summary was sent to Healey, who was in the United States, so that he could read it on the plane home. Healey called Hetherington, Richard Scott and Peter Gibbings to a meeting and announced that he had decided to exempt newspaper trusts from the proposed legislation.

This experience influenced the evidence which the company gave to the Royal Commission on the Press. On balance that evidence, submitted in October 1974, was strongly in favour of trust ownership for a number of reasons. Public service could be made the primary object of newspapers, which did not necessarily mean 'that they must be highbrow or of any particular political persuasion. The *Manchester Evening News*, for example, is a successful popular newspaper and independent in its political outlook.' Trustees were more ready than managements under commercial pressure to offset the losses of one paper against the profits of another. A Trust helped to guarantee editorial independence, although 'only if the trustees and those whom they appoint to run the business believe that editorial independence is a virtue . . . Most editors enjoy a fair measure of independence, whatever the form of ownership [but] trustees . . . are less likely to be tempted to interfere or to put any pressure on the editor and his staff.' Trust ownership could also, 'on occasions', lead to easier labour relations. 'While the *Guardian* and the *MEN* have had their quota of industrial difficulties, it is probably true that the mood among our staffs is generally more friendly and cooperative than in some other offices.'

Against these advantages, however, had to be set the impossibility of raising new equity capital on the market; capital for expansion could be raised only by accumulating retained profits or by borrowing. Although borrowing for short-term purposes was possible, to borrow for long-term investment, paying high interest rates, was undesirable, and given the highly cyclical nature of the newspaper industry could endanger the Trust ownership of the papers.

An added disadvantage, however, lay in the uncertainty about how the law on trusts would be interpreted, particularly by the Inland Revenue, and whether it would change. 'Both at its inception and more recently the Scott Trust has had to take long and costly legal advice about its status.' Through a technicality in the law a trust of the Scott variety (a discretionary rather than a charitable trust) had to provide for ultimate disposal at the end of the trust period. The 1948 settlement could run for twenty years after the death of the survivor of a number of persons then living, but not later than the year 2030; it could also be wound up at an earlier date, and upon disposal the capital and income should go in such proportions as the trustees thought fit to (a) Adult employees, then or within the previous ten years, of the company; (b) any issue of the age of thirty of any of the settlors, who were L.P. Scott, C.P. Scott (grandson of the namesake), L. Montague, R.F. Scott, R. Ebbage (former company secretary), and A.P. Wadsworth; (c) any issue over the age of thirty of E.A. Montague and E.J. Scott (another descendant of C.P.); and (d) the company. It was never intended that any of these individuals should in fact benefit. The crucial clause 9 of the Trust Deed states:

The Settlors whilst not purporting to impose any binding trust or obligation in that respect desire that the persons becoming entitled to the Settled Funds shall use their best endeavours to procure that the business of the Company shall be continued and that the *Manchester Guardian* and *Manchester Evening News* or any other paper or papers or other medium for collecting and disseminating news comment or opinion in which the Company the Company's successors or any subsidiary company of either of them shall then be interested shall be carried on as nearly as may be upon the same principles as they have heretofore been conducted and carried on while under the guidance of the said John Russell Scott and his family and the Trustees of the 1936 Settlement.

In spite of this injunction the drafting of the deed required that if the trustees failed to provide beneficiaries from the above list the properties should go in equal parts to all the then living adult descendants of the five settlors, if no adults then to minors, if no minors then to the last survivor. In addition to this stipulation the trustees themselves were, of course, collectively free to do so as they wished with the company's ordinary shares. These niceties made the trustees and the Trust as a whole vulnerable to the very sort of caprice of the Revenue which J.R. Scott had striven to avoid in 1936.

Hetherington, Peter Gibbings and Peter Preston all gave oral evidence but the commission evidently felt that the Scott Trust was an isolated example of altruism, and in its final report made no direct allusion to the benefits, nor did it recommend a similar act of self-abnegation to other moguls of the press.

To pursue the discussions of the Trust in more recent years is beyond the scope of this book. The tendency under Hetherington, however, was in a slightly more interventionist direction, and it would probably be true to say that Preston may not always have come to expect the unequivocal support from the Trust chairman upon which his predecessor had been able to rely. As the group expanded, and the nature of daily journalism changed, questions which had barely arisen in 1936 and 1948 about the future direction of the *Guardian* became more pressing, and by the end of this narrative had been so complicated by the shifting values of daily journalism that the Trust felt obliged to look again at its priorities and consider its duties not only to the *Guardian* but to the manifold other enterprises under its control.

CHAPTER 25

Double Bubble

HIGH summer for the *Guardian* of the recent past, before its stylistic transformation early in 1988, may have begun with the Conservative general election victory of May 1979, or with Roy Jenkins's Dimbleby Lecture (stiffening the centre) in November of that year. It was certainly being enjoyed at about the time Dr David Owen and friends issued their Limehouse Declaration in January 1981. It ended with the launch of the *Independent* in October 1986.

As in most summers the sky was not cloudless. The paper suffered the hailstorm of the Tisdall case in 1983–4.* Thunder echoed nightly, and with increasing menace, through the composing room as the print unions fought their costly rearguard action against the advance of the new technology. (It is another story, better told by others, but something perversely enjoyable was lost when the barracking suddenly stopped and the silent anonymity of the Atex computer screen took over.) Strange though it was, when tens of thousands of copies were being lost nightly through 'unofficial industrial action' personal relations rarely broke down, and the *Guardian*'s horror stories are less horrific than those of other papers at that time. The father of one of the more stubborn printing chapels telephoned the managing director at home one night and demanded of his wife 'Is he there? Put him on!' When Taylor went to the phone the FoC said, 'Look, Gerry, apologise to your missus will you? I was putting on a show for the lads.'

Banter could not, however, disguise the threat which the paper faced. In February 1985 the Scott Trust met on an evening when the Imperial Chapel had prevented production altogether after a month in which losses of circulation had been reaching 100,000 copies a night. It was a sombre meeting. With any other paper in the group the management could have truthfully said to the staff that it would do all it could to sustain the paper; but if action by the staff made the paper unprofitable it could be closed. But the *Guardian* was unique, and its management felt impeded from saying anything

---

* See Chapter 19.

comparable. If disruptive action led to the closure of the paper, which by then had become conceivable, the trustees would have to secure its continuity by other means, some of which, like using the *Guardian Weekly* to provide continuity of editorial policy and work for the staff, had almost an air of desperation. The crisis was overcome by a combination of gritted teeth at the *Guardian's* end and full-scale assault on the NGA and Sogat by Rupert Murdoch in taking his titles to Wapping.

Another cause of friction, which strictly concerned only the *Manchester Evening News*, nevertheless had some fall-out on the *Guardian*. The *MEN* journalists' chapel had taken the management under Harry Roche to court claiming that special allowances paid along with salary should be pensionable. The chapel lost when the case was decided in the High Court in May 1985 and was landed with costs in six figures. But the acrimony attached, quite unfairly, to Roche himself. When he became managing director of the *Guardian* later that year on the retirement of Gerry Taylor he was deemed to be anti-NUJ. Things do not normally work that way, with simple pro- and anti-attitudes, but it would not have been surprising if relations between management and NUJ on the *MEN*, which had been sour for years and remained so, should cause what doctors call referred pain when Roche went to London.

Yet in spite of these vicissitudes everything in the paper seemed, from about 1980 to 1986, to fall together. It was the focus for discontent with the new Tory radicalism and what were seen, rightly or not, as its consequences. The riots of 1981 in Toxteth, Brixton, North London and elsewhere were material for the sort of probing – by Melanie Phillips, Malcolm Dean and others on the staff and by assembled academics on the features pages – in which the *Guardian* had been accustomed to excel. These reports and commentaries foreshadowed in close detail the findings[1] of Lord Scarman's subsequent inquiry: unemployment among young blacks and their consequent despair and alienation, coupled with insensitive policing and the lack of an independent police complaints procedure. The paper had a good Falklands war.* It had a good miners' strike under Keith Harper, the labour editor, Malcolm Pithers, Peter Hetherington and others. It sympathised with the miners and their families, giving much space to their privations, but not with their leaders Arthur Scargill and Peter Heathfield; with the policemen behind their riot shields but not with the government which, if it did not operationally deploy them, took satisfaction in their deployment. The cartoonists Gibbard, McAllister, and Posy Simmonds were part of *Guardian* readers' households. John Ezard kept up his all-round descriptive writing; David Hencke kept up his scoops. And every Tuesday on the leader page James

* See Chapter 18.

*"In real life, a crowd that size would
be attacking the police."*

*At the occasion of the wedding of Prince Charles and Lady Diana Spencer, 30 July
1981. Copyright © Bryan McAllister, 1981.*

Cameron, a famous name among veteran foreign correspondents, wrote a
popular (though sometimes populist) column.

In the early 1980s also the paper adopted a new style for TV promotions in
which, first of all, sports and entertainment celebrities – Peter Ustinov and
Spike Milligan were among them – talked enthusiastically about what they
liked in it. As a development of this the celebrities were intermixed with
other readers chosen fairly randomly and interviewed in the street. The result
was the same: they adored Nancy Banks-Smith, the TV critic, and some of the
stars in the *Guardian*'s sports galaxy of the day – Frank Keating, David Lacey,
John Rodda. On one such occasion Gerry Taylor invited to the office several of
the readers who had been interviewed for the commercial. One or two walked
around the board room silently, almost reverentially, fingering the furnishings. Finally one plucked up courage to ask, 'Could you do me a favour? Could
you show me where Derek Malcolm sits?' Taylor said certainly, but he didn't
think Derek Malcolm would be in at that particular time. The interviewee

The spirit of the age: 12 July 1977. Copyright © Bryan McAllister, 1977.

said he wouldn't dream of disturbing him: he was a devotee of the film reviews and wanted to see where they were written.

Circulation seemed to be unstoppable. It went up in those five and a half years from 380,000 to 524,000. *The Times* introduced its bingo game, Portfolio, in June 1984 and that caused a slight blip when the *Guardian* lost some 7,000 in the following 6 months. But no more than a blip, and the paper did not feel constrained to follow into that labyrinth. The editorial, advertising and circulation staff felt a self-confidence about the paper's success and about the open road before it which they had not enjoyed for many years. John Gardner, the deputy news editor, and Geoffrey Andrews, transport correspondent, used now and then to have breakfast at the Progressive Working Class Restaurant opposite the Mount Pleasant sorting office at the top of Farringdon Road. This institution, discovered when the *Guardian* moved to its new premises, had benches like church pews, but facing one another across a table, and served good food cheap and without adornment. You did not have to claim working-class credentials to go there, though several on the staff would have been glad to do so (and even gladder had the claim been true). The breakfast menu always included bubble and squeak to go with the bacon. When Gardner and Andrews were especially happy with that day's paper they would tell the office afterwards that it had justified double bubble.

The chief reason for the *Guardian*'s success in the early 1980s was that the Social Democratic Party was founded in its pages and the battle for the soul of the Labour party fought out there. The paper stood towards the SDP much as it had done towards CND in the 1950s and 60s. It did not endorse either group but it was essential reading for those in the constituencies anxious about the rise of the radical Right and the decline of the consensus Left, as it had been two decades earlier on the Aldermaston marches or the demos in Trafalgar Square. There was one important difference. The *Guardian* actively disagreed with unilateralism; it did not actively disagree with the Social Democrats. If it did not endorse the SDP it was so highly critical of the Labour Left which dominated the party that readers were not left in much doubt where the paper's sympathies lay.

Formal endorsement would have been contrary to Peter Preston's style and to the way he tackled the responsibilities of the leader column. Hetherington's leaders had usually been prescriptive; Preston's were discursive and reflective. Hetherington would set down points one, two and three on which action needed to be taken. Preston would gently recommend. He would wonder aloud, sometimes leaving strange linguistic vapour-trails for readers (and staff) to gaze upon. Yet the perception in the Labour party at large was that the *Guardian* had become an SDP newspaper, and that would have been hard to deny.

Over the years both the editorials and the Peter Jenkins political column had urged the same complaints against Labour as the SDP now urged. John Torode, as industrial and occasionally political leader-writer, had fought Norman Lamont for Labour at Kingston-upon-Thames in 1979. He was a former Labour correspondent who, like others in that speciality, came to identify with his subject and especially with its practitioners among old-style trade union leaders (of whom his father had been one) against the more far-flung idiosyncrasies of the constituency parties. Torode was close to a number of Labour MPs, most of them centrist, and it was known in the PLP which way he and several of his colleagues on the *Guardian* were beginning to think.

There was also a history of latent SDP-ism, going back to Hetherington's day when he had repeatedly advocated Lib–Lab cooperation. Towards the end of his tenure he had had a long-running dispute with Michael Foot, most of it carried on in the paper's leader columns and some at the Department of Employment, about the effect on editorial freedom of the Trade Union and Labour Relations (Amendment) Bill introduced into the Commons at the end of 1974. The bill was designed to restore to trade unions the right, taken away from them in the Conservative government's Act of 1971, of requiring employers to operate a closed shop.

If Hetherington erred in labour relations, either nationally or in dealing with the NUJ chapels, it was on the side of generosity towards the unions, possibly because he was conscious that his own academic background had removed him from shop-floor anxieties and felt he needed to give the benefit of doubt to those who had not enjoyed that privilege. Thus he was not in principle opposed to the closed shop. The leader columns took up the theme of the labour specialists that the closed shop could in many cases make negotiations easier by preventing overlapping claims.

But Hetherington believed, and so did other Fleet Street editors for whom he acted as shop steward, that coupled with the NUJ's decision to remove from editors and their deputies the special 'associate' status they had previously enjoyed the bill would make it lawful for the NUJ to remove an editor, simply by throwing him out of the union if he failed to accept its instructions. Foot (who had been acting editor of Beaverbrook's *Evening Standard* in 1942) belittled those fears. He said the danger to editorial independence came not from the NUJ but from proprietors and management. The appointment of editors, he said, was like the coronation of Tsars 'in which the newly appointed autocrat would march in procession preceded by his father's murderers and followed by his own'.[2]

The Hetherington–Foot argument remained courteous on both sides, and the problem eventually went away when the Conservative government of 1979 came to office. In 1976, however, Peter Jenkins, who had often been a savage critic of Harold Wilson, turned the attention of his political column to Foot. He wrote:

> A famous industrialist summed up the position the other day when he threatened to commission a cartoon of David Low's famous TUC carthorse with Mr Foot on his knees licking its behind. It would be in bad taste but not unfair. Mr Foot's entire political position and contribution to the Government can be summed up as a trade union-licker . . . The Employment Protection Bill was drafted by Mr Foot handing his officials the TUC's shopping list and instructing them to legislate accordingly.[3]

On 8 September 1978 Callaghan upset virtually every political calculation by deciding not to hold a general election that year. The *Guardian* queried the decision, hoping it did not mean that he was looking to survive the winter with the aid of the Ulster Unionists. Peter Jenkins had some sympathy with him:

> People's sense of things getting better or getting worse often lags behind the reality, and from my own brief forays into the country recently it seemed that the people were not yet fully aware of the improvement in their living standards and still less certain that it would continue. So, even if the indicators were to be turning against Mr Callaghan by the spring, the recovery would have had another six months to seep into people's pockets. That's where elections are won and lost, not in the City columns . . . It requires courage, however, even to

court accusations of cowardice. He has stood against a veritable media stampede and that required some courage too. To have chosen the risks of continuing against the risks of not continuing seems to me in no way a dishonourable decision.

A month later[4] Harper was reporting from Blackpool the worst blow of Callaghan's premiership, amounting to a threat to his election chances, when the unions rejected his 5 per cent pay policy by 2–1 majority. The leader comment on that occasion summed up the way the paper's line had been developed, principally by Torode:

> In the words of Mr Joe Gormley 'For God's sake trust us.' That, it seems, is the wages policy which the Labour Party conference, against the advice of the Government and its own national executive committee, adopted . . . Wage control, of any kind, at any time, is repudiated . . . Those same market forces which are so vehemently and repeatedly denounced in all other contexts by speaker after speaker at every Labour Party conference are to be allowed to reign virtually unchecked. The Government, whose intervention Labour Party conferences so enthusiastically recommend in almost every other sphere of economic life, is here assigned the role of standing benignly by, arms folded, trusting in Mr Gormley. There is little in recent history, and nothing in yesterday's debate, to suggest that such simple trust is likely to be rewarded.

After the 'winter of discontent' in 1978–9, to which the 1978 Labour conference had been the prelude, Callaghan, defeated in the Commons, went to the country on 3 May. Preston, in one of his longer leaders (c. 2,400 words), ended:

> At the end we have [on the Tory side] only a steadily diminishing pining for 'change and not much else'. That is not enough. It reflects a lack of faith in the party of burning faith. And since there is scant faith, only a gritty determination to make the best of what we have by learning and unlearning and struggling, then Mr Callaghan, a compassionate struggler, is not merely the man we deserve but also, in probability, the man we need.

Jenkins's commentary concurred: Mrs Thatcher, he said, was not a woman of ungenerous spirit, but 'the paternal warmth which usually accompanied Tory radicalism is lacking from her market creed. I cannot see the country working for her.'

Commenting on Mrs Thatcher's victory the paper said: 'The have-nots, the have-littles and the have-problems bent only slightly in the wind of change whilst the have-plentys and the want-mores were eager to clip along with the Conservatives.' Preston ended with a reference to two people he much admired:

> No single moment from the entire media campaign, perhaps, will stay longer in the memory than five BBC TV minutes yesterday afternoon when a bone-

Oh, What a Lovely Monetary Policy!

Copyright © Les Gibbard, 1980.

weary and resolutely cheery Shirley Williams stood on a Hertfordshire lawn and heard Norman St-John Stevas lament her cruel defeat. It was not merely that her defeat was indeed viciously unmerited; it was her long-time Conservative adversary across the floor of the House alone finding the eloquence to wrap a tragedy in affection and admiration. That was a good beginning to a new administration: a spirit of comradeship to cherish and remember.

Peter Jenkins likened the Labour party's conference that autumn (1979) to an impeachment trial of James Callaghan with Tony Benn as prosecutor.

> Mr Benn's vision of the future, which he sketched with lightning artistry for the Labour Party conference yesterday, is full of gloom and full of cheer. The bad news is the coming slump; the good news is that capitalism is in its death throes and socialism is on the way.

Summing up on 6 October Jenkins wrote:

> Both in the fifties and in the aftermath of the third successive defeat in 1959 the rows took place between those who essentially, or so they were accused, saw the Labour Party as a crusading force and those who saw it as a party of government.
>
> The Left, it used to be said, secretly – and sometimes not so secretly – preferred opposition to government. Mr Michael Foot, for example, was more at home ranting in Trafalgar Square than down the road in Whitehall

wandering lost in what C.P. Snow, at about that time, had christened the corridors of power. The late Richard Crossman, some will remember, wrote a pamphlet after 1959 which was wrong on the most lavish scale. In it he predicted, and indeed advocated, virtually permanent opposition for Labour until the patent superiority of the centrally planned economies of Eastern Europe brought about a crisis of capitalism of such magnitude that Labour's unsullied radicalism could have its day.

In November 1979 Roy Jenkins, then chairman of the European Commission, delivered the Dimbleby Lecture regretting the polarisation of politics, advocating proportional representation, and calling for the strengthening of the political centre. The *Guardian* sympathised but was not awestricken. As a contribution to practical politics the lecture was intriguing but marginal. 'But for those who want to file the cuttings away it could be more relevant a year or two from now.'

The following year, 1980, the Labour conference voted to pull out of the EEC, of which decision the paper commented[5] that if Britain were to slink away from its European destiny that would not be

> the triumph of Mr Peter Shore's sub-Churchillian rhetoric, but the bleakest admission of failure. European failure; British failure; and Labour Party failure too. Mrs Shirley Williams is right and right again to keep on reminding the comrades around her of their international heritage. You cannot pull up the drawbridge and build socialism alone in one Castle Gloriana. If the Labour Party appeals only to the old and the frightened and the insular, the Labour Party will perish.

Michael Foot replaced Callaghan as leader in November 1980 by vote of the PLP, and a special one-day party conference was called at Wembley towards the end of January 1981 to decide how future leaders should be elected. The *Guardian* was now becoming more remote from Labour because of the difficulty in discerning what the Labour party was. It noted[6] that at meetings with the Left, Foot deplored the fissile tendencies of the Right. At meetings with the Right, he held out hopes that the triumph of the Left would not be total. He had come to the leadership 'in the midst of the worst internal crisis to hit Labour in fifty years, and at a time when less attention is paid to what leaders say than at any time in recent party history'. The paper likened Labour to the Stephen Leacock character who, mounting his horse, rode off furiously in all directions.

The purpose of the Wembley conference was to start changes in the structure of the party and especially in the method of electing the leader. There was to be an electoral college in which Foot wanted the PLP to have 50 per cent of the votes. In the event, a switch of votes by one trade union ensured that the PLP would have 30 per cent, the constituencies 30 per cent, and the unions 40 per cent. On that same heavily charged weekend David Owen, William Rodgers and Shirley Williams were joined by Roy Jenkins to issue their manifesto from Dr Owen's home in Limehouse. There was plenty to write about in Monday morning's editorial blockbuster.

> More than five million people voted on Saturday to 'change the course of history' (as Mr Benn put it) at Wembley . . . Many thousands of them were unaware that they had done so. Many were at the supermarket, watching the football, or busy in the garden. Others are members of the Conservative Party, the Liberal Party, the Communist Party, even the National Front. Still others do not even exist. They are simply deemed to exist, for the purpose of block votes wielded by unions.

Of the Limehouse Declaration it said:

> What will emerge out of the portentously named Council for Social Democracy will not be a Centre Party. The idea of a party uniting Left and Right, Heathite alongside Gang of Three Labour, is an illusion. It would be a coalition of negatives. Even the present Gang of Four (the original Gang plus Mr Jenkins) may not be easy to reconcile. The egalitarianism which makes Mrs Williams ready to see the end of private education is hardly a distinguishing mark of Mr Jenkins . . . [The policy statement expected in summer] is more than likely to produce a platform which will come far closer to the true positions of Mr Healey, Mr Hattersley, and many more of those who stay within the Labour Party than with the manifesto on which Labour fights in 1983–4 . . .The new grouping will not expect anything like the surge of support which the polls have indicated. What the polls do suggest, however, is that there is a ground left untenanted by Mrs Thatcher's conservatism and Labour swinging Left where people are hunting anxiously round for some grouping which reflects their own beliefs.

In other words, the breakaway party would not sweep Labour out of sight, but it could take enough constituency support to deny Labour in the marginals.

The Gang of Four immediately received more than 8,000 messages, and decided to capitalise on their support with an advertisement in the *Guardian* of 5 February asking for names, addresses and money. The ad was in the names of 100 people, many of them political, academic or arts celebrities. Within a month 80,000 letters had been received and the response encouraged the CSD to become the fully fledged SDP. Hugh Stephenson commented not long afterwards:

> In the year or so up to Limehouse, the *Guardian* had increasingly been adopted by the protagonists of a new centre or social democratic party as the Fleet Street newspaper in which they best liked to air their views. The unquestioned choice of the paper to be the sole organ of the national press to carry the first call for

public support was a subconscious recognition of the kind of membership to which they would appeal.[7]

The episode recalls a full-page advertisement by CND in the *Guardian* of 21 May 1962, paid for by 'a sympathetic businessman', which reprinted articles from *Tribune* by Michael Foot and David Boulton explaining 'the frustrations' which led to hostile receptions for Hugh Gaitskell and George Brown by unilateralist crowds at May Day rallies in Glasgow and London respectively. It foreshadowed the advertisement in the *Guardian* of 30 November 1988 which was the public launch of Charter 88. In all three cases, readers of the *Guardian* were the advertisers' natural target.

The Labour Left took no heed of cautionary words from its friends. When Mrs Williams captured Crosby from the Conservatives on 26 November 1981 the paper put its finger on the reasons for the SDP's inexorable rise in its sharpest leader on the subject, written by David McKie:

> The SDP/Liberal surge is in no small part a revolt against parties where the manifesto matters above all, or where you are required to mortgage much of your life to the party's activities before you are regarded as fit to have any conclusive influence over the way the country is run. It is a revolt against those who believe that long hours on the doorstep in the pouring rain or in the committee room passing resolutions late at night is the beginning of political wisdom and the overriding qualification for political decision-making; and that decisions so arrived at ought to stand, whatever the weight of evidence marshalled against them by people outside.
>
> That, certainly, is how many now see Labour: a party in which a fanatical approach to politics has in recent times greatly prospered. And so a party which, on many counts, should have much going for it – a Government in power which has richly deserved the people's censure; an approach to issues like Europe and the nuclear threat which catches the mood of many people in the country – remains tethered in a state of snarling irrelevance as the SDP and Liberals get on with the cherished work of turning Tories out.

A couple of days earlier, in one of the *Guardian*'s Terry Coleman interviews, Roy Jenkins had given his famous repudiation of the word 'socialist'. 'I don't use the word. I haven't used the word socialist, or socialism, for some years past . . . I regard it as more obfuscating than clarifying.'

Peter Preston's handling of the general election of 9 June 1983 kept the paper's distance from the Tories without bringing it closer to Labour:

> We have admired Mrs Thatcher's native wit and adroit grip on so many emotions. We have watched her in war fighting against her own diplomatic frailty. We can understand why she seems so dominant and why she expects to win. But there is no hope – no prospect of building afresh or staunching decline by our own efforts – which lies that way . . .
>
> One cannot, for example, square Mrs Thatcher's glorious invocations of

British scientific genius with the hacking, even in recession, of great technological universities like Aston and Salford. It doesn't make sense; it is stupidity;
one day soon, in despair, the role of government in seeking to create the climate
of progress will have to be reasserted.

He looked for a society 'where wealth is created for use with compassion' and
took comfort that such a balance was addressed as directly by David Owen as
by Peter Shore. 'However it comes, it is the next stage in the process of change
and upheaval of which Alliance is a volcanic symbol. We have watched and
looked for that process since Mr Grimond first turned his troops in search of
the gunfire. We cannot tell how it will end: but we would not wish to see it
lost on Thursday at the random whim of the electoral system.'*
     This was as close as the *Guardian* came to an endorsement. There was no
point, it said, 'in consistently, though vainly, attempting to advise a party
that is losing touch with its constituency, and then mindlessly blessing it,
come what may'. Peter Jenkins, on the Monday before polling, took it as read
that Labour had lost:

> The guilty men and women are the self-indulging ideologues and the hypocriti-
> cal careerists, the guilt-ridden middle class leftists and the cowardly trade
> union bureaucrats, the sentimentalists, the romantics, and the Don Quixotes
> who have split and, for the time being, destroyed the party to which millions
> looked as their instrument of reform and progress and as their chief hope.

Four *Guardian* journalists, three of them leader-writers, stood for the SDP:
Malcolm Dean at Bath (against Christopher Patten); John Torode at Saffron
Walden; Christopher Huhne at Reading East; and Polly Toynbee (wife of
Peter Jenkins) at Lewisham East. James Lewis, a Welsh speaker and political
reporter based in Manchester, stood as a Liberal at Clwyd North West against
Sir Anthony Meyer. None of them got in; all came second with five-figure
votes except Polly Toynbee, whose 9,351 votes helped to unseat the sitting
Labour man and let in Colin Moynihan for the Conservatives.
     Of the four, Malcolm Dean was and remained the strongest influence on the
social policy of the *Guardian*, in education, social security, legal matters and
race relations. He was anything but the dry old stick which such a formidable
list of topics calls to mind: he had the loudest voice and one of the most
infectious laughs in the office. He never wrote in a vacuum of theory. Over a
period of twenty years he was a member of a dozen advisory bodies, among
them the Dangerous Offenders Committee, the Holloway Board of Visitors,

---

* To help Labour in its most divisive question of defence, the editorial columns recommended
the manifesto 'Defence without the Bomb' (Taylor & Francis, 1983) drawn up by the
Alternative Defence Commission based on the Peace Studies Department at the University of
Bradford. The report came too late in the campaign, however, to be as influential as it might
otherwise have been.

Guy's Hospital Community Medicine, The Royal College of Psychiatrists legislative review body, and the Commission for Racial Equality advisory group. In order better to understand race relations he went to live where the going was likely to be toughtest, in Stockwell in South London. He had made his own way in journalism, doing four years on local papers in Cheshire before travelling round the world for four years, attending Ruskin College, Oxford, and taking a Harkness fellowship at the University of Chicago. To learn more about the inner workings of government he took leave of absence from the paper for six months to become a special adviser to the Secretary for Health and Social Security towards the end of the Callaghan administration. He started the *Guardian*'s social policy page which became Society Tomorrow and then Society Guardian.

Tony Benn joined the mêlée. After his defeat at Bristol South-east, he was given a regular column on the Agenda page in Monday's *Guardian* which he frequently used to complain about 'the media'. (He was heard to compare his column with papers smuggled out of prison, presumably like those of Dietrich Bonhoeffer.) His first column, on 20 June, argued that an important result of the election 'that has passed virtually without comment in the media' was that for the first time since 1945 a political party with an openly socialist policy had received the support of over 8½ million people. As recently as 1979 the Labour manifesto, drafted in Downing Street, had been in essence an SDP policy statement, and the Lib–Lab pact had been the direct forerunner of the Liberal–SDP alliance. '. . . It is indeed astonishing that Socialism has reappeared once more upon the national agenda and has won such a large vote when you consider the obstacles that had to be overcome.' By contrast on the same page David Selbourne, tutor in politics at Ruskin College, Oxford, wrote a piece arguing that 'Tory populism with its deep reach into the working class has made suckers of the slow-thinking socialist Utopians'.

SDP-ism pervaded the leader-writers' room. The Labour loyalists on the staff – of whom there were many, including Julia Langdon, political correspondent, Melanie Phillips, Martin Linton (ex-*Labour Weekly*) and the labour staff – failed to convince their friends in the party that the *Guardian* had not deserted it. Ian Aitken was the longest-standing of the committed Labour supporters in the office and doubtless he disapproved of what some of his colleagues were up to.* But he disapproved equally of Benn's part in Labour's downfall. Some years later, reviewing Benn's volume of diaries *Against the Tide*,[8] He wrote:

> But as one trudges through page after page of Benn's complaints against Wilson, and notes the repeated breaches of collective responsibility, one begins

* Even so he had earlier been arraigned before a consistory court of his colleagues for the alleged deficiency of his zeal. His prosecutors were two departmental editors, W.L. Webb (books) and Elizabeth (Liz) Forgan (women).

to feel growing sympathy for poor old Harold. One wonders whether a prime minister has ever been so put upon by a sanctimonious colleague, and is tempted to rejoice when he at last blows the whistle. For when Wilson threatens to sack Benn, the great rebel backs down. As Eric Heffer, a more consistent rebel, tells him: 'You grovelled'.

They were tumultuous years for the Left and Centre of British politics, and the engagements were carried out between what a previous generation of *Guardian* writers would perhaps have called the Scylla of the Falklands campaign and the Charybdis of the miners' strike. The National Union of Mineworkers under its new leader Arthur Scargill imposed an overtime ban on 31 October 1983. Its strike, the longest and bitterest since the general strike of 1926, began the following spring.

On Monday 19 March Patrick Wintour and Malcolm Pithers led the paper with what was to become about the most controversial of topics in the Coal Board's and government's handling of the strike: the 'massive police operation' to prevent flying pickets from Kent and Yorkshire travelling to the Midlands and Derbyshire. Nick Davies reported on the same page: 'The movements of miners' flying pickets are being monitored and blocked by a new form of police operation which has marshalled 20,000 officers from all over England and Wales in one centrally directed effort . . . The operation started on Thursday and is being run from a room on the 13th floor of New Scotland Yard.'

During the next twelve months the *Guardian* did appear to have, from the trade union and political side, as well as in the tea and sympathy, an instinct for what was important. At the outset Keith Harper wrote:

Arthur Scargill's determination to bring about his revolutionary change in society is threatening to produce an important casualty in the NUM.

The wounds from which it is currently bleeding are self-inflicted because he has failed to stick to the rules drawn up so carefully by the NUM's forefathers, observing the lessons of the 1926 general strike. To win the battle, you have to secure the hearts and minds of the troops.

When the NUM's leaders gained their sweeping victories against government policies in the 1970s, they did so by using the ballot box . . . Mr Scargill has been rebuffed by his membership so frequently in his first two years of office that he has now resorted to letting areas like Yorkshire and Scotland have their heads by picketing other areas and relying on the traditional solidarity of the miners not to cross picket lines . . . The miners neither know, nor have they been clearly told, why they are being called upon to fight at the end of a winter where coal stocks are at the highest level they have ever been . . . He brooks no criticism of his actions and is inwardly nurtured by his political philosophy . . . His tactics are half-heartedly questioned by an ineffective caucus who have neither the authority nor the unity to win arguments. The overall result of the

*"To show there are no hard feelings I
think I might offer to pay the NUM
fine out of my overtime."*

hostilities which Mr Scargill has aroused in the Labour movement – and which, it is fair to say, do not worry him – has been the loss of membership on the national executive committee of the Labour party and a diminishing voice within the TUC . . . [9]

Martin Linton considered the effects of the strike on the Labour party which had closed the gap on the Tories but now slipped back again.

The immediate cause may well be the miners' strike. It is certainly true that since the strike started – on March 12 – Labour's rating has fallen from 40 to 38 and now 37 per cent. There may also be a secondary effect that the coal strike draws attention away from the other issues, such as the health service and education, which Neil Kinnock has been putting in the political limelight, and it also detracts from the wider strategy of giving the Labour Party a more forward-looking image. Coal strikes just make people think back to 1972 and 1974.[10]

The worst scenes of violence were at Orgreave coking plant near Rotherham, Yorkshire, with cars burned, stones and bottles thrown and policemen lashing out with truncheons. Malcolm Pithers was early on the scene:

> The battle lasted for 10 hours of horrific clashes. At the end 93 had been arrested and 79 injured – 51 of them pickets and 28 police officers . . .
>
> Miners began converging on the Orgreave plant at 3 am yesterday. Some had travelled from Scotland, Wales, the North-east of England as well as Yorkshire.
>
> At one stage they practically overwhelmed police units. There were pitched battles inside the coking plant for the first time since picketing began, and the frustration on both sides spilled over into sickening scenes of miners being batoned and of police being attacked with bricks, slivers of glass as well as containers of fuel.
>
> Although the police lines eventually held, officers did react violently. Truncheons were drawn and used on individuals by snatch squads.
>
> The day produced unreal, pitiful scenes. Cars were rolled downhill towards policemen and ignited to make a flaming barricade.
>
> At one point I heard a policeman yell at a photographer to take photographs of a hero. He was pointing to a mounted police officer whose arm was bleeding badly. An ambulanceman was holding the wound to stem the flow of blood.
>
> It was equally sickening to hear policemen clapping and cheering as a picket, bleeding heavily from a head wound, was helped into an ambulance . . .

Not all was violence and solemnity. Terry Coleman wrote:

> Since the NUM was holding a special delegate conference on the following day, I went the day before to the Sheffield Trades and Labour Club, and asked the secretary if I might come in to speak to some of the members. Now this is a pretty awful district, among high rise council flats inflicted on the city by some barbarians. No one should have to live in such a place. Just down the road is an old public baths which now calls itself a 'Swimming Improvement Centre'. Just opposite is the Salvation Army.
>
> 'No,' said the man he approached.
>
> 'Tell him that yourself,' said the secretary.
>
> I then introduced myself, saying I was from the *Guardian*.
>
> 'Nothing to say to you,' said the man.
>
> A second man said, 'See that sign?'
>
> I asked what sign.
>
> He pointed to the green exit sign above the door. 'You're a social enemy,' he said. 'I'd like you to leave the club.'
>
> A social enemy. Outside of a Marxist tract I have never come across the phrase. The man cannot have known me from Adam. If he thinks the *Guardian* is a social enemy, then he must consider the miners' only remaining friend the *Morning Star* . . . I looked around. None of the members present, 20 or so, said

a word. So I said goodnight and left. This is a small incident, but I think it shows in a small way how isolated the militant miners have made themselves.[11]

Or compare Michael White at the TUC conference that year:

Striking miners poured into Brighton on Monday to witness the TUC's historic decision to write a blank cheque for their struggle and its prudent decision not to sign it.

For many of the strikers it was their first visit to the South Coast resort which is the home of one of Britain's traditional heavy industries — adultery. They were evidently enchanted with the town and it with them, for there was no trouble all day. The visitors' fears that these closely knit communities in the south are lawless hooligans were quickly dispelled.

Miners cheerfully rattled tins at the public in search of funds and publicans rattled cash registers at the miners, who responded generously, for Brighton's adultery-based industries have been severely hit by the recession and the growth of the do-it-yourself market to Hove and beyond.

Outside the Brighton conference centre a large and, by the standards of this dispute, good-natured crowd of policemen, miners and miners' friends (including the banner of the Hemel Hempstead Miners' Support Group) had gathered by 9 o'clock. There was an eerie silence as they waited to cheer — or boo — the grandees of the General Council as they arrived.

Those confident of a warm reception walked close to the miners' barrier to make sure they got it. So did the *Mirror*'s Mr Maxwell on the mistaken assumption that his peace-making efforts would make up for his refusal to put another bingo £1 into the miners' tins.

Union bosses, more shrewdly expecting to be called 'Scab' or 'Judas', like Bill Sirs of the ISTC and — if anyone had recognised him — the electricians' new leader, Mr Eric Hammond, took advantage of the wide pavement to keep their distance. Mr Clive Jenkins walked down the middle where he will one day get run over.

. . . In the midday sunshine Mr Dennis Skinner MP described the amiable Sussex coppers under Mr Roger Birch . . . as 'Mrs Thatcher's Gestapo' and wholesome young people from the revolutionary fringe who have only seen coal in coal scuttles chanted 'TUC get off your knees! Organise a general strike!' But would they? This was definitely not the big question after lunch . . . [12]

But what about the actual issue in supposed dispute, the forthcoming pit closures? On 1 May an editorial disagreed with the maximalist line Hattersley had taken in a TV interview.

. . . And then there is Mr Hattersley's near-endorsement of the view that all pits now open should survive. Did he stand, he was asked, for no closures? 'I think I probably do', he replied — though that was modified (rationality reasserting itself against emotion?) a moment later; the present level should be 'more or less' maintained. But Mr Hattersley is a potential Chancellor as well as a potential deputy prime minister. He would be confronted at the Treasury with the same cruel jostling of priorities which racked his Labour predecessors. To deny that the MacGregor closure programme represents the best and most rational course for the industry is reasonable enough; that is why we have suggested an independent reassessment. But to come out so nearly in favour of the status quo is hardly in line with the new realism which over the past six months has been one of the most persuasive ingredients in Labour's rehabilitation.

Through all this time Michael Parkin in Leeds wrote about the hardships of the Yorkshire miners and Jean Stead especially, the embodiment of the *Guardian*'s reputation for 'social concern', about those in Scotland. She was constantly in the mining towns. On Christmas Eve she wrote about the generosity of helpers. By early the previous week £240,000 had been pledged and £100,000 collected for the Women Against Pit Closures Christmas Appeal. At Fallin sleepless women stayed up to wrap the villagers' share of 100,000 toys sent for miners' children by French trade unionists.

> In Scotland, where the strike is nearly solid and there has been strong financial help from district and regional councils, the distribution of food has been tightly controlled from the start. Soup kitchens are general and that is where the pit families eat their main meal of the day. The Glasgow and West of Scotland branch of Sogat last week distributed 10,000 frozen chickens for the miners' Christmas dinners. Robert Gillespie, the Sogat secretary concerned, said 'We had some of the wives and children at our convalescent home for a stay in the summer. We would put the children to bed and then we would open the bar for the wives to have a drink. That was when the tears started to flow and they told us what it was really like. Otherwise, they're too proud to let outsiders know.' A mother in a colliery near Barnsley said 'If the pit shuts, there's no other job, and what will happen to [their sons]? You worry about the kids who leave school with no jobs to go to and turn to drugs and crime. That's why we're not giving in . . .'

Scottish women had been getting £6.40 a week in social security plus family allowance. The fathers got nothing. 'The miners' families agreed that the single miners who get nothing – no social security, no strike pay, and no food parcels – are the worst off.'

Selected quotations notwithstanding, the *Guardian* and the people on it loved Michael Foot, but on the back benches rather than the front. It was no surprise when the *Guardian* welcomed Neil Kinnock's election as leader with, on the so-called dream ticket, Roy Hattersley as his deputy. Both men had close personal friends on the paper. Aitken and McKie were close to Kinnock; Julia Langdon had lived for a while at the home of Neil and Glenys.

Kinnock stood for the Shadow Cabinet in 1979. The first twelve automatically qualified for a place but Foot persuaded Callaghan to offer Kinnock, who at fourteenth might have expected a lowly post, the grander one of education. On 19 June Ian Aitken called it 'an astonishing leg-up to one of the most charismatic figures in the much-maligned Tribune Group'.[13] Back in 1977 the paper had found him a favourite at party conference when he helped to organise, and starred in, a revue: *The End of the Peers Show*. Two days after Kinnock's shadow appointment Martin Wainwright, then running the diary, learned that because of his heavy new responsibilities Kinnock was planning to give up the boards. Wainwright deeply regretted it. Kinnock had 'brought down the house with that song about Ole Man Callaghan: "He must know somethin'", sang Kinnock, "But he don't do nothin". The Brighton Pavilion shook.'

At the party conference that year Michael White wrote in his sketch of the standing ovation given to Kinnock unusually early in his career: 'As a politician he has a big credibility problem. People like him. Worse, so do the media. This is partly because he makes good jokes and partly because you can only run one Bogy Man at a time; and on Mr Benn's days off the deputy bogy man is currently Eric Heffer.'[14]

When the next leadership contest was held in the autumn of 1983 the *Guardian* said that if the four contestants had 'been judged solely in terms of the intellectual content of their analysis and prescription Mr Peter Shore would now be leading the field. As it is, he seems destined to finish last with a humiliating share of the vote.' That evidently did not mean, though, that the paper was judging candidates by intellectual quality alone. Three days later when it was clear that Kinnock was going to win, it quoted its previously expressed view that

> If anyone is to resurrect Labour Mr Kinnock and Mr Hattersley are the people to do it. Mr Kinnock says his aim will be to unify and to organise for victory, but, as he knows, the second objective is unlikely to be achieved without some cost to the first. Over the past few years, and conspicuously since the disastrous events of 1981, Mr Kinnock has emerged as the leading representative of the Realist Tendency on the left of the party, and he has disclosed enough of his intentions since June 9 [polling day] to demonstrate that he means to bend every effort to set the party as a whole on a far more realistic course than it has taken since the defeat of 1979.[15]

By 1987 the Liberal–SDP Alliance was beginning to falter and it was the *Guardian*'s duty to say so.

> What's really fresh about 1987 is that Labour is fighting the campaign it wishes it had fought in 1983 – and fighting it with an élan which appears . . . to make it look the new, moderate show in town. Last time the Alliance achieved lift-off as Michael Foot wandered into the sands. This time merely being in the middle (whatever its pragmatic virtues) leaves the Alliance reacting to anything even

marginally interesting that Mr Kinnock or Mrs Thatcher may have to say, but not being able to call its own shots.[16]

The paper still did not believe that Labour had put forward a credible defence policy and Denis Healey had failed to demonstrate how he could do a deal with Moscow which would allow for British nuclear disarmament. 'We think that Labour's defence policy is a bit of a mess,' the final election leader said on 10 June. 'So, alas, do rather a large number of voters who might otherwise have backed Mr Kinnock this time . . . and consider what a difference that 5 per cent might have made.' But the leader was headed 'Verdict: If she can do it, so can we', and the 'we' included a larger Labour than Alliance element. Readers were left in no doubt that the *Guardian* felt able to return to its home base.

Before that election the skies had begun to darken for the *Guardian*. Eddie Shah with his *Today* newspaper and Rupert Murdoch with his *Times* and *Sun* at Wapping had shown that newspapers could be produced without benefit of the 'old Spanish customs' with which generations of production managers and composing room overseers had had to make themselves familiar. But there was discontent among editorial staff at both *The Times*, where Murdoch's methods had given innovation a bad name, and at the *Daily Telegraph*, where an impression of stagnation had overtaken the life's work of the decent old Lord Hartwell. Andreas Whittam Smith, at one time on the *Guardian*, but never of it, and then on the *Telegraph* conceived the idea of a new quality newspaper which was evidently to compete more with the other qualities than with the *Guardian*. That expectation, coupled with the failure of the original *Today*, may have influenced the *Guardian*'s attitude towards the approaching launch. (The *Independent* began life with 115 experienced journalists[17] which was its great initial advantage. Of those only four were from the *Guardian*, including John Torode, who had been first to apply. About one third came from the Murdoch titles at Wapping and nine from the *Daily Telegraph* and *Sunday Telegraph*.)

One of Preston's early innovations had been to introduce the 'Tuesday conferences' at which a celebrity – minister, trade union leader, sportsman, ambassador – would be invited to speak to and answer questions from anyone on the staff who cared to turn up. The meeting would be followed by a small lunch in the board room for those staff members mostly closely concerned with the subject discussed.* In 1986 John Biffen MP visited the *Guardian* on 29 April, having attended a similar function at *The Times* the week before. He said as the meeting dispersed from the editor's office that he had found everyone at *The Times* very worried about the forthcoming launch of the

---

* In 1982 the Archbishop of Canterbury, Dr Runcie, accompanied by Terry Waite, expressed himself agreeably surprised at the friendly tone of the questions. He had expected a battering about women priests and sexist language in the liturgy.

Independent whereas they had no need to be, and at the *Guardian* he had found people were not worried whereas they had reason to be. Indeed when the *Independent* took the unprecedented step of circulating advance dummies to its rivals an editorial executive on the *Guardian*, who left for another paper not long afterwards, commented that 'There's not much there to worry about'. Preston commented on the launch issue: 'For a new paper it's lacking in new ideas. It looks a bit like *The Times* of five years ago. They need to offer something entirely different. This is absolutely the same.'[18]

In the event there was a great deal to worry about. Not only was the *Guardian* missing editions through labour disputes but its once-important letters columns had become a playpen for paranoiacs, nihilists and hard-left freaks, who were a caricature of the paper's following and with whom the more serious readers clearly did not wish to be identified. Within months *Guardian* writers found that their friends had switched papers. Within eighteen months the paper had lost nearly 10 per cent of its circulation, falling from 524,264 in January–June 1986 to 474,017 in October 1987–March 1988, in which time the *Independent* had bolted to 376,750 from a standing start. The rival was producing a clean, crisp newspaper; the *Guardian*, using ancient presses and only intermediate technology, was often turning out a scruffy product – scruffy and late, so that newsagents took the opportunity, when their *Guardians* failed to arrive, to introduce their customers to something new.

In one important respect, however, the new paper did influence the *Guardian*'s political reporting, and that was in its attitude to the Downing Street Lobby briefings. The Prime Minister's press secretary, Bernard Ingham, formulated the wording of her policy without any attribution to the source, so that Fleet Street had developed an elaborate code of circumlocutions ('All the signs are that . . .'; 'Sources close to the Government have suggested . . .'). The *Guardian* had bridled against this system in Hetherington's day and Preston's, and under Wilson, Heath and Callaghan as well as Margaret Thatcher. The outcome in 1986 may best be recounted from the attributable source of Peter Hennessy and David Walker:

> The new paper made it plain it would have nothing to do with the Lobby; it would operate outside the club from the start. The editor . . . recruited his team of Westminster and Whitehall specialists on that understanding. As a result Peter Preston . . . with the unanimous backing of his political journalists and commentators, decided, though he did not acknowledge this when announcing it in his paper, to break the cardinal Lobby convention of non-attribution. In future, briefings by the No. 10 Press Secretary would be attributed to 'a Downing Street Spokesman'.[19]

Preston, according to this source, tried to persuade Charles Wilson of *The Times* and Max Hastings of the *Daily Telegraph* to join him, but failed. He had an acrimonious correspondence with Ingham (a former *Guardian* reporter) in which it became clear that Ingham would allow no such attribution. The *Guardian* therefore withdrew altogether, not going back until it had reached satisfactory terms with the incoming press secretary after Mrs Thatcher and Mr Ingham had departed.

During this period of turbulence in and around Fleet Street (which was rapidly ceasing to be their geographical location) Preston was engaged for weeks, indeed months, in negotiation with the NUJ chapel about the introduction of the new technology which *The Independent* had had from the beginning and was using to good effect. Shortly after negotiations ended the Father of the Chapel left. The editor stayed, to transform and rebuild his newspaper and staunch its wounds. The gap which had threatened to close between himself and Whittam Smith was widened again. And in Preston's frequent words when he exhorted his staff to yet greater dynamism: 'That's showbiz'.

Experiments on a new design for the paper, commissioned from David Hillman, occupied the latter months of 1987. The first issue, in two sections, appeared on Friday 12 February 1988. The tough sans-serif type stood in stark contrast to the delicacies of the Century type family with which readers had become so familiar. As one would of course expect, the protests outnumbered the congratulations. Even within the office the resident design specialist, Michael McNay, had to keep a sharp eye on the recidivist tendency to revert to old typographical ways, earning himself the title of Head of the Thought Police. Preston had, after all, seemed to ignore the advice of an acknowledged master of the trade, Harold Evans, who wrote: 'There is a good deal to be said for conservatism in matters of newspaper typography and layout. When it is not necessary to change, it is necessary not to change. It is no advance for civilisation, simply because it is technically possible, to subject the reader to styles and manners of printing type which defy . . . settled habits of reading'.[20]

Was it then 'necessary to change'? Hindsight does not allow much doubt. The old design was looking tired, and the *Guardian* had vigorous competitors to contend with. As time went on, as readers adapted to what was certainly a radical challenge, as the part-italic and part-roman title-piece took on a life of its own and influenced typography elsewhere, the paper's fresh appearance began to acquire a new authority, even an inevitability. But that is a tale still to be told.

A Guardian Chronology

1821	5 May. *Manchester Guardian* founded as a weekly by J.E. Taylor, price 7d.
1855	Becomes a daily, price 2d.
1857	Price reduced to 1d.
1872	C.P. Scott becomes editor.
1907	C.P. Scott becomes proprietor.
1924–30	Acquisition of *Manchester Evening News*.
1932	Death of C.P. Scott. Younger son and successor as editor, E.T. Scott, dies. Elder son J.R. Scott becomes chairman. W.P. Crozier becomes editor.
1936	Scott Trust formed.
1944	A.P. Wadsworth becomes editor.
1948	Terms of Scott Trust revised. Laurence Scott succeeds his father, J.R. Scott, as chairman.
1952	29 September. News on front page.
1956	Alastair Hetherington becomes editor. Richard Scott becomes chairman of Scott Trust.
1959	24 August. 'Manchester' dropped from title.
1961	11 September. First issue printed in London.
1964	February. Editorial headquarters move to London.
1965–6	Abortive moves for merger with *The Times*.
1969	3 February. Paper redesigned with new mast-head.
1970	29–30 August. Manchester office moves to new building.
1972	1 February. Education Guardian introduced.
1973	7 June, Laurence Scott retires. P.W. Gibbings becomes chairman.
1975	21 March. Peter Preston appointed editor. Purchase of *Rochdale Observer* group.
1976	29 August. Move to new offices in Farringdon Road, London.
1977	Purchase of *Stockport Advertiser* series.
1978–9	Purchase of *Surrey Advertiser* group.
1984	R.F. Scott retires from chairmanship of Scott Trust. Hetherington appointed successor.
1984	First income from Reuters shareholding.

1987   Autumn: trials at new printing plant at Isle of Dogs.

1988   12 February. Retirement of P.W. Gibbings. Harry Roche becomes group chairman. First issue of new design.

Notes

CHAPTER 1

1. Hammond, p. 99.
2. *The* Manchester Guardian: *A Century of History*, pp. 25–8. Mills describes the yeomanry as 'the quintessence of local Toryism'.
3. See Ayerst, Chap. 22: The War of the Taylor Succession.
4. Ibid., p. 492.
5. November 1966.
6. *New Statesman*, 15 October 1971.
7. Hammond, p. 300.
8. *The Glorious Privilege*, Magnus Magnusson et al., Nelson, 1967, p. 166.
9. *Forgetting's No Excuse* (Virago edn.), pp. 67–8.
10. *Have Pen, Will Travel*, J.M.D. Pringle, Chatto & Windus, 1973, p. 130.
11. Personal recollection by Ayerst.

CHAPTER 2

1. *The History of* The Times, vol. V, Times Books, 1984, p. 217.
2. *Three Centuries of Anglo-Jewish History*, V.D. Lipman, Jewish Historical Society, 1961.
3. *Jewish Life in Britain*, Sonia and Vivian Lipman, Saur, 1981.
4. *MG*, 22 November 1915, quoted in *The Balfour Declaration*, Leonard Stein, Valentine Mitchell & Co. Ltd, 1961.
5. *Great Britain and Palestine*, Sidebotham, Macmillan, 1937, p. 29, quoted in Stein, p. 302.
6. Stein, op. cit., pp. 466–7.
7. Ibid., p. 664.
8. Letter to *The Times* after the Balfour Declaration.
9. Pringle, op. cit., p. 36.
10. Harman Grisewood, *One Thing at a Time*, Hutchinson, 1968, pp. 198–204.

11.   Ayerst, p. 622.

CHAPTER 3

1.   The 1914 version might have used a separate title. See Ayerst, pp. 230 and 354.
2.   *After I was Sixty*, Thomson, p. 170.
3.   LPS–board, 12 February 1962.
4.   LPS–board, 7 August 1963.
5.   *The Right to Know*, Francis Williams, Longman Green, 1969, p. 309.
6.   *Gdn*, 11 September 1986.
7.   Interview.
8.   Laurence wrote to Hetherington early in 1964: 'Allen Clarke [London manager, later company secretary] has had some discussion with union hq before we decided to ask Daly to come. In the end it sounded as though union hq were about as glad that Daly was willing to come as we ourselves were.'

CHAPTER 4

1.   The two papers in the 1950s are compared by T.S. Matthews in *The Sugar Pill*, Gollancz, 1957.
2.   GY, p. 368.
3.   More correctly, between supporters of factions within the nationalist movement which later split to become the largely Shona ZANU (Zimbabwe African National Union) and Joshua Nkomo's ZAPU (Zimbabwe African People's Union).
4.   Mrs Keatley's own African expertise was of service to the Archbishop of Canterbury, Dr Robert Runcie, when she became his press secretary.
5.   *Gdn*, 21 March 1962.
6.   GY, p. 267; Clare Hollingworth, *Front Line*, Jonathan Cape, 1990, p. 191.
7.   Ibid., p. 212.
8.   Morris–Hetherington, 10 May 1956.
9.   See Fred Halliday in *The Media in British Politics*, ed. Seaton and Pimlott, Avebury, 1987.
10.   *Gdn*, 27 July 1970.
11.   Halliday, op. cit.
12.   *The Sugar Pill*, op. cit., pp. 136–7.
13.   Ayerst, p. 577.
14.   Cooke–Hetherington, 16 December 1963.

CHAPTER 5

1. *The Spectator*, 4 November 1960.
2. *Forgetting's No Excuse*, Virago edition, p. 112.
3. Letter to the Editor, 17 February 1961.
4. 22 and 25 February 1961.
5. LPS–AH, 17 March 1961.
6. GY, p. 132.
7. Quoted from *The* Guardian *in Words and Music*, ed. Veronica Wedgwood, Collins, 1981.
8. Paul Johnson, *DNB*.
9. Letter to author.
10. GY, p. 136.

CHAPTER 6

1. 1 November 1960.
2. LPS retrospect, December 1966.
3. GY, p. 157.
4. Hetherington papers.
5. Laurence handwritten note, 30 January 1966.
6. Haley–Laurence Scott, 10 January 1966.
7. Laurence–Richard Scott, 22 January 1954.
8. Laurence memo to board and Trust, 29 March 1965.
9. Meeting of 22 August.
10. For biographical notes, see Ayerst, p. 532.
11. Letter to author.
12. Hetherington–Laurence, 12 August 1966.
13. Author's personal recollection.
14. Roy Jenkins, *European Diary 1977–1981*, Collins, 1989; entry for 18 May 1978.

CHAPTER 7

1. *After I was Sixty*, Thomson, p. 173.
2. Interview with David Astor.
3. LPS evidence to MMC, 28 October 1966.
4. The chairman was Ashton (later Lord) Roskill QC and the members Brian Davidson, W.E. Jones, E.L. Richards, Professor B.S. Yamey, and three co-opted for the hearing: Lord Annan, Lord Francis-Williams and Donald Tyerman.
5. Notes of meeting, 10 November 1966.

6. In 1970 top people's pay in *Guardian* management and editorial was, the chairman excepted, of the order of £12,000.

CHAPTER 8

1. *Two Lives, Two Worlds*, Sheila Chichester, Hodder & Stoughton, 1969, pp. 100 et seq.
2. Leader, *Gdn*, 11 October 1965.
3. *Gdn*, 7 March 1966.
4. *Daily Telegraph*, 24 January 1974.
5. Martin Walker, *Gdn*, 28 November 1978.
6. Hetherington–Anderson, 10 July 1967.
7. *Gdn*, 27 May 1967.
8. Anderson–Hetherington, 14 February 1967, quoting the Japanese Ambassador to the US.
9. *The Ulysses Factor*, Hodder & Stoughton, 1970.

CHAPTER 9

1. 6 May 1965.
2. Letter to author.
3. *Gdn*, 21 January 1966.
4. Leader 6 February 1967.
5. 14 February.
6. *Vietnam*, Mary McCarthy, Weidenfeld & Nicolson, 1967.

CHAPTER 10

1. GY, p. 242.
2. 8 June.
3. Letter to author.
4. 19 February 1968.
5. Adams–Hetherington, 28 May.
6. Hetherington–Adams, 30 May.
7. Hetherington to foreign ed., 17 December 1968.
8. 16 June 1968.
9. 5 June.

CHAPTER 13

1. 12 January 1981.
2. Hammond, pp. 61 et seq.
3. Ibid., p. 68.
4. Ibid., p. 120.
5. Winchester anglicised the name of Ruairi O Bradaigh. Stevenson, who was English, gaelicised his name to Sean McStiofan.
6. *In Holy Terror*, Winchester, Faber & Faber, 1974, p. 111.
7. *Violence and Civil Disturbances in Northern Ireland in 1969*, Belfast, HMSO, Cmd 566, April 1972, p. 5.
8. 21 March 1973.
9. 11 September 1973.
10. 6, 7, 8 July 1981.

CHAPTER 14

1. 9 November 1960.
2. Quoted 9 November 1960.
3. The statement about advertising appears in correspondence with Lord Reith, who asked (5 August 1965) for permission to quote Laurence's evidence to the 'Advertising Commission'. The full quotation, headed Political Discrimination, ran: 'A few attempts at the time of Suez produced very little effect. Mr Laurence Scott stated that the *Guardian* lost "a very insignificant amount", but he explained that this was in connection with the advertising of company meetings, "where the placing of an advertisement would depend rather on the whim of the chairman of the company than the advertising agent".' Laurence had previously given the opinion that advertisers took space where it would be effective, regardless of politics.
4. Hetherington–Sachs, 22 April 1971.

CHAPTER 15

1. Searle memorandum – The Logic of Deansgate, March 1969.
2. *New Technology and the Press. A study of experience in the United States.* By Rex Winsbury and the Acton Society Press Group for the Royal Commission on the Press, HMSO, 1975.
3. *Industrial Relations in the National Newspaper Industry*, Cmnd 6680, 1976, Ch. 3.
4. 11 September 1986.
5. Hetherington file note, 10 November 1970.

6. Gibbings memorandum, 6 November 1972.

CHAPTER 16

1. Interviews with Cole and Jones.
2. GY, pp. 342–3.
3. Ibid.
4. In earlier years the assumption had always been otherwise. In 1953, during discussion of a proposed debenture issue, the conditions suggested by the brokers included '. . . (d) on the editorial side Mr Wadsworth to proceed as soon as possible with the training and selection of his eventual successor.'

CHAPTER 17

1. GY, p. 140.
2. Stott–Hetherington, 15 August 1968.
3. *Sunday Times*, 17 February 1991.
4. 3 July 1972.
5. 10 November 1975.

CHAPTER 18

1 *Gotcha! The Media, the Government and the Falklands Crisis*, Robert Harris, Faber & Faber, 1983, pp. 19–20.
2. Minutes of evidence, 28 July 1982.
3. *Gdn*, 3 May 1982.
4. 28 April.
5. 5 May.
6. 10 May.
7. 26 May 1983.
8. Ayerst, p. 280.
9. Carney, p. 129.
10. Carney, p. 124.
11. Carney, p. 187.
12. *MG*, 19 May 1900.
13. *MG*, 15 March 1900.

CHAPTER 19

1. 5 February 1965.
2. A full account is given by Hetherington in GY, Ch. 11.

3. 11 May 1971.
4. 9 July 1971.
5. 1 November 1983.
6. Leader, *Observer*, 18 December 1983.
7. 'Let the mole beware', *The Times*, 17 December 1983.
8. Letter to *The Times*, 28 March 1984.
9. Contempt of Court Act 1981, Section 10.
10. The NUJ code of conduct, item 7, states simply: 'A journalist shall protect confidential sources of information.'
11. The reference is apparently to Sylvester Bolam, editor of the *Daily Mirror*, whose paper identified the 'acid bath murderer', John Haigh, before his trial (1949); and Brendan Mulholland of the *Daily Mail* and Reginald Foster of the *Daily Sketch*, who refused to name sources in the Vassall affair. The comparisons are not wholly appropriate.
12. *Granta*, 12, Summer 1984.
13. *Daily Mail*, 16 August 1984.
14. 23 June 1986.
15. Leading article, 12 July 1986.
16. 8 September 1987.
17. Private information.

CHAPTER 20

1. *MG*, 27 December 1917.
2. *Gdn*, 28 March 1969.
3. *Gdn*, 25 April 1984.
4. 23 October 1988.
5. 6 November 1980.
6. 23 March 1955.
7. 4 February 1960.
8. 4 January 1978.
9. *European Diary*, Collins, 1989, entry for 15 March 1978.
10. Ibid., 18 May 1978.
11. Ibid., 4 May 1979.
12. 19 March 1980.
13. Private information.

CHAPTER 21

1. *Gdn*, 22 September 1972.
2. 20 July 1967.
3. 18 September 1961.

4.   21 March 1978.
5.   27 September 1986.

CHAPTER 22

1.   Obituary of J.G. Crowther (P.A. Tucker), 31 March 1983.
2.   Chatto & Windus, 1962.
3.   GY, p. 66.
4.   Rupert Sheldrake: *A New Science of Life: the Theory of Formative Causation*, Granada, 1983.
5.   Author's personal inquiry.

CHAPTER 23

1.   Report to the board, October 1969.
2.   Report, HMSO, 30 April 1975.
3.   *Good Times, Bad Times*, Harold Evans, Weidenfeld, 1983.
4.   Ayerst, pp. 142–6.
5.   *Reuters' Century*, Graham Storey, Max Parish, 1951, p. 10.
6.   *DNB* entry on Sir Roderick Jones.
7.   Storey, p. 213; *The Price of Truth – The story of the Reuters millions*, John Lawrenson and Lionel Barber, Mainstream, 1985, pp. 82–3.
8.   *A Life in Reuters*, Jones, Hodder & Stoughton, 1951, p. 451 et seq.
9.   Lawrenson and Barber, op. cit., p. 156 et seq.
10. Ibid., pp. 31 and 142–3.

CHAPTER 24

1.   L.P. Scott memorandum, 'Allocation of Resources', 8 January 1967.
2.   Trust document, 16 April 1973.
3.   'The purpose and principles of the Scott Trust', memorandum by LPS, 25 February 1969.
4.   1986; circulated privately.
5.   GY, p. 358.

CHAPTER 25

1.   25 November 1981.
2.   HoC, 5 December 1974, quoted in GY, p. 350.
3.   17 March 1976.

4. 3 October 1978.
5. 1 October 1980.
6. 23 January 1981.
7. *Claret and Chips: the rise of the SDP*, Stephenson, Michael Joseph, 1982.
8. Hutchinson. Aitken's review was on 28 September 1989.
9. Reprinted in *Guardian Weekly*, 28 March 1984.
10. Ibid., 6 May 1984.
11. Ibid., 24 August 1984.
12. Ibid., 9 September 1984.
13. Quoted in *The Making of Neil Kinnock*, Robert Harris, Faber & Faber, 1984.
14. 2 October 1979.
15. 3 October 1983.
16. 4 June 1987.
17. *The Making of* The Independent, Michael Crozier, Coronet Books, 1988, p. 63.
18. Ibid., p. 120.
19. In *The Media in British Politics*, ed. Jean Seaton and Ben Pimlott, Dartmouth, 1987.

Index

Persons are indexed under the name or title used in the text, with cross-references where necessary to alternative names. Page numbers in *italics* refer to cartoon illustrations. Major page references are in **bold** type, footnotes represented by n. The following abbreviations have also been used: AH (Alastair Hetherington); *G* (Guardian); *MEN* (Manchester Evening News)